MW01258893

Praise for
RECLAIMING SEXUAL WHOLENESS

As a therapist who treats those suffering with sex and pornography addiction, the chapter on the Neuroaffective Model is indispensable. My clients are often focused on getting rid of their acting-out behaviors, and rightfully so. However, so much is going on beneath the surface that needs to be tended to. This chapter in particular gives clients and therapists the language necessary to get to the deeper issues and to focus the therapeutic effort on trauma treatment and dismantling shame. Dr. Todd Bowman and the other clinicians with whom he has collaborated have written an essential book that not only seeks to treat sex and pornography addiction but seeks to treat the whole person who is created in the image of our Creator. This is a must-read for those offering hope and healing in a sexually broken world.

CHRIS ELLMAN, MSW, LCSW, SATP, CSAT,
EMDR trained

Reclaiming Sexual Wholeness deftly shares practical wisdom and clinical insights from a who's who of leaders in the sexual-addiction treatment field. Dr. Bowman and his fellow authors lay out a comprehensive understanding of the breadth and depth of sexual addiction with many nuanced points, as well as evidence-based treatment approaches that also address how the faith of those affected by the addiction can be a resource. You would be hard pressed to find a book on this topic that is more clinical and Christian.

KENYON KNAPP, PhD, LPC, NCC, dean,
School of Behavioral Sciences, Liberty University

Great book written to bring clarity, understanding, and wisdom for those who have suffered with unwanted sexual behaviors. The contributing authors are experts and practitioners in the field of sexual addiction, all with many years and untold numbers of clients that report successful experiences. With carefully researched science, the reader will come away refreshed by the straightforward and systematic thinking around such a complex topic as problematic sexual addiction. As I think of what I would have wanted to know as a pastor leading those who struggle, this is the exact kind of book I would ask for.

PATRICK NORRIS, founder of Red Ink Revival

As a therapist who works with individuals who have experienced trauma, loss, and disruptions in their attachment relationships, I see the remnants of individuals who are seeking to piece together fragments of a disorganized self, like that of putting together a shattered glass mirror. Just as the individual is a complex, multifaceted human person, the need exists for a holistic treatment model of sexual addiction that helps meld the pieces of one's heart and life back together. Dr. Bowman's *Reclaiming Sexual Wholeness* provides an integrated model for treating the disconnected sense of self and includes not only the clinical but also the spiritual within the Christian narrative. By doing so, *Reclaiming Sexual Wholeness* brings about the hope of 1 Corinthians 13:12, as these interconnected yet fragmented pieces come to be restored, and the individual comes to know himself or herself more deeply in relationship with God and with others.

ANDREW RYAN, MA, LCPC

RECLAIMING SEXUAL WHOLENESS

RECLAIMING SEXUAL WHOLENESS

AN INTEGRATIVE CHRISTIAN APPROACH
TO SEXUAL ADDICTION TREATMENT

TODD BOWMAN,
GENERAL EDITOR

ZONDERVAN
ACADEMIC

ZONDERVAN ACADEMIC

Reclaiming Sexual Wholeness
Copyright © 2022 by Todd Bowman

Requests for information should be addressed to:
Zondervan, *3900 Sparks Dr. SE, Grand Rapids, Michigan 49546*

Zondervan titles may be purchased in bulk for educational, business, fundraising, or sales promotional use. For information, please email SpecialMarkets@Zondervan.com.

ISBN 978-0-310-09313-8 (audio)

Library of Congress Cataloging-in-Publication Data

Names: Bowman, Todd, 1981- editor.
Title: Reclaiming sexual wholeness : an integrative Christian approach to sexual addiction treatment / Todd Bowman.
Description: Grand Rapids : Zondervan, 2022. | Includes bibliographical references and index.
Identifiers: LCCN 2022009990 (print) | LCCN 2022009991 (ebook) | ISBN 9780310093107 (hardcover) | ISBN 9780310093114 (ebook)
Subjects: LCSH: Sex addiction--Religious aspects--Christianity.
Classification: LCC BV4627.L8 R43 2022 (print) | LCC BV4627.L8 (ebook) | DDC 241/.664--dc23/eng/20220331
LC record available at https://lccn.loc.gov/2022009990
LC ebook record available at https://lccn.loc.gov/2022009991

The information in this book has been carefully researched by the authors and is intended to be a source of information only. Readers are urged to consult with their physicians or other professional advisors to address specific medical or other issues. The authors and the publisher assume no responsibility for any injuries suffered or damages incurred during or as a result of the use or application of the information contained herein. Names and identifying characteristics of some individuals have been changed to preserve their privacy.

All Scripture quotations, unless otherwise indicated, are taken from The Holy Bible, New International Version®, NIV®. Copyright © 1973, 1978, 1984, 2011 by Biblica, Inc.® Used by permission of Zondervan. All rights reserved worldwide. www.Zondervan.com. The "NIV" and "New International Version" are trademarks registered in the United States Patent and Trademark Office by Biblica, Inc.®

Scripture quotations marked ESV are taken from The Holy Bible, English Standard Version. ESV® Text Edition: 2016. Copyright © 2001 by Crossway Bibles, a publishing ministry of Good News Publishers.

Scripture quotations marked NLT are taken from the *Holy Bible*, New Living Translation, copyright © 1996, 2004, 2015 by Tyndale House Foundation. Used by permission of Tyndale House Publishers, Inc., Carol Stream, Illinois 60188. All rights reserved.

Any internet addresses (websites, blogs, etc.) and telephone numbers in this book are offered as a resource. They are not intended in any way to be or imply an endorsement by Zondervan, nor does Zondervan vouch for the content of these sites and numbers for the life of this book.

All rights reserved. No part of this publication may be reproduced, stored in a retrieval system, or transmitted in any form or by any means—electronic, mechanical, photocopy, recording, or any other—except for brief quotations in printed reviews, without the prior permission of the publisher.

Cover design: LUCAS Art & Design
Cover photos: © Ryan Franco; Kristy Kravchenko; Designecologist / Unsplash
Interior design: Kait Lamphere

Printed in the United States of America

22 23 24 25 26 27 28 29 30 31 32 /TRM/ 15 14 13 12 11 10 9 8 7 6 5 4 3 2 1

In memory of Mark Laaser,
beloved colleague, mentor, and friend

CONTENTS

PART 3: TREATMENT STRATEGIES
AMONG SPECIAL POPULATIONS

PART 1

UNDERSTANDING PROBLEMATIC SEXUAL BEHAVIOR

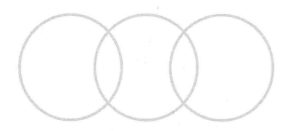

CHAPTER 1

SEXUAL ADDICTION:
A Contextual Overview

Todd Bowman, PhD, CSAT-C, and Mark Laaser, PhD

With the growing diversity of sexual content and experiences introduced in the modern world, and the corresponding uptick in reported distress and dysfunction reported among those who struggle, the helping professions have worked to conceptualize and respond to the suffering evidenced in this space. There is Scott, a 47-year-old abuse survivor who compulsively watches porn and masturbates in his basement, disengaged from his wife and children and hoping that his secret online behavior won't be discovered. There is Allison, a 19-year-old college student who has had seventeen hook-ups in her first semester of college, pleading, "I don't know what I am doing and I can't stop. Please help me!" There is Stefon, a 14-year-old student whose mom walked in on him watching porn on the iPhone she gave him for his birthday. There is Victoria, a 49-year-old wife and mom who walked in on her husband having an affair in their home with a neighbor from across the street. These stories, and the millions of others for which there is not space to share, serve as the examples of how the sexual shift has created immense distress in our relationships, families, and churches. If you are a therapist, a pastor, or a student in either field reading this book, you are invited to help participate in the alleviation of this suffering by offering quality assistance to those in need of it. As you read, you will find a blend of content from various experts, from brain scientists to clergy to educators to therapists. As such, the style of writing will vary some between chapters. Some of the content might be foreign to you, overwhelming to you, or simply not applicable given your profession. Regardless of the role you serve, I invite you to engage all the content and pull from these pages whatever principles may equip you to be an agent of healing in the overwhelming expressions of brokenness in the world today.

The sexual revolution in Western societies through the middle of the twentieth century birthed a new framework for understanding the human person and initiated numerous cultural shifts, many of which are still being felt over fifty years later. Perhaps the most fundamental shift that transpired in this "sexual awakening" is that the constraints of human sexuality came to be defined differently than the largely heterosexual, monogamous standard Western societies have used for centuries. Replacing this foundational understanding of human sexuality was a mindset that emphasized novelty, offered a diversity of sexual experiences, and normalized a noncommittal posture in sexual relationships. In many ways, the belief that we can have sex as much as we want, with whomever we want, however we want, whenever we want, with little to no consequences has come to shape the sexual imagination of Western cultures.

Inherent in this belief is the notion that the human person is first and foremost sexual and that satisfying this sexual dimension is of utmost importance. Pornography, then, emerged as a powerful driver in resetting these cultural norms. And the widespread normalization of this misguided belief system opened the door for sexual addiction to emerge as a legitimate construct in the clinical nomenclature.

Building on the work done by Orford in the 1970s (Carnes et al. 2012), Pat Carnes popularized the term *sexual addiction* in his work that led to the publication of *The Sexual Addiction*, which was later published under the title *Out of the Shadows: Understanding Sexual Addiction*. Since that time, therapists, academics, pastors, and clients have all wrestled with the nature of this construct, with hard lines often emerging between those who recognize its validity and those who hold the position that all sexual behavior is valid unless it involves an abuse of power or violates personal consent. Other ideas have been postulated to better understand and explain this phenomenon, such as sexual compulsivity, sexual obsession, problematic sexual behaviors, and hypersexuality, to name a few. A helpful definition provided by Riemersma and Sytsma reads, "'sexual addiction' is broadly defined as a disorder characterized by compulsive sexual behavior that results in tolerance, escalation, withdrawal, and a loss of volitional control despite negative consequences" (2013, 308). At its core, sexual addiction can be understood as "a pathological relationship with a mood-altering behavior" (Carnes 2015, 43). More specifically, this definition indicates that sexual addiction involves an individual participating in self-absorbed, other-objectifying sexual behaviors in an attempt to escape their distressing mood states in lieu of engaging in the healthy self-giving, other-honoring dynamics that human sexuality is intended to embody in healthy relationship.

The most sensible starting point in examining sexual behavior as potentially addictive is a universally understood definition of addiction, followed by an examination of the degree to which sexual behavior meets this established clinical definition. As a leading authority in the arena of addiction assessment and treatment, the American Society for Addiction Medicine's public policy statement defines addiction as

> a primary, chronic disease of brain reward, motivation, memory, and related circuitry. Dysfunction in these circuits leads to characteristic biological, psychological, social and spiritual manifestations. This is reflected in an individual pathologically pursuing reward and/or relief by substance use and other behaviors. (2011)

In short, addiction can be understood as a sequence of brain-related changes that come to impact the total functioning of the individual, including spiritual function, that leaves the individual pursuing the object of their desire (chemical or process addictions) for hedonic gain—that is, to experience pleasure or to avoid some undesirable state (e.g., pain, boredom, anxiety). Toward this end, Levine suggests a clinical framework for sexual addiction that involves,

> The clinical perception of sexual addiction is based on behaviors that are obviously destructive to somebody—the person himself or herself, the spouse, lover, family, employer, or society (Goodman, 2001). These behaviors may occur at a high frequency or occupy a large amount of time. They are sometimes expensive in economic, psychologic, and social terms. They may persist despite negative consequences. The patient may not be able to stop the behavior when he or she states that goal. Most of the behaviors are kept a secret, although some partners know about their presence but not their extent. (2010, 262–63)

In researching the development of sexual addiction, Carnes (1992, 11–12) identifies ten criteria for operationalizing sexual addiction as a construct, with the presence of three or more criteria serving as the cutoff score for positive identification of sexual addiction:

- A pattern of out-of-control behavior
- Severe consequences due to sexual behavior
- Inability to stop despite adverse consequences
- Persistent pursuit of self-destructive or high-risk behavior
- Ongoing desire or effort to limit sexual behavior
- Sexual obsession and fantasy as a primary coping strategy

- Increasing amounts of sexual experience because the current level of activity is no longer sufficient
- Severe mood changes around sexual activity
- Inordinate amounts of time spent in obtaining sex, being sexual, or recovering from sexual experience
- Neglect of important social, occupational, or recreational activities because of sexual behavior

Individuals presenting with sexually addictive behaviors will not likely endorse all of these criteria, but identifying those that comprise the individual's reported struggle helps increase the accuracy of intervention and treatment. To streamline the assessment process, Carnes and colleagues (2012) developed a brief screening tool for sexual addiction called PATHOS. The items comprising the PATHOS screening include the following:

- **Preoccupied:** Do you often find yourself preoccupied with sexual thoughts?
- **Ashamed:** Do you hide some of your sexual behaviors from others?
- **Treatment:** Have you ever sought help for sexual behavior you did not like?
- **Hurt others:** Has anyone been hurt emotionally because of your sexual behavior?
- **Out of control:** Do you feel controlled by your sexual desire?
- **Sad:** When you have sex, do you feel depressed afterwards?
  (Carnes et al. 2012)

With a cutoff score for determining the presence of addiction set at three, Carnes and colleagues (2012) report significant accuracy in determining differences between healthy subjects and sex-addicted participants. One consideration for using the PATHOS screening in Christian contexts is that a sensitivity to guilt or shame may lead to overresponding and erroneously inflated scores. Grubbs and Hook suggest that conservative Christian ideals can lead to "stricter sexual values . . . higher levels of guilt when transgressing sexual values . . . greater sexual dysfunction," while also noting that these ideals serve a protective function in the relationship and lead to "enhanced levels of sexual satisfaction" (2016, 156). As such, it may be beneficial to use one of the more robust instruments discussed in chapter 8 when screening for sexual addiction with this population.

The criteria identified in Carnes's work have significantly influenced the conversation surrounding sexual addiction as a viable psychological construct. In the transition to the fifth edition of *The Diagnostic and Statistical Manual for Mental Disorders* (DSM-5), the concept of sexual addiction is rigorously investigated for inclusion under the concept of Hypersexual Disorder, which is defined "as a repetitive and intense preoccupation with sexual fantasies, urges, and behaviors, leading to adverse consequences and clinically significant distress or impairment in social, occupational, or other important areas of functioning" (Reid 2015, 221). Reid's proposed criteria included the following (2015, p. 222):

a. Over a period of at least six months, recurrent and intense sexual fantasies, sexual urges, and sexual behaviors in association with four or more of the following five criteria:
1. Excessive time is consumed by sexual fantasies and urges, and by planning for and engaging in sexual behavior.
2. Repetitively engaging in these sexual fantasies, urges, and behavior in response to dysphoric mood states (e.g., anxiety, depression, boredom, irritability).
3. Repetitively engaging in sexual fantasies, urges, and behavior in response to stressful life events.
4. Repetitive but unsuccessful efforts to control or significantly reduce these sexual fantasies, urges, and behavior.
5. Repetitively engaging in sexual behavior while disregarding the risk for physical or emotional harm to self or others.
b. There is clinically significant personal distress or impairment in social, occupational or other important areas of functioning associated with the frequency and intensity of these sexual fantasies, urges, and behavior.
c. These sexual fantasies, urges or behaviors are not due to the direct physiological effect of an exogenous substance (e.g., a drug of abuse or a medication), a co-occurring general medical condition, or to manic episodes.
d. The person is at least 18 years of age.
Specify if [the behavior involves]: Masturbation, Pornography, Sexual Behavior with Consenting Adults, Cybersex, Telephone Sex, Strip Clubs

While the American Psychiatric Association made the determination to exclude any variant of compulsive sexual behavior in their final version of DSM-5, in spite of a growing body of supportive findings on the shared neurological underpinnings of process and chemical addictions, the eleventh edition of *The International Classification of Disorders* (ICD-11), published in 2018, includes Compulsive Sexual Behavioral Disorder, which frames the phenomenon in terms of compulsivity rather than in terms of addiction (Kraus et al. 2018). These authors propose the construct is present when one or more of the following criteria are met:

a. engaging in repetitive sexual activities has become a central focus of the person's life to the point of neglecting health and personal care or other interests, activities and responsibilities;
b. the person has made numerous unsuccessful efforts to control or significantly reduce repetitive sexual behaviour;
c. the person continues to engage in repetitive sexual behaviour despite adverse consequences (e.g., repeated relationship disruption, occupational consequences, negative impact on health); or
d. the person continues to engage in repetitive sexual behaviour even when he/she derives little or no satisfaction from it. (Kraus et al. 2018, 109)

The ICD-11 also recommends caution with using the diagnosis when the symptoms are better accounted for by another mental illness and recommends that self-identification or moral/spiritual distress are insufficient features to qualify for this diagnosis (Kraus et al. 2018). This distinction is essential in providing proper care for a Christian population that may be inclined to adopt a label of addiction as a way to make sense of or potentially minimize responsibility for their problematic sexual behavior. As Levine notes in his work, perhaps the best conceptualization for the clinical dynamics associated with sexual addiction is that "sexual addiction is a behavioral complex not a diagnosis" (2010, 262). In their work clarifying sexual addiction as a disease, Carnes, Hopkins, and Green (as cited in Phillips, Hajela, and Hilton 2015, 172) state,

> Given almost 50 years of controversy regarding diagnostic criteria among researchers of problematic sexual behavior, the literature is surprisingly congruent when distilled from an atheoretical perspective. Although disagreement remains as to the nomenclature (e.g., sexual addiction, hypersexuality), researchers across several perspectives are relatively consistent with regards to descriptions of related phenomena. Controversy can generally be attributed to either a lack of empirical investigation for proposed criteria (e.g., duration of symptoms) or a focus on etiology rather than phenomenology. As the literature was otherwise congruent, we assert that reasonably accurate measurement of the construct of sexual addiction should be possible apart from any consideration of etiological theories.

Regardless of the label that is used to understand this construct, many individuals, approximately 6–10 percent of the population (Ferree 2010), experience this phenomenon, which has a negative impact on their physical, emotional, spiritual, relational and interpersonal functioning. As such, the most sensible starting point for assessment and treatment is to examine the convergence of the individual's reported symptoms and experiences. Despite this wealth of data that undergirds the notion of sexual addiction, there remains opposition to establishing formal diagnostic criteria and providing treatment for those who experience the unwanted consequences of problematic sexual behavior.

Those who oppose the notion of sex addiction typically take one of the following three positions: (1) Sexual behaviors and/or pornography cannot possibly be an addiction since they are not drugs or chemicals injected, ingested, or inhaled and therefore do not fit the longstanding framework for defining addiction. (2) Sexually addictive behaviors are better accounted for by other diagnostic constructs (e.g., bipolar disorder, obsessive-compulsive disorder). (3) Sex positivity does not allow for a sexual behavior to be pathologized unless it involves coercion or the violation of another's rights, and any expression of one's sexuality should be celebrated so long as these criteria are maintained. These three positions and other, less common beliefs that seek to invalidate the reality of sexual addiction are somewhat surprising against the breadth of research on process addictions and the associated neuroscience. These findings consistently offer further clarification for the concept of sexual addiction for clergy and therapists alike and validate the millions of anecdotal stories shared by men and women whose lives have been negatively impacted by this struggle. Phillips, Hajela, and Hilton summarize this body of findings by suggesting,

> The research and scientific revelations related to addiction confirm that the behavioral or process addictions, including sex addiction, are not merely based on the chemical dependency model but are based on the scientific understanding that there are common brain mechanisms at work in the brain related to all addiction. (2015, 173)

The research demonstrates common variables, both biological and nonbiological, for sexual behavior to qualify as an addiction, yet there is a strong reluctance among some to integrate these findings into our shared understanding of human sexuality. It makes one wonder why the American Psychiatric Association, an international leader in issues pertaining to mental health, has only been willing to consider the *underfunctioning* of one's biology as problematic or worthy of diagnosis (e.g., erectile dysfunction, hypoactive sexual desire disorder), while simultaneously claiming that a dimensional model (problematic behavior occurring as a result of both underfunctioning and overfunctioning) has the most explanatory power in understanding the human experience. Dismissing the reality of hyperactive sexual desire or compulsive models of sexual behavior emerges as a fundamentally inconsistent position to hold when examined against the organization's logic for classifying problematic behavior of a diagnosable nature. Both ends of the continuum (i.e., hypo- and hyper-) entail varying types of disordered behavior yet create similar levels of distress in the social, emotional, and physical functioning of those who present for treatment.

This reluctance to acknowledge the reality of sexual addiction seen in certain fields and subgroups of the helping professions should not be surprising given the degree to which the distorted logic introduced by the sexual revolution is held in the current cultural and professional mindset. How quickly as a society we look to the brain to validate the constructs we prefer to support, oftentimes erroneously, while quietly dismissing the neuroscientific findings that frame a healthy sexual ethic when we interpret this data in an objective, unbiased fashion. How many confirmatory brain studies will it take for our clinical imagination to integrate this notion of sexuality as a potentially addictive phenomenon? One challenge is that for culture to set boundaries with regard to sexual behaviors would mean undermining the relativistic hedonism that has come to define our postmodern sexual mentality; such boundaries would implicitly validate the history of church teachings and Christian theology pertaining to the image of God borne in the human person and the significance given human sexuality in the Scriptures, two concepts that are actively being deconstructed in the current worldviews and beliefs about human sexuality popularly adopted in Western societies.

With the sexualization of the human person in many cultures around the world, human sexuality has become a significant topic for pastors and theologians alike. The navigation of this space has impact for the future of the church and its relevance in the cultural imagination. Sexualization tends to birth objectification of others, which results in seeing others as a commodity to be consumed or transacted rather than a human person to love well. In managing the tension between cultural pressures and theological continuity, many in the church have opted for compromise to the permissive sexual standards of the world rather that persisting in faithful adherence to Scripture as the primary determinant of truth. As those who courageously walk the healing path of recovery know so well, for themselves or alongside those who are suffering, the words of Christ ring true:

> Enter through the narrow gate. For wide is the gate and broad is the road that leads to destruction, and many enter through it. But small is the gate and narrow the road that leads to life, and only a few find it. (Matt. 7:13–14)

SEXUAL ADDICTION MODELS

As the construct of sexual addiction has become more widely understood and applied, a number of models have emerged as best efforts to continue exploring the concept as it matures through scientific inquiry and clinical application. Rather than modifying the primary definition for sexual addiction, these models enhance our framework for conceptualizing the manifestation of sexually addictive struggles in different populations in different contexts at different points in time. Rather than competing for primacy in the theoretical landscape, they are best understood as adjunctive models that bring dimensionality to an ongoing conversation.

Carnes's Model of Sexual Addiction

Carnes's (2015) model of The Addictive System suggests that life experiences in dysfunctional family environments, which are then amplified by other life events, birth a *belief system*, or a series of core beliefs about the self. These beliefs emerge early and are subtly refined over time in the life of the individual. Those struggling with sexually addictive behavior tend to report the following core beliefs:

1. "I am a bad, unworthy person."
2. "No one would love me as I am."
3. "My needs are never going to be met if I have to depend on others."
4. "Sex is my most important need." (Carnes 2015, 46)

Shame is a prominent emotional experience that weaves itself through these beliefs and plays a critical role in the perpetuation of the cycle of sexual addiction. Shame in the context of addiction and recovery will be explored in greater detail in chapters 3 and 7, respectively. These core beliefs and the resultant shame combine to birth *impaired thinking*, or a distorted perception of reality and loss of awareness of things that are occurring around oneself (Carnes 2015). Out of this space emerges an *addiction cycle*, which begins with a sense of *preoccupation*, or "obsessing about being sexual or romantic," which eventually leads to the loss of control over one's behavior (Carnes 2015, 45).

Carnes continues by suggesting that obsessions tend to be intensified through behavioral rituals, with the *ritualization* process creating "further distance between reality and the sexual obsession," which fosters a type of "trance" and decreases the individual's ability to say "stop" (2015, 45). *Acting out* behaviors emerge from this trance-like state and can include a variety of sexual behaviors, as well as co-occurring addictive behaviors involving drugs or alcohol (Carnes 2015). This acting out process falls under the *sexual compulsivity* phase of the addiction cycle, with Carnes suggesting, "compulsivity simply means that addicts regularly get to the point where sex becomes inevitable, no matter what the circumstances or the consequences" (2015, 45). The cycle culminates with *despair*, or feelings of depression, emptiness, or hopelessness (Carnes 2015). *Unmanageability* then emerges in this addictive system, which reinforces chaotic living and distorted core beliefs, in turn furthering impaired thinking, and the cycle continues (Carnes 2015). The primary mood-altering function of sexually addictive behavior, then, is found in the experience of arousal, numbing, escape, or control (Carnes 2015, 308–12).

On the inverse side of compulsive sexual behavior, Carnes proposes a restrictive response, a type of binging and purging cycle among some individuals dealing with sexual addiction. He names this response *sexual anorexia* and suggests that it is defined by features such as a pattern of resistance to anything sexual; going to extremes to avoid sexual contact or attention; maintaining rigid, judgmental attitudes about one's own sexuality and that of others; extreme shame and loathing about sexual experiences and one's own body and finding that one's sexual aversion interferes with life, work, relationships, hobbies, and other aspects of normal daily living (Carnes and Moriarity 1997). Carnes (2015) also suggests that sexual anorexia operates similarly to sexual addiction, with the key differences in the cycle of addiction being distancing strategies and sexual aversion in the place of ritualization and sexual compulsivity.

Another foundational contribution made by Carnes's work is the idea of an *arousal template*, or a sexual scanning of familiar patterns, which is shaped in early developmental years and modified over time. Influences include family messages about sexuality, experiences of nurturance or the lack thereof (i.e., neglect, abuse), early sexual experiences, and social influences, such as the church, media, and more (2015). The arousal template will often shape the behaviors that come to define one's acting out behaviors, and understanding the arousal template is a significant part of recovery. The twenty categories of sexually addicted behavior identified by Carnes (2015, 86–87) include the following:

- Fantasy and consequences
- Paying for sex, commercial, prostitution
- Pornography use
- Paying for sex, power, paying for sex in relationships
- Networking for anonymous sex
- Phone sex
- Swinging and group sex
- Voyeurism and covert intrusions
- Cruising behavior
- Exhibitionism

- Relationship addiction
- Exploitative sex, trust
- Conquest behavior
- Exploitative sex, children
- Intrusive sex
- Home-produced pornography
- Humiliation and domination
- Object sex, using objects or sex toys
- Pain exchange
- Drug interaction, using sex in combination with drugs and alcohol

While Carnes's work has historically focused on individuals whose addictions entail a wide range of sexual behaviors, the emergence of cybersexuality and its propensity toward addiction have forced a reconceptualization of the nature of sexual addiction. Specifically, Riemersma and Sytsma (2013) have proposed a "classic" model of sexual addiction and a "contemporary" variation in light of these changes in culture and technology.

Riemersma and Sytsma's Classic versus Contemporary Model

In their model of contemporary sexual addiction, Riemersma and Sytsma emphasize the *chronicity* of exposure to sexual materials or experiences, the availability of more graphic *content* by way of the internet, and the *culture* of sexual permissiveness found in American society: "Rapid-onset addictive patterns are the result of the '3C' toxic cocktail of content, chronicity, and culture, with special concern warranted for children and youth whose age of first exposure interrupts normal biopsychosexual development" (2013, 315). Riemersma and Sytsma differentiate "classic" and "contemporary" sexual addiction by the following items (307):

Classic Sex Addiction
- History of abuse is common
- Insecure attachment patterns
- Disordered impulse control
- Gradual onset
- Typically catalyzed by cross-addiction or comorbid mood or anxiety disorders
- Defined by shame and personal worthlessness

Contemporary Sex Addiction
- Chronic exposure to sexually graphic content
- Cultural trends toward virtual or nonrelational sex
- Disordered neurochemical, sexual, emotional, and social development
- Rapid onset
- Can result in cross addictions or comorbid mental health issues
- Defined by early sexualization

Given the differences that exist between these proposed models of sexual addiction, the process of treatment will look different depending on which category the individual best fits and the unique elements of their personal narrative. Scott Brassart suggests treatment is similar for the trauma-driven/classic sexual addiction patient and the digital-age/contemporary sexual addict but differs in a few unique ways. He states:

> Early in the healing process, treatment for these two groups is, in most respects, the same. The primary focus is on identifying and halting the compulsive/addictive behavior. As treatment progresses, however, the approach diverges. This divergence is necessary because although the two categories of compulsive/addicted porn users may look the same on the surface, they are quite different beneath the surface. The underlying issues driving the behavior are just not the same. Thus, longer-term treatment is also not the same. (Brassart 2021)

From there, however, work with contemporary sex or porn addiction focuses on fostering appropriate social, relational, and sexual development; diversifying coping skills; and rebooting their neurological responses to sexual stimuli (Riemersma and Sytsma 2013; Weiss, n.d.). For classic sex addicts, however, a process of breaking through denial; facilitating trauma resolution; managing comorbid dynamics such as attention-deficit/hyperactive disorder and other impulse-control concerns, mood disorders, and anxiety-related disorders; and addressing co-addictive behaviors is required (Riemersma and Sytsma 2013; Weiss, n.d.).

Ferree's Model of Female Sex and Love Addiction

One significant contribution to the sexual addiction literature is found in the publication of *No Stones: Women Redeemed from Sexual Addiction* by Marnie Ferree (2010). This volume was one of the first of its kind to examine the differences between men and women in the experience of sexually addictive behavior. Regarding female sexual addiction, Ferree frames the construct as an umbrella term, with subcategories including relationship or love addict, romance addict, fantasy addict, and pornography or cybersex addict. Ferree indicates female sexual addiction can include masturbation, exhibitionism, selling or trading sex, or partnering with another sex addict, as well as falling into patterns of sexual binging and purging, and "acting in" by way of sexual anorexia (2010, 68). Providing insight into its function, Ferree suggests, "female sexual addiction, for those women addicted to relationship, romance and fantasy, can involve an important element that's often overlooked: the incredible feeling of power" (2010, 70). Ferree provides additional insights into female sex and love addiction in chapter 14.

Hall's Opportunity, Attachment, and Trauma Model

Another contemporary model for conceptualizing sexual addiction emerged with Paula Hall's Opportunity, Attachment, and Trauma (OAT) model (2013). Developed with the goal of "moving beyond the traditional model of attachment" for sexual addiction, this model focuses on opportunity, attachment, and trauma as the primary constructs to consider in sexual addiction assessment and treatment (Hall 2013, 279). This paradigm provides four distinct categories of sexual addiction: opportunity-induced, attachment-induced, trauma-induced, and attachment/trauma-induced. She indicates that "'opportunity' is everywhere and people, with or without a background of trauma and/or attachment difficulties, can now experiment with and indulge their sexual desires in the privacy of their home and at the click of a button" (282). With opportunity as a necessary feature of these four models of sexual addiction, the OAT model places a high value on exploring the individual's personal narrative for a history of trauma and impaired attachment processes in better understanding how to tailor the treatment process to maximize clinical outcomes.

One dynamic to consider with the OAT model is that a history of exposure to sexual content or experiences does not automatically qualify an individual for sexual addiction, and religious individuals may overreport the impact of this exposure due to the heightened sense of guilt or shame that may occur in communities of faith that emulate a rigid, disengaged family system. As such, utilizing additional screening tools to gain a clearer picture of the scope and nature of their sexual behaviors is essential in both assessing and treating problematic sexual behaviors.

Katehakis's Psychobiological Approach to Sex Addiction Treatment (PASAT)

The emergence of research specifically fostering an understanding of the role of biological and neurological processes in the development of human relationships has given way to a newfound emphasis on these variables in the etiology of sexually addictive behavior. Katehakis (2016) weaves together a holistic model of conceptualizing and treating sexually addictive behavior through the lens of interpersonal neurobiology, specifically emphasizing the attachment narrative in human development and its impact on psychobiological functioning throughout the lifespan. She examines the corrective impact of a holistic treatment paradigm that focuses on "intellectual, behavioral, somatic, and relational fronts to generate real and enduring transformation" and uses the strength of the therapeutic alliance to facilitate this process (2016, 5). PASAT places dual emphasis on the treatment of addictive behaviors in the short-term, initial phase of treatment, while transitioning to focus on the processing of trauma through the middle and later stages of the recovery process. While borrowing concepts from psychodynamic theory in framing the therapeutic relationship, this holistic approach also integrates psychological assessment, Cognitive-Behavioral Therapy, twelve-step work, trauma resolution models such as Somatic Experiencing (SE) or Eye Movement Desensitization and Reprocessing (EMDR) as needed, and Affect Regulation Theory.

Skinner's Reaction Sequence in Pornography Addiction

In researching and treating pornography addiction, Skinner (2005) proposes a reaction sequence to explain the development of porn addiction, which also serves as a model for facilitating treatment. Specifically, this model proposes that vulnerable times awaken the desire for stimulation, which in turn activates a series of thoughts, emotions, and chemical release in the brain. Consequently, a body-language response is initiated by this chemical release, which initiates thoughts of rationalization or justification, reinforces negative hypotheses or beliefs about the self (e.g., "I am a bad person"), and eventually leads to engagement in the behavior associated with pornography use. Like Carnes's model, Skinner's concludes with the experience of remorse in the aftermath of the behavior, which is carried forward until the next space of vulnerability. Skinner proposes a recovery game plan model that seeks to reduce vulnerable times by increasing self-awareness and interpersonal contact, while getting active in alternative activities to redirect thoughts and emotions, thereby interrupting the reaction sequence and replacing the problematic behavior with healthy alternatives.

Barta's Trauma Induced Sexual Addiction (TINSA)

In his model of Trauma Induced Sexual Addiction, Barta (2018) identifies and differentiates between the various types of trauma in the human experience and their impact on the development of sexually addictive behavior. Regarding "big-*T* traumas," he includes events in one's life such as "sexual assault or abuse, physical assault or abuse, emotional or psychological trauma, serious accidents, illnesses, or medical procedures, disasters, witnessing violence, school violence, including bullying, traumatic grief or separation, war on terrorism and betrayal or relational trauma" (2018, 14). And while these big-*T* traumas can lead to addiction, many who present for treatment of sexually addictive behaviors frequently endorse "little-*t* traumas" or neglect, including lack of attunement, thwarted emotional development, lack of protection, invalidation, abandonment, wounds to vulnerability, and wounds to authenticity (Barta 2018). The recovery process for those individuals who experience trauma-induced sexual addiction, according to Barta, focuses on three things: (1) helping the client recognize the impact of self-regulating behaviors on their addiction; (2) fostering a greater capacity for outer regulation, or the ability to trust others enough to let them help in the recovery process; and (3) developing inter-regulation, or a state of attunement, interdependence, and security.

CHRISTIAN SPIRITUALITY AND SEXUAL ADDICTION

Building on the notion within Sexaholics Anonymous of lust being "an attitude demanding that a natural instinct serve unnatural desires" (1989, 40), Mark Laaser spent his career extending recovery work into the realm of Christian spirituality, with one of his most influential works being *Healing the Wounds of Sexual Addiction* (2004), a landmark publication in Christian sex addiction recovery. Laaser likens sin to addiction: "Sin and addiction have common characteristics. Like addiction, sin is uncontrollable and unmanageable. . . . Addictions, being unmanageable, also lead to destructive consequences. Addictions destroy lives, break up families and ruin careers. Sin too has its consequences" (24). Where the definition for addiction provided by the American Society for Addiction Medicine includes spiritual implications arising out of the disease, little specific attention has been paid to the theological and clinical intersection with sexual addiction beyond the work of Laaser and, more recently, Ted Roberts. Yet spirituality is understood to be a driving force in the recovery process within the Sexaholics Anonymous literature: "We will use the word *spiritual* in referring to that aspect of ourselves underlying and determining all our attitudes, choices, thoughts, and behavior—the very core of personality, the very heart of the person" (1989, 46). Exploring a framework for understanding sexually addictive behavior that is rooted in clinical best practice and is simultaneously honoring of traditional Christian anthropology is critical to understand the distortions of human sexuality evident in the modern world and the process of reclaiming sexual wholeness that is congruent with God's design for the human person.

The reality is that sexual addiction is a bio-psycho-socio-spiritual condition, one that has consequences in every part of the human experience. It has the power to entice men and women into physical acts with their bodies that cross lines they swore they would never cross. It ravages one's ability to feel certain emotions and incapacitates one's ability to regulate others appropriately. It fosters secrecy in the place of transparency and leaves a trail of destruction in the areas of trust and intimacy in marriage. It breeds tremendous strain and disconnection within family systems, and it distorts one's identity from a beloved son or daughter of the Heavenly Father to the "wretched man" that Paul describes in

Romans 7. It would follow, then, that our best strategy for treating such a holistic phenomenon would be to address each of the specific domains systematically and intentionally where the impact is felt. That is, any approach that does not include addressing the biological (brain and body), psychological (cognition and emotion), sociological (family systems and social context), and spiritual (grace/forgiveness and spiritual formation) fails to address the total impact of sexual addiction in the life of the individual, thereby leaving the individual prone to subsequent relapse and prolonged struggle. The wisdom of the twelve steps, covered in chapter 9, and its intentional inclusion of spirituality at its genesis with Alcoholics Anonymous has more validity to it than the many models of treatment and recovery that have historically discounted spirituality on the one hand or overspiritualized sexual addiction on the other. As a patient once reflected, "The church basement [at an SA meeting] is the place where I finally met the God I have been looking for in the sanctuary for my entire life."

BUILDING-BLOCK BEHAVIORS

In considering the etiology of sexual addiction, Laaser (2004) suggests there is a constellation of behaviors that increase an individual's probability of struggling with compulsive sexual acts that fit the aforementioned definition generated by Patrick Carnes. Namely, Laaser identifies sexual fantasy, masturbation, and viewing pornography as the triad of behaviors that serve as these building blocks. While a number of conditions detailed in the previously identified models serve as antecedent variables that accelerate this process (e.g., insecure attachment styles, traumatic experiences, and more), the concepts of opportunity (Hall 2013) and chronicity (Riemersma and Sytsma 2013) suggest, even apart from these antecedent variables, that addictive behaviors can begin to take root simply due to exposure over time.

Fantasy

Fantasy is the first building-block behavior identified by Laaser (2004) in the development of sexual addiction. It serves as an escape from the current moment individuals find themselves in and at its core contains a high potential for a mood-altering response (Carnes 2015). In addition, fantasy is a space in which we maintain a high degree of control over the narrative playing in our minds; it is a space where we can have unfettered access to the things from our world that would be otherwise off limits or inaccessible to us. The novelty afforded in such a space loads on addictive potential because our pleasure centers are highly responsive to the dopamine generated by novel stimuli. This novelty dimension is a key ingredient in pornography's addictive power in the human experience. Lastly, fantasy provides us with the ability to use various compensatory strategies to offset the disappointments of our lived experience. Who among us has not fantasized about the big game going a different way if only we had been on the field or how we would spend the billion-dollar prize if we held the winning lottery ticket?

In many ways, fantasy, especially sexual fantasy, operates as a distortion of our capacity for imagination. Imagination is a beautiful outgrowth of our creativity capability and a reflection of God's image within us. However, a key distinction between fantasy and healthy imagination is the role the self plays in the mind's story. Fantasy is an egocentric phenomenon, with the gratification or validation of the self serving as the focus of the narrative, whereas healthy imagination is much broader in emphasis, and the focus is largely outside of the self. In exploring the emotional needs that drive fantasy, Laaser writes, "Every sexual act symbolizes some form of excitement, acceptance, love, nurturing, power, or control; sexual acts are ways we symbolically try to solve our emotional issues" (2011, 98). As such, taking the time to identify the legitimate needs evidenced in one's sexual fantasy becomes an essential aspect of the recovery process, allowing them to serve as reflections from the soul about what the heart truly desires and priming relational interactions that will get those needs met in legitimate ways (Laaser 2011).

Masturbation

The second building block for sexual addiction identified by Laaser (2004) is masturbation. This move from the novelty of the mind to an embodied experience of pleasure is of critical importance in understanding how the biology of human sexuality can become addictive. Coria-Avila, Herrera-Covarrubias, Ismail, and Pfaus (2016) suggest that a significant response of sedation, relief, and relaxation corresponds with orgasm. In the context of addiction, the aggregate effect is one of temporary relief or escape from an undesired mood state (e.g., boredom, anxiety, sadness), a fleeting moment of self-medication that often results in the intensification of the undesired mood state. Specifically, the intensity of orgasm gives it a special place in the pantheon of human neurochemical responses, and its power has a highly reinforcing effect, increasing the probability that the behaviors leading to the orgasm will be repeated in the future (Coria-Avila et al. 2016). Struthers (2009) suggests that the chemical effects of orgasm initiate a bonding response to whatever stimuli are present at the time of orgasm. While the neurophysiological intent of this beautiful reality is intended, from a Christian perspective, to deepen the sense of trust, safety, commitment, and attunement shared by lovers within the covenant of the marriage vows, human biology is largely susceptible to manipulation. The reality of consequences emerging from this manipulation is unavoidable, namely, bonding to the images that serve as the cues for sexual arousal associated with the masturbatory behavior.

While there are a variety of opinions regarding the role of masturbation in the life of the believer, as well as its place in the process of recovery, Sexaholics Anonymous (SA) holds the position that solo-sexual activities constitute a breach of sobriety: "Any form of sex with one's self or with partners other than the spouse is progressively addictive and destructive" (1989, 202). Given its function as a building block behavior in the etiology of sex addiction and from the perspective of church history and the theology of the body, it would follow that the primary function of orgasm is to deepen unitive and procreative ends of the human experience, and, therefore, should occur exclusively within the context of sexual expression within marriage.

Pornography

The use of pornography as a sexual stimulus is the third building block that Laaser (2004) identifies as a factor in sexual addiction, and his position is supported by a wealth of scientific literature that demonstrates the addictive potential of pornographic imagery. Generally understood, pornography can be described as any explicit materials—printed, auditory, or visual—that are intended to stimulate sexual or erotic feelings. Regarding the addictive nature of pornography, late Stanford psychologist Al Cooper proposes a model he calls the Triple-A Engine to provide insight into this phenomenon. Cooper's model emphasizes the *accessibility, affordability,* and *anonymity* of online pornography in determining its addictive capacity, where others have added factors such as *acceptability, approximation,* and *accidental* to this list of features that explain how it comes to have such power in the lives of those who become addicted to it (Cooper et al. 2003).

In their research on the prevalence of pornography viewing in the United States, Regnerus and colleagues (2015) found that 46 percent of men and 16 percent of women reported intentionally viewing it in any given week. Stoner and Hughes (2010), editors of *The Social Costs of Pornography*, suggest that high pornography viewers are more likely to endorse belief in the rape myth (the belief that victims of sexual assault wanted or deserved to be raped), be more accepting of violence toward women, endorse adversarial sex beliefs, report a higher probability of engaging in rape or forced sexual acts, and report a higher degree of sexual callousness. As such, pornography is not a value-neutral stimulus that exists toward the end of personal gratification; it is a social force that desensitizes the individual viewer and reshapes beliefs about the nature of human sexuality. In its objectification and dehumanization of others, it is fundamentally inconsistent with God's design for human relationships.

Sexualization

Given the prominence of sexual materials in many forms of media available to children in Western cultures, these building-block behaviors may be quietly socialized into one's life by way of *sexualization* (Hall 2013; Riemersma and Sytsma 2013). According to the American Psychological Association (APA), sexualization occurs when any one of the following conditions is present:

1. A person's value comes only from his or her sexual appeal or behavior, to the exclusion of other characteristics;
2. A person is held to a standard that equates physical attractiveness (narrowly defined) with being sexy;
3. A person is sexually objectified—that is, made into a thing for others' sexual use, rather than seen as a person with the capacity for independent action and decision making; and/or
4. Sexuality is inappropriately imposed on a person. (2007, 1)

This would suggest that movies, television shows, music, video games, and other common activities that children and youth participate in have an impact on the formation of their sexual self-concept, as well as normalizing their implicit acceptance of sexual behaviors and attitudes. Children with a more permissive sexual self-concept based on messaging from family and engagement in activities that have a higher probability of sexualization (e.g., unsupervised time online, inappropriate apps, and more) are more likely to explore building block behaviors earlier in their lives. Beyond the development of problematic sexual behaviors with early sexualization, additional areas of impact can include body dissatisfaction and appearance anxiety, changes in cognitive and physical functioning, disordered eating, low self-esteem, and negative attitudes and beliefs about self-worth for young women (APA 2007).

While sexualization will be explored in greater detail in later chapters, it is important to note that in the context of an increasingly sexualized society and the inherent vulnerability to exploring building block behaviors for sexual addiction among those who experience early sexualization, one preventative factor that should be considered is a greater emphasis on sex education starting at younger ages than has traditionally been provided. While a great deal of diversity exists within the church regarding sexual attitudes and beliefs, the essential factors that should be communicated to children from an early age center around the names and physical aspects of their genitalia, an understanding of consent to touch the body and what constitutes healthy versus unhealthy touch, and how to identify and report inappropriate images/pornography when they come across them. In effect, building a healthy sexual mentality that can offset the power of sexualization and the curiosity around these building block behaviors starts by socializing them into open conversation around issues of sexuality when they are young and helping parents establish themselves as experts on the issue of human sexuality rather than defaulting to popular culture to fill in the deafening silence.

THE ROAD TO RECOVERY: THE SEVEN PILLARS OF FREEDOM

Many Christian sexual addiction recovery resources have been created to assist those who strive to integrate their faith into the recovery process. One comprehensive Christian sexual addiction recovery program is *The Seven Pillars of Freedom Workbook*, developed by Dr. Ted Roberts. This resource is unique in that it draws on the work of Pat Carnes through an intentionally Christian perspective, while contributing several significant insights to sexual addiction recovery. These seven pillars focus on fostering restoration by developing biblically informed life competencies in the process of recovery:

1. Break through denial.
   - Understands the characteristics of denial and self-delusion.
   - Identifies the presence of self-delusion in life.
   - Knows personal preferred patterns of thought distortion.
   - Accepts confrontation.

2. Understand the nature of sexual addiction.
   - Knows information on addictive behavior.
   - Applies information to personal life.
   - Understands sexually compulsive patterns.
   - Knows specific stories/scenarios of the arousal template.

3. Surrenders to process.
   - Acceptance of addiction in life.
   - Knows personal limitations.
   - Discerns difference between controllable and non-controllable events.

4. Limits damage from behavior.	• Has internal skills for anxiety reduction. • Develops resolution for change and commitment.
5. Establish sobriety.	• Uses clearly stated boundaries of sobriety. • Manages life without dysfunctional sexual behavior.
6. The battle is in your mind.	• Emotional healing.
7. Develops and implements a spiritual growth plan.	• Maintains a lifestyle of spiritual growth.

An additional tool that Roberts utilizes in the recovery process entailed in the workbook is the FASTER scale, which was adapted from the Genesis Project and Michael Dye. The FASTER scale provides a model of self-reflection for individuals in recovery to assess where their behavior is with regard to the potential for relapse. This mindfulness tool is holistic in its design, focusing on a range of physical, social, emotional, and spiritual variables in the process of facilitating recovery. As Roberts states, "One of the hardest skills for a guy coming out of sexual bondage is . . . being present" (2015, 9). The FASTER scale includes a sequence of emotional and behavioral processes that culminate with relapse when left unchecked. Developing self-awareness of these items and choosing appropriate responses when they are present help the individual remain on the road to recovery. The six points on the FASTER scale include,

- **Forgetting priorities:** focusing on the circumstances instead of God and recovery; leads to
- **Anxiety:** fear begins to grow, emotional energy increases; leads to
- **Speeding up:** getting busy, always in a hurry, skipping responsibilities; leads to
- **Ticked off:** getting energy from anger, aggression, or adrenaline; leads to
- **Exhausted:** loss of physical and emotional energy, depletion, depression; leads to
- **Relapse:** returning to the place you swore you would never go again.

Admittedly, there is much more to the process of sexual addiction recovery than simply generating an awareness of where one is regarding probability of relapse.

This complex process involves the development of strategies for breaking through denial; taking thoughts captive; identifying tools for regulating difficult emotional experiences; deepening a sense of understanding one's family dynamic and its impact on their relational template; allowing for a new experience of the self to emerge in relationship to others in the context of group; taking daily inventory of thoughts, feelings, and behaviors; allowing oneself to give and receive forgiveness where it is needed; and much more. *The Seven Pillars of Freedom Workbook* is simply a guide for walking this process of healing with rigor and accountability.

RECONNECTING SEXUALITY AND CHRISTIAN SPIRITUALITY

The church needs to exert time and energy toward understanding the reality of sexual addiction, both in the world it is called to minister to and in the body of the church. While one might assume the tenets of Christian spirituality serve to buffer the effects of sexualization and minimize the probability of sexually addictive behavior among believers, the research suggests this is not true in all contexts. Karaga and colleagues (2016) note that while about half of the articles they examined support this protective influence of spirituality on problematic sexual behaviors, there were notable exceptions. In fact, the authors suggest that "a few studies actually found a positive relationship between religion/spirituality and perceived addiction" (Karaga et al. 2016, 177). That is, rigid religiosity that masks as Christian spirituality can lend itself toward a false positive identification of sexual addiction in instances where the best explanation for the sexual behavior lies elsewhere (Grubbs and Hook 2016). Similarly, Reid, Carpenter, and Hook state, "It is important to consider whether religious attitudes and discrepancy are the source of distress for some, rather than hypersexuality per se, and whether 'repressed' sexual behavior arising from efforts to abstain actually contributes to sexual acting out" (2016, 298). At both a theological level and a practical level, the process of reconnecting Christian beliefs to an appropriate understanding of human sexuality is essential for equipping the church to create a space to care for those within the church and outside of it who are caught in the struggle.

Beyond the theoretical rationale for this call to reintegrate Christian spirituality and human sexuality, the current stats on problematic sexual behaviors within the church echo the need for a new conversation. With regard to pornography use, the Barna Group (2016) found that 72 percent of males between ages thirteen and twenty-four who are not practicing Christians report frequent porn use, and 41 percent of self-identifying Christian males in this age group report frequent use, with the twenty-five-and-over male demographic endorsing frequent pornography use at 55 percent for non-Christian identifying, and 23 percent for Christian identifying participants. Regarding female pornography use in participants not identifying as Christian, 36 percent of the thirteen- to twenty-four-year-old demographic and 17 percent of the twenty-five-and-over demographic reported frequent use, with 13 percent of practicing Christian females thirteen to twenty-four and 5 percent of female Christians twenty-five and over reporting frequent use.

These stats resemble a study conducted by the Barna Group in 2014, which found that among eighteen- to thirty-year-old Christian men, 77 percent look at pornography at least monthly, 36 percent view pornography at least daily, and 32 percent admit being addicted to pornography, with another 12 percent who report thinking they may be addicted. Among the thirty-one- to forty-nine-year-old Christian male demographic, the study found that 77 percent looked at pornography while at work in the past three months, 64 percent view pornography at least monthly, 18 percent admit to being addicted to pornography, and another 8 percent report thinking they may be. While the possibility of overreporting problematic sexual behaviors among self-identifying Christians may explain a portion of these results, the broader picture indicates that, sexually addicted or not, a significant percentage of Christian men struggle with behaviors that are incongruent with their self-described spiritual values and beliefs. And these concerns are not contained to the laity; the 2016 Barna study suggests that 64 percent of youth pastors and 57 percent of pastors struggle with pornography currently or have in the past. And lest the conversation be confined to Christian men, Ferree (2010) suggests that approximately 40 percent of the individuals in the general population struggling with sexually addictive behavior are female.

> The reintegration of healthy sexual practices and a robust understanding of love for God, self, and others exists at the heart of Christian sexual addiction recovery work. Giblin speaks beautifully to this need to recapture a godly vision for the human person and the sexual nature: "Society as a whole, particularly men, is sorely in need of an integrated vision of sexuality and spirituality. In the absence of such a vision, men experience their sexuality as burden not blessing, as nonrelational sexuality, and unconnected lust. Men are at risk of preoccupation with sexual fantasy, pornography, affairs, sexual addiction, and abuse." (2014, 74)

The following chapters of this text are intended to help foster deeper reflection into this process of reintegration with specific emphasis on assisting those who present with problematic sexual behavior in a pastoral context or in the clinician's office. The collective expertise provided by the contributing authors points to the tip of the iceberg in comprehending the nature of sexual addiction and the process of treatment. Engaging the primary resources referenced throughout the book will further assist the reader in deepening this process of reintegrating human sexuality with Christian spirituality to help the church fully embody Paul's words in his first epistle to the church in Corinth:

> Flee from sexual immorality. All other sins a person commits are outside the body, but whoever sins sexually, sins against their own body. Do you not know that your bodies are temples of the Holy Spirit, who is in you, whom you have received from God? You are not your own; you were bought at a price. Therefore honor God with your bodies. (1 Cor. 6:18–20)

REFERENCES

2014 Pornography survey of Christian Men (n.d.). Retrieved from http://www.christian newswire.com/news/3446774899.html.

American Psychiatric Association. 2013. *Diagnostic and Statistical Manual of Mental Disorders*. 5th ed.

American Psychological Association, Task Force on the Sexualization of Girls. 2007. *Report of the APA Task Force on the Sexualization of Girls*. http://www.apa.org/pi/women/programs/girls/report-full.pdf.

American Society of Addiction Medicine. 2011. *Public Policy Statement: Definition of Addiction*. August 15, 2011. https://www.asam.org/docs/default-source/public-policy-statements/1definition_of_addiction_long_4-11.pdf?sfvrsn=a8f64512_4#:~ :text=Short%20Definition%20of%20Addiction%3A&text=Addiction%20is%20characterized%20by%20inability,and%20a%20dysfunctional%20emotional%20response.

Barna Group. 2016. "Porn in the Digital Age: New Research Revealing 10 Trends." April 6, 2016. www.barna.com/research/porn-in-the-digital-age-new-research-reveals-10-trends/.

Barta, M. 2017. *Trauma Induced Sexual Addiction (TINSA): A Neurological Approach to the Treatment of Sexual Addiction*. Self-published, CreateSpace.

Brassart, S. 2021. "Treatment for Porn Compulsivity/Addiction: Part 2, Digital-Age 'Conditioned' Users." https://sexandrelationshiphealing.com/blog/treatment-for-porn-compulsivity-addiction-part-2-digital-age-conditioned-users/. February 8, 2022.

Carnes, P. 1992. *Don't Call It Love: Recovery from Sexual Addiction*. New York: Bantam Books. Kindle.

———. 2015. *Facing the Shadow: Starting Sexual and Relationship Recovery*. 3rd ed. Carefree, AZ: Gentle Path.

Carnes, P., and J. Moriarity. 1997. *Sexual Anorexia: Overcoming Sexual Self-Hatred*. Center City, MN: Hazelden.

Carnes, P., B. Green, L. Merlo, A. Polles, S. Carnes, and M. Gold. 2012. "PATHOS: A Brief Screening Application for Assessing Sexual Addiction." *Journal of Addiction Medicine* 6, no. 1: 29–34.

Sexual Addiction • 27

Carnes, P., T. Hopkins, and B. Green. 2014. "Clinical Relevance of the Proposed Sexual Addiction Diagnostic Criteria: Relation to the Sexual Addiction Screening Test-Revised." *Journal of Addiction Medicine* 8, no. 6: 450–461.

Christian News Wire. 2014. "2014 Pornography Survey of Christian Men: Shocking New National Survey Reveals High Levels of Pornography Use and Rampant Extramarital Affairs among Christian Men." October 7, 2014. http://www.christiannewswire.com/news/3446774899.html.

Cooper, A., M. A. Mansson, K. Danebeck, R. Tikkanen, and W. Ross. 2003. "Predicting the Future of Internet Sex: Online Sexual Behaviors in Sweden." *Sexual and Relationship Therapy* 18, no. 3: 277–291.

Coria-Avila, G., D. Herrera-Covarrubias, N. Ismail, and J. Pfaus. 2016. "The Role of Orgasm in the Development and Shaping of Partner Preferences." *Socioaffective Neuroscience & Psychology* 6, article 31815. http://dx.doi.org/10.3402/snp.v6.31815.

Ferree, M. 2010. *No Stones: Women Redeemed from Sexual Addiction.* Downers Grove, IL: InterVarsity.

Giblin, P. 2014. "Men Reconnecting Spirituality and Sexuality." *Journal of Spirituality in Mental Health* 16, no. 2: 74–88.

Grubbs, J., and J. Hook. 2016. "Religion, Spirituality and Sexual Addiction: A Critical Evaluation of Converging Fields." *Sexual Addiction and Compulsivity* 23, no. 2-3: 155–166.

Hall, P. 2013. "A New Classification Model for Sex Addiction." *Sexual Addiction and Compulsivity* 20, no. 4: 279–291.

Karaga, S., D. Davis, E. Choe, and J. Hook. 2016. "Hypersexuality and Religion/Spirituality: A Qualitative Review." *Sexual Addiction and Compulsivity* 23, no. 2-3: 167–181. DOI: 10.1080/10720162.2016.1144116.

Katehakis, A. 2016. *Sex Addiction as Affect Dysregulation.* New York: W. W. Norton & Company.

Kraus, S., R, Kreuger, P. Briken, M. First, D. Stein, M. Kaplan, V. Voon, C. Abdo, J. Grant, E. Atalla, and G. Reed. 2018. "Compulsive Sexual Behavior Disorder in the ICD-11." *World Psychiatry* 17, no. 1: 109–110.

Laaser, M. 2004. *Healing the Wounds of Sexual Addiction.* Grand Rapids: Zondervan.

———. 2011. *Taking Every Thought Captive.* Kansas City: Beacon Hill.

Levine, S. 2010. "What Is Sexual Addiction?" *Journal of Sex and Marital Therapy* 36, no. 3: 261–275.

Phillips, B., R. Hajela, and D. Hilton, Jr. 2015. "Sex Addiction as a Disease: Evidence for Assessment, Diagnosis, and Response to Critics." *Journal of Sexual Addiction and Compulsivity* 22, no. 2: 167–192.

Reid, R. 2015. "How Should Severity Be Determined for the DSM-5 Proposed Classification of Hypersexual Disorder?" *Journal of Behavioral Addictions* 4, no. 4: 221–225.

Reid, R., B. Carpenter, and J. Hook. 2016. "Investigating Correlates of Hypersexual Behavior in Religious Patients." *Sexual Addiction and Compulsivity* 23, no. 2-3: 296–312. DOI: 10.1080/10720162.2015.1130002.

Regnerus, M., D. Gordon, and J. Price. 2015. "Documenting Pornography Use in America: A Comparative Analysis of Methodological Approaches." *The Journal of Sex Research* 53, no. 7: 1–9. DOI: 10.1080/00224499.2015.1096886.

Riemersma, J., and M. Sytsma. 2013. "A New Generation of Sexual Addiction." *Journal of Sexual Addiction and Compulsivity* 20, no. 4: 306–322.

Roberts, T. 2019. *The Seven Pillars of Freedom Workbook*. Troutdale, OR: Pure Desire Ministries International.

Sexaholics Anonymous. 1989. *The White Book*. Brentwood, TN: Sexaholics Anonymous.

Skinner, K. 2005. *Treating Pornography Addiction: The Essential Tools for Recovery*. Provo, UT: GrowthClimate.

Stoner, J., Jr., and D. Hughes, eds. 2010. *The Social Costs of Pornography: A Collection of Papers*. Washington, DC: The Witherspoon Institute.

Struthers, B. 2009. *Wired for Intimacy: How Pornography Hijacks the Male Brain*. Downers Grove, IL: InterVarsity Press.

CHAPTER 2

SEX ADDICTION:
Circuits, Synapses, and Sobriety

BILL STRUTHERS, PHD

In this chapter we will consider the use of the term *addiction* and examine how it has been used in relation to problematic patterns of human sexual expression. We will present the overlap of behavioral, psychological, and neurological research on sexual arousal, motivation, and behavior alongside the brain regions and neurotransmitters involved in substance abuse and drug addiction. While overlap between these independently researched systems is not surprising, there is considerable debate about whether the clinical terminology associated with drug addiction should be used when describing problematic sexual behaviors. Is it appropriate to refer to a sexual behavior that a person finds themselves unable to control as an *addiction*? Should a pattern of being unable to stop sexually acting out be understood as a sexual addiction, hypersexuality, or a sexual obsessive-compulsive disorder?

The use of the term *addiction* has been employed by many therapists and counselors when working with those struggling with seemingly uncontrollable, excessive, maladaptive, and/or distressing patterns of sexual behavior. If these sexual problems can be understood as similar to drug addictions and have significant overlap with the neurological mechanisms underlying drug addiction, might the recovery of healthy forms of sexual expression be envisioned in parallel to neurobiological models of recovery for drug addiction (i.e., sobriety)? Demonstrating an overlap between the brain's systems for sexual behavior and drug addiction may play a significant part in answering these questions.

ADDICTION DEFINED

Addiction is often defined as a cycle of binging, withdrawal, and craving (that leads back to binging) (Volkow et al. 2016). An addiction cycle carries with it an implicit notion that the pattern is both maladaptive and beyond the individual's capacity to control. This lack of self-control often is closely associated with drug craving—a preoccupation with the drugs—even in light of the clear negative consequences associated with drug use. The compulsion to consume / act out / ingest the drug is so strong that addicts will report a loss of self-control to resist taking it (Hancock et al. 2018). An inability to resist is often accompanied by a resignation of personal agency and responsibility by the addict when they resolve to re-administer the drug (i.e., relapse).

In cultures where there is a heavy emphasis on personal agency and responsibility for one's behavior, the concept of addiction impacts how we see others (Room et al. 2015). More than just the term used to describe someone's problematic pattern of drug consumption, *addiction* carries with it the implication that this cycle of behavior is particularly irrational and illogical; it is beyond the addict's capacity to stop on their own (Glantz 2013). This emphasis of a disordered capacity for decision-making, behavioral habits, and moral responsibility in relation to a disrupted internal locus of control is vital to address for those working with addicts in therapeutic and counseling contexts (Volkow and Boyle 2018).

Not everyone who ingests a drug becomes an addict. Drinking a glass of wine doesn't inevitably make someone an alcoholic, and there are many who try cocaine or methamphetamine who don't develop addictions to them. Many nonpharmacological factors—genetics, personality, a history of trauma, and social pressures—influence someone's vulnerability to the development of an addiction. Discovering those vulnerabilities and risk factors and how they are involved in addiction is critical. The pharmacological properties and neuroactive profiles of some drugs, however, make them more likely to be drugs of addiction (e.g., heroin, methamphetamine).

Prior to the latter half of the twentieth century, many theories understood addiction as resulting from a personality trait, childhood upbringing, or moral weakness. But the last several decades have seen a movement toward emphasizing the brain when explaining mental health issues and disorders (Leshner 2001; Volkow et al. 2016). Many in scientific, counseling, and public health communities have championed understanding addiction as a brain disease. The current view of addiction is tied to explanations of neurochemical and brain circuitry disruptions based on discoveries in the neurosciences and pharmacology (Bickel et al. 2018).

Contemporary explanations now defer to how drugs act on the brain to produce the maladaptive and problematic cognition, behaviors, and emotions. How do these patterns emerge and play out in the life of an addict? What brain regions are critical in the development of an addiction? What neurotransmitters are involved? Questions like these have been researched with the aid of modern brain imaging and with the precision of cellular and molecular pharmacological research in animal models.

It is now possible to examine the impact of drugs on various neurotransmitter systems, and we can peer into the brains of those who are struggling with addictions or given drugs. We can examine at a cellular level the impact of drugs delivered directly to a variety of brain regions in animals to discover which neural circuits addictive drugs selectively activate. This research frames the current professional and public discussions on addiction and by extension how we theorize and evaluate a diagnosis of sexual addiction.

UNDERPINNINGS OF ADDICTION

Pharmacological explanations of addiction are the most straightforward aspect of the brain disease model of addiction (Volkow et al. 2016). Drugs of addiction act as exogenous compounds that mimic endogenous compounds in the body and brain to activate reward and motivational systems within the brain (Wise and Robble 2020). The molecular attributes of a drug enable it to directly bind to neurotransmitter receptors. The location and function of these receptors play a critical role in whether an addiction will develop. Why does a person become addicted to amphetamines but not to aspirin? Why does a person become addicted to opium but not to antibiotics? In essence, it boils down to the characteristics of the drug and their mechanisms of action within the brain.

Located in the brain are neurological systems designated for the experience of pleasure, decision-making circuits, and hubs for forming behavioral habits (Berridge and Kringelbach 2013). Every aspect of our psychological experience has its roots or correlates in our brain. When we examine these systems in light of the criteria for addiction, it's not surprising that they overlap with one another. Systems important for natural reinforcers having hedonic salience, brain regions evaluating future consequences of actions, and those coordinating the development of automated behavioral patterns are all disrupted in drug addicts. These systems are also important for sexual motivation, sexual arousal, and sexual behavior (Berridge and Kringelbach 2015). Integrated neural systems that process natural reinforcers such as food, water, and sex are part of the brain's developmental blueprint in the limbic system. Without them, motivated behavior that keeps the organism alive would be compromised. Circuits in the cerebral cortex assess likely outcomes of potential choices against previous experience to determine the best option available, and these decisions set in motion (and often rely upon) previously established habits and responses organized by the basal ganglia. A drug only has an addictive potential inasmuch as it can activate these natural hedonic, decision-making, and habit-formation systems.

A common pharmacological and neurological aspect of addictive drugs (e.g., cocaine, amphetamine, opium, or heroin) is that they directly act on neurotransmitters (e.g., dopamine, norepinephrine, and endorphins) and their circuits known to be involved in these natural hedonic, decision making, and habit-forming processes (Self and Nestler 1995; Nestler 2005; Badiani et al. 2011; Nestler and Lüscher 2019; Wise and Robble 2020). Addictive drugs take advantage of the brain's plasticity and neuroadaptive processes within these aforementioned systems to develop what can be called a *gain of function* (Lüscher 2016). This gain of function is established when a drug alters the adaptive synaptic plasticity of the brain and creates a long-lasting trace for future responses. This trace is resistant to change so that any new, negative consequences resulting from the drug do not impair the trace's power or capacity for continued influence. The system's original preference is overridden, or hijacked, so that the drug now takes precedence. The addict now relies upon the drug. Caught in a pharmacologically altered neural web of addiction, they now feel a need for the drug that did not exist prior to their ingesting it. It has supplanted other needs and has become their preferred goal.

A *need* can be understood as a physiological requirement or something necessary for survival—things like water, oxygen, and glucose. But we also talk about a need for shelter and a need to regulate body temperature. We can frame needs as not just limited to what enables survival but as a tiered set of things that build upon one another (e.g., Maslow's Hierarchy of Needs). Instincts and reflexes are goal-directed and innate patterns of behavior that aren't due to learning and experience, and needs are often triggered by deprivation. Deprivation of a need produces what might be referred to as a *drive*, and a drive will motivate an organism to want to satisfy that need. We are activated and aroused to satisfy these needs, and we experience pleasure when we get what we want. Each of these terms—*needs, drives, motives, wants, likes, arousal*—influence the way neuroscientists and pharmacologists research and interpret many of the issues that are relevant to psychological experience, sexuality, and mental health issues and addiction. Many theories on addiction and sex addiction in particular will appeal to these different constructs, so we should take care to use them precisely. Unfortunately, we often use them in careless and flippant ways, not realizing that they can be easily misunderstood and lead to wrongheaded ways of thinking about ourselves.

For example, is it appropriate to frame sexual activity as a need? If a need is something required for an individual's survival like water and oxygen, then sexual activity is not a need. One does not die from virginity or abstinence. But most adults have experienced sexual impulses and drives for erotic and sensual connection that they would describe as a need. When this need is felt, its frustration or nonsatisfaction can be profoundly distressing. This human sexual drive is powerful (Kringelbach and Berridge 2016). It is not only important for reproduction within the species, but it also serves to establish social and parenting bonds between partners. Those who do not satisfy these sexual desires and impulses can experience considerable distress. While lack of sexual activity is not necessarily fatal, it can dramatically impact the quality of a person's life experience.

On a psychological level, sexual desire can be linked to orgasm or to a longing to connect with a partner (Aron et al. 2005), along with a variety of other psychological motivations and needs. It is widely understood that people have sex for many different reasons. Some will engage in sexual activity to feel closer to an intimate partner. Others might engage in a sexual act when the motivation for intimacy is absent, out of a sense of obligation to a mate. It is not uncommon for some to engage in sexual encounters to advance themselves socially or professionally. Others will have sex to care for their partner, to act upon their sexual curiosity and a sense of play, or to self-soothe when they are distressed. Some people feel a strong desire to have sex, but others do not yet have sufficient motive to engage in sexual activity. Additionally, there are varying levels of enjoyment of sex. Some may have sex and not enjoy it at all. They may not want to have sex but still be sufficiently motivated to have it. They may feel uncomfortable or disappointed when they engage in sex with their partner or when they masturbate.

Suffice it to say that human sexuality is complex. But does this complexity and ability to meet multiple needs open the door for it to have a *gain of function* capacity? Are there sexual stimuli (e.g., pornography) that possess an ability to trigger addictive patterns within a vulnerable individual (e.g., a child going through puberty)? Is it possible for pornography-aided masturbation or other sexual habits to develop into uncontrollable coping strategies for dealing with a variety of stressors and motivational states? Might the hedonic and physiological consequences of sexually acting out serve to temporarily distract someone from their stress, avoid the ongoing impact of trauma, or manage unresolved psychological problems? Could a framework that incorporates the neuroscience of drug addiction overlap with human sexuality in such a way to predict or explain sexual habits as addictions? Not everyone who views pornography becomes a porn addict, but are there similarities between drug and pornography addiction?

HEDONIC SYSTEMS

The satisfaction that comes from eating a sweet morsel when you are hungry, the pleasure of quenching your thirst with a delightful beverage when you are thirsty, and the heightening of erotic excitement culminating in orgasm all have a dopaminergic element to them. Opioid drugs are known to produce ecstatic highs and release/relief from pain or tension. Opiates accomplish this through the activation of endorphin receptors in the septum (part of the limbic system linked to orgasm) (Berridge and Kringelbach 2015). Stimulant drugs, such as amphetamines, are also known to act on dopamine systems involved in sexual excitement and arousal. Initially, dopamine activity was believed to be part of the high of orgasm. It was thought that dopamine release in a specific brain region (the nucleus accumbens—more on this later) was the underlying chemical substrate of pleasure, but this is now believed to be more opioid-dependent. The combined actions of dopamine and opiates form hedonic associations. Ingesting a drug that acts on these systems to produce a high (the initiation of a connection between drug and high) begins the *gain of function* process whereby the drug overrides the natural hedonic system.

The hedonic value for a natural reinforcer such as food or sex can be understood as having a natural upper limit that is influenced by deprivation. This is why a bland piece of food tastes so much better when you are hungry, a glass of water is so much more refreshing when you are thirsty, and an orgasm can feel more intense when there has been a prolonged period of abstinence. When a drug-naïve, natural hedonic system has been perturbed by a drug, the systems within this pathway are reset to expect the drug, the *gain of function*. This gain results in significant negative consequences where the original workings of the neural systems (*sans* drug) are no longer the default. The system has now adapted because of the drug exposure. This diminished state is what causes withdrawal. These negative consequences are tied to brain cells adapting and developing a tolerance toward the drug and serve as the cue to trigger the memory of the drug's effects. Prior hedonic rewards associated with eating, drinking, sex, or other pleasures become secondary to the drug. This serves to redirect the system and elicits a preoccupation with the drug (craving), increased intensity of negative withdrawal to be managed, and binging.

As mentioned earlier, opioids can produce highs that users will often compare to sexual release (Nestler 1996). That is not surprising since a burst of endorphins is released as part of sexual orgasm (Levin 2014; Coria-Avila et al. 2016). Opioids (particularly synthetic opiates such as heroin and oxycontin) have profound addictive potential. Other drugs, such as stimulants, have their addictive impact by preferably acting upon dopamine systems. Discrete dopaminergic systems are known to be involved in movement, attention, arousal, and habit formation. Dopamine is also critical for neurological processing of natural rewards and reinforcers.

Early studies on dopamine systems' involvement in motivated behavior and as a model for addiction can be traced to a study by Olds and Milner published in 1954. In their landmark study, James Olds and Peter Milner (Olds and Milner 1954; Olds 1962) discovered a neurological system in rats where they would work to self-administer small electrical shocks through an electrode implanted in their brain. Ensuing research over the next several decades produced a rich understanding of how dopaminergic connections between deep midbrain tegmental portions of the brainstem extend into the septum, ventral striatum of the basal ganglia, and the cortex and how these connections are involved in motivated behavior.

This mesolimbic system relies heavily on the midbrain regions' triggered release of dopamine into higher limbic and cortical brain regions (Salamone and Correa 2012). One part of this mesolimbic circuit, the ventral tegmental area (VTA) of the midbrain, maintains a dopaminergic projection to the ventral striatum (also known as the nucleus accumbens, or NuAc), which then connects to the nearby ventral pallidum. Dopamine release into the NuAc was discovered when hungry animals were given food, when water-deprived animals were given sugar water, and when animals would mate. Dopamine could also reliably be released by administering a variety of addictive stimulant drugs. Initially proposed as the Dopamine Hedonia Hypothesis, it was postulated that the NuAc and ventral pallidum were pleasure sites, with dopamine its pleasure neurotransmitter. Dopamine activation of the NuAc and ventral pallidum produced a hedonic experience of "liking" (or enjoyment) that animals would be motivated to work for. This was also supported by evidence that a blockade of dopamine activity in the NuAc prevented these behavioral responses (Salgado and Kaplitt 2015). Dopamine blocking drugs produced *anhedonia* when administered in these regions. Additional research, however, has shown that this is an incomplete way of understanding dopamine's role in this region.

It appears that dopamine activity in the NuAc and ventral pallidum, while certainly having a hedonic component, is also involved in related reward processes. Within the NuAc and ventral pallidum are several small subregions better understood as hotspots (Robinson et al. 2005; Berridge and Robinson 2016; Berridge 2019). Some of these hotspots appear to be directly tied to the experiencing of hedonic pleasure, but not all of them. Dopamine release into these hotspots has been connected to what researchers call incentive salience, an object's capacity or power to provoke attention. Incentive salience is when an object calls attention to itself and attracts you to it. It is one thing to take notice of something in the environment and be attracted to it, but it is another thing to want it. Dopamine in these types of hotspots may be best understood as an underlying desire. This can be linked to incentive cues about the object or a history of reward that is associated with them—the *gain of function*. This implies the potential for a learned process by which something can make itself increasingly attractive. A stimulus (e.g., a drug) can take on incentive salience because you have indulged in it, or it may have natural stimuli that are attention-grabbing or distracting as part of a predisposition of the system (e.g., sexual cues in a postpubertal brain). Dopamine plays a significant role in these hedonic (liking) and incentive salience (wanting) NuAc and ventral pallidum hotspots. The distinction between these two systems can also be beneficial when considering why addicts might want something (such as drugs or orgasm), even though they may experience a diminished liking of it.

In the life of an addict, the dissonance between increased wanting and diminished liking of the drugs can contribute to a downward spiral. Dysregulation, tolerance, and the accompanying neurological and pharmacological adaptations resulting from drug use serve to disrupt natural reward systems. Attempts to stop ingesting an additive drug become difficult. As tolerance to the drug increases, its hedonic value diminishes. As withdrawal symptoms increase, drug use becomes more about withdrawal avoidance than a pursuit of a high (Chamberlain et al. 2016). The distress related to the withdrawal leads to a vulnerability to relapse. Each relapse deepens the drug's trace and its gain of function on the hedonic systems. Relapse vulnerability can also be tied to normal developmental issues. The brains of an infant, toddler, child, adolescent, teen, and adult can be dramatically different with varying levels of plasticity, resiliency, and vulnerability to addictions.

DECISION HUBS AND LOOKING INWARD

A second neurological set of systems disrupted by drug addiction (and also important for sexual behavior) is connected to executive functioning and decision-making (Bickel et al. 2018). These networked cortical systems are involved in predicting likely outcomes of behaviors, regulating emotional responses, and gatekeeping of downstream behavioral responses. These executive regions include the dorsolateral prefrontal cortex (dlPFC), the orbitofrontal cortex (OFC), and the anterior cingulate cortex (ACC). The dlPFC serves to evaluate future outcomes important for determining which behavioral responses should be selected. As a need is generated (such as withdrawal symptoms, deprivation, or incentive salience), the NuAc, amygdala, and other limbic regions are activated. The promise of pleasure, fear of missing out on a reward, and deprivation generate internal distress within limbic and cortical systems. The OFC is involved in managing this emotional activity in light of ongoing decision-making cortical activity (e.g., the dlPFC). Eventually, the ACC serves as the launching point for the execution of the selected behavioral response or habit to deal with the need. Each of these cortical regions are disrupted by drugs of addiction but are also relevant when considering human sexual response.

The insula is a cortical region that is primarily involved in what is referred to as interoception, the mapping of visceral bodily states (Namkung et al. 2017; Ibrahim et al. 2019). The insula serves as the nexus where we integrate these visceral bodily signals. These include autonomic, genital, and tactile sensations. The insula is interconnected with the dlPFC and plays a role in moral decision-making. This cortical region is where the visceral response of withdrawal is felt in an addict and where the ache of sexual longing is likely situated. When we get sick to our stomach at the thought of a moral failure or when we are rejected, the insula serves as a locus for this interoceptive experience. When we combine the interoception of the insula with the incentive salience of a stimulus and its dopamine release in the NuAc and incorporate amygdaloid activity generated by the distress of deprivation, we get a better picture of the psychological and neurobiological components of craving and withdrawal within the addictive cycle—but also of sexual longing and motivation. These systems can be conceptualized as interconnected hubs working in concert with one another to produce the complexity of both drug addiction and sexual motivation.

OVERLAPPING SYSTEMS

Extensive literature exists on the neurobiology of reproductive behavior in a variety of animal species. This comparative work often sets a framework alongside which human sexual behavior is placed. Male and female organisms develop biologically, and their reproductive drives are influenced by circulating hormones, availability of mates, and mating strategies. In primates, sexual activity does not exclusively serve reproductive purposes; it also possesses a social dimension. Sexual development, motivation, and behavior is complex. By examining animal patterns of attraction, arousal, appetitive behaviors, and copulation, the relevant neural processes present in males and females have been thoroughly investigated (Ågmo 1997; Pfaus et al. 2015).

Mammalian female and male brain regions (and connected systems) important for reproduction include the hypothalamus, amygdala, NuAc, midbrain, and cortex (as well as the spinal cord). Species' specific sensory systems detecting sexual cues and indicating sexual availability feed into these systems. Many mammals use pheromones, auditory signals, or visual cues to indicate their sexual status or availability. In the presence of these cues and under the right motivational conditions, sexual arousal and behavior can be initiated. Much of the interconnectivity and pharmacology in both male and female systems is well understood. Reproduction in adult animals involves a series of sequenced stages (nuanced as male or female) with mating-oriented (or auto-sexual) behaviors through which an organism progresses. Much has been revealed by experimental manipulation through surgical lesions, altering the presence of gonadal hormones, direct pharmacological manipulation, and direct behavioral assessment.

While there are many striking similarities between humans and nonhuman primates, it is critical to remember that human sexuality cannot be completely separated from nonhumans, nor should it be seen as functionally and organizationally equivalent to nonhumans. The human brain is critically involved in the organization of our sexual lives. It coordinates our reproductive development from childhood, through puberty, and into adulthood. It is integrated with other bodily organ systems, such as the genitals and gonads, and generates sexual motivation. It responds to sexual cues in the environment, develops sexual scripts for appropriate sexual behaviors, coordinates our sexual behavior, and is the center of our psychological sexual experience. The natural hedonic systems that govern sexual pleasure, eating, drinking, and other needs that generate human behavior are also linked to drug addiction.

Discussions of human sexuality must include a neurobiological component that covers its emotional, motivational, behavioral, and cognitive aspects (Georgiadis and Kringelbach 2012). Sex research on humans would suggest that humans can have multiple motives, different cues, and different ways of coordinating their sexual behaviors (Georgiadis et al. 2012). A complex system of contextual neurobiological factors that are acquired, deliberated upon, triggered, and acted upon go into human sexual behavior. Higher brain systems (such as the visual cortex, which detects sexual cues in the environment, as well as other parts of the cerebral cortex) directly related to sexual thoughts and experiences are connected to subcortical regions involved in generating sexual motivation and emotions. In the brainstem, the hypothalamus has long been known to play a critical role in sexual development. As a site rich in gonadal hormone receptors, the hypothalamus is involved in generating sexual drives and coordinating sexual responses to incoming sex-relevant cues.

During puberty, dormant sexual drive systems within the hypothalamus are activated, triggering changes across the brain. As these systems go online, reproduction drives emerge, and previously innocuous sensory cues can contain newfound sexual incentive salience. Moving through adolescence into adulthood and sexual maturity causes changes to multiple organ systems. Brain regions that are oriented toward reproductive and erotic sensitivity have newfound properties. Sexual incentives and experiences become available in a way that a prepubertal childhood brain is not open to. The hypothalamus and other brain regions are integrated with peripheral systems, such as the genitals, that generate psychogenic responses, reactions, and reflexes, which increase the salience and intensity of the sexual experience (Georgiadis and Kringelbach 2016). These systems have the blueprint for the reproductive and erotic aspects of human sexuality, but they can be impacted by behavioral conditioning, observational learning, cultural scripts, and cognitive frameworks (Baldwin and Baldwin 2002; Baldwin and Baldwin 2012). Of note, the hypothalamus is also a region through which the mesolimbic dopamine pathways run to connect the VTA with the cortex and NuAc.

The impact of brain lesions on the control of human sexual behaviors reveals several cortical and subcortical regions as crucial (Baird et al. 2006). Frontal lobe lesions can be accompanied by an impairment in controlling sexual responses, and parietal cortex lesions near the insula impact interoceptive genital sensation. Lesions of the amygdala as well as lesions of the surrounding temporal cortex (i.e. Klüver Bucy Syndrome) can produce sexual drive disorders (an elevation of libido). Case studies of Parkinsonian patients receiving dopaminergic drugs or deep brain stimulation near mesolimbic projection systems reported an increase in sexual impulses not present prior to treatment (Barbosa et al. 2018).

Brain imaging research on individuals seeking treatment for problematic pornography use reveals disruptions of NuAc/basal ganglia, amygdala, cortex, and hypothalamus, as well as further implicating these regions as sex-relevant in nonclinical populations (Gola, Miyakoshi, and Sescousse 2015; Brand et al. 2016; Gola et al. 2017; Kraus et al. 2016; Gola and Drap 2018). While this research is not without controversy (primarily associated with the diagnostic and public discourse surrounding pornography and sex addiction), the underlying brain regions known to be involved in human sexual function overlap considerably with those related to drug addiction. In truth, much of the research related to pornography and sex addiction appeals to this overlap as part of its justification for use of addiction terminology.

A THOUGHT EXPERIMENT ON SEXUAL ADDICTION

As part of normal development, adolescents undergoing pubertal changes will find themselves being newly attuned to erotic/mating/sexual cues. These sexual cues will have a newfound incentive value that grabs their attention. A naked form may produce sexual urges or desires they will need to navigate. A familiarity with sexual scripts (either by directly viewing, reading, or being instructed about sexual behaviors) will inform their response. An increase in sexual interest, sexual motivation, and sex-oriented behavior can be informed by these scripts.

Consider the example of an adolescent viewing pornography for the first time. Out of sexual curiosity, an adolescent (visual sexual cues can play a significant role in triggering sexual arousal) may feel an interoceptive pressure (insular and amygdala activity), be hypnotized by the images (incentive sexual salience due to emerging dopamine activity in NuAc hotspots), and develop a sexual behavior repertoire by observing the participants and reading the video's comments (dlPFC). As they attempt to manage these feelings (OFC), the combined experience may direct them to experiment with masturbation (ACC). The resulting stimulation and orgasm (release of endorphins in the septum) is consolidated into memory. An association between the needs, feelings, behavior, and outcomes is likely established through this process. For the developing adolescent, however, by repeating this pattern to cope with other, nonsexual motivations (e.g., social isolation or rejection, parental neglect, depression, anxiety), a potential *gain of function* could develop whereby pornography paired with masturbation could become their preferred means of dealing with a variety of stressors. This may limit their willingness to seek out alternative coping mechanisms or more appropriate responses.

CONCLUSION

It is important to question the way we theorize about, frame, categorize, diagnose, and treat symptoms and problems experienced by those who identify as sex addicts. Rather than thinking of sex as a drug, why not think of sex as, well, sex? Rather than talking about pornography as "cocaine for the eyes," why don't we talk about opium as an injected orgasm that bypasses foreplay and other embodied aspects of sexual intimacy? Drugs are the hijackers, sending multiple neurological systems designed for sexual responses into addictive patterns. Perhaps this is an entirely appropriate way to frame the issue at hand.

The complexity identified in this exploration of the neurobiological dimensions of sexuality and addiction raises even more questions and future directions for scientific inquiry. Should addiction terminology be used when talking about recurring maladaptive and problematic sexual behaviors? Does it matter that we use the terminology linked to drug use as a way of talking about disrupted and pathological forms of sexual expression? Does it put the cart before the horse? If we use the "exogenous" language of drugs to describe "endogenous/natural" sexuality, what limitations are set in place? Or what frontiers might be opened? As researchers and practitioners engage in discussions about sexual addictions, how do we coalesce around the common neurological and pharmacological elements while reminding ourselves of the important commonalities and differences between drugs and human sexuality? Coming together around a testable theory and critically evaluating it is the best way to approach the phenomenon, to describe its symptoms, diagnose it, and form a response. Ultimately, we are striving to find the best way to understand the problem presented by many and to deal with it. There is good reason to describe these problems as "sex addiction." Considerable overlap exists with these behaviors and drug addiction. But this terminology should also be used cautiously, with full awareness of its limitations and with willingness to consider alternate frameworks to address these issues.

Assimilating the habits that are found in the life of people struggling with problematic and repeated sexual behaviors into a diagnostic framework such as addiction (or some other term) can be limiting as much as it can be freeing. Whether it is referred to as recovery, sobriety, or reorganization of sexual habits, reliance on the same adaptability of the human brain that led to the addiction is also needed to plot a path forward. And it is relationship that most powerfully and comprehensively activates this neurobiological potential for growth and change. Throughout his earthly ministry, Christ makes it a regular habit to see those who had been rendered invisible within his cultural context. Much like he engaged the Samaritan woman at the well, as helpers we are called to perceive and respond to the legitimate needs of those who struggle with problematic sexual behavior, help them examine their personal narrative, and, most importantly, provide them with a glimpse of the same mercy and grace they encounter in relationship with him.

REFERENCES

Ågmo, A. 1997. "Male Rat Sexual Behavior." *Brain Research Protocols* 1, no. 2: 203–9. https://doi.org/10.1016/S1385-299X(96)00036-0.

Aron, A., H. Fisher, D. J. Mashek, G. Strong, H. Li, and L. L. Brown. 2005. "Reward, Motivation, and Emotion Systems Associated with Early-Stage Intense Romantic Love." *Journal of Neurophysiology* 94, no. 1: 327. https://doi.org/10.1152/jn.00838.2004.

Badiani, A., D. Belin, D. Epstein, D. Calu, and Y. Shaham. 2011. "Opiate versus Psychostimulant Addiction: The Differences Do Matter." *Nature Reviews Neuroscience* 12, no 11: 685–700. https://doi.org/10.1038/nrn3104.

Baird, A. D., S. J. Wilson, P. F. Bladin, M. M. Saling, and D. C. Reutens. 2007. "Neurological Control of Human Sexual Behaviour: Insights from Lesion Studies." *Journal of Neurology, Neurosurgery and Psychiatry* 178, no. 10: 1042–49. https://doi.org/10.1136/jnnp.2006.107193.

Baldwin, J. D., and J. I. Baldwin. 2002. "Sexual Behavior." In *Encyclopedia of Human Behavior* 309–22. Academic Press.

———. "Sexual Behavior." 2012. In *Encyclopedia of Human Behavior*, 2nd ed., edited by Vilayanur S. Ramachandran, 418–24. Amsterdam: Elsevier.

Barbosa, P. M., T. Grippe, A. J. Lees, S. O'Sullivan, A. Djamshidian, and T. T. Warner. 2018. "Compulsive Sexual Behaviour in Parkinson's Disease Is Associated with Higher Doses of Levodopa." *Journal of Neurology, Neurosurgery and Psychiatry 89, no. 10:* 1121–23. https://doi.org/10.1136/jnnp-2017-317298.

Berridge, K. C. 2019. "A Liking versus Wanting Perspective on Emotion and the Brain." In *The Oxford Handbook of Positive Emotion and Psychopathology,* edited by J. Gruber, 183–96. Oxford: Oxford University Press. https://doi.org/10.1093/oxfordhb /9780190653200.013.13.

Berridge, K. C., and M. L. Kringelbach. 2013. "Neuroscience of Affect: Brain Mechanisms of Pleasure and Displeasure." *Current Opinion in Neurobiology 23, no. 3:* 294–303. https://doi.org/10.1016/j.conb.2013.01.017.

———. 2015. "Pleasure Systems in the Brain." *Neuron 86, no. 3:* 646–664. https://doi.org /10.1016/j.neuron.2015.02.018.

Berridge, K. C., and T. E. Robinson. 2016. "Liking, Wanting, and the Incentive-Sensitization Theory of Addiction." *American Psychologist 71, no. 8:* 670–679. https:// doi.org/10.1037/amp0000059.

Bickel, W. K., A. M. Mellis, S. E. Snider, L. N. Athamneh, J. S. Stein, and D. A. Pope. 2018. "21st Century Neurobehavioral Theories of Decision Making in Addiction: Review and Evaluation." *Pharmacology Biochemistry and Behavior 164*: 4–21. https://doi .org/10.1016/j.pbb.2017.09.009.

Brand, M., J. Snagowski, C. Laier, and S. Maderwald. 2016. "Ventral Striatum Activity When Watching Preferred Pornographic Pictures Is Correlated with Symptoms of Internet Pornography Addiction." *NeuroImage 129*: 224–232. https://doi.org/10.1016/j .neuroimage.2016.01.033.

Chamberlain, S. R., C. Lochner, D. J. Stein, A. E. Goudriaan, R. J. van Holst, J. Zohar, and J. E. Grant. 2016. "Behavioural addiction—A rising tide?" *European Neuropsychopharmacology 26, no. 5:* 841–855. https://doi.org/10.1016/j.euroneuro.2015.08.013.

Coria-Avila, G. A., D. Herrera-Covarrubias, N. Ismail, and J. G. Pfaus. 2016. "The Role of Orgasm in the Development and Shaping of Partner Preferences." *Socioaffective Neuroscience & Psychology 6*, no. 1: article 31815. https://doi.org/10.3402/snp.v6.31815.

Georgiadis, J. R., and M. L. Kringelbach. 2012. "The Human Sexual Response Cycle: Brain Imaging Evidence Linking Sex to Other Pleasures." *Progress in Neurobiology 98*, no. 1: 49–81. https://doi.org/10.1016/j.pneurobio.2012.05.004.

———. 2016. "Intimacy and the Brain: Lessons from Genital and Sexual Touch." In *Affective Touch and the Neurophysiology of CT Afferents*, edited by H. Olausson, I. Morrison, J. Wessberg, and F. McGlone, 301–321. New York: Springer. https://doi .org/10.1007/978-1-4939-6418-5_18.

Georgiadis, J. R., M. L. Kringelbach, and J. G. Pfaus. 2012. "Sex for Fun: A Synthesis of Human and Animal Neurobiology." *Nature Reviews Urology 9, no. 9:* 486–498. https:// doi.org/10.1038/nrurol.2012.151.

Glantz, M. D. 2013. "The Terminology of Addictive Behavior." In *Principles of Addiction*, edited by P. Miller, 13–22. Amsterdam: Elsevier.

Gola, Mateusz, and M. Draps. 2018. "Ventral Striatal Reactivity in Compulsive Sexual Behaviors." *Frontiers in Psychiatry 9*: 546. https://doi.org/10.3389/fpsyt.2018.00546.

Gola, M., M. Miyakoshi, and G. Sescousse. 2015. "Sex, Impulsivity, and Anxiety: Interplay between Ventral Striatum and Amygdala Reactivity in Sexual Behaviors." *Journal of Neuroscience 35*, no. 46: 15227–15229. https://doi.org/10.1523/JNEUROSCI.3273-15.2015.

Gola, M., M. Wordecha, G. Sescousse, M. Lew-Starowicz, B. Kossowski, M. Wypych, S. Makeig, M. N. Potenza, and A. Marchewka. 2017. "Can Pornography be Addictive? An fMRI Study of Men Seeking Treatment for Problematic Pornography Use." *Neuropsychopharmacology 42*, no. 10: 2021–2031. https://doi.org/10.1038/npp.2017.78.

Hancock, D. B., C. A. Markunas, L. J. Bierut, and E. O. Johnson. 2018. "Human Genetics of Addiction: New Insights and Future Directions." *Current Psychiatry Reports 20*, no. 2: 8. https://doi.org/10.1007/s11920-018-0873-3.

Ibrahim, C., D. S. Rubin-Kahana, A. Pushparaj, M. Musiol, D. M. Blumberger, Z. J. Daskalakis, A. Zangen, B. Le Foll. 2019. "The Insula: A Brain Stimulation Target for the Treatment of Addiction." *Frontiers in Pharmacology 10*: 720. https://doi.org/10.3389/fphar.2019.00720.

Kraus, S. W., V. Voon, and M. N. Potenza. 2016. "Neurobiology of Compulsive Sexual Behavior: Emerging Science." *Neuropsychopharmacology 41*, no. 1: 385–386. https://doi.org/10.1038/npp.2015.300.

Kringelbach, M. L., and K. C. Berridge. 2016. "Neuroscience of Reward, Motivation, and Drive." In *Recent Developments in Neuroscience Research on Human Motivation*, edited by S. Kim, J. Reeve, and M. Bong, 23–35. Vol. 19 of *Advances in Motivation and Achievement*. Bingley, UK: Emerald Group.

Leshner, A. I. 2001. "Addiction Is a Brain Disease." *Issues in Science and Technology 17*, no. 3: 75–80.

Levin, R. J. 2014. "The Pharmacology of the Human Female Orgasm—Its Biological and Physiological Backgrounds." *Pharmacology Biochemistry and Behavior 121:* 62–70. https://doi.org/10.1016/j.pbb.2014.02.010.

Lüscher, C. 2016. "The Emergence of a Circuit Model for Addiction." *Annual Review of Neuroscience 39*, no. 1: 257–276. https://doi.org/10.1146/annurev-neuro-070815-013920.

Namkung, H., S.-H. Kim, and A. Sawa. 2017. "The Insula: An Underestimated Brain Area in Clinical Neuroscience, Psychiatry, and Neurology." *Trends in Neurosciences 40*, no. 4: 200–207. https://doi.org/10.1016/j.tins.2017.02.002.

Nestler, E. J., and C. Lüscher. 2019. "The Molecular Basis of Drug Addiction: Linking Epigenetic to Synaptic and Circuit Mechanisms." *Neuron* 102, no. 1: 48–59. https://doi.org/10.1016/j.neuron.2019.01.016.

Nestler, E. J. 1996. "Under Siege: The Brain on Opiates." *Neuron 16*, no. 5: 897–900.

Nestler, E. 2005. "Is There a Common Molecular Pathway for Addiction?" *Nature Neuroscience* 8: 1445–49.

Olds, J. 1962. "Hypothalamic Substrates of Reward." *Physiological Reviews 42*, no. 4: 554–604.

Olds, J., and P. Milner. 1954. "Positive Reinforcement Produced by Electrical Stimulation of Septal Area and Other Regions of Rat Brain." *Journal of Comparative and Physiological Psychology 47, no. 6:* 419.

Pfaus, J. G., S. L. Jones, L. M. Flanagan-Cato, J. D. Blaustein. 2015. "Female Sexual Behavior." In *Knobil and Neill's Physiology of Reproduction*, edited by T. M. Plant and A. J. Zeleznik, 2287–2370. Amsterdam: Elsevier.

Robinson, S., S. M. Sandstrom, V. H. Denenberg, and R. D. Palmiter. 2005. "Distinguishing Whether Dopamine Regulates Liking, Wanting, and/or Learning about Rewards." *Behavioral Neuroscience 119*, no. 1: 5–15.

Room, R., M. Hellman, and K. Stenius. 2015. "Addiction: The Dance between Concept and Terms." *The International Journal of Alcohol and Drug Research 4*, no. 1: 27. https://doi.org/10.7895/ijadr.v4i1.199.

Salamone, J. D., and M. Correa. 2012. "The Mysterious Motivational Functions of Mesolimbic Dopamine." *Neuron 76*, no. 3: 470–485. https://doi.org/10.1016/j.neuron.2012.10.021.

Salgado, S., and M. G. Kaplitt. 2015. "The Nucleus Accumbens: A Comprehensive Review." *Stereotactic and Functional Neurosurgery 93*, no. 2: 75–93. https://doi.org/10.1159/000368279.

Self, D. W., and E. J. Nestler. 1995. "Molecular Mechanisms of Drug Reinforcement and Addiction." *Annual Review of Neuroscience* 18, no. 1: 463–95.

Volkow, N. D., and M. Boyle. 2018. "Neuroscience of Addiction: Relevance to Prevention and Treatment." *American Journal of Psychiatry 175*, no. 8: 729–40. https://doi.org/10.1176/appi.ajp.2018.17101174.

Volkow, N. D., G. F. Koob, A. T. McLellan. 2016. "Neurobiologic Advances from the Brain Disease Model of Addiction." *New England Journal of Medicine 374, no.* 4: 363–71. https://doi.org/10.1056/NEJMra1511480.

Wise, R. A., M. A. Robble. 2020. "Dopamine and Addiction." *Annual Review of Psychology 71, no.* 1: 79–106.

CHAPTER 3

THE NEUROAFFECTIVE MODEL
OF SEXUAL ADDICTION

Todd Bowman, PhD, CSAT-C

The world is changing quickly. New technology and new terminology leave us constantly trying to keep up. The evolution of sexual attitudes, beliefs, and behaviors is no different. New concepts and nomenclature emerge regularly, largely driven by the advances in technology and the accessibility afforded by the Internet. As chapter 1 highlights, numerous models attempt to capture the addictive aspects of these malleable sexual concepts. Pat Carnes's pioneering work is the primary example of one response that has been made with this cultural shift in sexual attitudes and behaviors. Beyond the realm of psychology, theologians have worked to clarify and communicate a biblical sexual ethic in response to these ever-evolving sexual norms and practices. Given these movements and the need to continually integrate new findings into a comprehensive framework, the Neuroaffective Model provides an expanded paradigm for understanding and treating sexually addictive behaviors, as well as emphasizing the importance of psychological and spiritual integration for the individual. Building on Carnes's early work, this model draws intentionally on Christian theology, advances in neuroscience, and a broad swath of clinical literature regarding problematic sexual behavior to best conceptualize the origins and ongoing functionality of sexually addictive behavior for the individual and the most effective interventions for therapists and pastors to utilize. The anthropology, physiology, and psychology used in this conceptual framework emerge from the biblical teachings regarding the human person, augmented by the psychological sciences. Where secular models of sexual-addiction recovery are significantly informed by religious expression (e.g., meditation) and personal spirituality (e.g., personal identification with a higher power) (Carnes, 2009), the Neuroaffective Model draws on Christian theology in positing that spirituality is the core of personhood and deems healthy relationship with God, self, and others as an essential dynamic in sustainable and successful sexual-addiction recovery.

Understanding the human holistically provides better insights into the driving factors of addiction and shapes how we think about interventions. Toward this end, Pardini and colleagues (2000) indicate that higher engagement in spirituality and religious practices increases the level of optimism in life orientation and perceived social support, results in higher resilience in the face of stressors, and lowers reported levels of anxiety among individuals seeking substance abuse treatment. In the research that has been produced in the two decades since this study was first published, the findings hold true time and time again: Personal spirituality and religious practices have a significant impact on the recovery process for those in substance abuse treatment, and this finding would likely generalize to recovery from other types of addiction as substance and process addictions share neurobiological substrates (Love, et. al, 2015; Nestler, 2005). Ongoing research continues to examine the role of spirituality and religious expression in relation to sexually addictive behaviors (see Karaga, Davis, Choe, and Hook, 2016; Reid, Carpenter, and Hook, 2016).

THE NEUROAFFECTIVE MODEL

At this intersection of physiology, psychology, and theology, interpersonal connection serves as a primary construct in understanding God's design for the human experience. The Neuroaffective Model operationalizes connection as the experience of feeling felt and being known and posits that this need for connection is shown in the human person's social and affective neurobiology, as informed and affirmed by the biblical narrative. Christian anthropology begins with the notion that humans are created for rich, meaningful connection in the image of an intrinsically relational God. Genesis 2:18 reads, "The LORD God said, 'It is not good for the man to be alone. I will make a helper suitable for him.'" This need for connection extends to all parts of the human experience: connection with God, with self, with others, and with creation as a whole. The disruption of this healthy sense of connection is a critical variable in the development of sexual addiction, and the process of recovery, healing, and transformation is by its very nature intended to facilitate reconnection across these domains, correcting the distortions that have taken root in the individual's lived experiences and reclaiming God's design for human sexuality. For the purposes of this model, Hall's Opportunity, Attachment, and Trauma model (2013) discussed in chapter 1 serves as the soil from which problematic sexual behavior tends to emerge. Specifically, the sexualization of the human imagination in the modern world by way of cybersexuality tends to increase objectification of the self and the other, as will be unpacked further in chapter 5. While possible, sexual addiction without sexualization is infrequent. In addition, human attachment systems that are distorted by way of environmental and interpersonal influence leave one more vulnerable to externalizing types of coping, as will be discussed in chapter 4. Lastly, trauma disorganizes an individual in ways that often inhibit self-awareness, overwhelm coping systems, and disrupts the process of developing trust and bonding with others. These traumatic moments include wounds of both abandonment (e.g., neglect) and intrusion (e.g., physical abuse, sexual abuse), labeled as "big-*T*" and "little-*t*" trauma in chapter 1. The process of recovery seeks to understand how the individual's unique experiences create a vulnerability to sexual behavior as a coping mechanism and empathically assist them in walking the path of recovery.

Where these three constructs in the OAT model serve as foundation for problematic sexual behaviors, shame is the primary catalyst in entrenching the behavior as addiction. Shame is an emotional experience that originates in disconnection and is both built and repaired through the felt experience of connection. Emerging at a preverbal stage of development, it is ubiquitous in the etiology of sexual addiction. Shame results in a self-appraisal of being intrinsically bad, which can be understood differently than guilt, in which the self is appraised as having *done* something bad rather than being *defined* by badness (Parker and Thomas 2009). Guilt tends to increase movement toward reconciliation and relationship, whereas shame leads to further disconnection, short-circuiting the necessary repair of relationship through behaviors such as covering or hiding, sabotaging, blame-shifting, or isolating. These interpersonal origins of shame are captured by Lopez, who states,

> Shame refers to the phenomenological experience of sudden and unexpected exposure, one that renders the self diminished or defective in some way. Pointing to the "quintessentially" social nature of shame, Lewis (1971) proposes that shame involves the failure of the central attachment bond, whereas Kaufman (1989, 1992) relates shame to the experience of being emotionally and psychologically cut-off from one's significant attachments. (Lopez et al. 1997, 188)

Shame, then, is the emotional experience of feeling exposed, deficient, and rejected birthed in the unexpected sense of disconnection from important people or caregivers, often beginning in infancy and continuing through human development. This framework for understanding shame as an interpersonal phenomenon is congruent with Christian anthropology. In the biblical narrative, we see shame emerge in the human experience in Genesis 3:7–8:

> Then the eyes of both of them were opened, and they realized they were naked; so they sewed fig leaves together and made coverings for themselves. Then the man and his wife heard the sound of the LORD God as he was walking in the garden in the cool of the day, and they hid from the LORD God among the trees of the garden.

Shame comes from the repeated and sustained breakdown of the primary attachment bonds. The primary behaviors elicited by this introduction of shame in the human experience include covering the self and hiding from connection with a primary attachment figure. These are both efforts to avoid consequences for one's behavior or to protect oneself from judgment.

Through this lens, it makes sense that shame-proneness is an antecedent condition in the etiology of sexually addictive behavior. The distorted sense of identity emerging from this developmental narrative leaves space for the maladaptive coping styles that lend toward externalizing behaviors, which are activities intended to change one's mood that do not rely on healthy interpersonal connection, including sexual self-soothing, substance abuse, cutting, disordered eating, and more. In a highly visual, sexualized society, it follows that these externalizing behaviors develop around appearance, body image, and sexual prowess. For those carrying high amounts of shame, impression management becomes a survival strategy. It is an attempt to cover perceived defects aimed at gaining the acceptance, validation, and belonging people should receive in healthy relationships. Sexually addictive behaviors are a fragmented foraging for connection without offering true vulnerability or intimacy in return. Despite the desire to feel felt, connected, and accepted, if the self is experienced as defective or deficient in some way, the threat of rejection chokes out any willingness to be truly vulnerable or fully known. Sexually addictive behaviors perpetuate the experience of being cut off from true intimacy and leave the individual settling for a "safe" (i.e., nonrejecting) alternative. This lack of intimacy and use of "safe" alternatives (e.g., pornography, fantasy, prostitutes, and more) reinforces the sense of self as defective or diminished in some way, which amplifies the sense of shame and leads to participation in behaviors that need to be covered to avoid consequences or judgment, both of which relate to rejection. This cycle is not easily broken, and it has powerful neurobiological underpinnings. Shame is a toxic psychological concept that pollutes the nature of connection we are created to experience in relationship with one another. Its role in the etiology of sexual addiction cannot be understated.

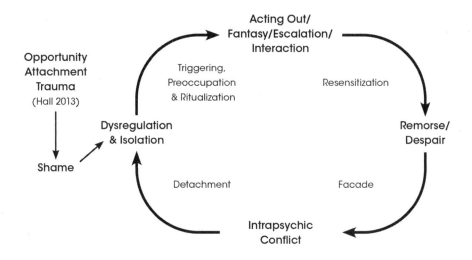

With shame as a primary emotional driver, the Neuroaffective Model argues that the origins of problematic sexual behavior are found in the need for persons to manage their dysphoric emotional experiences in relationship and that neglectful and abusive environments, various types of trauma, early sexualization, and unhealthy attachment experiences lead to a style of relating to the self and others that is inherently mistrustful or disengaged, inhibiting one's ability to effectively manage these affective experiences in relationship. We are created for both physical and emotional balance, and we regulate our physical and emotional experiences in safe, trusting relationships. When our relational world is unsafe or inconsistent, we eventually lose the ability to entrust ourselves to others completely, and shame is quick to fill this relational void. This lack of meaningful connection in the developmental narrative leaves a lasting impression on the human attachment process and reverberates throughout a person's life.

Our need for emotional homeostasis drives us to bond with parents and caregivers as a way to manage our emotional experiences, even from the earliest of ages. This design for balance suggests that a prolonged state of heightened emotional activation (underregulation) or dissociation/withdrawal (overregulation) is psychologically unsustainable. Intense emotion experienced for too long can birth general anxiety, panic attacks, and cardiovascular issues, whereas suppressing or ignoring emotion can lead to depressive disorders and somatic issues (e.g., pain disorders, impaired immune functioning, and more.). In the context of sexual addiction, the escape from these affective states is driven by the anticipation of (preoccupation), movement toward (ritualization), and/or experience of sexual stimulation (acting out or fantasy), even when the escape is short-lived and compounds one's experience of shame.

DYSREGULATION AND ISOLATION

Given the importance of connection in understanding the human person and the healthy management of emotion, the natural starting point for examining the phenomenon of sexual addiction is the disruption of connection. Dyadic regulation, or the drawing on physical proximity to or the internal representation of an attachment figure to regulate one's emotional state, is evident early in human development. Many infant behaviors invite a regulating response from an attachment figure or caregiver. These instinctual behaviors, such as clinging when afraid or crying when alone, indicate that emotions are intended to be soothed by physical and psychological contact, such as the touch of a hand or looking into the eyes. The inconsistency or unavailability of caregivers creates a working model of others as unresponsive, untrustworthy, and unreliable. The lack of access to connection over time leads to unmanaged emotional states (affective dysregulation) and leaves the infant prone to externalizing behaviors, which include thumb-sucking, clinging behavior, or inconsolable crying in infants. This fundamental breakdown in responsiveness and attunement in the infant's world lays the foundation for later addictive self-soothing. To this end, Katehakis suggests,

> If an infant or toddler is deprived of all caregiving, his cortisol level stays chronically high and he will decline into passive parasympathetic strategies of dissociation. Such chronic stress disables the child from responding effectively to any future danger, to which he responds uniformly by entering a withdrawn state. Habituation to either the active or the passive response programs the developing brain, and makes the repeated imbalanced state into a permanent trait: dysregulated anxiety or aggression, or dissociation. (2009, 5)

These intense responses of anxiety or aggression and dissociation, when reinforced frequently over time, can be understood as underregulated (feeling uncontrollably intense affect) and overregulated (dissociating or shutting off affect) self-states, respectively. As the individual ages, self-soothing behaviors, or emotional regulation strategies, are established and refined by continued exposure to the social environment. Maladaptive variations of self-soothing later in development include behaviors such as overeating, drug and alcohol abuse, cutting, gambling, and even sexual behaviors, all geared toward managing intense emotional behaviors by trying to feel emotion less intensely or moving out of dissociation by attempting to feel something at all.

The common denominator with these responses is that each holds the potential for addiction. The more any self-state is experienced, the more familiar it becomes. This suggests that the more integrated the problematic self-soothing behavior is, the more reflexive it becomes when the individual becomes emotionally dysregulated. When sexual behavior is integrated as a self-soothing strategy early in development due to early sexualization, it becomes a primary strategy for managing emotional distress, given its relative effectiveness in comparison to other potential responses. Katehakis indicates that these learned emotional regulation patterns become permanent traits and are more firmly fixed in the individual's psychological makeup, thus increasing the complexity of sexual addiction treatment (2009).

Trauma is another important construct to consider in the development of maladaptive coping strategies, especially given the strong relationship between trauma and shame. In their meta-analysis of shame and PTSD, Saraiya and Lopez-Castro state, "the emotional consequences of relational trauma and repeated traumas are linked with shame" (2016, 10). Schore suggests that "in human infancy, relational trauma, like exposure to inadequate nutrition during the brain growth spurt, to biological pathogens, or chemical agents that target developing brain tissue, and to physical trauma to the baby's brain, interferes with the experience-dependent maturation of the brain's coping systems, and therefore, have a long-enduring negative impact on the trajectory of developmental processes" (2001, 207). Trauma, then, activates an experience of the self as diminished and unworthy, which decreases movement toward relational regulation and diminishes the brain's capacity to foster healthy coping mechanisms. This finding is especially true for those who experience sexual violence as compared to nonsexual forms of trauma, with both groups demonstrating more shame response than individuals with no exposure to trauma (Saraiya and Lopez-Castro 2016). Forged in the rigid and disengaged family systems identified by Carnes, overregulation and underregulation as maladaptive styles of coping leave the individual turning to pathological soothing strategies to manage their emotional world (2015). Inherent in this process of managing stress and other emotions apart from relationship is the reinforcement of a toxic experience of the self: shame. Out of this experience of shame, an identity rooted in the core beliefs of sexual addicts identified in chapter 1 begins to emerge that further predisposes the individual to self-soothing sexual behavior, and the potential for addiction increases.

Self-sufficiency and an overt need to protect the self are inherent in the identity formed by these beliefs, leaving the individual prone to further isolation, loneliness, and a general detachment from self and others, especially when interpersonal trauma is at the root of shame. The shame implicit in these core beliefs is exacerbated as the individual lives out these beliefs. Participation in sexually addictive behaviors results in a growing sense of disconnection from others, further reinforcing the validity of these beliefs in the mind of the sexual addict. This chasm of disconnection and isolation renders the self vulnerable to the many self-soothing strategies that have been identified to have addictive potential—sex, drugs and alcohol, eating, spending, gambling, video games, and internet use, among others—and when used to escape undesirable mood states or disconnect from reality the cycle of addiction is born. As the sense of interpersonal connection in a culture diminishes, the utilization of these maladaptive self-soothing strategies grows in popularity and prominence. Successful treatment of sexual addiction resolves this core experience of shame, replaces dysfunctional core beliefs with healthy self-understanding, and properly boundaries and replaces acting out behaviors, ensuring they are not simply traded for equally unhealthy alternatives.

While much research exists examining the impact of isolation and loneliness on emotional and physical wellness, Nikmanesh and colleagues studied the relationship between loneliness and the abuse of drugs in Iranian culture (2015). They suggest, "The correlation between feeling of loneliness and difficulties in emotion regulation indicated a positive significant relationship between drug abuse and feeling of loneliness and emotion regulation difficulty among students" (Nikmanesh et al. 2015, 189). Given the shared neurobiology underlying process and chemical addictions, it is logical to posit that loneliness increases affective dysregulation, which factors into the development of sexually addictive behavior as well. In support of this claim, Yoder, Virden III, and Amin conclude, "This study's results regarding the ratio of Internet pornographic usage as it relates to loneliness clearly establishes that an association exists" (2005, 30). Loneliness is also cited as a psychological characteristic in hypersexual behavior in Reid, Bramen, Anderson, and Cohen's work (2014). Persistent disconnection from others, starting in the developmental narrative as unresolved shame and reinforced through negative life experiences, leaves us prone to the overregulation or underregulation of our emotions and largely incapable of managing strong affect without external means of coping (e.g. food, drugs, technology). When the context of healthy relationship is not adequately provided in critical periods of development, the search for surrogates shapes the emergence of one's coping skills through childhood, adolescence, and into young adulthood. These underdeveloped coping skills often come to prioritize immediate relief from distress and trend toward problematic sexual behaviors in later developmental periods.

For some, especially those with early sexualization and trauma, this loneliness and isolation attempts as self-soothing or emotional regulation by way of sexual acting out or fantasy. Carnes suggests, "Distorted fantasies and satiating behaviors . . . are used in an attempt to resolve the addict's desperate loneliness. Addiction can be viewed, then, as an intimacy disorder" (2015, 43). If isolation plays a significant role in the development and maintenance of sexual addiction, largely by way of shame, then connection serves as a necessary tool in authoring a story of hope and healing.

Comorbid Psychological Constructs

Regarding self-soothing, sexual addiction has been defined by Carnes as a pathological relationship with a mood-altering sexual experience (2009). Specifically, the term *pathological* used in this definition speaks to the idea of a significant distortion from what is normative within human development and points to the potential of comorbid disturbances or illnesses. To this end, a variety of psychological conditions and clinical phenomena can contribute to the emergence of sexually addictive behaviors. This psychological vulnerability to emotional dysregulation exists with concerns such as attention-deficit/hyperactive disorder, anxiety disorders, mood disorders, obsessive-compulsive and related disorders, personality disorders, and substance use disorders. According to Ragan and Martin, "Mood disorders, anxiety disorders, personality disorders and substance use disorders are the most frequently diagnosed disorders comorbid with sexual addictions" (2000, 166). Additionally, Briken and colleagues state,

> Sexual addictive symptoms in paraphilic as well as in nonparaphilic individuals can be accompanied by high rates of other psychiatric disorders: up to 40% have anxiety disorders (Kafka & Hennen, 2002; McElroy et al., 1999), 70% have mood disorders (Kafka & Hennen, 2002; Raymond, Coleman, & Miner, 2003), 30–50% have substance abuse disorders (Coleman et al., 2003; Goodman, 1993; Kafka & Hennen, 2002; McElroy et al., 1999). In an anonymous survey of 75 persons suffering from sexual addiction problems (Schneider & Schneider, 1990), 39% reported also having substance abuse problems, 32% had an eating disorder, 13% characterized themselves as compulsive spenders, and 5% as compulsive gamblers. Persons with sexual addiction may also present with complications to their physical health, such as sexually transmitted diseases or abuse of sexual performance enhancers (Coleman et al., 2003). (2007, 133)

Given the susceptibility to affective dysregulation occurring in these diagnostic categories and the power that sexual behavior contains in human neurophysiology, these comorbid concerns can leave the individual prone to engaging in self-soothing via sexual behavior. There is no endogenous neurochemical experience that can come close to the mood-altering significance of orgasm. Sexual addiction, in many instances, can be seen as a co-occurring clinical construct, not simply a constellation of sexual symptoms associated with these psychological disorders. As such, underlying psychological conditions and the problematic sexual behavior should be treated as distinct but related constructs with a similar etiology, each with unique psychological functions in the life of the patient unless the sexual behavior occurs exclusively in the context of the psychiatric condition (e.g., impulsive sexual decisions in the context of a manic episode).

An appropriate framework to borrow from in conceptualizing this relationship between psychological concerns and sexually addictive behaviors is the dual-diagnosis model found in the substance abuse community. Treating the underlying concern is essential to the individual's recovery from sexual addiction, in that treatment (e.g., therapy, medication) provides tools for managing mood, thought, and behavior more effectively. However, it is a faulty assumption to suggest that treating an underlying psychological disturbance is sufficient to eradicate sexually addictive behavior. Sexually addictive behavior can be a symptom of other psychological concerns, and treatment should target both the comorbid construct (e.g., depression, trauma) while also addressing the problematic sexual behavior directly. Adequate intervention addresses each clinical phenomenon appropriately and comprehensively.

Preoccupation and Ritualization

As this cycle of using sexual behavior to manage dysregulated self-states and dysphoric emotion takes root, the individual first begins to experience preoccupation about sexual behaviors and then begins to ritualize these behaviors. Carnes defines *preoccupation* as "obsessing about being sexual or romantic" and *ritualization* as a trance that puts distance between reality and one's sexual desire, which decreases the individual's ability to stop the behavior (2015, 45). In other terms, preoccupation is the pull of sexual energy toward expression that drives implicit decision-making for the individual, and ritualization is the step-by-step progression that precedes and includes the sexual acting out, and, in some cases, the behaviors that follow. Recovery rituals that do not involve bringing acting out behaviors to light perpetuate the struggle by leaving it in the dark. Operating largely outside of conscious awareness, these two dynamics tighten the grip of sexual addiction in one's life.

A significant aspect of sexual addiction treatment involves combatting ritualization and preoccupation by deepening the client's level of self-awareness, increasing their recognition of sensations, thoughts, and behaviors in the moment, with the goal of strengthening the will in choosing strategies for redirecting thoughts and behaviors toward a desired end, namely, connection and accountability. In this vein, mindfulness practices serve as important tools in the recovery toolbox and help to address the many concerns related to hypersexual behaviors, namely, anxiety, depression, impulsivity, and vulnerability (Reid et. al 2014). Interventions such as thought stopping, body scanning, diaphragmatic breathing, and guided imagery can be implemented to help the client be mindful of what they are paying attention to in their moment-by-moment experience. On a spiritual level, these mindfulness activities can include reading and meditating on Scripture, engaging in prayer and reflective journaling, and participating in corporate worship.

Sexual Acting Out/Fantasy

Preoccupation and the resultant ritual move the individual toward further fantasy and acting out behaviors. The building-block behaviors present in sexual addiction (i.e., fantasy, porn, and masturbation) were identified in chapter 1. While providing a helpful conceptual framework for thinking about the nature of sexually addictive behaviors, there is a much more diverse range of behaviors that may be present in an individual's struggle, identified below. In his proposed model of hypersexual disorder for inclusion in the DSM-5, Kafka includes specific acting out behaviors as different subtypes of this disease (2010). While hypersexuality was not ultimately included in that volume of acceptable psychological diagnoses, the framework he proposed is helpful in considering potential types of sexually addictive behavior. Although incomplete due to the quickly evolving clinical jargon, the model does highlight broad categories that an individual's acting out behaviors likely fall into:

- **Masturbation:** 75 percent of sexual addicts struggle with compulsive masturbation (Wines, 1997).
- **Pornography:** 51 percent of men seeking counseling report pornography dependence as a presenting problem (Reid et al, 2009).
- **Sexual Behavior with Consenting Adults:** This can also be considered promiscuity; 89 percent of men diagnosed with paraphilic disorders qualified as promiscuous (Kafka and Hennen, 1999).
- **Cybersex:** Online sexual activities such as talk, video chatting, and other online behaviors for the purpose of sexual pleasure (Shaughnessy, Fudge, and Byers, 2017).
- **Telephone sex:** Approximately 10 percent of sexual addicts present with this as the primary addictive behavior (Briken et al, 2007).

- **Strip clubs:** Erickson and Tewksbury state, "Based on the present research, 80 percent of the men that patronize strip clubs do so in the pursuit of a voyeuristic/ pornographic experience" (2000, 290).
- **Other:** These behaviors include cruising, exposing, voyeurism, etc.

In addition to these overt forms of sexual behavior seen in individuals in sexual addiction recovery, fantasy serves as another form of acting out. At times, this concept of euphoric recall is integrated into the individual's ritualization process, whereas at others, the fantasy alone serves as a type of acting out behavior. As such, euphoric recall, or replaying memories of previous sexual acting out while overlooking the negative consequences associated with these behaviors, serves as a threat to sustained sobriety and true recovery (Carnes 2015). Robert Saplosky indicates that anticipation of a desired outcome produces a large quantity of dopamine in the pleasure pathway (2004). This anticipatory surge can even surpass the dopamine hit experienced in the consumption of the desired experience. Thus, the novelty found in online pornography provides an ever-present opportunity to maintain heightened levels of dopamine production and avoid satiation. The same can be said of the escape to sexual fantasy as a way to avoid the relational, occupational, and emotional demands of living. In some instances, sexual fantasy falls under the category of euphoric recall used by Carnes, where an individual replays in their mind memories of previous pleasurable experiences, with the goal of managing their dysphoric mood state via sexual stimuli (2015). Gola and colleagues suggest that visual sexual stimuli (VSS) foster intrinsically rewarding responses in the brain and, with diminished responsiveness in individuals who present with problematic use of VSS, support the hypothesis of sex as an addictive behavior (2016).

Cross-Addiction/Addiction Interaction

Considering sexual behavior an addiction is controversial to some, yet there is a growing body of literature to support this position, emerging primarily from the neuroscience of addiction studies. Nestler states, "Early findings in the field raise the possibility that the similar behavioral pathology that characterizes drug addictions and certain natural addictions may be mediated, at least in part, by common neural and molecular mechanisms" (2005, 1445). These shared neurobiological underpinnings suggest that addictive behaviors have an influence on one another and can be conceptualized through the lens of cross-addiction or addiction interaction. Simply stated, where there is one, there is likely more. Marnia Robinson, author of *Cupid's Poisoned Arrow*, describes cross-tolerance: "One kind of intense stimulation (or its aftermath) can make someone more likely to reach for *other* potent stimuli, such as recreational drugs, alcohol, gambling, junk food, or reckless shopping" (2009, 147). In his work on addiction as an attachment disorder, Flores speaks to the relationship between impaired emotional regulation, drug/alcohol addiction, and natural rewards:

> Since it is biologically impossible to regulate our own affect for any extended period of time, individuals who have difficulty establishing emotionally regulating attachments are more inclined to substitute drugs and alcohol for their deficiency in intimacy. Because of a person's difficulty in maintaining emotional closeness with others, certain vulnerable individuals are more likely to substitute a vast array of obsessive-compulsive behaviors (e.g., sex, food, drugs, alcohol, work, gambling, computer games, etc.) that serve as a distraction from the gnawing emptiness and internal discomfort that threatens to overtake them. Consequently, when one obsessive-compulsive type of behavior is given up, another is likely to be substituted unless the deficiency in self-structure is corrected. (2004, 6–7)

Nestler's work advances Flores's model from "obsessive-compulsive behaviors" into a more appropriate framework of process addictions.

> Growing evidence indicates that the VTA-NAc [Ventral Tegmental Area-Nucleus Accumbens] pathway and the other limbic regions cited above similarly mediate, at least in part, the acute positive emotional effects of natural rewards, such as food, sex and social interactions. These same regions have also been implicated in the so-called 'natural addictions' (that is, compulsive consumption for natural rewards) such as pathological overeating, pathological gambling, and sexual addictions. Preliminary findings suggest that shared pathways may be involved: (an example is) cross-sensitization that occurs between natural rewards and drugs of abuse. (2005, 1445)

Robinson further states, "Since one addiction lowers the threshold for developing another, sex addicts are more likely to have problems with other addictive behaviors" (2009, 147). Given the correlation that exists between sexually addictive behaviors and other chemical and process addictions, assessing for addiction interaction/cross-tolerance is essential to sexual addiction treatment and recovery.

In their work on "bargaining with chaos," Carnes, Murray, and Charpentier address the reality of addiction interaction, suggesting, "Behavioral addictions are certainly the most controversial of the potential interactions among addictions. However, the evidence is clear that behavioral disorders such as gambling, compulsive shopping, sexual addictive behavior, and eating disorders substantially co-occur with substance abuse disorders" (2005, 21). Their research suggests that the most common cross-addictive behaviors for men receiving treatment for sexual addiction are alcoholism, substance abuse, caffeine addiction, compulsive spending, high-risk behavior/danger, compulsive spending/debt, nicotine, compulsive eating, and compulsive raging/violence. For women in treatment for sexual addiction, the research suggests the most common cross-addictive behaviors include alcoholism, substance abuse, caffeine addiction, compulsive working, compulsive eating, nicotine, high-risk behavior/danger, and bulimia/anorexia (Carnes, Murray, and Charpentier 2005). These concepts should be examined and assessed in individuals presenting for treatment with sexually addictive behaviors, and sexual addiction should be screened in patients who commonly present with these co-occurring compulsive and/or addictive behaviors.

Beyond identifying the processes or substances that are used as cross-addictions in those who struggle with sexual addiction, it is imperative to understand the specific manner by which these multiple addictions interact with one another. The primary dynamics of multiple addictions, according to Flores, include the following:

- **Switching:** "Suspending one compulsive behavior but initiating a new one" (2004, 8). This can manifest as *transferred-addiction recovery*, such as the initiation of smoking as one enters alcohol treatment, to help curb the negative effects of stopping an addictive behavior. Carnes indicates this process of mediating withdrawal by switching addictive behaviors is present in 56 percent of individuals seeking sexual addiction treatment (2009).
- **Masking:** "One addiction masks or excuses another" (Flores 2004, 8). An example is using social media or video game binges to excuse the pornographic content that is being sought out. Masking is reported by 45 percent of individuals seeking sexual addiction treatment (Carnes 2009).
- **Fusion:** More than one addiction must be present for the other to work" (Flores 2004, 8). An example would be needing to use a stimulant in order to engage in sexual acting out behaviors. This combining process in multiple addictions is reported by 46 percent of individuals receiving sexual addiction treatment (Carnes 2009).
- **Ritualizing:** "One addiction is part of the ritual for another" (Flores 2004, 8). This is evidenced in clinical narratives where foraging on the internet, such as seeking out celebrity photos, is a part of the excitatory preoccupation and ritualization of accessing pornographic content. According

to Carnes, 41 percent of sexual addicts presenting for treatment report ritualizing in their acting out behaviors (2009).

- **Numbing:** "Shame about one addiction is numbed by another addiction" (Flores 2004, 8). An example is workaholism serving to compensate for the shame of sexual acting out. Carnes notes that 54 percent of individuals seeking sexual addiction treatment endorse using sexual behavior as a numbing agent (2009).
- **Disinhibition:** "One addiction lowers inhibitions for another addiction" (Flores 2004, 8). This is seen in the abuse of alcohol to disinhibit participation in anonymous sex in some sexual addicts. Approximately 42 percent of sex addicts receiving treatment report disinhibition (Carnes 2009).
- **Alternation:** "An ingrained pattern of alternating from one addiction to another" (Flores 2004, 8). This can be an indicator of sexual anorexia as a part of the pattern of sexual addiction. Carnes's research suggests that 41 percent of individuals receiving sexual addiction treatment endorse alternating addiction cycles (2009).
- **Intensification:** "Mutual addictions intensify one another" (Flores 2004, 8). An example is the use of amphetamines to enhance sexual experiences in addictive acting out. This is the most frequently endorsed dynamic in sexual addicts seeking treatment, with 61 percent indicating intensification as a part of their sexual acting out (Carnes 2009).

Escalation

Another principle that is evidenced in patterns of sexually addictive behavior is *escalation*. Escalation can be understood as the drift into content or experience that is more hard-core or that increases the level of excitement in the acting out process, which can occur slowly over time or quite rapidly. An example of escalation is starting with movies that include nudity and sexual content to soft-core films to relatively generic pornography to more specific types (e.g., amateur, fetish, BDSM), to porn that is riskier or more thrilling in some way or involves money (e.g., camming, starting an online relationship), and, in some cases, to extreme forms of porn (e.g., child porn, rape porn) or offending behavior (e.g., voyeurism, exhibitionism). Similarly, escalation can occur in the physical realm, such as moving from cybersexual behavior (e.g., porn and masturbation) to crossing the flesh line (e.g., hooking up, anonymous sex), to paying for sex (e.g., escorts, prostitutes), to various types of offending behavior (e.g., frotteurism, voyeurism), yet not every individual's escalation will follow this specific pattern. The intensification from addiction interaction can also contribute to this concept of escalation, and movement from fantasy to physical acting out is a form of escalation as well.

While there is no standard trajectory for this process of escalation, the very nature of sexual addiction as a disease suggests that it is progressive. No two people will escalate with the same trajectory or at the same pace, as there are several factors at play in this process, such as arousal template, trauma history, sexual history, and more. However, escalation serves as the primary evidence of this progression of the addiction in the life of the individual, and this process is directly tied to human neurobiology. Escalation of sexually addictive behavior involves four major brain-related changes (Wilson 2014).

1. Desensitization

The first brain-related change is *desensitization*, or a numbed response to pleasure. Wilson states, "Reduced dopamine signaling and other changes leave the addict less sensitive to everyday pleasures and 'hungry' for dopamine-raising activities and substances. The addict may neglect other interests and activities that were once high priorities" (2014, 97). This desensitization is likely the first addiction-related change in the brain that users of pornography and other forms of acting out will notice. Over time, they require more and more stimulation to obtain the same high, in effect establishing tolerance. Escalation, then, is the mechanism by which more novelty and more intense experiences increase dopamine and adrenaline, actively resetting the threshold for arousal. This resetting of "normal" in the brain leaves the individual susceptible to *anhedonia*, or the diminished capacity to experience pleasure, which, in turn, creates the need for greater intensity to feel the excitement of acting out.

2. Sensitization

The second concept in this progression is *sensitization*, or an unconscious super-memory of pleasure that, when activated, triggers powerful cravings. "Rewired nerve connections cause the reward circuit to buzz in response to addiction-related cues or thoughts—the 'fire together wire together' principle. This Pavlovian memory makes the addiction more compelling than other activities in the addict's life" (Wilson 2014, 98). In effect, stimuli from the individual's lived experiences that have become associated with sexual behavior can implicitly awaken a desire for sexual acting out, even though the individual is unaware of the source of their desire in that moment. The men to whom I have provided counsel have often disclosed a subconscious process by which they scan the room for a glimpse of flesh or evaluate others based on hair color, body shape, age, or some other characteristic that has been shaped by their porn consumption or sexual acting out. Combating sensitization means reframing these pleasurable memories by becoming more aware of oneself, evaluating for underlying unmet needs (see Laaser and Laaser, *Seven Desires*, 2013), and initiating connection with God and others in place of acting out. Sobriety over time helps facilitate this reframing, even when the super-memory remains stored away in the memory center of the brain.

3. Hypofrontality

The third construct pertaining to escalation is *hypofrontality*, or reduced brain activity in the prefrontal regions of the brain, which weakens willpower in the face of strong subconscious cravings. "Alterations in the prefrontal regions' grey matter and white matter correlate with reduced impulse control and the weakened ability to foresee consequences" (Wilson 2014, 98). Neuroscientist Dan Siegel indicates that this region of the brain is responsible for important relational functions, such as empathy, insight and self-awareness, fear modulation and extinction, intuition, morality, response flexibility, affect regulation and emotional balance, attenuated communication, and body regulation (2007). These functions serve as the core constellation of personhood and give the individual the capacity to exist in healthy relationship to God, self, and others. In fact, these features hold a profound resemblance to what Paul describes as the fruit of the spirit in Galatians 5:22–23: "But the fruit of the Spirit is love, joy, peace, forbearance, kindness, goodness, faithfulness, gentleness and self-control." Given this neurological reality, sexual addiction results in a narrative where the individual is less capable of accessing the relational connection that would serve as antidote to their condition. As such, the progressive nature of addiction leaves the individual stuck on this hedonic treadmill, trapped in a downward spiral toward depravity, even when the pleasure derived from the behavior has long since ceased.

4. Decreased Stress Circuits

The final dynamic of brain function related to the process of escalation is *decreased stress circuits*, which can make even minor stress lead to cravings and relapse because they activate powerfully sensitized pathways (Wilson 2014). This inability to manage stressors effectively leads the individual to turn to sexual acting out as a form of relief or escape with more frequency, even to stressors that previously would not have elicited a sexualized coping mechanism. The functional consequences of decreased response flexibility manifest as the return to sexual fantasy or acting out to manage even minimally distressing affective states as other coping strategies go unutilized.

One way of conceptualizing this would be to imagine each individual with a set range of emotional tolerance that can be endured, and once the stress threshold is reached, the individual must enact coping strategies to manage this distress (Siegel 1999). Siegel states, "One's thinking or behavior can become disrupted if arousal moves beyond the window of tolerance" (1999, 254). This is certainly the case in sexual addiction. Prolonged use of sexually addictive behaviors effectively lowers this threshold, leaving the individual in need of increasingly intense coping responses for less and less significant stressors. Paired with diminished response flexibility, sexually addicted individuals utilize the same response (sexual acting out) to manage stressors that they used to manage without resorting to addictive behaviors. This feature of doing the same thing over and over despite the negative outcomes is also seen in patients with trauma, which supports the conceptualization of sexually addictive behavior as an outgrowth of unprocessed trauma or neglect.

Escalation from a Biblical Perspective

From a biblical perspective, Ephesians 4:17–24 speaks to this escalation process, albeit with somewhat different language, namely in the hardening of the heart and the loss of sensitivity that epitomize this escalation. Inherent in Paul's words is the loss of identity that occurs in this drift, and the call to connection as a restorative individual and social process. He writes,

> So I tell you this, and insist on it in the Lord, that you must no longer live as the Gentiles do, in the futility of their thinking. They are darkened in their understanding and separated from the life of God because of the ignorance that is in them due to the hardening of their hearts. Having lost all sensitivity, they have given themselves over to sensuality so as to indulge in every kind of impurity, and they are full of greed.
>
> That, however, is not the way of life you learned when you heard about Christ and were taught in him in accordance with the truth that is in Jesus. You were taught, with regard to your former way of life, to put off your old self, which is being corrupted by its deceitful desires; to be made new in the attitude of your minds; and to put on the new self, created to be like God in true righteousness and holiness.

At its core, sexual addiction recovery involves a series of new experiences of the self in healthy relationship with God, self, and others that fosters a sense of acceptance, vulnerability, rigorous honesty, and purified desires. It is impossible to walk this recovery road alone.

RESENSITIZATION

The next phase of the Neuroaffective Model is a process known as resensitization, where the individual begins to come out of the fog of sexual acting out or fantasizing, and there is a return to the emotional state that was present prior to the sexual self-soothing. The physical symptoms activated by the neurochemicals of sexual behavior—dopamine, adrenaline, and endogenous opiates, among others—offer a powerful but unsustainable moment of relief. Resensitization is the process by which the individual's psychological reality comes crashing back into conscious awareness, amplified by the waning of the physical sensations. In short, this transitional process indicates a return to the dysphoric state that the sexual behavior was intended to escape. For instance, if the sexual behavior was intended to escape an experience of boredom, the process of resensitization suggests that the neurochemical window afforded by orgasm will be short lived, and the gnawing sense of boredom will eventually creep back into the individual's awareness. The opponent-process theory of emotions applies here, with relief and a sense of escape being followed by previous emotional states, which are then further amplified by shame.

Remorse and Despair

Resensitization initiates the emergence of what Carnes identifies as despair in the sexual addiction cycle (2015). While there is certainly a despair that fills this psychological space that sexual addicts report, largely driven by the deepening sense of shame, the construct of despair can be somewhat egocentric if it suggests that the individual does not have the capacity to recognize the impact of his or her behavior on others. While there is a deficit in self-awareness that fosters this egocentricity within sexual addiction, the notion of remorse shown by some individuals in recovery suggests that despair may not be an exclusive psychological feature in this window after acting out. Remorse can be understood as the deep regret and pain felt through recognizing the consequences of the addict's behaviors on others, such as their spouse or family, affair partners or prostitutes, and others.

This dichotomy of despair and remorse point directly to the dichotomy of shame and guilt. Often used synonymously because of their tendency to emerge simultaneously, these emotional experiences serve different functions. As defined previously, shame centers on the self as inherently bad or unworthy in some way, whereas guilt is built around the notion of the self having *done* something wrong. Shame leads to covering and hiding (Gen. 3:7–8), whereas guilt leads to ownership and reconciliation. The negotiation of this tension of guilt and shame can lead to either intentional disclosure of the struggle with sexually addictive behavior, where the individual willingly divulges their sexual acting out, or it is compartmentalized and buried, often leading to unintentional discovery of the behaviors by the partner, where denial, minimization, evasion, lying, and even gaslighting are used by the addict to downplay the reality of their behavior. Regarding this differential in the function of guilt and shame in sexual addiction recovery, Gilliland, South, Carpenter, and Hardy state,

> The Shame component . . . has a significant, positive predictive relationship with hypersexual behavior . . . and the TOSCA [Test of Self-Conscious Affect] Guilt component has a significant, positive predictive relationship both with Motivation to Change and self-reported Change behaviors. Conversely, Guilt had a reliable negative predictive relationship with hypersexuality while shame had a reliable, negative predictive relationship with motivation to change and self-reported change behaviors. Clearly, these exploratory findings don't establish a causal link between shame and pornography use, but they are consistent with theories that hypersexual behavior may be engaged as a maladaptive substitute or deflection of existing shame rather than seeing shame only as the result of such behavior. This may lead to a vicious circle of behavior and consequence that feeds itself repetitively. (2011, 22)

One narrative from Scripture that highlights this difference between guilt and shame in the human experience is the confrontation of King David by the prophet Nathan in 2 Samuel 12. In a state of relative isolation, having sent his most trusted advisors and companions off to war (2 Sam. 11:1), David finds himself in a relative state of stress and loneliness, and his objectification of Bathsheba emerges shortly thereafter. In the verses that follow, we see the quintessential manifestation of shame in David's behaviors—namely, increasingly desperate attempts at concealing his sin by using Uriah as a pawn as his loss of control becomes more evident. While shame is very much a defining theme in this painful passage, we see guilt introduced by way of relationship in the person of Nathan.

Nathan's use of story to start this difficult conversation is a brilliant means by which to activate David's shame. By framing the narrative through the lens of sheep, a creature that would have had a special place in David's heart from his years as a young man shepherding his father's herds, Nathan is able to discretely awaken a sense of injustice and anger in David, while not yet confronting the reality of David's behavior directly. Then, in the perfect redemptive setup, Nathan offers those famous words, "You are the man!" in 2 Samuel 12:7. In the blink of an eye, we see the power of connection initiate the ownership of consequences, the utterance of repentance, and the initiation of reconciliation that David embraces in his response to this confrontation. Where shame is sustained in anonymity and isolation, guilt does its reparative work in a relational context defined by insight-building and empathic attunement. In shame the self is experienced as fundamentally bad to the core, whereas a sense of guilt allows one to retain perspective and understand the wrong they have done. It is a critical distinction. This is where therapy, a twelve-step support community, and working with a sponsor become essential in recovery, as they offer an experience of relationship where life stories can be processed and rigorous honesty can be pursued despite the consequences. Healthy relationships foster a sense of appropriate guilt, and appropriate guilt invites us to reconciliation rather than the covering and hiding so regularly observed with shame.

Carnes and Adams (2002) identify five elements of effective shame reduction within sex addiction treatment:

1. Identify the origins of the client's shame and how it functions in the addictive cycle.
2. Differentiate shame and guilt in the client's narrative.
3. Identify defenses utilized to deny the painful feelings that are created by the shame (denial, reaction formation, projection, displacement, etc.).
4. Utilize shame reduction techniques at critical junctures in the client's treatment process.
5. Modify negative core beliefs that reinforce shame.

Ultimately, overcoming shame means becoming more familiar and more comfortable with vulnerability on an appropriate level in relationships where there is trust, safety, and the exchange of knowing and being known (Struthers 2010). This fledgling vulnerability can be fostered first in the therapeutic relationship, in accountability relationships, and with others in the twelve-step community and eventually generalized to others in the individual's social world as it matures through recovery. Inability to escape the whirlpool of shame inevitably perpetuates the cycle of sexual addiction.

Façade

When shame permeates one's psychological experience, a façade begins to emerge as a survival tactic. The purpose of a façade is to provide a high-quality outward appearance, typically with a high-end finish or material. However, a physical façade is often constructed with cheap material designed to paper over or imitate the real thing, such as granite, stone, or marble. In the life of the individual struggling with sexual addiction, the function of a façade is social camouflage, appearing socially engaged and emotionally balanced in their spiritual, family, work, and other pursuits while simultaneously keeping others from getting close enough to discern that the public self they show the world is an empty shell of secrecy and shame. Specifically, this social camouflage may include being a trustworthy employee and maintaining an impeccable reputation with professional colleagues; presenting with a robust spirituality, such as serving as an elder or deacon within a religious community; or functioning as an accessible, attuned, and responsive parent or partner. More often than not, the ability to operate in this duality of the façade is learned in the family of origin and perfected over time. The revelation of this façade by disclosure or discovery is the epicenter of betrayal trauma, initiating a trail of destruction for the individual, their relationship, and at times, the entire family system.

Intrapsychic Conflict and Detachment

One interesting dynamic that emerges in the maintenance of the façade is a sense of dissonance within the individual—namely, internal wrestling about their acting out and the desire to no longer participate in these addictive behaviors. For a time, this dissonance is mediated by the belief that the addict is still in control and can stop whenever he or she would like to, which is a primary indicator of their delusion and evidence of denial. Successful treatment helps the addict break through this denial. Intrapsychic conflict describes a state of competition between one's values, desires, emotions, and impulses in any given moment. In their work on intrapsychic conflict and sexually deviant behavior, Garos, Bleckley, Beggan, and Frizzell found,

> Intrapsychic conflict and its relation to negative mood states is an important factor to consider. Support for the relationship between conflict, affective states, and deviant sexual behaviors was established in a study conducted by McKibben, Proulx and Lusignan (1994). These researchers found that the presence of conflicts and negative mood were strongly related to engagement in deviant sexual fantasies and increased masturbatory activities while fantasizing. (2004, 26)

This convergence between unregulated, negative mood and internal conflict, namely, internal conflict about participating in a sexual behavior, can exacerbate sexual fantasies and behaviors. This process is intensified further when a spiritual element is present. This forbidden-fruit syndrome multiplies the high of acting out when the behavior runs against deeply held morals and spiritual beliefs. The longer the individual attempts to manage this tension in their internal world, the more detached they become from their relational world. Like a raft drifting out to the open ocean, they are pulled toward the isolation that birthed the destructive pattern they are caught in. They look for a way out of the cycle but become trapped in the repetitive pattern that is sexual addiction. In Romans 7, Paul addresses this same dissonance in the human experience.

> I do not understand what I do. For what I want to do I do not do, but what I hate I do. (7:15)

> For I do not do the good I want to do, but the evil I do not want to do—this I keep on doing. (7:19)

> So I find this law at work: Although I want to do good, evil is right there with me. (7:21)

As Paul's words reveal, this process of internal conflict, the war between the flesh and the spirit, is not a novel construct. From the ancient world to the present context, this tension will continue to exist. This internal conflict is a fundamental aspect of the human experience, reflective of inborn sinful nature, that is intensified in the struggle of sexual addiction, and one that requires a relational response. Given the isolating nature of addiction, no self-contained approach to recovery will ever be successful. Recovery is a process of learning to live in harmony with God's design for the human person, namely, to exist in rich, meaningful relationship with him, with oneself, and in community with others (Luke 10:27). To this point, Paul writes, "What a wretched man I am! Who will rescue me from this body that is subject to death? Thanks be to God, who delivers me through Jesus Christ our Lord!" (vv. 24–25). The solution to our unmet needs and emotional distress is not found in things or experiences but rather in healthy relationships. Relationship with Jesus is the foundation of authentic faith. Likewise, relationship is the foundation of successful recovery. Specifically, a rigorously honest articulation of our brokenness and a subsequent deepening belief in and intimacy with Jesus is foundational to recovery. From this relationship with Christ, connection with self and others emerges as important processes in our healing and transformation.

Triggers

In sexual addiction, a trigger is any stimulus (e.g., video, image, memory, thought, situation) that primes foraging for sexual stimulation, including fantasy or euphoric recall. As such, triggers can be directly tied to the aforementioned concepts of preoccupation and ritualization. Triggers are often implicit experiences in the mind, meaning they go unrecognized until a slip has already taken place. Rewinding the tape and exploring what transpired in the hours, days, and weeks leading up to the slip can provide helpful clues about how to not be caught off guard in the future. Performing an autopsy of a slip or relapse helps the individual identify triggers, tying them to preoccupation and ritualization, and explore recovery tools that can help disempower them, suggesting the individual must sharpen their radar for recognizing the cues that cause the trigger. Four commonly reported categories of triggers include:

- **Emotional triggers:** Intense emotions often serve as triggers. These include anger, sadness, fear, shame, being overwhelmed, irritation, and fatigue. Even surprise, relief, and other positive feelings can trigger a sexual response.
- **Behavioral triggers:** Behavioral triggers are frequently tied to habits or sequences of behaviors that are difficult to relearn. If part of the addictive acting out has involved a ritual or predictable pattern of behaviors, engaging in *any* part of the series of behaviors may trigger the entire reflexive sequence.
- **Situational/physical triggers:** Certain contexts tend to serve as triggers, especially those that are paired with intense emotions. Places associated with previous acting out (e.g., workplace, streets, hotels, cities) may act as triggers, as well as relational situations (e.g., preceding intercourse, certain looks or questions from a spouse, interacting with abusive family members, etc.) can trigger foraging for acting out opportunities, as can bodily sensations or physical stimuli that have been associated with the addictive behavior (e.g., smells, textures).
- **Cognitive triggers:** Self-talk, especially self-defeating beliefs and self-criticism, tends to serve as a trigger. Memories, dreams, fantasies/daydreams, and other cognitive processes also serve as triggers that prime foraging if not processed.

FOUR CS OF RECOVERY

The narrative of sexual addiction starts early in life and involves a variety of complex and entrenched features. Treatment involves a multipronged approach over a significant period of time, typically years. Certified Sexual Addiction Therapists (CSATs) and other sexual addiction treatment providers have access to a variety of assessments, clinical tools, and professional expertise to help the individual navigate the journey toward health and wholeness. Yet the church has an important role to play in assisting those who have a relationship with Christ yet are stuck in the snare of sexual sin. The Four Cs of Recovery outline the space where the church can intervene.

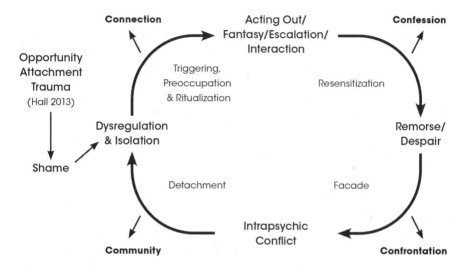

Community

The first space of intervention that the church body or pastoral staff can engage in is in the establishment of healthy community. Healthy church community operates similarly to healthy interpersonal relationships—with honesty, transparency, and vulnerability. Creating a culture where both sexual sin and sexual wholeness are discussed openly creates a space that invites parishioners to get real about their own struggles. Given the veil of shame and silence that has permeated the church around issues of human sexuality or the outright condemnation of others who struggle with sexual sin, it may take a while for this cultural shift to transpire in some congregations. One tool that can be helpful in fostering this cultural shift is the inclusion of Celebrate Recovery or some other twelve-step recovery ministry.

Connection

We are created for connection. Connection to trustworthy others allows us the space to explore our personal experiences more honestly and thoroughly. This sense of community within the church helps foster recovery as it provides individuals who struggle a space to become more honest about the reality of their addiction. In recovery, connection is the ultimate catalyst for sustained growth and change. Healing simply does not occur in isolation. Christ models healthy community and connection in his ministry. He develops relationships with each of his disciples and fosters a deeper level of connection with Peter, James, and John. David and Jonathan's covenant relationship [1 Samuel 18, 20] is also a strong model of this type of brotherhood. This deepened sense of mutual investment is seen in work with accountability partners, group members, and a sponsor, and phone calls become an essential variable in establishing comfort with reaching out for help in moments of temptation and struggle.

Confession

One outgrowth of healthy connection with group members, accountability partners, and a sponsor is the emergence of a space for confession. Recovery is a process of committing to reality at all costs and learning to live in rigorous honesty with ourselves and with others. Confession of slips or relapses that have occurred, updates to one's recovery plan, and all information that is pertinent to building a strong recovery should be made on a regular basis to sponsors and in group, as well as with a therapist. The formal disclosure process, which is discussed later, is a form of confession within the recovery process. James 5:16 speaks to the power of confession between members of the body of Christ: "Therefore confess your sins to each other and pray for each other so that you may be healed. The prayer of a righteous person is powerful and effective." Confession to another of slips and relapses indicates a commitment to rigorous honesty and helps to deepen the sense of trust. This confession of sin, when received in grace, heightens the sense of connection in relationships and helps to continue this shift within church culture toward sexual health.

Confrontation

Whereas confession is a proactive identification of sin and movement toward repentance by revealing it to a trusted individual or a group, confrontation is the flip side of the coin. A sponsor, accountability partner, or group member can identify something that exists outside the awareness of the individual. Galatians 6:1 provides a helpful model for how to initiate this process: "Brothers and sisters, if someone is caught in a sin, you who live by the Spirit should restore that person gently. But watch yourselves, or you also may be tempted." While this passage speaks directly to situations where someone is caught in sin, there are scenarios where confrontation occurs about suspicions or incongruence that others are perceiving. A spirit of gentleness is needed not only for those who offer the confrontation, but for the individual who is the recipient. When there is a sense of shared care, trust, and vulnerability in the relationship, rather than an affront or act of hostility, confrontation serves as an important means of grace.

REFERENCES

Briken, P., N. Habermann, W. Berner, and A. Hill. 2007. *"Diagnosis and Treatment of Sexual Addiction: A Survey of German Therapists."* Sexual Addiction and Compulsivity: The Journal of Treatment and Prevention 14, no. 2: 131–43. DOI:10.1080/10720160701310450.

Carnes, P. 2009. *Out of the Shadows: Understanding Sexual Addiction.* 3rd ed. Carefree, AZ: Gentle Path.

———. 2015. *Facing the Shadow: Starting Sexual and Relationship Recovery.* 3rd ed. Carefree, AZ: Gentle Path.

Carnes, P., and K. Adams, eds. 2002. *Clinical Management of Sexual Addiction.* New York: Brunner-Routledge.

Carnes, P. J., R. E. Murray, and L. Charpentier. 2005. "Bargains with Chaos: Sex Addicts and Addiction Interaction Disorder." *Sexual Addiction and Compulsivity: The Journal of Treatment and Prevention* 12, no. 2–3: 79–120. DOI: 10.1080/10720160500201371.

Erickson, D. J., and R. Tewksbury. 2000. "The 'Gentlemen' in the Club: A Typology of Strip Club Patrons." *Deviant Behavior: An Interdisciplinary Journal* 21: 271–93.

Flores, P. 2004. *Addiction as an Attachment Disorder.* New York: Jason Aronson.

Garos, S., M. K. Bleckley, J. Beggan, and J. Frizzell. 2004. "Intrapsychic Conflict and Deviant Sexual Behavior in Sex Offenders." *Journal of Offender Rehabilitation* 40: 23–40.

Gilliland, R., M. South, B. Carpenter, and S. Hardy. 2011. "The Roles of Shame and Guilt in Hypersexual Behavior." *Sexual Addiction and Compulsivity: The Journal of Treatment and Prevention* 18: 12–29.

Gola, M., M. Wordecha, A. Marchewka, and G. Sescousse. 2016. "Visual Sexual Stimuli— Cue or Reward? A Perspective for Interpreting Brain Imaging Findings on Human Sexual Behaviors." *Frontiers in Human Neuroscience* 10. DOI: 10.3389/fnhum.2016.00402.

Hall, P. 2013. "A New Classification Model for Sex Addiction." *Sexual Addiction and Compulsivity* 20, no. 4: 279–91.

Kafka, M. P., and J. Hennen. 1999. "The Paraphilia-related Disorders: An Empirical Investigation of Nonparaphilic Hypersexuality Disorders in Outpatient Males." *Journal of Sex and Marital Therapy* 25, no. 4: 305–19. DOI: 10.1080/00926239908404008.

———. 2002. "A DSM-IV Axis I Comorbidity Study of Males ($n = 120$) with Paraphilias and Paraphilia-Related Disorders." *Sexual Abuse: Journal of Research and Treatment* 14, no. 4: 349–66.

Kafka, M. 2010. "Hypersexual Disorder: A Proposed Diagnosis for DSM-V." *Archives in Sexual Behavior* 39, no. 2: 377–400. DOI 10.1007/s10508-009-9574-7.

Karaga, S., D. Davis, E. Choe, and J. Hook. 2016. "Hypersexuality and Religion/Spirituality: A Qualitative Review." *Sexual Addiction and Compulsivity: The Journal of Treatment and Prevention* 23, no. 2–3: 167–81.

Katehakis, A. 2009. "Affective Neuroscience and the Treatment of Sexual Addiction." *Sexual Addiction and Compulsivity: The Journal of Treatment and Prevention* 16, no. 1: 1–31.

Lopez, F., M. Gover, J. Leskela, E. Sauer, L. Schirmer, and J. Wyssmann. 1997. "Attachment Styles, Shame, Guilt and Collaborative Problem-Solving Orientation." *Personal Relationships* 4: 187–199.

Laaser, M., and D. Laaser. 2008. *Seven Desires: Looking Past What Separates Us to Learn What Connects Us.* Grand Rapids: Zondervan.

Love, T., C. Laier, M. Brand, L. Hatch, and R. Hajela. 2015. "Neuroscience of Internet Pornography Addiction: A Review and Update." *Behavioral Sciences* 5, no. 3: 388–433.

Nestler, E. 2005. "Is There a Common Molecular Pathway for Addiction?" *Nature Neuroscience* 8: 1445–1449.

Nikmanesh, Z., Y. Kazemi, and M. Khosravi. 2015. "Role of Feeling of Loneliness and Emotional Regulation Difficulty on Drug Abuse." *Journal of Community Health Research* 4: 55–64.

Pardini, D., T. Plante, A. Sherman, and J. Stump. 2000. "Religious Faith and Spirituality in Substance Abuse Recovery: Determining the Mental Health Benefits." *Journal of Substance Abuse Treatment* 19: 347-354.

Parker, S., and R. Thomas. 2009. "Psychological Differences in Shame vs. Guilt: Implications for Mental Health Counselors." *Journal of Mental Health Counseling* 31, no. 3: 213–24.

Ragan, P., and P. Martin. 2000. "The Psychobiology of Sexual Addiction." *Sexual Addiction and Compulsivity: The Journal of Treatment and Prevention* 7, no. 3: 161–75.

Reid, R., J. Bramen, A. Anderson, and M. Cohen. 2014. "Mindfulness, Emotional Dysregulation, Impulsivity, and Stress-Proneness among Hypersexual Patients." *Journal of Clinical Psychology* 70, no. 4: 313–21.

Reid, R., B. Carpenter, and J. Hook. 2016. "Investigating Correlates of Hypersexual Behavior in Religious Patients." *Sexual Addiction and Compulsivity: The Journal of Treatment and Prevention* 23, no. 2–3: 296–312.

Robinson, M. 2009. *Cupid's Poisoned Arrow: From Habit to Harmony in Sexual Relationships.* Berkeley, CA: North Atlantic Books.

Sapolsky, R. 2004. *Why Zebras Don't Get Ulcers.* 3rd ed. New York: Holt.

Saraiya, T., and T. Lopez-Castro. 2016. "Ashamed and Afraid: A Scoping Review of the Role of Shame in Post-Traumatic Stress Disorder (PTSD)." *Journal of Clinical Medicine* 5, no. 11: 94. DOI:10.3390/jcm5110094.

Schore, A. 2001. "The Effects of Early Relational Trauma on Right Brain Development, Affect Regulation, and Infant Mental Health." *Infant Mental Health Journal* 22, no. 1–2: 201–69.

Siegel, D. 2007. *The Mindful Brain.* New York: W. W. Norton.

———. 1999. *The Developing Mind: How Relationships and the Brain Interact to Shape Who We Are.* New York: The Guilford Press.

Shaughnessy, K., M. Fudge, and E. S. Byers. 2017. "An Exploration of Prevalence, Variety, and Frequency Data to Quantify Online Sexual Activity Experience." *The Canadian Journal of Human Sexuality* 26, no. 1: 60–75.

Struthers, B. 2010. *Wired for Intimacy: How Pornography Hijacks the Male Brain.* Downers Grove, IL: InterVarsity Press.

Wilson, G. 2014. *Your Brain on Porn: Internet Pornography and the Emerging Science of Addiction.* Kent, UK: Commonwealth Publishing.

Wines, D. 1997. "Exploring the Applicability of Criteria for Substance Dependence to Sexual Addiction." *Sexual Addiction and Compulsivity: The Journal of Treatment and Prevention* 4: 195–220.

Yoder, V., T. Virden III, and K. Amin. 2005. "Internet Pornography and Loneliness: An Association?" *Sexual Addiction and Compulsivity: The Journal of Treatment and Prevention* 12, no. 1: 19–44.

CHAPTER 4

SEXUAL ADDICTION AS AN ATTACHMENT DISORDER

Todd Bowman, PhD, CSAT-C

Secure emotional connection with another person is a primary human need. It cuts across the span of our lives, extending from the cradle to the grave. These relationships shift as we age, and our primary attachment figures transition from parents or guardians during much of childhood, to siblings and friends who help us explore the world and experience a sense of our individuality, to a partner or spouse who serves the role of trusted companion during our adult lives. Across these relationships, one constant remains: We long for connection, we desire to be desired, and we find these needs met in our primary attachment relationships (Johnson & Whiffen, 2003). Attachment theory was first developed by John Bowlby in the 1950s and later expanded by Mary Ainsworth in the 1960s and 70s. The concept can be understood as a relationship characterized by a secure emotional connection in which responsiveness and accessibility serve to insulate us from the isolation and loneliness of this world. It contains a rich emphasis on bonding to other human beings in close relationships as a mechanism of managing emotional states. Flores says, "Attachment is a fundamental motivation in its own right and cannot be reduced to a secondary drive" (2004, 40).

The central tenets of attachment theory elaborate on this need for secure emotional connection in relationship with another. These principles serve as a reflection of our original design in God's inherently relational image and model for us how to live in harmony with our families, our spiritual communities, and the world at large. The language used in this theory provides elaborate yet direct insight into the power of these important processes that define our human relationships and our Christian faith. As we understand and embody secure attachment, we can more completely reflect the nature of Christ in our lives and relationships through a sense of attunement to the needs of others and a faithful response to those needs. However, in the sexualized context we inhabit in the Western world in the twenty-first century, the deterioration of attachment bonds in the family system and among members of the community leaves us vulnerable to addictive patterns of behavior, which have steep psychological, spiritual, and social consequences. Flores further states,

> Addiction, therefore, can be viewed as an attachment disorder. Since it is biologically impossible to regulate our own affect for any extended period of time, individuals who have difficulty establishing emotionally regulating attachments are more inclined to substitute drugs and alcohol for their deficiency in intimacy. Because of a person's difficulty maintaining emotional closeness with others, certain vulnerable individuals are more likely to substitute a vast array of obsessive-compulsive behaviors (e.g., sex, food, drugs, alcohol, work, gambling, computer games, etc.) that serve as a distraction from the gnawing emptiness and internal discomfort that threatens to overtake them. (2004, 6–7)

In the context of sexual addiction and recovery, exploring the individual's attachment narrative becomes a central point of focus in creating a new experience of the self and establishing a new template for operating in relationship with God, self, and others. The narrative of addiction is largely shaped by the moments that have woven together the attachment style of individuals in recovery. Stories of rejection, loneliness, neglect, and invisibility permeate the emotional landscape for many who struggle with sexually addictive behaviors.

The published literature on the correlation between attachment style and sexual addiction provides a compelling rationale for exploring the two in more meaningful ways. Speaking specifically to this relationship between attachment bonds and sexual addiction, Katehakis says,

> We are only now beginning to appreciate the results of these blighted attachment patterns and how they favor sexually addictive behaviors. Research in affective neuroscience indicates that damaged attachment capacities impede not only emotional maturation (causing internally dysregulated states) but also the cognitive abilities needed to integrate information, attend to tasks, understand and use language, think abstractly, weigh decisions, comprehend ethical principles, and monitor one's own activity. Clearly, deficits in such crucial areas of affect regulation and thought in turn impact behavior and may manifest as hypersexuality and sexual addiction as well as depression, inattention, hyperactivity, difficulty with abstract reasoning, poor executive functioning and poor judgment. (2009, 3)

As such, attachment theory serves as an important Rosetta Stone to help interpret the influence of the individual's developmental experiences on the origins of their sexual addictive behavior, as well as helping a therapist translate those experiences into healthy emotional awareness and reciprocal responsiveness in attachment relationships. The model speaks to the power of the therapeutic relationship and connection shared between group participants in the recovery process. For helpers, exploring the stories that comprise the historical narrative of relationship with primary attachment figures throughout a client's life provides essential insight into the nature of their behavior and how best to facilitate the healing process. The power of these templates for relating suggests they get replicated in many ways across a wide array of relationships, but most powerfully in those relationships that involve physical/sexual or emotional closeness. What we discover there serves as the raw material to be used in the construction of a new experience of the self through the recovery process, in the context of individual, group, and couples counseling. Because sexual addiction infiltrates each facet of the human experience, the recovery process should be holistic in its addressing each of those facets, with human attachment and bonding as a core focus.

ATTACHMENT IS AN INNATE NEED

At the most fundamental level, attachment must be seen as an innate motivating force in human relationships. Simply stated, we are created for connection. From birth to childhood to marriage to older adulthood, we reflect the relational dimensions of our Creator. The process of establishing connection can be found in that first scream of an infant in the birthing room, in running to a parent after getting hurt as a child, and in romantic relationships in the joy of being with one's beloved. In addition to seeking connection, we are also powerfully motivated to maintain these connections; attachment bonds are the primary means by which they are fostered and sustained. Our propensity to reciprocate caring responses amid being given care demonstrates this motivation to maintain secure connection in our primary attachment relationships. Two-year-old children are exemplary at demonstrating the innateness of this principle: they share easily, protest loudly, cuddle sweetly, and fear intensely. Their unfiltered lives and implicit trust embody the essence of attachment. Until they are asked to share their favorite toy, of course! We are compelled by instinct to help them navigate the ups and downs of their emotional world. This reflexive responsiveness to the vulnerability of their emotional states is a profound example of how relationship is intended to operate in the human experience. The need is intended to be responded to by caregivers or attachment figures. However, when there is inconsistency in response from primary attachment figures, either in timing (e.g., after the felt emotion has passed) or accuracy (e.g., yelling at a child who is afraid), a rupture is birthed that creates an emotional space between child and parent (or between spouses, for that matter). Unresolved ruptures, over time, create a wedge between the injured party and the unresponsive party. In the developmental narrative, this process begins to shape a style of relating to the world that is clingy (or anxiously inclined), overly self-reliant (or avoidantly inclined), or a combination thereof.

Pain and loneliness are born out of unhealthy relational environments. Over time, people in these situations will grow in the perception that they are bad or unworthy, that they are not loved for who they are, that no one will meet their needs, and that sex is their most important need. These four core beliefs highlight the level of impairment in the attachment system among those who struggle with out-of-control sexual behavior. The natural progression toward shame-proneness and corresponding beliefs about the self tend to activate sexually addictive coping behaviors. Recalibrating the attachment system as a goal of recovery entails treating the shame, modifying these core beliefs, and creating new experiences of the self in relation to others to fill the psychological and relational space created by the cessation of the sexually addictive behaviors.

ACCESSIBILITY AND RESPONSIVENESS FACILITATE HEALTHY ATTACHMENT

Based on the foundational understanding of attachment as an innate need, it follows that accessibility (the conscious awareness that an attachment figure is approachable) and responsiveness (the perception that the attachment figure will meet physical and emotional needs) lay the foundation for secure attachment in human relationships. The perception of inaccessibility and the lack of responsiveness in the relationship drives the experience of relational distress and, over time, births a reflexive doubt about the trustworthiness of others, especially those who are closest. Actively responding to the emotional needs that exist in the attachment relationship communicates, "I am present with you, I hear you, and we are on the same page." The apex of distress is not experienced when there is an angry response from an attachment figure but rather when there is no response at all (Johnson and Whiffen 2003). Unresponsive childhood environments regularly feature in the attachment narratives of those who struggle with sexually addictive behavior. Carnes identifies this in his concept of the disengaged family system (2015).

Emotion lies at the heart of the attachment bond, and sexual acting out or addictive behaviors introduce relational carcinogens in the form of betrayal, resentment, and mistrust that squelch positive emotional experiences, instead sowing seeds of fear, depression, jealousy, anger, and resignation, among others. As one partner withdraws into a self-absorbed world of fantasy and acting out, their blank face leaves the other in a state of isolation and confusion, and responsiveness is replaced with inscrutability, lacking healthy emotional or sexual pursuit. As Pat Carnes writes, "The [sexual] addict's relationship with mood altering experience becomes central to his [or her] life" (2001, 14). As identified previously, shame plays an enormous role in driving the cycle of sexually addictive behaviors and in their development.

We traditionally view accessibility and responsiveness through the lens of the parent-child attachment dyad, such as in the case of a skinned knee or some other injury. The quintessential example is a child learning to ride a bicycle. Mastery of this complex set of coordinated motor functions and simultaneous fear management involves a series of trials and errors, many of which culminate with varying degrees of bodily harm. Tears flowing, the injured child often runs to his or her primary caregiver with a bump, scrape, or bruise in need of attention. This process typically involves a sequence of inquiring if the child is okay, followed by cleaning the wound, applying some sort of bandage to the afflicted body part, and a kiss or rub to make it all better. This series of caretaking behaviors serves as a ritual for feeling better and often ends with a hug, fist-bump, high five, or some other form of validating attention, which encourages the child to get back on the bike and ride. The wound, often as much or more emotional than physical, has been resolved with a satisfactory degree of care, and life as normal resumes.

In the parent-child dyad, the giving is designed as more unidirectional, from the attachment figure to the child. When this dimension in the parent-child dyad gets inverted, we begin to see "parentification" and a variety of unhealthy behavioral patterns in children as they attempt to serve as a primary attachment figure for their parent, including issues such as stuffing feelings, becoming an approval seeker, living afraid of authority, judging the self harshly, and others (ACA 2007). For many who were raised in addicted or dysfunctional family systems, this parentified style permeates the way they relate to others in social, romantic, and even occupational contexts. The Adult Children of Alcoholics Laundry List can serve as a self-assessment for sex addicts or partners of sex addicts about the reality of parentification and its impact on one's life and relationships. Items such as "We get guilt feelings when we stand up for ourselves instead of giving in to others" and "We became approval seekers and lost our identity in the process" speak to the attachment implications resulting from this parentified narrative (ACA 2007, iv).

It is important to note that marital attachment dyads involve a unique style of relating. While the bonding process is similar to the parent-child dyad, involving high amounts of focused attention, frequent physical proximity, the experience of feeling felt by the other, and intentional communication, the marriage attachment bond is distinct from parent-child bonds in that it is defined by the mutual giving of self and simultaneous receiving of the other on equal footing. This is both a physical/sexual and emotional reality. Rather than a parent caring for the injured child with no expectation of being cared for by the child in return, the marriage bond is defined by the mutual giving and receiving of care, affection, validation, and trust that is intended to define this most intimate of human relationships. This echoes the biblical narrative in Ephesians 5:21–28, where Paul writes,

> Submit to one another out of reverence for Christ. Wives, submit yourselves to your own husbands as you do to the Lord. For the husband is the head of the wife as Christ is the head of the church, his body, of which he is the Savior. Now as the church submits to Christ, so also wives should submit to their husbands in everything. Husbands, love your wives, just as Christ loved the church and gave himself up for her to make her holy, cleansing her by the washing with water through the word, and to present her to himself as a radiant church, without stain or wrinkle or any other blemish, but holy and blameless. In this same way, husbands ought to love their wives as their own bodies. He who loves his wife loves himself.

This mutual giving and receiving in the marriage dyad births an even more complex relational milieu: the vulnerability required for the giving of the self and the receiving of the other to occur. Vulnerability, the opening of oneself to another by articulating a felt need and depending on the other to respond with accurate understanding and empathic care, is a hallmark of securely attached relationships. It is an act of faith, trusting that the one you have bonded to and promised to live life with will share in the experience of woundedness, shortcomings, and failures with you and will honor you by creating a space of safety where these feelings can be felt and examined in a meaningful way. Paul's description of Christ's relationship with the church as a metaphor for the marriage dyad is both poetic and profound. This model of sharing life together shapes the imagination around healthy attachment behaviors in the marriage relationship and provides an example for the body of Christ to live in harmony with one another. Yet when the experience of the family of origin involves threat, coercion, fear, abuse, trauma, or addiction, the template that gets forged is one of heightened avoidance, anxiety, or both, and this insecurely attached narrative often underlies the development of problematic sexual behaviors, including sexual addiction (Hall 2013).

This notion of responsiveness to another's emotional experiences becomes critical for us to comprehend more deeply in understanding the body of Christ. While most of us prefer Paul's experience of God bursting onto the scene in an active demonstration of power that alleviates our habits, hang-ups, and hurts with blinding speed and effectiveness, most of us will have an experience more akin to Peter's: a process of slow, intentional growth marked by successful approximations toward a life defined by faithfulness, with the occasional realization that there is some additional area of surrender or growth that needs to occur as we strive toward a life defined by grace and truth. Quick transformation in sexual addiction recovery may be highly desired, but the validity of one's recovery is demonstrated in consistent and unrelenting ownership of consequences, repentance for sin committed, sustained transformation of emotional regulation and behavioral responses, and sufficient restitution facilitated in the lives of those who have been impacted by the addictive behavior. The adage "easy come, easy go" could not be more accurate in understanding the recovery process. Gains that are made easily do not last long. Surrender means giving up roles, relationships, sometimes jobs or friendships, certainly pride, and the unhealthy mechanisms of self-soothing that have existed for years or decades. Similarly, the healing process for the partner, the couple, and the family system is a slow, intentional one where the rebuilding of trust lays the foundation for secure attachment to fill the void left by addiction and betrayal.

Examining this principle of attachment opens an interesting path for conceptualizing the body of Christ. We pray for God to move in our lives, trusting that he will provide, yet in many Western churches we tend to isolate ourselves from the healthy community that God so often uses to answer these prayers. This is not to say that God lacks the ability to cut through time and space to intervene where he chooses; rather, as we explore the biblical narrative from an attachment perspective, we see that God regularly answers prayers by equipping his people to serve one another in love. Sometimes our looking up for an answer to prayer results in God telling us to look around and reach out to one another. Perhaps the caring for the stranger, the feeding of the hungry, the visiting of the imprisoned, and the care for the sick that Christ suggests are, in fact, participating in the answering of another's prayers (Matt. 25:35–40).

For the church to be a significant contributor in the restoration of sexual and emotional wholeness in a disturbingly sexualized culture, it must be defined by a sense of accessibility and appropriate responsiveness for those who come seeking assistance and relief from the burden of sexual addiction they are carrying, as well as for those who have been impacted by these behaviors. The church is best positioned to care for those who have been traumatized by sexual behavior and those who struggle with addiction or its impact. However, this opportunity to minister means we must get honest as the body of Christ about the problematic sexual behaviors that currently plague the church. After all, we profess Christ as the truth that will set the afflicted free (John 8:32). There is work to be done in the church living this truth out more completely.

ISOLATION AND LOSS EXPERIENCED AS TRAUMATIC

While we are created to connect richly and deeply with those we are closest to, attachment theory is in large measure a theory of trauma as it focuses explicitly on the individual's experience, real or perceived, of loss, rejection, and/or abandonment by the most important people in one's life: primary attachment figures, typically parents or other caregivers. Reflect on the toddler who is left at daycare or in the nursery at church. They experience the fear of a novel situation, being left with a complete stranger, while watching mommy or daddy, their source of comfort, protection, and acceptance, turn and walk away. Flores suggests, "Short separation provokes an acute response known as *protest*, while prolonged separation yields the physiological and psychological state of despair and eventual depression" (2004, 102). The screams of protest serve as an indicator that this experience is both overwhelming and terrifying for the child. Each time the caregiver leaves, the perception of potential or experienced abandonment heightens, and tremendously powerful emotional responses are evoked in the face of such a threat unless they are able to develop a bond of trust with an adult who can serve as a surrogate until their parent returns. If this rupture is not repaired, it has significant influence in shaping the individual's relational template, namely an anxious or avoidant style of relating to self and others.

This developmental trauma impacts personality development in many ways, including the shaping of one's ability to manage big emotions caused by other stressors across the lifespan. Allen Schore states, "Because attachment bonds are vitally important for the infant's continuing neurobiological development, these dyadically regulated events [repairing ruptured attachment bonds] scaffold an expansion of the child's coping capacities, and therefore, adaptive infant and later adult mental health" (2001, 205). This process of managing our varying states of emotion is known as affective or emotional regulation, and a functional deficit in this area is a hallmark feature of sexual addiction. We are not created to persist in this state of loss, confusion, or disconnection, nor in the state of emotional dysregulation that emerges as a result of prolonged distress. And if we do get stuck here, our bodies move toward whatever coping options are available to help escape the distress.

This experience of disconnection in the primary attachment relationship serves as the foundation of shame, which if left unchecked, births coping mechanisms that focus on isolated self-soothing rather than finding soothing in the context of healthy relationships. When attachment needs go unmet—the relational responses of comfort, presence, security, validation, and acceptance are not appropriately provided consistently or accurately in the relationship—a process of protest emerges. Stereotypical protest behaviors include anger, clinging, depression, anxiety, and even despair. Without appropriate responsiveness, these protests eventually give way to a position of detachment in the relationship. This element of unmet attachment needs is a defining feature of the family systems that Carnes (2015) identifies as fertile soil for sexual addiction. This same process of protest can be seen in relationships where sexually addictive behavior is present and can become more pronounced in the context of betrayal trauma.

FEAR AND DISTRESS TRIGGER ATTACHMENT NEEDS

Human relationships provide the opportunity for the entire range of emotions to be experienced by the individual and serve the function of assisting with regulating the emotions that get too big for us to manage on our own. From evoking joy to causing sorrow and every possible emotional experience in between, relationships allow us to feel deeply. Humans are designed for emotion, both the giving and the receiving of affect, and the ability to use relationship as a source of soothing is experience dependent, suggesting "to attain a healthy self-regulating system [one] must first have the early experience of interactive regulation" (Katehakis 2009, 7).

In the most intimate of our attachment relationships, these emotions are experienced even more intensely. When a stranger in the parking lot criticizes us, we feel a certain degree of emotion, such as fear, anger, or embarrassment, depending on the circumstances. When a parent or spouse uses those same words, they tend to cut more deeply and are more likely to be believed. Much like a fire, emotion can keep one warm and nurtured—stray too far from the fire and you freeze. But lean in too close and you get burned. The experience of big emotion, especially fear and distress, serves to elicit attachment needs of seeking comfort and longing for presence, which ideally activates emotion regulating behaviors from attachment figures, such as healthy touch, affirming words, gentle tone of voice, and soft facial expressions.

Healthy emotional regulation in relationship involves responses such as reaching for help and exhibiting vulnerability, whereas unhealthy responses include fear-based behaviors, such as withdrawing or freezing. Sexually addictive behaviors, such as viewing online pornography, masturbation, or sex with a prostitute, tend to be misaligned attempts at soothing a valid emotional need. They serve as evidence that attachment needs have gone unmet in the life of the individual for a long period of time.

When attachment needs go unmet and the appropriate relational responses are not present in the relationship, a process of protest tends to emerge. Stereotypical protest behaviors include anger, clinging, depression, anxiety, and even despair; without appropriate responsiveness these protests eventually give way to a position of detachment in the relationship, which is compounded over time. Psychiatrist Bessel van der Kolk suggests, "Early exposure to extreme threat and inadequate caregiving significantly affects the long-term capacity of the human organism to modulate the sympathetic and parasympathetic nervous systems in response to subsequent stress" (2003, 301). As such, survival strategies such as fight, flight, and freeze responses have their relational origins in unresponsive or intrusive attachment experiences. We are created for connection, and when we persist in a state of relational disconnection over long periods of time, unhealthy self-regulation begins. Rather than reaching toward healthy connection and intimacy, those caught in the snare of addiction reflexively reach to an illusion of connection that lacks the depth and vulnerability inherent in authentic intimacy.

THE BENEFITS OF HEALTHY ATTACHMENT

While attachment theory focuses on navigating the distress of separation from primary caregivers, this sense of loss highlights not only the significance of human relationships for us as human beings but also the goodness inherent in the bonding that takes place between attachment figures. While this model was developed examining infants and children, it also applies to husbands and wives as they deepen relationship with one another over time. The benefits of healthy attachment are essential for personal and relational flourishing, and inherent in them you will see how God reveals himself to us as an attachment figure throughout Scripture.

Attachment Provides a Secure Base

One of the telltale signs of development that parents often look to is how their children engage and explore the world around them. In this process of responding to their environment, children use parents and caregivers as a secure base they can return to in the event of distress or anxiety, promoting the confidence to learn, to take appropriate risks, and to test working models for understanding self and others. In the same way, adults are designed to rely on our attachment relationships to help us manage the anxieties and stresses of our world. Having a secure base from which to operate enhances our capacity for compassion, morality, communication, insight, and empathy, each a key component of healthy psychological and relational functioning.

The Strange Situation is a scenario developed by Mary Ainsworth that has been used for decades to research attachment style among infants. In this scenario, the infant must navigate the comings and goings of the caregiver, as well as the introduction of a stranger, and their emotional reactions serve to indicate the style of relating they have internalized due to their experience of the caregiver. The amount of exploration the child engages in is also important in the experiment as the idea of a secure base from which to explore the world helps to evidence the presence of secure attachment. However, the transition to an autonomous adult leaves the individual with more freedom to explore their world, and attachment style has a direct impact on *how* the individual goes about exploring their internal and relational world.

This relationship between attachment style and exploration strategy appears to indicate a tension between breadth of exploration versus depth of exploration. Breadth of exploration suggests a superficial style of navigating the world, wherein the individual settles for shallow experiences and feelings due to an intense fear or avoidance of depth of connection, which are hallmark features of insecure attachment styles. Conversely, secure attachment contains a depth of processing that establishes healthy boundaries between the self and others, which allows for a deeper level of experience of the other in relationship. As such, securely attached individuals are far less likely to present with sexually addictive behaviors (Zapf, Greiner, and Carroll 2008; Faisandier, Taylor, and Salisbury 2012). In the words of Flores, "Attachment theory, with its emphasis on the importance of a secure base, helps explain an important paradox about treatment: secure attachment liberates" (2004, 149).

This notion of orientation toward breadth versus depth in how one explores their experience has significant spiritual implications. Christian theology centers on a depth of knowing and being known by God in which we are called to explore who we have been created to be and to explore the creation we have been charged to steward. Conversely, Scripture is full of reminders that exploration without depth leads to a conformity to ungodly behavior. Deuteronomy 6:4–5, 14 reminds us that we are created for depth of relationship and not breadth or superficiality: "Hear, O Israel: The LORD our God, the LORD is one. Love the LORD your God with all your heart and with all your soul and with all your strength. . . . Do not follow other gods, the gods of the peoples around you." In his epistle to the church in Rome, Paul also indicates this notion of pursuing depth of relationship rather than breadth: "Do not conform to the pattern of this world, but be transformed by the renewing of your mind. Then you will be able to test and approve what God's will is—his good, pleasing and perfect will" (Rom. 12:2).

Attachment Provides a Safe Haven

Accessible attachment figures, such as parents, children, and spouses, provide relational responses that further the growth of healthy interdependence in the relationship. These responses include comfort, protection, emotional regulation, security, and validation, all of which foster healthy emotional and intellectual development. This safe-haven environment entails a reduction in unsafe vulnerability and stress. Inversely, a lack of accessibility with attachment figures and responsiveness to felt needs generates intrapersonal and interpersonal distress, creating an environment wherein unpredictability and stress stunt healthy growth. This emotional failure to thrive culminates with what Katehakis describes as "isolating regulatory strategies" or externalizing behaviors, such as problematic sexual behavior, drug and alcohol abuse, and other addictive processes (2016, 66). Just as the loss of a safe haven contributes to the development of sexually addictive behavior, the experience of betrayal trauma for spouses of sex addicts also threatens this idea of the relationship as a safe place where emotions can be shared, deepest thoughts can be divulged, and vulnerability will be honored.

Healthy Dependence Facilitates Greater Autonomy

We are inherently social creatures, but contemporary Western culture creates a web of isolation and individualism we frequently get stuck in. We are bombarded with messages promoting the idea that reliance on another is indicative of weakness and that self-sufficiency is to be valued above all else. From an attachment perspective, the ideas of independence and overdependence are somewhat nonsensical. Attachment theory assumes that each person is biologically dependent on human relationships; the million-dollar question is this: How healthy or effective is that dependence? Although some would argue that autonomy and dependence are opposing poles on the continuum of relational identity, attachment theory argues that a healthy level of dependence generates a greater sense of autonomy and liberates us to experience a fuller sense of self.

In this model, the healthiest position to adopt is one of interdependence, the reciprocal expression of felt need and relational response. The work of recovery involves increasing the individual's ability to accurately identify their affective state and invite another to appropriately respond to their need, while simultaneously improving their ability to perceive the felt experiences of others and to respond accordingly.

ATTACHMENT STYLES AND SEXUAL ADDICTION

As attachment theory has become popular outside of the realm of psychology, the most evident reflection of this collective awareness of its principles is the growth of interest in individual attachment styles and their impact on an array of psychological principles and relational dynamics, including problematic sexual behavior and sexual addiction.

In their research, Beck and McDonald state, "Positive relationships with caregivers are associated with more loving and nurturing God images. Conversely, it appears that negative relations with caregivers are associated with God being experienced as more demanding and authoritarian" (2004, 93). This research indicates that the quality of the bond between a child and their caregiver has a direct impact on one's perception of God's nature and character. It should be of no surprise, then, that Jesus invites the little children to come to him (Matt. 19:14) and that his parables are multilayered, addressing spiritual issues while directing us to relational and psychological truths as well.

While there have been different models used to make sense of how human beings attach or bond with one another, the primary dynamics inherent in each model center around the management of anxiety or distress upon separation of the attachment figure and degree of receptivity or disengagement/avoidance upon the return of the attachment figure (Beck and McDonald 2004). Bartholomew and Horowitz suggest that the reciprocal navigation of these dynamics between the child and caregiver, called *co-regulation*, birth internal working models of the self (dependence) and the other (avoidance) in the child, which can be either high or low, resulting in four possible styles. These styles are understood as Secure, Preoccupied, Dismissing, and Fearful (Bartholomew and Horowitz 1991).

Secure

The defining feature of securely attached children is that they have a low level of anxiety within themselves and a low level of avoidance of others, given the deep sense of connection, trust, and safety they have experienced in relationship to their caregivers. They demonstrate a healthy range of emotional expressions, such as crying at the departure of a caregiver, but can draw on their internal working model of the caregiver to soothe themselves healthily until the caregiver's return.

Securely attached individuals are more likely to be defined by qualities such as "happy, friendly, . . . expressive, . . . relationally warm." They have trusting and longer lasting relationships, and they "believe love persists through time, . . . consider themselves more likeable, . . . and believe others are well-intentioned" (Zapf, Greiner, and Carroll 2008, 162). Bartholomew and Horowitz suggest that secure attachment births "a sense of worthiness (lovability) plus an expectation that other people are generally accepting and responsive" (1991, 227).

Preoccupied

The preoccupied style emerges out of a high level of anxiety about the departure of the caregiver, where there is a low level of avoidance upon return. In many ways, the anxiety screams, "I am not okay without you!" This style is perhaps best understood through the clinging to the caregiver seen by the child at the anticipation of departure and the calming and connection that occurs upon reestablishing contact with the caregiver. As such, this attachment style embodies an internal working model of the self as overly dependent on the caregiver (low dependence on self) to be emotionally regulated, and minimal avoidance of the caregiver. In the preoccupied style, the child's need to develop autonomy to have space to grow and explore is infringed upon, and excessive dependence on or intense fear of being away from their primary caregiver fills the child with anxiety. This process stunts neurological maturation in the prefrontal cortex, the relational center of the human brain, resulting in emotional and relational immaturity over time.

There are numerous features that have been identified for individuals who fall into this preoccupied style identified by Bartholomew and Horowitz, namely a general sense of unworthiness and unlovability, as well as a striving "for self-acceptance by gaining the acceptance of valued others" (1991, 227). Zapf, Greiner, and Carroll go on to identify additional attributes of the preoccupied style: "more self-doubts, extreme jealousy, feel under-appreciated and misunderstood, fall in love easily, overly expressive, lower self-perceived attractiveness, lower self-esteem, clingy in relationships, and labile emotions" (2008, 162).

Dismissing

Contrary to the preoccupied style, the dismissing attachment style is defined by low dependence on another and a heightened sense of avoidance. This style tends to operate under the assumption, "I don't need anyone close to me." Rather than overly depending on an external feature to regulate effectively, individuals with this style become extremely self-reliant and tend to internalize their emotional regulation strategies to an unhealthy extreme. This style is perhaps best understood in the lack of emotion exhibited when the caregiver departs and in the relative indifference that is exhibited upon their return. In the context of a dismissing style, relationships tend to come and go quickly with very little actual entrusting of the self to another.

Bartholomew and Horowitz describe this dismissing style as one that involves perceiving the self as worthy of love but holding a simultaneous "negative disposition toward other people," which leads individuals to "protect themselves from disappointment by avoiding close relationships and maintaining a sense of independence and invulnerability" (1991, 227). Zapf, Greiner, and Carroll suggest individuals who operate with a dismissing style tend to express features such as "minimize emotional intimacy, fear intimacy, emotionally cold, lower personal relationship standards, more likely to use drugs, self-doubting, fewer concerns over relational mistakes, and drink more heavily" (2008, 162).

Fearful

Where the preoccupied and dismissing styles involve an elevation in either anxiety or avoidance, the fearful style presents in a much more disorganized fashion given the elevation in both anxiety and avoidance. This style of relating sends the message, "I need you close to me, but I don't want to need you close to me." This conflicting posture can be seen in those fearfully attached children who are inconsolable when their caregiver departs, and upon reunification allow the caregiver to hold them, but refuse to receive affection from them, often coinciding with an unwillingness to look face to face with the caregiver. This fearful style longs for connection to the caregiver to regulate, yet subsequently rejects the attempts of the caregiver to console their distress. There is a noticeable need for physical proximity and comfort, followed by subsequent rejecting or avoidance of emotional closeness from the same person, which in turn creates a template that is difficult to build and sustain relationship with.

This fearful style, as described by Bartholomew and Horowitz, involves the perception that the self is inherently unlovable and unworthy, while simultaneously holding the belief that others are untrustworthy and will be rejecting. Bartholomew and Horowitz state, "By avoiding close involvement with others, this style enables them to protect themselves against the anticipated rejection by others" (1991, 227). Zapf, Greiner, and Carroll describe features specific to this fearful style, including "lack true intimacy, lower self-confidence, unable to rely on others, lower levels of self-disclosure, unexpressive, unassertive, and consider self to be undeserving of love and support" (2008, 162).

These insecure styles of attaching render the individual more susceptible to sexually addictive behavior in later life. Hall states, "If attachment is disordered or disengaged, someone is more likely to turn to an addiction for comfort, rather than depend on a person" (2013, 283). Zapf, Greiner, and Carroll's study indicates that among men accessing online help for sexual addiction, 28% of respondents presented with a preoccupied style, 20% presented with a dismissing style, and 44% presented with a fearful style. Faisandier, Taylor, and Salisbury report similar results among male and female research participants in their study of New Zealand residents completing an online questionnaire regarding sexually addictive behaviors (2012). With regard to sexual behaviors and attachment style, Zapf, Greiner, and Carroll indicate that clients presenting with sexual addiction who have a preoccupied style will typically report "extreme sexual attraction, earlier first intercourse, higher levels of erotophilia (high responsiveness to sexual cues), more sexual partners, and greater infidelity" (2008, 162). They report the avoidant style more likely to present with "more frequent unwanted sexual experiences, less restrictive sexual beliefs, and sexual fantasies of someone other than partner," while the fearful style is "more interested in emotionless sex" (Zapf, Greiner, and Carroll 2008, 162).

RUPTURE, REPAIR, AND RECOVERY

The process of rupture and repair in the attachment dyad is central to determining the depth and quality of the bonds of the relationship. As previously identified, secure attachment is not defined as the absence of relational ruptures, but rather by how well ruptures are repaired within the relationship. Much like the building of strong physical strength occurs through micro-tears in the muscles being repaired stronger after the strain of exercise, relational resilience emerges from the successful repair of the small oversights, hurtful comments, thoughtless errors, and unavoidable moments of inaccessibility that transpire over the course of relationship.

Ruptures of pain can be considered the actual or perceived experience of betrayal, shame, abandonment, and/or trauma in the attachment relationship. The child is left feeling weak, small, and vulnerable, questioning their sense of self, their abilities, and their place in the world. The parent who constantly criticizes their child is introducing a pain-based rupture into the life of the child. The bond that connects the two has been strained by this experience of negative feedback from the parent to the child. This same principle holds true for other primary attachment dyads, namely the spousal relationship. The child or spouse might protest this rupture by crying, yelling back, stomping off, or shutting down and absorbing this negativity into their understanding of self. Depending on their developmental state, they will use their words and behaviors to exhibit this protest, an innate attempt at communicating their need for a corrective experience.

Protest is an important part of pain-based rupture as it is intended to be a source of feedback to the attachment figure that what is happening is not okay, that they are hurting, and that they desire this relationship to serve as a balm for fear, hurt, sadness, and other emotional experiences. Ruptures of pain emerge in relationships where sexually addictive behaviors are present. The attachment bonds become threatened by the introduction of a competing stimulus, namely the images of pornography, other sexual partners, and even emotional affair partners. However, given the power of the addiction, many who struggle are unable to receive the feedback of protest from their spouse in a way that responds to their needs in a healthy way. In some situations, disordered family of origin experiences, such as parentification, previous trauma, and other factors, inhibit a healthy protest response from the spouse. This loss of one's voice and feeling of minimal influence in the relationship contributes to the sense of betrayal trauma upon disclosure or discovery of the sexual addiction by their partner.

Not all ruptures in relationship, however, are ruptures of pain. To identify a physiological metaphor for ruptures of pain, we can look to the world of running. Running is a wonderful physical exercise that stretches our muscles and gets our blood flowing, which in turn increases concentration and memory, alleviates depressed and anxious moods, increases metabolism, and helps take off those last few hard-to-lose pounds, among other health benefits. Running, however, induces a state of rupture in a variety of systems of the human body. The cardiovascular system is stretched and grown through running as the heart works to keep oxygen flowing to the muscles through the blood, which carries carbon dioxide to the lungs for expulsion. Major muscle groups experience a literal tearing down as our stride carries us around the track, down the road, or on the treadmill. This process of stressing the various systems of the body to enhance their functioning is known as *eustress*. Just enough demand is placed on the body to increase optimal performance without overwhelming it. When learning to roll over, crawl, stand up, fight with a sibling, ride a bicycle, catch a ball, or open a bag of chips, the brain and the body are working synchronously to master the behavior. As the brain adjusts to the nuances of the demand, muscle groups practice the behavior and, in doing so, are strengthened. A neural connection is tied to a specific set of behaviors that accomplish a given task.

From a relational perspective, much of our development across the lifespan is designed to follow this principle. In fact, infants epitomize it. Once their capacity for vision is more fully developed, babies feel joy by lying on their back and gazing into their caregiver's eyes. However, this gaze does not persist blankly; there is a connective dimension to the eye contact that is synchronizing the right brain of the child with that of the caregiver. When the infant is full emotionally, he or she will reflexively look away, almost as if to say, "I am full, I am connected, and now I can explore." The rupture induced in this parent-child dyad moment serves the function of increasing the optimal functioning of the caregiver as a nurturer and the child as an explorer of their environment with an autonomous sense of self. Over the course of development, setting limits, providing corrective feedback, and enforcing healthy boundaries all serve as gain-based forms of relational rupture that serve to increase individual well-being and enhance healthy psychological, social, and spiritual development for the child. Schore and Schore summarize this developmental process.

> Attachment experiences shape the early organization of the right brain, the neurobiological core of the human unconscious. . . . Thus, emotion is initially regulated by others, but over the course of infancy it becomes increasingly self-regulated as a result of neurophysiological development. These adaptive capacities are central to self-regulation, i.e. the ability to flexibly regulate psychobiological states of emotions through interactions with other humans, interactive regulation in interconnected contexts, and without other humans, autoregulation in autonomous contexts. (2008, 10–11)

CONCLUSION

In many ways, the process of sexual addiction recovery uses identical concepts to the notion of repairing injured attachment bonds. For instance, the setting of limits or enforcing of boundaries in recovery pertains to one's commitment to change their behavior in an effort to eliminate the sexual struggle, and the reciprocal giving and receiving of corrective feedback in the context of 12-step group participation, are essential ingredients in reclaiming sexual wholeness. This recovery process also includes taking personal responsibility and ownership for past behaviors and their impact on others, providing a full disclosure if partnered, seeking forgiveness where warranted, offering it to others when necessary, rebuilding trust in relationship, utilizing appropriate emotional and physical proximity to deepen bonds of connection, and living with rigorous honesty and intentional integrity in all one does. When we understand sexual addiction as an attachment disorder, we understand that activating healthy strategies for attachment becomes a part of the solution. Far more than just an interpersonal reality, this construct of attachment extends to one's personal identity in a spiritual sense, how one understands him or herself as a beloved son or daughter of God and receives the grace, forgiveness, and transformation that emerges out of relationship with him. Understanding betrayal trauma and repairing attachment wounds caused by sexual addiction will be addressed in later chapters.

REFERENCES

Adult Children of Alcoholics. 2007. *Twelve Steps of Adult Children Steps Workbook. Adult Children of Alcoholics.*

Bartholomew, K., and L. Horowitz. 1991. "Attachment Styles among Young Adults: A Test of a Four-Category Model." *Journal of Personality and Social Psychology* 61, no. 2: 226–244.

Beck, R., and A. McDonald. 2004. "Attachment to God: The Attachment to God Inventory, Tests of Working Model Correspondence, and an Exploration of Faith Group Differences." *Journal of Psychology and Theology* 32, no. 2: 92–103.

Carnes, P. 2001. *Out of the Shadows: Understanding Sexual Addiction.* 2nd ed. Carefree, AZ: Gentle Path.

———. 2015. *Facing the Shadow: Starting Sexual and Relationship Recovery.* 3rd ed. Carefree, AZ: Gentle Path.

Faisandier, K., J. Taylor, and R. Salisbury. 2012. "What Does Attachment Have To Do with Out-of-Control Sexual Behavior?" *New Zealand Journal of Psychology* 41, no. 1: 19–29.

Flores, P. (2004). *Addiction as an Attachment Disorder.* New York: Jason Aronson.

Hall, P. 2013. "A New Classification Model for Sex Addiction." *Journal of Sexual Addiction and Compulsivity* 20, no. 4: 279–291.

Johnson, S., and V. Whiffen, eds. 2003. *Attachment Processes in Couple and Family Therapy.* New York: Guilford.

Katehakis, A. 2009. "Affective Neuroscience and the Treatment of Sexual Addiction." *Journal of Sexual Addiction and Compulsivity* 16, no. 1: 1–31.

———. 2016. *Sex Addiction as Affect Dysregulation: A Neurobiologically Informed Holistic Treatment.* New York: W. W. Norton & Company.

Schore, A. 2001. "The Effects of Early Relational Trauma on Right Brain Development, Affect Regulation, and Infant Mental Health." *Infant Mental Health Journal* 22, no. 1-2: 201–269.

Schore, J., and A. Schore. 2008. "Modern Attachment Theory: The Central Role of Affect Regulation in Development and Treatment." *Clinical Social Work Journal* 36, no. 1: 9–20.

van der Kolk, B. 2003. "The Neurobiology of Childhood Trauma and Abuse." *Child and Adolescent Psychiatric Clinics of North America* 12, no. 2: 293–317.

Zapf, J., J. Greiner, J. Carroll. 2008. "Attachment Styles and Male Sex Addiction." *Journal of Sexual Addiction and Compulsivity* 15, no. 2: 158–175.

CHAPTER 5

THE DARK SIDE OF THE WEB:
Cybersex in the Twenty-First Century

Brent Moore, PhD, SATP

The times are changing, as always, but the current pace at which changes are happening is unprecedented. Technology is partially responsible for the rapid change in personal, occupational, and relational spheres (to name a few), but to complicate matters, technology is continually updating and morphing in a sphere of its own. Keeping up to date with technological progress is important for stakeholders in most spheres because it improves conditions and offers safety. For example, business ethicists concern themselves with data breaches on social media sites because it serves the public's best interest (Hand 2018). In medicine, policy makers scrambling to crack down on opioid abuse offer one solution of integrating IT systems of patient care organizations with online prescription drug monitoring programs (Landi 2018). Ensuring the fidelity of electronic databases continues to be a priority as all online users and information holders as they attempt to achieve security. The bottom line is that keeping up to date with technology matters.

Therapists working with gaming addiction or cybersex addiction are eager to deepen their knowledge and skills for assisting the clients they serve. However, conceptualizations, constructs, and mediums by which people engage and interact with technology are continually shifting. Concerning cybersex specifically, popular fetishes, virtual reality technologies, and remote-controlled sex toy technologies emerge faster than one can say "teledildonics." In a 2003 editorial article introducing a series on cybersex, the author remarks that the "five senses are often lost or distorted during Internet interactions" (Delmonico 2003, 259). The sixth sense that provides cues about first impressions, he says, is absent. "Perhaps this is what the Internet will never replace" (259).

Fast-forward a decade-and-a-half, and the internet as we know it offers an immersive experience. Not only have internet capabilities replaced sight and sound, such as "8D audio" on YouTube using headphones, but often preference is given to those stimuli given their intensity, even at the expense or neglect of person-to-person contact. For instance, it's not uncommon to see a parent at the park pushing a child on a swing while looking at the phone screen. According to Cockayne, Leszczynski, and Zook, "The proliferation of screens may at once facilitate estrangement, distraction and felt distance between those who are physically close" (2017, 1120). Unlike technology use in the early 2000s, sight, sound, and touch can be manipulated rather than lost, whereby the participants remain acutely oriented toward gratification-relevant stimuli during an internet encounter. The emergence of virtual reality technology stands as one primary indicator of this ongoing shift toward the intensification of privatized sensory experience at the expense of human contact.

Apparently, more is better. Participants of one study were prompted to complete a story stem about a male character preparing to encounter his first virtual reality (VR) pornographic experience. The researchers state, "Stories were noteworthy in that they often featured non-visual elements such as touch, taste, smell and sound" (Wood, Wood, and Balaam 2017, 5448). Remarkably, it was not out of the question for participants to expect all of the senses to be activated in an idealized, VR pornographic scenario. The technology is burgeoning to stimulate olfactory (Amores et al. 2018) and taste (Karunanayaka et al. 2018) senses in internet and VR applications, with experimentation well underway on these phenomena (Cheok and Karunanayaka 2018). Mainstream entertainment has profited from the development, manufacturing, and delivery of 4D films, and the business sector is also refining sensory experiences to optimize consumer revenue (Porcherot et al. 2018). Make no mistake, if we had ten senses, research and development teams around the globe would be designing ways to artificially manipulate them. At this point, a number of questions come to mind. One that is central to this chapter is this: "Why the need to augment reality?"

CLASSIC SEXUAL ADDICTION

For decades a fundamental conceptualization of sexual addiction has offered an answer to this question. The conceptualizations, constructs, and mediums by which people engage and interact with technology are continually shifting. We will cover all of these in an (ultimately futile but necessary) attempt to keep up with the rapidly evolving landscape involving cybersex. Let's start with operationalizing the conceptualization of what Riemersma and Sytsma refer to as "classic" sex addiction (2013). Sex addiction is generally marked by compulsive sexual behavior that leads to tolerance, escalation, withdrawal, and loss of volitional control in spite of adverse consequences. Central to addicts' lives is their relationship with a mood-altering experience, which can be so powerful as to lead over time to unmanageability (Carnes 2001).

As discussed in the previous chapter, Patrick Carnes was the pioneer of labeling and understanding sexual addiction, and he remains an essential figure in this field of study. Carnes (1991) asserts in research with sex addicts that the majority had experienced prior emotional (97%), physical (72%), and sexual (81%) abuse (as cited by Riemersma & Sytsma, 2013). Lasting treatment of sexual addiction often includes elements of trauma work to address issues of abuse. Not without controversy, these conceptualizations regarding the formation of sexual addiction from abuse were regarded by Gold and Heffner as a "conjecture about etiology" (1998, 375) due to underreporting of methodology and the participants being in advanced recovery. However, a proliferation of studies has supported various forms of abuse as contributing factors to the etiology of sexual addiction (Ferree 2003; Giugliano 2006; Schwartz and Southern 2000). Abuse is a distinctive feature of the classic sexual addiction model and continues to be a relevant source of inquiry and work in the treatment of sex addiction.

When abuse is carried out by the caregiver(s), a rupture occurs because the functional roles of protection, comfort, acceptance, and/or overall safety have been violated (Ainsworth and Bowlby 1991; Kobak and Mandelbaum 2003). Even if the caregiver is not the perpetrator of abuse but allows abuse to continue without intercession on the other's behalf, a rupture still occurs. In this sense, there is some overlap between abuse and insecure attachment. Preoccupied, fearful, and dismissing attachment styles (Bartholomew and Horowitz 1991) can derive from a caregiver's extreme mood disorder(s), insecurity, inconsistency, boundary violations, or separation, as well as perceived histories of trauma to the parent or child. While this is not an exclusive listing of etiologies, the myriad of possible origins related to attachment issues results in the outcome of unfulfilled needs, poor relational and coping skills, problems with intimacy, and dysfunctional forms of communication. In short, an outcome of chronic attachment ruptures is dysregulation.

Self-soothing, as described in chapter 3, can be a means to regain a sense of management in order to help control intense emotional behaviors. Bowman outlines insecure attachment styles with a potential unmet need that sex could artificially and temporarily fill (2013). Anxiously attached individuals might use sex as a way to seek approval. Avoidantly attached individuals tend to use sex for self-soothing, even at the expense of others. Those who relate with a fearful attachment can approach sex chaotically, dissociate, or use it as a means to exert power. People with secure attachment styles understand that the primary function of sex is about connection and offer protection, comfort, and acceptance with the expectation of mutuality.

Impulse control disorders, comorbid mood disorders, and co-addictions are also indicated as defining characteristics highlighted by classical sexual addiction (Riemersma and Sytsma 2013). The review of current scientific literature confirms high comorbidity rates of attention-deficit/hyperactivity disorder (ADHD) with excessive sexual behavior (Karaca et al. 2017), but also cautions that a great majority of hypersexual patients diagnosed with ADHD comprise the inattentive subtype (Reid 2007; Reid et al. 2011). The typical progression of ADHD moves from hyperactivity and/or impulsivity in childhood and adolescence to inattentive symptoms in adulthood. Nevertheless, childhood ADHD continues to share a relationship with excessive adult sexual behavior and abnormal sexual activity (Karaca et al. 2017).

CONTEMPORARY SEXUAL ADDICTION

With the features of classic sexual addiction being sexual, physical, and emotional abuse; impaired attachment and shame; impulse control disorders; comorbid mood disorders; and co-addictions, Riemersma and Sytsma (2013) further propose an emerging contemporary sexual addiction. They recognize and highlight the influence of chronicity, content, and culture as distinct and, at times, overlapping aspects with classical sexual addiction. These variables are of particular interest in relation to cybersex.

Chronicity

Chronicity refers to chronic exposure to stimuli. The internet offers a barrage of stimuli that can further produce enticement due to access, affordability, and anonymity (Cooper 1998). In reference to self-soothing, gratifying online behaviors become a quick, cheap (or free), no-strings-attached fix. Contemporary sexual addiction work emphasizes prevention and early intervention (Riemersma and Sytsma 2013) with the recognition that first exposure to pornography is trending at younger ages. While data simply cannot stay current with actual prevalence rates and trends, one source purported that the average first exposure to pornography is age 9 (Collier 2018). Yes, this means some children are first exposed at ages 8 and 7 years or younger. While neurological consequences of pornography are realized by reward or pleasure centers in the brain among adolescents and adults, less is known about the direct biopsychological and developmental effects of pornography on young children. The dopaminergic pathway associated with cocaine use is activated when viewing pornography (Landau, Garrett, and Webb 2008), so it does not take a wild imagination to speculate about pornography's consequences on a child's developing brain.

While the growth of internet pornography has skyrocketed exponentially due to accessibility, affordability, and anonymity, Mark Laaser includes "accidental" exposure as an additional explanation (1999). During the 1990s, "cybersquatters" purchased domain names hoping to sell them back to companies that might value them for a sizeable profit (Spaulding, Upadhyaya, and Mohaisen 2016). Often, these domains were populated with pornographic content in an effort to exploit the company into paying top dollar to take control of the domain and not have a public relations nightmare to navigate. This led to some unfortunate surprises for unsuspecting internet users. For anyone hoping to purchase quality products at competitive prices from Dick's Sporting Goods online prior to January 25, 2011, this might spur a flashbulb memory if you entered www.dicks.com.

Another strategy employed by profiteers involves redirecting to sites when wrong keystrokes are made when manually typing a URL. This is called "typosquatting" (Gilwit 2003). Deliberately registering a domain name that closely resembles another with malintent can have devastating consequences for young children and older crowds. Spaulding, Upadhyaya, and Mohaisen report one typosquatted domain name that targeted children and adults who mistyped the disneystore.com as "disenystore.com," which redirected to a website containing sexually explicit content (2016). For those who lack the capacity to type or spell, selecting links through the click of a mouse, strike of a touchpad, or tap of a touchscreen will also suffice for discovering porn accidentally. This intentional populating of the Web with "accidental" discovery moments by placing pornography on sites that are likely to be accessed in search of a legitimate website speaks to how incredibly present it is in our modern world and how children are often the target of this industry. When a young person is exposed to pornography early in their development, chronicity tends to increase as well, largely due to curiosity of what has been seen paired with a sense of secrecy and shame that permeates the conversation around human sexuality in Western cultures, especially in the church (Bowman, 2013).

The axiom "neurons that fire together, wire together" should be noted in chronic behavior or exposure (Hebb 1949). This simplistic understanding as scientific expression is troublesome when considering pornographic exposure (Bi and Poo 2001). When it overlaps with the classic sexual addiction notion of tolerance, the imagery of a frog in boiling water comes to mind. Intrusive obsessions and compulsions related to pornography can start with provocative images, such as television advertisements during Sunday afternoon football games or an accidental exposure to a pornographic website, then develop to more sexually explicit material (Ford, Durtschi, and Franklin 2012). In order to achieve a similar effect, the degree of sexual exposure becomes more explicit. As arousal diminishes, more graphic forms of pornography are required for physical and emotional stimulation. A biobehavioral cycle continues involving chronicity.

Content and Culture

Content and culture are explained by Riemersma and Sytsma as distinct entities in contemporary sexual addiction (2013). They are also inexorably linked. The Comstock Laws passed by the United States Congress on March 3, 1873, served to suppress trade in and circulation of obscene literature and articles of immoral use. The outcome forbade distribution of obscenity, sex toys, and visual or written erotica—including personal letters with sexual content—using the US Postal Service. The fine for violation was up to $5,000 or imprisonment up to five years or both. Political structures, in relation to culture, limited content in ways that would be unthinkable by today's standards.

Contextualizing sexuality and the practices that surround it is a moving target. According to Hubbard, "Identities like homosexual and heterosexual only have a meaning in relation to the society in which they exist" (2002, 365). A heteronormative love letter containing written erotica would have condemned its author to a prison sentence less than 150 years ago if sent through the US Postal Service. However, trading sexually explicit words, pictures, sound clips, and videos between consenting adults (i.e., cybersex) has now been normalized.

Culture has the ability to drive the context of normality, even outside of the law. A common sentiment by high-school-aged boys in my practice is that viewing indecent sexted pictures of girls is expected as the screen is being passed around. "I would be labeled weird if I didn't look" is a familiar response, despite the campaigns aimed at tackling this issue. Sexual attitudes, practices, norms, and preferences have shifted and will continue to shift (Bowman 2013).

It is challenging to treat a disorder that is difficult to understand. Many therapists are exceptional at treating clients with presenting issues of anxiety and depression. These are common ills that frequently walk through the doors of our practices, and there is something very familiar about anxiety and depression. We know how it feels to experience the symptoms that make up these conditions, even if only to a slight degree. Likewise, lust is familiar to the human condition, which intuitively assists with understanding some sexual addiction. However, the content of some pornography has become so bizarre and deviant in a variety of technologically diverse forms that the therapist's understanding could be potentially compromised. While the fundamentals of helping in such circumstances might not be compromised (e.g., empathy, attunement), knowledge about cybersex, the web, and technology in general will serve the therapist well. The following serves as a guide for navigating issues of cybersex and the trends that are emerging.

DEFINING CYBERSEX

As the world has become more integrated into and largely dependent on technology, a shift toward sexual experience being more available in a variety of forms has emerged. Far beyond pornography, cybersexual behavior often involves direct interaction with another person through a chat or a camera, and more recently through virtual reality and in online gaming platforms. A review of the literature covering "cybersex" will yield other important constructs such as "online sexual activity" (OSA), "internet addiction," and "pornography addiction."

Online Sexual Activity as Cybersex

OSA is broadly defined as online activities and behaviors that involve sexual content, topics, and stimuli (Shaughnessy, Fudge, and Byers 2017). The content of OSAs and intent of the person accessing OSAs are divergent. Shaughnessy, Fudge, and Byers distinguish OSA experiences in the following three categories: *non-arousal* (e.g., looking for information about sexual health online—STIs, contraception, fertility, looking for advice about sexual relationships or problems online); *solitary-arousal* (e.g., viewing sexually explicit pictures, video, or stories); *partnered-arousal* (e.g., engaging in sexual acts for someone watching over webcam, participation in an online sexual chat or discussion group for arousal, avatar participation in sexual activity) (2017, 66).

Some definitions of cybersex have included solitary and interactive activities (Cooper and Griffin-Shelley, 2002), but cybersex is nearly universally defined as a partnered-arousal OSA. In other words, cybersex is a subtype of OSA in much of the literature. Technically, defining "partnered-arousal" is complex with the advent of bots and artificial intelligence. The above study referenced by Shaughnessy, Fudge, and Byers (2017) inquired about eighteen partnered activities with fifteen out of eighteen prompts using the words "someone" or "person" (examples above are only a sampling of prompts). These person-to-person sexualized experiences have arguably become normalized (although the majority of people do not engage in them according to the literature). Not considered in the study but germane to cybersex is the encounter that includes more technologically mediated and more nonhuman yet partnered experiences. In other words, we are entering a time when partnered-arousal could include "something" rather than "someone" or a "person."

A subtle example of technologically mediated partnered-arousal comes through a prompt on the survey by Shaughnessy, Fudge, and Byers that identifies individuals who have "participated in an online sexual chat or discussion group for arousal" (2017, 69). The prompt is straightforward, and the assumption is that a chat or discussion group facilitates person-to-person interaction. In 2015, Ashley Madison, a "leading married dating service for discreet encounters" was exposed by a hacking group, The Impact Team. Data analyses revealed that 70,572 bots (70,529 programmed as female; 43 programmed as male) were engaging with human users in an attempt to make up for disproportionate female to male user accounts; male users received 20,269,675 messages from female bots, while female users received nearly 1,500 messages from male bots (Newitz 2015). Whether or not users suspected nonhuman interaction with the Ashley Madison service, nonhuman algorithmic entities were creating the "partner-to-partner" experience. This constitutes a less proximate, more technologically mediated interaction.

Another example of less proximate, more technologically mediated/non-human form of partnered OSA is "Bot2Bot" sex (Cockayne, Leszczynski, and Zook 2017). This could include watching "sex executed independent of human intervention between algorithms that are scripted without a sense of or requirement for physical proximity" (2017, 1126). Viewing could be a form of solitary-arousal or partnered-arousal (cybersex). Human-to-bot encounters involving masturbation with feedback by either human or nonhuman entities could be considered partnered. Other human-to-bot experiences could include sex games, or either party (human or bot) acting out instructed sexual stories. As artificial intelligence advances, cybersex will need to be further operationally defined.

Bot2Bot sex as a form of partnered-arousal, or cybersex, might seem out of the question for attempting to conceptualize. It should be difficult to conceptualize. In the Bible, the story of the Tower of Babel (Gen. 11:1–9) emphasizes human desire for independence and self-sufficiency apart from God. Robots and/or dolls designed for isolated or partnered-arousal mirror the intentions that motivated the creation of a tower that reaches to heaven. Technology is not inherently evil, nor is creating a robot. When God's creation, made in his image (*imago Dei*), attempts to create a representation of itself that in turn opposes God's will and purpose, then the emotions of confusion, repulsion, and disgust should be normalized. God's design needs no substitute. "For we are his workmanship, created in Christ Jesus for good works, which God prepared beforehand, that we should walk in them" (Eph. 2:10 ESV).

Internet Addiction

As the name suggests, internet addiction can be generally defined as the inability to control internet use, which leads to significant distress and/or functional impairment in normal activities (Pies 2009). Under the internet addiction umbrella can be situated smartphone addiction, gaming addiction, and cybersex addiction. Internet gaming disorder is identified in section III of the DSM-5, warranting more research prior to inclusion as a classified disorder. Smartphones and the internet act as the modality of delivery, so the internet itself is not addictive but instead the "medium through which certain behaviors may become addictive" (Baggio at al. 2018, 569).

Internet addiction in Korea was recognized as the top health problem experienced by children and adolescents (Ministry of Science 2015). Video game playing, gambling (Gainsbury 2015), and even social media (Carbonell and Panova 2017) have been deemed problematic behaviors. A common thread that weaves through internet-mediated addictions is fast access to stimuli. Whether swiping up, down, left, or right on the screen, data is delivered seamlessly.

Our expectation in the modern world for immediate gratification is confirmed by the academic literature (Ang and Lee 2017). Individuals in one study who were identified with internet gaming disorder exhibited high experiences of impulsivity by functional magnetic resonance imaging (fMRI), impaired insular function in error processing, and more activation of the fronto-striatal network to regulate their response inhibition performance (Ko et al. 2014). Translation: those with internet gaming disorder tendencies were more impulsive, less sensitive to feedback loops that inform their own actions, and less able to self-regulate than control participants.

Pornography Addiction

"Pornography addiction" is predominately a solitary-arousal OSA. Since this is a chapter on cybersex (considered a partnered-arousal OSA), its inclusion calls for an explanation. The term *pornography addiction* has been called into question, with criticism regarding poor experimental designs, methodological limitations, and lack of consensus on operationalized definitions (Ley, Prause, and Finn 2014). Each use of "pornography addiction" is set apart in quotations in this chapter due to the controversy surrounding it. However, Ley, Prause, and Finn also prefer the term *visual sexual stimulus* (VSS), expressing condemnation for the term *pornography* because it is loaded with negative bias. Advocates of this change in terminology also report the benefits of VSS because it enhances attitudes toward sexuality (McKee 2007), improves [perceived] quality of life

(Hald and Malamuth 2008), and provides a legal outlet for desires that are illegal if acted upon interpersonally (Diamond 2009). The authors also note that people viewing VSS have greater likelihood of anal and oral sex, emphasizing VSS's *positive* effects (Häggström-Nordin, Hanson, Tydén 2005).

Pornography can be renamed VSS in an attempt to reduce its stigma. Likewise, yams can be called sweet potatoes, but in the end, people will eventually use the terms synonymously. Pornography has a negative stigma for a reason. The idea of it still brings up feelings of anger and disgust for many (Voss 2015). It could be argued that this stigma is socially constructed to preserve conservative and historically normative ideologies (e.g., the Comstock Laws). But pornography is not part of God's intention. "The eye is the lamp of the body. So, if your eye is healthy, your whole body will be full of light, but if your eye is bad, your whole body will be full of darkness. If then the light in you is darkness, how great is the darkness!" (Matt. 6:22–23 ESV). The eye in this passage is similar to the heart in Jewish literature. The lamp is indicative of the quality of a person's character. More encompassing than vision related to pornography use, this passage identifies healthy eye habits with loyal devotion to God and "bad" eye habits with moral corruption (ESV Study Bible).

General agreement does not exist on cybersex as an exclusively partnered-arousal activity. Some literature considers "pornography addiction" to be a form of cybersex, which is why it is included in this chapter. A widely cited article by Laier and Brand denotes cybersex as involving both "interactive (e.g., sex chatting, self-displaying sexually or watching others perform sexual actions via webcam)" and "passive (e.g., watching pornography)" dynamics (2014, 306). Another contentious recognition is that although some academic literature vilifies the terms "pornography" and "pornography addiction," others embrace the terms. The article by Love et al. addresses the neuroscience of *internet pornography addiction* and is well worth the read for those interested in addictions work (2015).

In 2017, PornHub.com boasted sixty-eight years' worth of videos uploaded to their site with 28.5 billion visits (81 million each day). Of those visits, there were 25 billion searches performed. Streaming a two-hour movie would involve about two to six gigabytes of memory, depending on if it is a standard or high-definition version. One petabyte is equivalent to a million gigabytes. Pornhub alone transferred 3732 petabytes in 2017, which is enough data to fill the memory of every iPhone currently in use around the world. In 2019, 6.83 million new videos were uploaded to Pornhub. For some perspective, if one started viewing those videos today and watched all of them, they would have to watch continuously until the year 2179 to view them all. In their 2021 Year in Review, PornHub reported a *decrease* of nearly 30 seconds per visit to their website and boast this is due to a more enhanced search algorithm and slower internet speeds, with 83% of all visits coming from mobile devices.

To summarize, cybersex addiction and problematic pornography use are conceptually situated under internet addiction. As defined by many (but not all), cybersex is distinct from obsessions or compulsions to engage with pornography unless it involves partnered-arousal. Internet pornography poses a risk by continuing to release dopamine in the brain's pleasure center, the nucleus accumbens, which in turn leads to neurofunctional changes over time with chronic use so that maps for sexual excitement are altered (Doidge 2007). Chronic problematic pornography use increases activation of the ventral striatum, part of the brain's reward system, and corresponds with the severity of compulsive sexual behavior, amount of pornography viewed during a week, and frequency of masturbation (Gola et al. 2003). The addictive potential for either internet or pornography exists, especially for certain dispositions (see diathesis-stress framework by Davis 2001). Use of pornography is inherently obsessive and compulsive in nature, and the easy availability, quick gratification, and buffet of pornographic genres the internet offers adds fuel to the fire.

CONNECTING SEXUAL ADDICTION MODALITIES TO CYBERSEX

Merging sexual addiction modalities to current technological realities that surface in cybersex forms and variations is a formidable task due to constant shifts. Nevertheless, effective treatment relies on a solid framework for conceptualization and clearer understanding of the issues at hand. Again the work of Riemersma and Sytsma is a catalyst for teasing apart a distinct proposal for classic and contemporary sexual addiction (SA):

> [Classic SA] emphasizes family of origin (Willingham, 1999), attachment (Flores, 2004), and trauma resolution work (Feree, 2010; Laaser, 2004), and [contemporary SA] emphasizes prevention, early intervention to promote neurochemical reprogramming (Katehakis, 2009), social and relation skills training, and in some instances, adolescent clinical specialization. (2013, 307)

Contemporary sexual addiction work recognizes that many sexual behaviors available online can be characterized by depersonalization and dehumanization. Sexual objectification is a result of treating another person as an object to be valued for its use by others. For example, "A woman's body or body parts are singled out and separated from her as a person and she is viewed primarily as a physical object of male sexual desire" (Szymanski, Moffitt, and Carr 2011, 8).

For those who understand cybersex as a solitary-arousal experience, the encounter is marked by objectification. It is that simple. Cybersex as partnered-arousal is most likely trading the function of healthy sexuality for a feel-good experience. Sex is often reduced to a rush of excitement or a physiological high with relational and intimacy-building qualities treated as non-entities. The problem with denying the byproducts of sex is that they still exist. Oxytocin and vasopressin are released to bond users to stimuli (Cotiga and Dumitrache 2015; Moberg 2003). Bonding with images on a screen or body parts of a known human lover through video-mediated technology leads to unintended consequences.

The history of perversion is historically deep, which is why the Bible addresses it specifically (Eph. 5:3–17). Internet pornographic content has changed dramatically to include extreme perversion (highlighted later in this chapter), which was not as readily available at the time of Carnes's early writings and formation of classic sexual addiction, if it existed at all. Even family of origin dynamics, unhealthy attachments, and history of trauma do not explain some of the bizarre sexual arousal templates that present in practice. Our intuitions should be firing, "There's something else in the water." A vast array of perverse content helps to explain this shift and informs treatment.

In Greek mythology, Peitho, the goddess personifying persuasion and seduction, is regularly conflated with Aphrodite, the goddess of love or desire. In Greek culture, the close relationship between Aphrodite and Peitho parallels the connection between persuasion or seduction and desire. Drawing on social learning theory, it is possible to empirically link persuasion to desire. Perverse and unusual behaviors once reserved for secretive spaces are now readily available online. Social learning and persuasion subconsciously reinforce practices that later become normative. Unimaginable desires prior to exposure become essential features of arousal even when repulsion warns the conscience to stop.

In addition to content as a propelling force in cybersex, chronicity and culture collide with the objectification of women in commercials, prime-time television programs, movies, music lyrics and videos, magazines, advertising, sports media, video games, and internet sites (APA 2007). Mass media reaches everyone, including young children. People are socialized in all ecological contexts about what constitutes normal. As culture continues to normalize graphic content and chronicity (age of exposure) trends younger (Bowman, 2013), the need for intervention has grown. Treatment for contemporary sexual addiction stresses early intervention, the ability to treat younger clients, behavioral interventions (e.g., internet filtering, computers in public places), and relation-skills training

(Riemersma and Sytsma 2013). Those in the helping profession must take up advocacy efforts to alter systemic structures that promote dehumanization.

THE EXPLOSION AND IMPLOSION OF SEXUAL SCRIPTS

How people develop sexual beliefs and behaviors involves interaction between cultural, interpersonal, and intrapersonal levels (Gagnon 1990). Sexual beliefs and behaviors have always been restricted to personal histories, experiences, sensations, and imaginations. Compare the breadth of sexual possibilities perceived by a forty-year-old man living in Colonial America in 1770 to a sixteen-year-old adolescent male currently living in a similar geographic location who has been regularly watching free clips of online pornography for the past month. Given that the top five searches on PornHub.com in 2017 were lesbian, hentai, MILF, step-mom, and step-sister (PornHub 2018a), the adolescent's imagination is able to conjure up sexual scenarios that could not be conceived by the Colonial forty-year-old. In 2021, this list was largely unchanged, with the top four search terms on PornHub.com include hentai, Japanese, MILF, and lesbian (PornHub 2021).

Arousal is a significant subject in this chapter because it is the major purpose of cybersex for most users. Arousal templates, previously explored in chapter 1, inform an individual's sexual script, with both virtual content and lived experiences contributing to their development. Masters et al. state, "Sexual scripts are cognitive schema that instruct people how to understand and act in sexual situations" (2013, 409). On the south end of Boston, one high school arranges an opportunity for sophomores, juniors, and seniors to take a "Porn Literacy" course. It meets for two hours each week for five weeks with the aim of reducing sexual and dating violence. Jones reports her afternoon spent with the class on the third week of curriculum delivery (2018). The teacher of Sexual Literacy in Southside Boston exemplified this when she told her students in front of a marked-up whiteboard, "This is called a vulva. . . . This is a clitoris. . . . This is where women get most pleasure. Most women do not have a G spot. If you want to know how to give a woman pleasure, it's the clitoris" (Jones 2018).

Aspects of the curriculum that promote the reduction of sexual and dating violence could be presented here for a balanced perspective, but the method of content delivery trumps the learning objective. Watching pornography is not a prerequisite for attending the class, but the students, most of whom are minors, are taught how to watch videos. Even just describing the material brings to mind salacious imagery, piquing curiosities for those still naïve. A similar course on "Drug Literacy" could be developed to describe drugs, their effects, where to safely purchase them, and how to optimize safety while using them.

Facilitated group discussions could affirm individuals' preferences for particular drugs with nonjudgmental attitudes. However, the course would be forestalled because drugs are harmful, not to mention illegal. Just as drugs of various classifications and quantities are illegal to acquire, accessing pornographic content by minors is illegal. This is but one public space in which sexual socialization will have a dramatic influence on sexual scripts.

The debate about using "porn as pedagogy" in secondary schools is not a new discussion (Albury 2013). It is a response to children's accessibility to it. Biblically grounded discourse surrounding pornography and its devastating impacts should be a part of responsible childrearing in Christian homes. This is one of many preventative and early intervention strategies suggested by Riemersma and Sytsma (2013).

Cybersex is connected to the conversation about pornography. Besides people receiving sex education from pornography, a common message is that it serves as an acceptable partnered-arousal activity. In other words, relational OSA (specifically engagement with pornography) is believed to be "a means of enhancing and expanding a couple's sexual repertoire or as a means of fostering sexual communication" (Grov et al. 2010). An example of a sexual act commonly featured in pornographic films is a "facial," whereby a man ejaculates on a woman's face. In one study of nearly 300 youth aged fourteen to eighteen who reported watching porn, 25 percent of girls and 36 percent of boys reported watching this particular behavior in film (Herbenick as cited in Jones 2018). So, yes, pornography can expand a couple's sexual repertoire—but that does not mean it will improve their physical or emotional, sexual, or spiritual health.

The former examples serve to demonstrate the change in sexual scripts due to exposure by the ubiquitous availability of screens with access to the internet. Less subtle is the implosion of sexual scripts that are espoused by queer theory. By deconstructing dominant social narratives, queer theory advocates for lifestyles and practices that deviate from heteronormality, "a term describing the social privileges given to heterosexuality, assuming it is the 'natural' and 'normal' sexual orientation" (Wood, Wood, and Balaam 2017, 5447). Since the connection between sexuality and the gendered body (Hubbard 2002) is called into question given the tenets of queer theory, every single sexual script imaginable becomes available to an individual. Queer theory also continues to nonhumans. Cockayne et al. argue that "sexual relations propagated in digital space and with non-humans [should be taken] seriously (Payne, 2014), and not dismissing them as 'less real' or 'less intimate' than human:human sex" (2017, 1121). Be prepared for celebrations of diversity that include robots and dolls (see Davecat in Knafo 2015).

Dean (2009) suggests that heterosexual relationships are founded on predispositions of being "fetishistic" toward the opposite sex's genitals (as cited by Cockayne et al. 2017, 1121). As for queer theory, this is enough to "depathologize" other forms of sex, no matter the object. So humans are objectified, and objects are just as real and just as capable of intimacy as humans. According to queer theory, ideally, nothing should constitute perversion because standards would not exist. "Anger" and "disgust" directed toward pornography, as demonstrated earlier in this chapter, would not be an involuntary emotional reaction since acceptance and inclusion would reign overall. "Normal" sexual scripts within current gender roles would no longer be delineated; instead, identity would be a constellation of multiple and fluid sexualities. Sexual identity would become so fragmented by potentially vacillating genders, practices, and simultaneous combinations of conflicting positions that sexual scripts would implode.

ROMANCING THE STONE

One definition of romance is "a quality or feeling of mystery, excitement, and remoteness from everyday life." Coupling this definition with stones as inanimate objects, we have a fitting characterization of many OSA pursuits. Blurring popular trends with fantasy is characteristic of the porn industry. Each year, PornHub.com makes available an annual report of data that provides user insights from the previous year. In 2017, "fidget spinner" (a propeller-shaped toy with a ball bearing at the center) was deemed one of the top searches that defined the year on the pornography site. This is telling about the age demographic of porn users and the bizarreness of their fetishes. The number two most searched term or genre for the eighteen- to twenty-four-year-old demographic was "hentai."

Hentai (manga) porn parallels Japanese comics with sexually explicit themes and graphic portrayals of sexual acts and fetishes (Uidhir and Pratt 2013). In this genre, sexual encounters are depicted using anime characters with flawless and often exaggerated attributes. "After discovering hentai porn, regular porn became boring," is not an uncommon sentiment on discussion boards that follow articles about hentai. With chemical drug addiction, users want *more* to achieve the same effect. With pornography addiction, users often want *different* (Zimbardo and Duncan 2012).

Different is sometimes offered in the way of "monster (car)toon porn." Paasonen writes, "In monster toon porn, demons, zombies and hulk-like creatures copulate with elves, Hollywood starlet look-alikes and female game characters, huge bodies penetrate tiny ones and human-like bodies sprout novel sexual organs" (2017, 1). According to the statistics available from PornHub, the eighteen- to twenty-four-year-old age group searches "cartoon" 55% more and "hentai" 65% more than other age groups. Besides the 10 p.m. to 1 a.m. traffic on PornHub, the second most popular time to view pornography is 3 p.m. to 5 p.m., around the time that the school day ends. Again, the concepts of chronicity, content, and culture inform "normality" and impact arousal templates and sexual scripts. A child can go from playing Fortnite, a cooperative shooter-survival video game, to watching pornography involving the game's characters (real or computer-generated) performing any kind of sex act imaginable in seemingly infinite combinations, all while staying on the online gaming system (e.g., Xbox, PlayStation, Nintendo Switch). According to PornHub, their "development team works tirelessly to make sure that users can enjoy their experience on a wide variety of devices, and that includes visiting PornHub on game consoles" (2018). Through 2018, Fortnite has stayed on PornHub's top twenty-five searches with the most searched terms "Fortnite hentai" followed by "Fortnite porn." People are seeking mysterious, exciting escape and remoteness from everyday life by interacting with the inanimate.

In Martin Buber's work *I and Thou*, originally published in 1923, people are noted as using word pairs "I-It" and "I-Thou." (2010). I-It can be a form of "using" as an externalized way of addressing the world or "experiencing" as an internalized way of addressing the world. I-It is a selfish, self-serving relationship with the world that objectifies. I-It can also be a way to describe using others, even the inanimate, as a means to an end for self-gratification. The I-Thou relationship or encounter is fully engaged and involves mutuality and reciprocity. For Buber, God is the essential Thou, and the way we relate to the world around us involves him. What a tremendous responsibility we have been given! Our interactions with everything from people to inanimate objects have the potential to bring glory to God.

EMBODIMENT MATTERS

Synchronicity plays an important part in physiological and psychological bonding between caregivers and their infants, as well as between adults throughout life. From eye gaze to prosody to breathing, presence helps to define encounters. Perhaps Delmonico was right when he wrote that the internet will never replace that sixth sense, at least for now (2003). Despite attempts to recreate the "felt" experience that humans share through person-to-person contact, something is lost when transmitted from screen-to-screen. Cybersex in the form of partnered-arousal tends to focus on erotic pleasure rather than the connection or bonds that are forming between the individuals.

Solitary-arousal OSA perverts God's designs for intimacy in his creation. One argument in favor of solitary-arousal is that no one else is involved, therefore nobody is impacted. When synchronicity is traded for a one-sided experience (at the expense of individuals hurt by the porn industry), consequences follow. In van der Kolk's *The Body Keeps the Score*, readers navigate narratives marked by trauma and the biophysiological, psychological, and social consequences of various acute and chronic traumatic events. He writes that traumatic experiences "also leave traces on our minds and emotions, on our capacity for joy and intimacy, and even on our biology and immune system" (van der Kolk 2015, 1). Until just recently, people have not been able to systematically, at will, embark on voyeuristic sexual acts. It is feasible for solitary- or partnered-arousal OSA to reach beyond the realm of a person's psychological capacity so that it resembles trauma. With unparalleled access to devious acts notwithstanding, internet users consume content that can potentially lead to feelings of shame and remorse. All experiences leave traces, no matter how latent, on our minds and emotions. Involvement of the sympathetic nervous system just stamps an exclamation point on the memory and/or body (either knowingly or unknowingly to the user).

Embodied cognition underscores the notion that more than just the brain is at play with regard to mental activity. While studies involving neurophysiology provide evidence to support neurological pathways that parallel drug addiction or craving, taken alone these findings can be reductionistic. The brain does not act in isolation from our experiences but requires interplay with the sending and receiving of information from the body in relation to context. Arguably, nowhere is this more sacred than through the sexual encounter. Though the authors of the following quote are not writing specifically about sex, pay attention to how well their explanation of embodied cognition fits with the physical and nonphysical dimensions of intimacy:

> Theories of embodied cognition thus make it clear that we think with records of experiences gained as our bodies interact with the world. Human nature is emergent from more than just a complex brain, but from entire bodily systems involved in behavioral interactions with the world and their consequences in ongoing sensory feedback about the outcomes of such actions. Thus, as culture and its social and physical artifacts proliferate and become increasingly complex, the developmentally self-organizing mental capacities of persons get more diverse and complex. (Brown and Strawn 2017, 415)

Academics in the field of interpersonal neurobiology highlight that the mind does not exist without a body, relationships, or a society from which to develop

(Siegel 2016). Further, the theory of extended cognition incorporates "physical, cultural, or social aspects of the environment that are, at the moment, enmeshed in the current, ongoing mental transactions" (Brown and Strawn 2017, 415). Reciprocal and interactive exchanges define moments of mental processing, which include the surrounding environment. Instead of Mom saying, "You are what you eat," a more encompassing yet equally accurate aphorism is, "You are what you consume, and what you consume is also impacted by your consumption of it." The consumption of arousal-based OSA impacts mental capacities that extend beyond neurotransmitters to philosophical spheres. How do the emotional and cognitive aspects of one's self adapt to responses to sexual stimuli that exist solely for the purpose of self-gratification? How does this impact future person-to-person encounters?

SEXUAL WELLNESS IS NOT SEXUAL WHOLENESS

In early 2017, PornHub launched a "Sexual Wellness Center" (www.pornhub.com/sex/) with the intention of providing visitors with a "truly holistic approach to informing themselves on becoming healthier, happier and more responsible when it comes to sex" (Pornhub 2018b). Site content is organized by topics, ranging from anal sex to BDSM to sex toys. It is common for articles to link to pornographic videos on the site or to external content leading the curious down a rabbit trail. An example article is titled, "Six Steps to Start Exploring the Swinging Lifestyle" (Pornhub 2018c). Clearly, *wellness* is a term that can be operationally defined.

Sexual wholeness involves sexual wellness as outlined in God's Word, but sexual wellness does not necessarily imply sexual wholeness. By paying closer attention to cognitions, emotions, and the body, it is possible to recognize a fuller picture of the integrated self, which is dramatically impacted by relationships. This includes interpersonal relationships but can also comprise *all* relationships with the world around us. It is fair to claim that the mind "emerges from environmental interactions during human development," and it "encompasses external artifacts or situations" (Brown and Strawn 2017, 412, 416). Interactions with sexualized content will impact cognitions, emotions, and the body. The user then faces a crossroad when dealing with the consequences of those experiences. New potential exists for putting novel sexualized behavior into practice or even adding to one's sexual repertoire. Another possibility is to deny the significance of interactions with sexualized content, which perpetuates disintegration. Conversations about the function of cybersex and sexual wellness should include the ways in which their use relates to sexual wholeness. McClone states, "Wholeness and holiness derive from the same root and healthy sexuality calls us to the best of both" (2011, 9).

Peter writes in his first letter, "Be self-controlled and sober-minded for the sake of your prayers. Above all, keep loving one another earnestly, since love covers a multitude of sins" (1 Pet. 4:7–8 ESV). While the former part of this passage is often referenced for the purpose of harnessing behavioral and cognitive capacities, the simple wisdom of the latter part needs emphasizing. It is not possible to love others in the way God intends and simultaneously reduce them to an object, as cybersex often does. A fitting conclusion to a chapter covering "the dark side of the web" includes a call to love one another. Consider these questions posed by McClone:

- Do I seek to align my sexuality with God's call to love?
- Do I live in a way that is consistent with my spiritual values?
- What role does my faith play in dealing with sexual relationships?
- Is my behavior a choice that honors the commitments I have made, or does it draw me away from those commitments? (2011, 8)

REFERENCES

Ainsworth, M. D. S., and J. Bowlby. 1991. "An Ethological Approach to Personality Development." *American Psychologist* 46, no. 4: 331–341.

Albury, K. 2013. "Porn and Sex Education, Porn as Sex Education." *Porn Studies* 1(1–2): 172–181.

Amores, J., R. Richer, N. Zhao, P. Maes, and B. M. Eskofier. 2018. "Promoting Relaxation Using Virtual Reality, Olfactory Interfaces and Wearable EEG." 15th International Conference on Wearable and Implantable Body Sensor Networks, Las Vegas, Institute of Electrical and Electronics Engineers.

Ang, C. S., K. F. Lee. 2017. "Ability to Resist Temptations of Technology Use: A Qualitative Analysis of Children's Views on Factors Associated with Delay of Gratification." *The Journal of Genetic Psychology: Research and Theory on Human Development* 178, no. 5: 291–297.

American Psychological Association, Task Force on the Sexualization of Girls. 2007. *Report of the APA Task Force on the Sexualization of Girls*. Retrieved from http://www.apa.org/pi/women/programs/girls/report-full.pdf.

Baggio, S., J. Studer, O. Simon, G. Gmel, V. Starcevic, S. M. Gainsbury, and J. Billieux. 2018. "Technology-Mediated Addictive Behaviors Constitute a Spectrum of Related yet Distinct Conditions: A Network Perspective." *Psychology of Addictive Behaviors* 32, no. 5: 564–72.

Bartholomew, K., and L. Horowitz. 1991. "Attachment Styles among Young Adults: A Test of a Four-Category Model." *Journal of Personality and Social Psychology* 61, no. 2: 226–44.

Bi, G., and M. Poo. 2001. "Synaptic Modification by Correlated Activity: Hebb's Postulate Revisited." *Annual Review of Neuroscience* 24, no.1: 139–66.

Bowman, T. 2013. *Angry Birds and Killer Bees: Talking to Your Kids about Sex.* Kansas City: Beacon Hill.

Brown, W. S., and B. D. Strawn. 2017. "Beyond the Isolated Self: Extended Mind and Spirituality." *Theology and Science* 15, no. 4: 411–423.

Buber, M. 2010. *I and Thou.* Mansfield Centre, CT: Martino.

Carbonell, X., and T. Panova (2017). "A Critical Consideration of Social Networking Sites' addiction Potential." *Addiction Research and Theory* 25: 48–57.

Carnes, P. 1991. *Don't Call It Love.* New York: Bantam Books.

———. 2001. *Out of the Shadows: Understanding Sexual Addiction.* 3rd ed. Center City, MN: Hazelden.

Cheok, A. D., and K. Karunanayaka. 2018. *Virtual Taste and Smell Technologies for Multisensory Internet and Virtual Reality.* New York: Springer.

Cockayne, D., A. Leszczynski, and M. Zook. 2017. "#HotForBots: Sex, the Non-Human and Digitally Mediated Spaces of Intimate Encounter." *Environment and Planning D: Society and Space* 35, no. 6: 1115–33.

Collier, C. 2018. "The Neuroscience of High-Risk Behavior: Implications for Prevention and Treatment in Youth." *Journal of Recovery Science* 1, no. 2: 12.

Cooper, A., and E. Griffin-Shelley. 2002. "The Internet: The Next Sexual Revolution." In A. Cooper, ed., *Sex and the Internet: A Guidebook for Clinicians*, 1–18. New York: Brunner-Routledge.

Cooper, A. 1998. "Sexuality and the Internet: Surfing into the New Millennium." *Cyberpsychology and Behavior* 1, no. 2: 187–93.

Cotiga, A. C., and S. D. Dumitrache. 2015. "Men's Sexual Life and Repeated Exposure to Pornography. A New Issue?" *Journal of Experiential Psychotherapy* 18, no. 4: 40–45.

Davis, R. 2001. "A Cognitive-Behavioral Model of Pathological Internet Use." *Computers in Human Behavior* 17, no. 2: 187–95.

Delmonico, D. 2003. "Cybersex: Changing the Way We Relate." *Sexual and Relationship Therapy* 18, no. 3: 259–60. DOI: 10.1080/1468199031000153892.

Diamond, M. 2009. "Pornography, Public Acceptance and Sex Related Crime: A Review." *International Journal of Law and Psychiatry* 32, no. 5: 304–14.

Doidge, N. 2007. *The Brain That Changes Itself: Stories of Personal Triumph from the Frontiers of Brain Science.* New York: Penguin.

ESV Study Bible. 2008. Wheaton, IL: Crossway.

Ferree, M. C. 2003. "Women and the Web: Cybersex Activity and Implications." *Sexual and Relationship Therapy* 18, no. 3: 385–93.

Ford, J. J., J. A. Durtschi, and D. L. Franklin. 2012. "Structural Therapy with a Couple Battling Pornography Addiction." *The American Journal of Family Therapy* 40, no. 4: 336–48.

Gagnon, J. H. 1990. "The Explicit and Implicit Use of the Scripting Perspective in Sex Research." *Annual Review of Sex Research* 1, no. 1: 1–43.

Gilwit, D. B. 2003. "The Latest Cybersquatting Trend: Typosquatters, Their Changing Tactics, and How to Prevent Public Deception and Trademark Infringement." *Washington University Journal of Law and Policy* 11, no. 1: 267–96.

Gainsbury, S. M. 2015. "Online Gambling Addiction: The Relationship Between Internet Gambling and Disordered Gambling." *Current Addiction Reports* 2, no. 2: 185–93.

Giugliano, J. 2006. "Out of Control Sexual Behavior: A Qualitative Investigation." *Sexual Addiction and Compulsivity* 13, no. 4: 361–75.

Gola, M., M. Wordecha, G. Sescousse, M. Lew-Starowicz, B. Kossowski, M. Wypych, S. Makeig, M. N. Potenza, and A. Marchewka. 2003. "Can Pornography Be Addictive? An fMRI Study of Men Seeking Treatment for Problematic Pornography Use." *Neuropsychopharmacology* 42, no. 10: 2012–2031.

Gold, S. N., and C. L. Heffner. 1998. "Sexual Addiction: Many Conceptions, Minimal Data." *Clinical Psychology Review* 18, no. 3: 367–81.

Grov, C., B. J. Gillespie, T. Royce, and J. Lever. 2010. "Perceived Consequences of Casual Online Sexual Activities on Heterosexual Relationships: A U.S. Online Survey." *Archives Sexual Behavior* 40, no. 2: 429–39.

Häggström-Nordin, E., U. Hanson, and T. Tydén. 2005. "Associations between Pornography Consumption and Sexual Practices among Adolescents in Sweden." *International Journal of STD & AIDS* 16, no. 2: 102–107.

Hald, G. M., and N. M. Malamuth. 2008. "Self-perceived Effects of Pornography Consumption." *Archives of Sexual Behavior* 37, no. 4: 614–625.

Hand, D. J. 2018. "Aspects of Data Ethics in a Changing World: Where Are We Now?" *Big Data* 6, no. 3: 176–190.

Hebb, D. 1949. *The Organization of Behavior.* Hoboken, NJ: Wiley.

Hubbard, P. 2002. "Sexing the Self: Geographies of Engagement and Encounter." *Social and Cultural Geography* 3, no. 4: 365–381.

Jones, M. 2018. "What Teenagers Are Learning from Online Porn." *The New York Times Magazine.* February 7, 2018. https://www.nytimes.com/2018/02/07/magazine/teenagers-learning-online-porn-literacy-sex-education.html.

Karaca, S., A. Saleh, F. Canan, and M. N. Potenza. 2017. "Comorbidity between Behavioral Addictions and Attention Deficit/Hyperactivity Disorder: A Systematic Review." *International Journal of Mental Health Addiction* 15, no. 3: 701–724.

Karunanayaka, K., N. Johari, S. Hariri, H. Camelia, K. S. Bielawski, and A. D. Cheok. 2018. "New Thermal Taste Actuation Technology for Future Multisensory Virtual Reality and Internet." *IEEE Transactions on Visualization and Computer Graphics* 24, no. 4: 1496–1505.

Knafo, D. 2015. "Guys and Dolls: Relational Life in the Technological Era." *Psychoanalytic Dialogues* 25, no. 4: 481–502.

Ko, C. H., T. J. Hsieh, C. Y. Chen, C. F. Yen, C. S. Chen, J. Y. Yen, P. W. Wang, and G. C. Liu. 2014. "Altered Brain Activation During Response Inhibition and Error Processing in Subjects with Internet Gaming Disorder: A Functional Magnetic Imaging Study." *European Archives of Psychiatry and Clinical Neuroscience* 264, no. 8: 661–72.

Kobak, R., and T. Mandelbaum. 2003. "Caring for the Caregiver: An Attachment Approach to Assessment and Treatment of Child Problems." In *Attachment Processes in Couple and Family Therapy,* edited by S. M. Johnson and V. E. Whiffen, 144–64. New York: Guilford.

Laaser, M. 1999. *Faithful and True: Sexual Integrity in a Fallen World.* Nashville: LifeWay.

Laier, C., and M. Brand. 2014. "Empirical Evidence and Theoretical Considerations on Factors Contributing to Cybersex Addiction from a Cognitive-Behavioral View." *Sexual Addiction and Compulsivity* 21, no. 4: 305–321.

Landau, J., J. Garrett, and R. Webb. 2008. "Assisting a Concerned Person to Motivate Someone Experiencing Cybersex into Treatment: Application of Invitational Intervention; The ARISE Model to Cybersex." *Journal of Marital and Family Therapy* 34: 498–511.

Landi, H. 2018. "Top Ten Tech Trends 2018: In the Fight against the Opioid Crisis, Providers Are Turning to Technology." *Healthcare Informatics*. August 30, 2018. https:// www.hcinnovationgroup.com/population-health-management/article/13030657/top -ten-tech-trends-2018-in-the-fight-against-the-opioid-crisis-providers-are-turning-to -technology.

Ley, D., N. Prause, and P. Finn. 2014. "The Emperor Has No Clothes: A Review of the 'Pornography Addiction' Model." *Current Sexual Health Reports* 6, no. 2: 94–105.

Love, T., C. Laier, M. Brand, L. Hatch, R. Hajela. 2015. "Neuroscience of Internet Pornography Addiction: A Review and Update." *Behavioral Science* 5, no. 3: 388–433.

Masters, N. T., E. Casey, E. A. Wells, and D. M. Morrison. 2013. "Sexual Scripts among Young Heterosexually Active Men and Women: Continuity and Change." *The Journal of Sex Research* 50, no. 5: 409–420.

McClone, K. 2011. "Sexual Health: A Christian Perspective." *Human Development* 32, no. 1: 3–9.

McKee, A. 2007. "The Positive and Negative Effects of Pornography as Attributed by Consumers." *Australian Journal of Primary Health* 34, no. 1: 87–104.

Ministry of Science, ICT and Future Planning, and the National Information Society Agency. 2015. "The Survey on Internet Overdependence." Seoul: National Information Society Agency.

Moberg, K. 2003. *The Oxytocin Factor: Tapping the Hormone of Calm, Love, and Healing.* Boston: Da Capo Press.

Newitz, A. 2015. "Ashley Madison Code Shows More Women, and More Bots." *Gizmodo.* August 31, 2015. https://gizmodo.com/ashley-madison-code-shows-more-women-and -more-bots-1727613924.

Paasonen, S. 2017. "The Affective and Affectless Bodies of Monster Toon Porn." In *Sex in the Digital Age*, edited by P. Nixon and I. Düsterhöft, 10–24. New York: Routledge.

Pies, R. 2009. "Should DSM-V Designate 'Internet Addiction' a Mental Disorder?" *Psychiatry (Edgmont)* 6, no. 2: 31–37.

Porcherot, C., S. Delplanque, N. Gaudreau, M. Ischer, A. De Marles, and I. Cayeux. 2018. "Immersive Techniques and Virtual Reality." In *Methods in Consumer Research*, Volume 2, edited by G. Ares and P. Varela, 69–83. Cambridge, UK: Woodhead.

Pornhub. 2018a. "Pornhub Insights: 2017 Year in Review." Accessed November 28, 2018. https://www.pornhub.com/insights/2017-year-in-review.

———. 2018b. "Announcing the Pornhub Grant for Sexual Wellness Research." Accessed November 28, 2018. https://www.pornhub.com/sex/pornhub-grant-sexual-wellness -research/.

———. 2018c. "Six Steps to Start Exploring the Swinging Lifestyle." Accessed November 28, 2018. https://www.pornhub.com/sex/?s=Six+Steps+to+Start+Exploring+the +Swinging+Lifestyle.

———. 2019. "Pornhub Insights: 2019 Year in Review." https://www.pornhub.com/insights /2019-year-in-review.

———. 2021. "Pornhub Insights: 2021 Year in Review." https://www.pornhub.com/insights /yir-2021.

Reid, R. C. 2007. "Assessing Readiness to Change among Clients Seeking Help for Hypersexual Behavior." *Sexual Addiction and Compulsivity* 14, no. 3: 167–86.

Reid, R. C., B. N. Carpenter, R. Gilliland, and R. Karim. 2011. "Problems of Self-Concept in a Patient Sample of Hypersexual Men with Attention-Deficit Disorder." *Journal of Addiction Medicine* 5, no. 2: 134–40.

Riemersma, J., and M. Sytsma. 2013. "A New Generation of Sexual Addiction." *Sexual Addiction and Compulsivity* 20: 306–22.

Schwartz, M. F., and S. Southern. 2000. "Compulsive Cybersex: The New Tearoom." *Sexual Addiction and Compulsivity* 7, no. 1–2: 127–44.

Shaughnessy, K., M. Fudge, and E. S. Byers. 2017. "An Exploration of Prevalence, Variety, and Frequency Data to Quantify Online Sexual Activity Experience." *The Canadian Journal of Human Sexuality* 26, no. 1: 60–75.

Siegel, D. J. 2016. *Mind: A Journey to the Heart of Being Human*. New York: W. W. Norton.

Spaulding, J., S. Upadhyaya, and A. Mohaisen. 2016. "The Landscape of Domain Name Typosquatting: Techniques and Countermeasures." https://arxiv.org/pdf/1603.02767.pdf.

Szymanski, D. M., L. B. Moffitt, and E. R. Carr. 2011. "Sexual Objectification of Women: Advances to Theory and Research. *Journey to The Counseling Psychologist* 39, no. 1: 6–38.

Uidhir, C. M., and H. Pratt. 2013. "Pornography at the Edge: Depiction, Fiction, and Sexual Predilection." In *Art and Pornography: Philosophical Essays*, edited by H. Maes and J. Levinson, 137–160. New York: Oxford University Press.

van der Kolk, B. A. 2014. *The Body Keeps the Score: Brain, Mind, and Body in the Healing of Trauma*. New York: Penguin Group.

Voss, G. 2015. *Stigma and the Shaping of the Pornography Industry*. London: Routledge.

Wood, M., G. Wood, and M. Balaam. 2017. "'They're Just Tixel Pits, Man': Disputing the 'Reality' of Virtual Reality Pornography through the Story Completion Method." *Virtual Reality*, 5439–451.

Zimbardo, P. G., and N. Duncan. 2012. "The Demise of Guys: Why Boys Are Struggling and What We Can Do about It." N.p.: TED.

CHAPTER 6

SEX, ADDICTION, AND THE DIVINE IMAGE

Fr. Sean Kilcawley, STL, PSAP

In chapter 3, sexual addiction was referred to as an intimacy disorder, and many recovering sexaholics refer to themselves as "love cripples." In short, sexual addiction reveals the fact that we have a love problem. From a theological perspective, we therefore can look at sexual addiction and recovery through the lens of a theology of love, and more precisely through the lens of what we call the "image of God." Each human person is created in this image of God who is love, and each of us is called to love as God loves. The spiritual dimension of recovery from sexual addiction involves the redemption of the image of God in our lives and movement toward living in a way that is congruent with the truth of love as revealed by God himself. Therefore, we need a theology of love that will serve as a point of reference for relationship. The theology of the body provides that reference point and serves as something of a roadmap for those who seek to rid their lives of addiction and live in accordance with the image of God written on our hearts.

Saint John Paul II was the leader of the Roman Catholic Church from October 16, 1978, until his death on April 2, 2005. In many ways he was ahead of his time. In 1960, as Archbishop of Krakow, he published *Love and Responsibility*, a moral treatise regarding human love and sexuality, culminating in a final section dedicated to sexology. The content of that book reveals that the Bishop of Krakow had a great desire to walk with couples as they navigated marriage in the context of the sexual revolution. His desire was to enter into the lives of his people and to help them love as God loves. When he was elected by the college of cardinals and became the 264th pope, he continued his work by giving a series of Wednesday reflections on "Human Love in the Divine Plan," where he gave a deep biblical reflection on what it means to be created in the image of God and what it looks like to live in conformity with that image. Those reflections spanned five years and are collectively now known as *The Theology of the Body.*

The Polish pope opens his reflections with a meditation on Jesus's encounter with the pharisees in the nineteenth chapter of Matthew's Gospel. When asked, "Is it lawful for a man to divorce his wife for any and every reason?" our Lord responds, "Haven't you read ... that at the beginning the Creator 'made them male and female,' and said, 'For this reason a man will leave his father and mother and be united to his wife, and the two will become one flesh'? So they are no longer two, but one flesh. Therefore what God has joined together, let no one separate." (Matt. 19:3–6). Jesus does not answer their question regarding divorce directly but points them back to the beginning. Their question is not really about the law or the rules, it is a more fundamental question of what it means to be human. In pointing them to the beginning, he quotes Genesis 1:27 and Genesis 2:24, indicating that the answer to the real question at hand is contained in these two chapters of the Torah.

Yet the Pharisees insist on the question of divorce: "Why then ... did Moses command that a man give his wife a certificate of divorce and send her away?" Jesus responds that it was "because your hearts were hard" and that "it was not this way from the beginning" (Matt.19:7–8). Here we see an indication that something from the beginning was lost due to the sin of our first parents. The law of Moses provided a kind of compromise with our sinfulness, but Jesus now calls the people to live in a new way and to recognize that "anyone who divorces his wife, except for sexual immorality, and marries another woman commits adultery" (19:9). He is calling them to live in a redeemed way, and what he calls us to he also enables. Just as he called a crippled man to walk and restored sight to the blind, so too, when he calls us to live a redeemed life of love, he will enable us, through his grace, to do so.

From this passage, John Paul II continues to unpack what it means to return to the beginning. The theology of the body is an attempt to propose an *adequate anthropology* for dealing with not only the question posed by the Pharisees, but with every question that touches on what it means to be human. He writes,

> I think that among the answers that Christ would give to the people of our times and to their questions, often so impatient, fundamental would still be the one he gave to the Pharisees. In answering these questions, Christ would appeal first of all to the "beginning." He would perhaps do so all the more decidedly and essentially, inasmuch as man's inner and simultaneously cultural situation seems to

move away from that beginning and assume forms and dimensions that diverge from the biblical image of the "beginning" to points that are evidently ever more distant. (John Paul II 2006, 219)

The theology of the body is not simply a theological reflection on marriage and sexuality, it is an *adequate anthropology* that is fundamental to understanding what it means to be created in the image of God. For those who seek healing and freedom, particularly in the area of sexuality, it can be a roadmap for coming to understand one's story in the context of the story of salvation and a path to true recovery and conversion.

CREATED FOR LOVE

When we speak of being created in God's image, we traditionally attribute the image of God to self-knowledge and self-determination. Humans have reason and free will. What John Paul II notes throughout his teaching is that the image of God also includes our capacity for love, which is fundamental to the human experience. In his first encyclical letter, John Paul II wrote, "Man cannot love without love. He remains a being that is incomprehensible to himself. His life is senseless. If love is not revealed to him, if he does not encounter love, if he does not experience it and make it his own, if he does not participate intimately in it" (John Paul II 1979, 10). We are created for love and connection. Love is first revealed in the experience we have with the love of our parents for one another. Then we come to encounter the love our parents have for us. As we grow in this experience of love, we make it our own and eventually participate in it as we fall in love with another.

In this context, we see sexual addiction as a countersign to love. Sex addicts live in pursuit of a love they never find. What is revealed in pornography is void of any true connection and leads to loneliness and isolation in the psychological experience of the viewer. What we see in addiction is the fulfillment of Jesus's words to Peter at the Last Supper, "Simon, Simon, Satan has asked to sift all of you as wheat" (Luke 22:31). The enemy's plan is to divide, and just as a sifter divides each grain of wheat from the others, so too sin separates us from the communion we are created for. This is especially evident in the lives of sex addicts who struggle to connect with real people at a deep level. Therefore, the task of every addict is to learn to love well, or perhaps, to learn to love again. The Christian therapist or pastor has the task of presenting the gospel in such a way that it might facilitate a new beginning with the Lord. This is the same task that was undertaken by John Paul II in *The Theology of the Body.*

THEOLOGY OF THE BODY AND THE
NARRATIVE OF SALVATION

When Jesus spoke to the Pharisees, he referred to different periods of salvation history. He referenced *the beginning* in Genesis 1–2. He spoke of a period of *hardness of heart* that is marked by sin. This is the period that spans from the fall of man in Genesis 3 until the coming of Christ. He then gave a new commandment and calling to live on a higher level. This is echoed throughout the Sermon on the Mount in the series of "you have heard it said . . . but I say to you" statements. As John Paul II unpacks his *adequate anthropology*, he reflects on each of these time periods and finishes with a reflection on our destiny in heaven. The four parts are commonly referred to as follows:

- **Original man,** covering the period between creation and the sin of our first parents. Here we find a reflection on what love was meant to be like in the beginning. It is also referred to as the period of *original innocence*.
- **Historical man fallen,** reflecting on the dynamism of sin and the experience of love, which is distorted after sin enters into the world.
- **Historical man redeemed,** reflecting on the dynamism of redeemed love beginning from the time Jesus entered the world and gave us new life through his passion, death, and resurrection, and ending with the end of time.
- **Eschatological man,** reflecting on the destiny of love—we will participate in the divine love of God in heaven (John Paul II, 2006).

This structure provides us with a framework for reflecting on both the biblical narrative and our personal narrative through the lens of love and relationality. The biblical narrative is a story of love that is lost and found again. It is a love story which begins with a marriage in Genesis 1–2 and ends with the wedding feast of the Lamb in the book of Revelation. It is the narrative that we hold in common as Christian men and women, and it is the narrative of every addict in recovery. Simply stated, the narrative form is that God created everything, and it was very good. Then darkness settled in: after the sin of our first parents, love became distorted. Then dawn broke: Jesus Christ entered the world in order to redeem us so that we can grow in clarity and virtue, and then will come the end of our lives when we enter into the divine life in heaven. Within this narrative are key boundary experiences that mark the end of one phase and the beginning of another. The sin of Adam and Eve in Genesis 3 marks the boundary between original innocence and historical sinfulness. The passion, death, and resurrection of Jesus Christ mark another boundary between historical sinfulness and redeemed life. The final boundary experience will be the second coming of Christ at the end of time.

This narrative, found in the entirety of Sacred Scripture, is also the narrative of our own lives. As we find ourselves within this narrative, we can also identify the times in our lives of some form of innocence. There are experiences of rupture, trauma, and sin which can mark a transition from that state of innocence to a state of sinfulness. Hopefully we have other experiences of redemption and healing that mark a transition to living in recovery and freedom—redeemed love. For example, I was born into the world, and everything was good. Then darkness crept in: my mother died when I was two years old, I felt emotionally distant from my dad throughout adolescence, I was exposed to pornography at eleven years of age at a neighbor's house, I was exposed to my first pornographic movie at fourteen, in high school I had weak masculine identity, and the upperclassmen spread rumors that I was gay. All of these distorted my thinking about who I was, how I perceived who God is, and what I understood about right relationship between men and women. Then life arrived: Jesus entered into my life to reveal to me who I am, to heal what was wounded, to supply what I hadn't received, to make me a new creation in him so that I can now walk in clarity and virtue and someday get to heaven.

The way an individual tells her story is a window into her healing process. It is also telling about a person's conversion. Is a person able to articulate the distortion part of their story, or do they brush over it? How do they feel about the broken parts of their story? Do they see their life as one story or many disjointed ones? Do they have a redemption story? Is there a clear experience of how Christ entered into the distortion to bring clarity?

I was speaking with a mother of an adolescent girl who came looking for resources for talking to her daughter about God's plan for sex. When I pointed her to a book that is recommended, she said, "Father, I can't say those words!" *Interesting,* I thought. *Why don't you think you can say them? What was your experience with sex education growing up?* I learned that she had very little education from her own parents. As a young girl, she had experienced some peer-to-peer abuse, which led to a problem with promiscuity in college. Then, at a certain point, she converted and decided to change her life. She now tries to live according to biblical principles and follows the teachings of the Catholic Church with regard to sexual morality.

The phases of the biblical narrative are present here. She had various experiences of rupture as a young person. The abuse she experienced distorted her view of love and sexuality, then her own sinful behaviors grew out of those wounds and distorted her view of herself. Then she decided to make a change, but her present was somehow cut off from her past. She changed but wasn't transformed. The faithful Christian adult version of her seemed disconnected from the wounded young person version of her. I asked her, "What do you think of 'College You' (the distorted version of yourself)?"

"Father, I hate that person."

"How does Jesus see that person?"

"I don't want to think about that!"

"What if Good Christian Mom You and College You were both in the room, and Jesus knocked on the door?"

"I'd kick college me out of the room."

"So who do you think Jesus would rather hang out with, You or College You?"

"Hopefully both."

"In the Gospels, who would Jesus go to dinner with, You or College You?"

"Ugh, Father! College Me."

"So, for your assignment, go to chapel and spend some time praying as College You. Let Our Lord encounter you just as he encounters the sinful woman in John chapter 8."

The next time I met this woman, she came into the office and said, "Father, I read the book, and it was amazing!" What was needed in this case was the integration of her story. Her personal narrative was split at the frontier between fallen and redeemed. She needed to encounter Jesus in the place of her woundedness. When she allowed him to encounter the part of her that was still stuck in her shame about her past, he transformed her and integrated the past with the present. This is also the story of every recovering addict. We all have a story of how love was distorted in our own lives, and in our recovery, we learn to love again.

THE ANTHROPOLOGICAL ORDER

In the first chapter of Genesis we read, "God created mankind in his own image, in the image of God he created them; male and female he created them" (Gen. 1:27). From the beginning, we are created male and female in the image of God. We also believe that God from all eternity is Father, Son, and Holy Spirit. The Trinity is a communion of life and love that has existed from all eternity. Reflecting on the image of God, the German theologian Joseph Ratzinger says,

> The real God is by His very nature entirely being for (Father), being from (Son), and being with (Holy Spirit). Man, for his part, is God's image precisely insofar as the "from", "with", and "for" constitute the fundamental anthropological

pattern. Whenever there is an attempt to free ourselves from this pattern, we are not on our way to divinity but to dehumanization, to the destruction of being itself through the destruction of the truth. (Ratzinger 1996, 28)

These words from Ratzinger provide a profound theological insight about the triune God who is love and the implications for us who are created in his image. Within the love of the Trinity, he identifies three movements or dynamisms of love. The Father is entirely "being for." The Father is the source of all. He pours himself out in love toward the Son. This means the Father's love is an active love, a self-giving love. It is the love that says, "Your needs are more important than my needs." It is the love that lays down one's life for one's friends. The traditional words we use to describe this act of love are *to will the good of the other*. In more colloquial terms, it is sacrificial love.

The Son is entirely "being from" the Father. In the life of Jesus, we see this evidenced as he says, "the Son can do nothing by himself; he can do only what he sees his Father doing" (John 5:19); "anyone who has seen me has seen the Father" (John 14:9); "believe me when I say that I am in the Father and the Father is in me" (John 14:11); and "I and the Father are one" (John 10:30). The love of the Son responds to the Father's love. The language we use to describe this movement is more difficult. What is the proper response to a love that is willing to give its very life for you? Gratitude, receptivity, and returning the Father's love are all ways this may be described. Another way of describing the love of a son or daughter is *entrusting oneself entirely to the other*. To entrust oneself signifies that one gives oneself to the other, but particularly that one gives oneself into the other's care. One places one's heart into the other's hands. This is how Jesus responds to the Father's love as he prays from the cross, "Father, into your hands I commit my spirit" (Luke 23:46).

The Holy Spirit is entirely "being with" the Father and the Son. The Holy Spirit is the bond of love between the Father and the Son, which also constitutes a third person within the Trinity. This signifies a kind of interdependent love, which we see in friendship or spousal relationships. We all love in each of these ways. We will the good for others in relationships in which we serve as a caregiver: as father, mother, teacher, therapist, pastor, doctor, or nurse. We entrust ourselves to others in relationships where we are cared for or on whom we are dependent: son, daughter, patient, or student. We experience interdependent love in our peer relationships, friendships, sibling relationships, or amid colleagues. The image of God is revealed in us as we love in each of these ways. Most importantly, we reveal the image of God as these three dynamics form the pattern of love in our lives.

The anthropological pattern taught by Ratzinger provides a deeper insight into the *adequate anthropology* of John Paul II. Ratzinger states, "Man is God's image precisely insofar as the 'from,' 'with,' and 'for' constitute the fundamental anthropological pattern" (1996, 28). In our human development, our first experience of love is the experience of being sons and daughters who entrust ourselves completely to our parents. It is a relationship of complete dependence and attachment. Later we learn to "be with" another in our sibling relationships and friendships. These are interdependent relationships of love. Finally, one of those friendships becomes a marriage, and through the bearing of children we become a mother or father who is "for" their children. Maternal and paternal love always seeks good for the child and is willing to lay down their lives for that child. This anthropological pattern is a hermeneutical key for understanding how love is distorted by sin and addiction and how recovery involves restoring the anthropological pattern or anthropological order in our lives.

Ratzinger indicates how the order of love is distorted, saying, "Whenever we attempt to free ourselves from the pattern, we are not on our way to divinity but to dehumanization, to the destruction of being itself through the destruction of the truth." An attempt to free ourselves from the pattern is indicated when we rearrange or reprioritize the order of love. Another way of putting it is that we forget the order. Any time we forget the order, we free ourselves from the pattern. If we attempt to live a life of sacrifice ("being for") without first entrusting ourselves to another who loves us with a sacrificial love, we are attempting to give what we do not have. A pertinent question for every Christian is this: What is first, to love or to be loved? What is more important, to love or to be loved? Very often the answer people give is "to love." Yet we cannot give what we do not have. St. John reminds us, "This is love: not that we loved God, but that he loved us" (1 John 4:10).

Another way we can wrongly order the pattern is when our identity becomes tied to our "being for" or "being with" relationships rather than our "being from" God. We can find our identity in what we can accomplish rather than in being a child of God, or we can find our identity in who we are attracted to or who we are aroused by rather than where we are from. From a theological point of view, our identity is always to be found in our "being from" relationship. As Christians, we believe that Jesus reveals to us who we are, and Jesus's identity is Son of God. His identity is not first and foremost bridegroom of the Church ("being with") or Savior of the world ("being for"), it is Son of God. Mark introduces his writing as "the good news about Jesus the Messiah, the Son of God" (1:1). At the baptism, we hear the words of the Father, "This is my Son, whom I love; with him I am well pleased" (Matt. 3:17). At the transfiguration, "This is my Son, whom I have chosen; listen to him" (Luke 9:35). At the conclusion of Matthew's Gospel, we hear the affirmation, "Surely he was the Son of God!" (Matt. 27:54). The gospel proclamation is a proclamation of who Jesus is: the Son of God. Therein we find his identity. St. Paul affirms that we too are sons and daughters by adoption (Rom. 8:15). So anytime we seek to find our identity in what we do, what we produce, whom we are attracted to or aroused by, or who is attracted to us, we are attempting to reorder God's pattern. And the work of recovery is to come to know and live into our identity as beloved sons and daughters of the Father.

ORIGINAL INNOCENCE AND THE GENESIS 2 NARRATIVE

In Genesis 2 we see that we are created according to this anthropological order. God first creates Adam and places him in the garden, only giving one commandment: "You are free to eat from any tree in the garden; but you must not eat from the tree of the knowledge of good and evil, for when you eat from it you will certainly die" (Gen. 2:16–17). Implied in this commandment is a relationship between Adam and the Lord. Because God wants good for Adam, he commands him not to eat from the fruit of the tree of knowledge of good and evil. Adam believes the Lord, he trusts the Lord, and he entrusts himself to the Lord, and everything is good. John Paul II calls this relationship an experience of original solitude, which means that Adam finds himself alone with the Lord. He is not alone by himself, but alone with the Lord. He is a "partner of the Absolute" (John Paul II, General Audience 6, 1979, 151). He is in relationship with the Lord as a son to a father. This is what makes him unique in the created world.

The experience of original solitude also reveals a longing to find another someone to relate to. Reflecting on the experience of being a son before the fall, we can imagine Adam discovering the world around him. He notices the things that are like himself and the things that are not. He might pick up a rock, noticing that both he and the rock are composed of matter, yet the rock lacks the ability to move about or communicate, so what Adam learns is that he is not like the rock and therefore must be like God—at least more like God than the rock. He might also notice a tree and realize the tree is alive just as he is alive, yet the tree also lacks the ability to move about or communicate, so he is more like God than the tree. Adam is the only part of God's creation with the capacity for self-knowledge and self-determination, or reason and free will. Therefore, he finds himself alone with the Lord.

John Paul II points out that it is precisely the structure of the body that reveals that Adam is a person created in the image of God. "The structure of the body is such that it permits him to be the author of a genuinely human activity.

In this activity, the body expresses the person. It is thus, in all its materiality ('he formed man with dust of the ground'), penetrable and transparent, as it were, in such a way as to make it clear who man is (and who he ought to be) thanks to the structure of his consciousness and self-determination" (John Paul II, General Audience 7, 1979, 154). Two characteristics he notes are that the body is penetrable and transparent. Insofar as our bodies are penetrable, we can be wounded. Others can act toward us. This also gives us the ability to receive another person. Insofar as they are transparent, our bodies reveal to others who we are. Our bodies and what we do with them matters.

The Lord knows this: "It is not good for the man to be alone. I will make a helper suitable for him" (Gen. 2:18). In the state of original solitude, Adam only experiences that first movement of love "to be from." His heart, however, longs to find someone to "be with." As the Lord creates all of the animals, Adam continues to differentiate himself from them, and "no suitable helper was found" (Gen. 2:20). So the Lord casts a deep sleep on Adam, and when he wakes from that sleep he encounters a new creature. Her body is both like and unlike his own body. When he looks into her eyes, he can see she knows the same God he knows. She is a daughter of the same father: "This is now bone of my bones and flesh of my flesh" (Gen. 2:23). In other words, this is someone for Adam to "be with."

John Paul II teaches that their "being with" love, which he calls "original unity," is built on the foundation of the original solitude experienced by each of them. "The meaning of original solitude enters and becomes part of the meaning of original unity, the key point of which seems to be precisely the words of Genesis 2:24. . . . 'A man will leave his father and mother and unite with his wife and the two will become one flesh' (Mt. 19:5)" (John Paul II, General Audience 8, 1979, 156–157). The delight that each experienced before the Lord is now a delight shared for one another.

Adam sees in Eve the same image of God he experiences in himself. She is also a "being from" the Lord. In his encounter with her, he sees in her person the same anthropological order, calling to mind the expression found in Song of Songs: "my sister, my bride" (Song 4:9–10). He first sees her as a daughter of the same father, and because this is true, he can unite with her as his bride. Whereas in the trinitarian love of God the movements are absolute (the Father only wills the good for the Son, the Son only entrusts himself to the Father), in human beings these movements are mixed. Adam can now love his wife with the love he has received from the Lord. As God wants the good for Adam, he wants the good for his wife, and Adam also entrusts himself to her care. As Eve has entrusted herself to the Lord, she entrusts herself to her husband, and she also wills the good for him.

When that love is expressed in the most complete, profound, and bodily way, a third person comes forth: "With the help of the LORD I have brought forth a man" (Gen. 4:1). In this way, according to God's original plan, Adam can love as a son, husband, and a father, and Eve can love as a daughter, wife, and mother, and everything is good. What we see here is that the sexual embrace is also a manifestation and participation in the love of God. It is a place where God is experienced as the one who has given my spouse to me. It is also a place where Adam and Eve collaborate with God in the creation of new life.

LOVE IS DISTORTED ACCORDING TO THE PATTERN

As sin enters the world in Genesis 3, we see that it distorts love according to the pattern. The first temptation is against the identity of our first parents, and it is the same temptation that each of us faces each time we fall into sin. It is a temptation to doubt the fact that God wants the good for us: "Did God really say, 'You must not eat from any tree in the garden'?" (Gen. 3:1). Eve replies, "God did say, 'You must not eat fruit from the tree that is in the middle of the garden, and you must not touch it, or you will die'" (Gen. 3:3). Then come the key words of temptation: "'You will not certainly die,' the serpent said to the woman. 'For God knows that when you eat from it your eyes will be opened, and you will be like God, knowing good and evil'" (Gen. 3:4–5). The primary temptation says, *God doesn't really want the good for you. He wants to keep you down. He wants you to be slaves rather than sons and daughters.*

When we are presented with this temptation and doubt is cast on the fact that God wants the good for us, it follows that we no longer can entrust ourselves to him, leading us to declare our autonomy from him. In the biblical narrative, our first parents eat the fruit they were commanded not to touch, and the Spirit is evicted from their hearts, constituting the loss of their identity as children of God.

Then the order of love continues to become distorted. Rather than seeing the image of God in the other, we cannot see past the void of God's love and presence in our own hearts. Rather than loving his wife with the love he first received from the Lord, Adam may think, *If God is not trustworthy, neither is this woman; but maybe she can fill the void in my heart.* Eve may think the same: *If God isn't trustworthy, neither is this man; but maybe he can fill the void in my heart.* Rather than a relationship of willing the good for one another and mutually entrusting their hearts to one another, they fall into a relationship marked by domination and manipulation: "Your desire will be for your husband, and he will rule over you" (Gen. 3:16).

Once married love is distorted, parental love quickly suffers the same fate. This distortion commonly manifests when there is a distorted marriage, and in turn, each parent turns to a child and begins to rely on the child to meet their needs. Or in cases of emotional incest, a child is made the emotional partner of the parent. The son becomes the "being with" his mother rather than "being from" his mother. This distortion of parental love can be illustrated in the story of Jacob and Esau in Genesis 27.

Isaac had grown old and was planning to give his blessing to Esau, his firstborn son. He asked Esau to go hunting and prepare a tasty dish for him. Overhearing this, Rebekah instructed Jacob, the younger, to impersonate his brother so Isaac would be tricked into blessing Jacob rather than Esau. Jacob is put into a position where he can either obey his mother and betray his father, or he can disobey and displease his mother and be faithful to his father. It is a situation not unlike that of many children of divorce who grow up moving back and forth from Mom's house to Dad's house, navigating different rules in each household. The question for many of them is, "How do I meet the needs of these two parents?" or "How do I be the parent of my parent?" Then children become the "being for" their parents rather than the "being from" their parents and lose their identity as children. The distortion in parental love begets a next-generation distortion in childhood, and the cycle repeats.

REDEEMED LOVE

We were created to love according to the fundamental anthropological pattern: as sons and daughters, husbands and wives, mothers and fathers. Love is distorted according to the same pattern. The good news is that love is redeemed according to that pattern. Just as the original sin was a boundary experience marking the frontier between original and historical man, the cross is a second boundary experience marking the frontier between fallen and redeemed man. It is the moment from which all graces flow. In the Catholic tradition, we hang crucifixes in our rooms, offices, and church sanctuaries because they remind us of that pivotal moment that Jesus spoke about to Nicodemus: "Just as Moses lifted up the snake in the wilderness, so the Son of Man must be lifted up, that everyone who believes may have eternal life in him" (John 3:14–15). The critical question for a person seeking to move from fallen man to redeemed man is, "When you look at the crucifix, what do you see?"

Do you see the fact that "God so loved the world that he gave his one and only Son, that whoever believes in him shall not perish but have eternal life" (John 3:16)? Do you believe St. Paul when he says, "while we were still sinners,

Christ died for us" (Rom. 5:8)? Do you believe that at your worst moments, at the height of your addictive acting out, our Lord's response was to give his life for you so that you might live? The crucifix reveals the moment in which God proved that he wants the good for you, and if we believe that is true, then we can entrust ourselves to him. We can place our hearts in his hands, and when we do so, we will find ourselves living into our identity as beloved sons and daughters.

HEALING AND THE ANTHROPOLOGICAL PATTERN

As previously stated, this theological narrative found in salvation history is the narrative of our own lives, and in each of our lives we find these same boundary experiences which mark the frontier between innocence and distortion and then distortion and redemption. Healing takes place when we bring the moment of redemption into the moment of rupture. For addicts, one of the clear moments of rupture is their first exposure to pornography. Today, it is more common for parents to call me when this happens than it would have been in the past. In one case, a father and son came to my office because the son (twelve years old) was struggling with pornography and masturbation. His first exposure was at the end of fourth grade. He typically viewed pornography at home on the public computer. When I asked how he found it or who exposed him, he answered that there was a pop up add on a game, which led to pictures and then to videos.

"How did that make you feel?" I asked.

"My heart was racing, I was sweating, and I wanted to look away but couldn't."

"That's totally normal," I said. Then I asked, "How do you think Jesus felt?"

"I don't want to think about that."

"If he was in the room, what do you think he would do?"

"He would be in the corner staring at me."

"What do you think he would say?"

"He would say, 'That's bad for you, it's a sin, you're hurting people, you should know better.' It's like I'm hammering the nails into his hands!"

Then I responded, "You're a kid. You're just a kid. Jesus says, 'Whoever causes one of these little ones to sin it would be better for them if a millstone were placed around their neck and they be thrown into the sea.' If Jesus were in the room with you, he would be angry at pornography, not at you. And he would kneel down in front of you, pull your head into his shoulder, and say 'I'm sorry this happened to you. This shouldn't have happened to you. I will always love you. I will never leave you.'" After repeating those phrases several times, the boy began to get tears in his eyes as he was reencountering the love of our Lord.

The moment of rupture was his exposure to pornography. It brought shame, fear, and doubt that Jesus would love him. The moment of redemption was brought in as the truth of Jesus's love and mercy was spoken into the place of rupture. It is there that our identity as sons and daughters is restored, and subsequently, we begin to love others in healthy ways. Eventually the healing extends to our love as mothers and fathers. We are healed according to the pattern. As we are healed, we begin to act in conformity with the image of God. We begin to love as God loves in all areas of our lives.

SEX AND GOD:

Toward a Theology of the Body

Todd Bowman, PhD, CSAT-C

If you are anything like me, at some point in your life, your understanding of sex and God looked like oil in a cup of water. They do not blend well. There is a clear distinction between the two elements when they are brought together; even after you mix them, they tend to return quickly to their segregated resting state. I believe the broad misunderstanding of God and sex we have historically negotiated in the Christian tradition has more to do with fear than it does biblical truth. Our theology has regularly been more defined by reacting to the shifting sexual sands of the secular culture around us than by proclaiming the fullness of the sexual makeup that God gifted us with. In many Protestant churches, there is little formal communication of a theology of the body to help guide an understanding of how God reveals himself to us through the human body and sexual intimacy. Christ uses the analogy of a husband and wife to describe his relationship with the church (see Matt. 9:15; Mark 2:19; Luke 5:34). Yet this is often about as far as we go in exploring sex. It remains a mystery, described in biblical euphemism and often little more: "he *knew* her," "two become *one flesh.*" We often refrain from mining the depths of insight into the Word given our limited comfort discussing sexual things and our inability to see God and sex as more than simply oil and water. If discussed, sex is often reduced to a biological act that culminates with pleasure or leads to pregnancy, and we operate with a fragmented understanding of this divine engagement. Simply being Christian does not facilitate this shift in understanding sexuality; it only happens with great intentionality. Tearing the veil of silence and shame that shrouds the topic of sex in the church is an important part of helping those who struggle with problematic sexual behavior find the freedom they seek.

If we look to what leaders in the church are saying, we see that the ingredients are there for a more comprehensive theology of sexuality, but like baking a cake, what matters most is the relationship between the ingredients. A few years ago, author Josh McDowell started the *Just1ClickAway* campaign to raise awareness of the societal impact of pornography and to keep the church from losing a generation of members. Additionally, *Straight Talk to Your Kids about Sex* outlines the ingredients necessary for this theology, including the intimacy factor, the pleasure factor, and the procreation factor (McDowell and McDowell 2012). While identification is a necessary foundation (we need to know what goes in the cake), many churches still lack a framework for how these ingredients are designed to come together to create something beautiful. Mixing ingredients without a recipe can be disastrous! While it would be far too great of an undertaking to provide a comprehensive theology of sexuality in this chapter, it is worth examining the necessary components of this theology as well as exploring an understanding of the relationship between these constructs.

THE *3P* APPROACH

As I have explored the McDowell's model in recent years, the three primary constructs within a theology of the body I see emerging are nearly identical: pleasure, procreation, and pair-bonding. In the model, the *pleasure* dynamics inherent in human sexual experience—the gratification and related neurochemical changes that transpire before, during, and after sex—are addressed. The second dynamic of human sexuality captured in the model is *procreation*, namely, the human capacity for producing *offspring*. This construct is designed to encompass the totality of the reproductive processes and capabilities we have been endowed with. Finally, *pair-bonding*, which examines oxytocin, the brain chemical associated with trust and cuddling, represents the attachment dynamics inherent to the sexual process as the third dimension. While intimacy is the natural outgrowth of this process, the process of deepening attachment bonds is a more central tenet for understanding human sexuality. In this approach to understanding human sexuality, each construct has a unique function; however, these three constructs mutually influence one another and enrich sexuality when it is understood within the fullness of God's intended design.

The Social Approach: Orgasm

As with many things in our culture, implicit social messages shape the manner in which these dimensions of sexuality are understood to coexist. The sexual revolution emphasized access to intercourse with as many potential partners as one could find, as frequently as one desired sexual gratification, with as many partners who were willing, with no real consequences. In many ways, this shipwreck of a movement actually accomplished what its champions were hoping for. The ethos of permissiveness and hedonistic pursuit is now embedded in seemingly every corner of the culture we currently inhabit. The clearest way in which that's true is the emphasis on increasing the intensity of pleasure in the sexual experience. From online advertisements for a variety of creams, pills, and wipes to magazines that have been promising "the best sex ever" for the past thirty years—which, one would think after so many articles that we would have finally discovered by now—we are confronted with numerous implicit and explicit messages about increasing sexual pleasure in our lives. As a culture, we are obsessed with it, it would seem. There is a reason orgasm is known as the "big O." When orgasm is the sole focus of sexuality, we lose sight of God's full design for the human person. We are created for more than pleasure for pleasure's sake.

The neurotransmitter dopamine spikes during orgasm. It is also released when we receive sexual cues. It has been shown to play an important part in the reinforcement of behaviors and preferences, as well as why humans experience cravings (Struthers 2009). Not only is dopamine powerful in that moment, but it also has a strong tie to our implicit memory. Our brains are always telling us we need to remember where and how good things happen. I found this principle to be true on a trip to Home Depot one rainy day. We had to park in a different area of the lot that fateful day, so we entered through a side door. That is when I saw it: a crisp, clean ten-dollar bill smiling up at me. Now to understand the impact of this moment, you must understand my past. As a child, I learned that checking under the couch cushions for spare change could yield enough money to buy a pack of baseball cards. Finding money was a big deal, as it gave me the resources to buy the baseball cards, and those cards were an immense source of anticipatory pleasure! As I picked up the cash, I was baffled that my wife, who was walking in front of me, hadn't even seen it, and subsequently I floated my way through the store on cloud nine. Time passed, and eventually I put that experience out of my mind. Then, on a busy Saturday morning the following spring, we were selling our house and needed flowers to spruce it up. The Home Depot parking lot was full, so we parked in a spot near where we did during the aforementioned ten-dollar trip. As soon as we walked through those same side-entry doors, I found myself scanning the ground. My pulse quickened, and my breaths got short. It took me a few seconds to recognize what was going on in my body. The implicit memory of the ten-dollar bill had flooded my brain with dopamine, and I was full of anticipatory pleasure to the point of losing control of simple voluntary behaviors. As you can see, dopamine is not the ideal chemical for deepening relational connection or raising offspring.

Marnia Robinson, author of *Cupid's Poisoned Arrow*, states that the dopamine crash following orgasm can induce a dopamine hangover, which lasts up to two weeks. During this time, we are more depressed, and we view our partners as less attractive. In addition, we become irritable, stressed, and fatigued. Sounding familiar? Culture provides us a variety of ways to self-medicate during this time: substances such as the caffeine found in coffee and soda, alcohol, nicotine and other drugs, food, shopping, internet gaming, and the list goes on. After finding the ten-dollar bill at the store, I bought candy for myself and my boys. As I look back, I can see that it was a mindless attempt at trying to keep the high of excitement flowing by consuming sugar, a subconscious attempt at maintaining a temporary state. While we can try to run from the consequences by using other dopamine-raising behaviors, the true antidote to our longings is oxytocin, produced in loving, connected relationship.

The resolution process begins to take on new meaning when we see that it serves as a protective and preventative influence in our marriages. Simply put, oxytocin production signals the shutdown of dopamine production, keeping us from dopamine hangover and enhancing the experience of safety, trust, and connection in the relationship. This neurological process is reflective of a profound spiritual truth, found in Luke 11:24–26. When we sweep the house clean, we must replace what was there, otherwise we will be worse off than before. When it comes to the brain and sex, this principle is fundamentally true. Sex without healthy resolution, meaning post-orgasmic cuddling and caressing as our bodies flush and our neurochemistry activates the deepening of trust and attunement, short-circuits the sexual cycle and opens the door to ongoing sexual struggle, as well as other vices. God intended intimacy in our marriages, and our bodies reflect that truth. You won't be reading this in an issue of *Cosmopolitan* anytime soon; our culture thrives on depression, dissatisfaction, and dysfunction. Exhibit A: the evening news. It is easy to develop a sense of sexual entitlement when we believe the world is crumbling around us. When pleasure is our primary orientation to one another as Christian husbands and wives, our children receive an even more disturbing message about love and relationship: the church is no different than the world.

Pleasure cannot sustain a godly marriage, but it certainly does enhance a godly marriage. This distinction is important for our children to know. Sex should have an important place in our marriages, but it cannot be the centerpiece. Where some suggest that sexual pleasure is worldly and not to be pursued, God reveals the importance of incorporating pleasure into the marriage covenant. When sex in the marriage comes from a place of pure intent, mutual understanding, and honest communication, God's design for our bodies and relationship is honored. We are created to experience the joys of shared pleasure, as Solomon writes in the Song of Songs:

> How delightful is your love, my sister, my bride!
> How much more pleasing is your love than wine,
> and the fragrance of your perfume
>   more than any spice!
> Your lips drop sweetness as the honeycomb, my bride;
>   milk and honey are under your tongue. (Song 4:10–11)

The Scientific Approach: Offspring

Similar to the social approach, the scientific approach provides an incomplete perspective of the relationship between pleasure, procreation, and pair-bonding when it is the only aspect that shapes our understanding of human sexuality. It approaches sexuality with a primary emphasis on the biology of the reproductive process, and the mingling of genetic materials involved in the sexual cycle. In the scientific approach, pleasure is a secondary gain in the reproductive process, and pair-bonding is an afterthought. It reminds me of what I witnessed with my wife when we visited Las Vegas.

As a young faculty member, my wife and I managed a vacation to Las Vegas late one summer. It was the cheapest getaway we could find, and rightly so. Scorching heat greeted us as we stepped off the plane, and it made anything but lounging in the coolness of the pool simply unbearable. We braved the heat to go sightseeing each evening, and what we encountered provided a perfect description of the scientific model. At some point, we entered the MGM Grand and followed the crowds to the famous lion exhibit. As we examined those beautiful creatures, they must have heard the keeper preparing dinner, because the imposing male lion stirred from his slumber, stood up, and checked his food bowl. The throng of people, many consuming their favorite adult beverages, began to ooh and aah. And then it happened. The lion, finding his food bowl empty, looked to his left and saw one of the many lionesses lying close by, asleep. He sauntered over to her, squatted down, and began to thrust. The crowd erupted, chanting in unison, "Go! Go! Go! Go!" Three pumps and a quiver later, he stood triumphantly, examined his still-empty food bowl, and flopped back to the ground to the continued cheers of the delighted onlookers.

The lion's excuse for this typical mammalian behavior is simple: he's a lion. His brain operates in a much more straightforward fashion than a human's, and his reflex was to participate in the reproductive process that lions engage in, especially during *estrus*, or mating season. Unfortunately, the longer I work in the field of human sexuality, the more I see human sexual patterns mirroring this lion's approach, even in Christian marriages. Wake up, survey the calendar, look for coffee or food, navigate daily responsibilities, go home, watch television, have routine sex, then go to sleep. When sex is simply viewed as a task or to-do item within the relationship, there tends to be little experience of bonding with one's spouse. Conversely, for many of the teens I have worked with, there is little else of meaning they would like to participate in. They are seemingly trapped by their biological urges, driven by this innate desire, and yet not capable of fully comprehending the implications of their decisions.

Some couples struggling with infertility are keenly aware of this phenomenon of emotionally disconnected sex. As the months pass by and pregnancy remains elusive, sex can begin to take on a rather lifeless, routine, and even mechanical essence. The passion is gone, the pleasure is fleeting (if present at all), and the pair-bonding in the relationship is strained by the lingering doubts about a child ever arriving. In circumstances involving infertility, much care must be given to nurturing the sexual and nonsexual aspects of the relationship during this delicate season, lest the relationship crumble under the intensity of emotional turmoil, as many do. We are designed for purposes far greater than empty, mechanical sexual experiences, especially in the context of marriage.

"Be fruitful and multiply," Scripture states (Gen 1:28 ESV), an affirmation of the procreation that defines the scientific approach within this model. In many ways, menstruation in the reproductive cycle is designed as an important system of checks and balances in our marriages. It provides a necessary ingredient for new life to form, but it also demands that we bond through practices other than sex. As a civilization, we have come a long way from the bleeding tents mentioned in the Old Testament, where women were sent away during their times of menstruation. In light of this progress, there are times when the pendulum has swung too far, and we wreak havoc on the sensitive physical aspects of human reproduction. The sexual revolution, as has been mentioned, sought to "liberate" us sexually as a culture. Many of the contraceptive practices used in American culture were popularized in the 1960s and 70s. To this day, these practices allow sexual contact during any point of the menstrual cycle, without the consequence of pregnancy. In some circumstances, these contraceptives limit the menstrual cycle to three days out of the entire year or eliminate it altogether. Under the guise of liberation, the fullness of femininity was reduced to sexual objectification. For men to have more sex, pleasure was elevated, and the beauty of the female reproductive cycle was vilified, seen as too inconvenient. Freud and his wandering uterus hysteria must not be overlooked in this progression. The impact on culture from this period of American history is still being felt. Being stewards of our sexuality, we must pay attention to our physical design and work with it rather than against it.

As detailed in the Synoptic Gospels of Matthew, Mark, and Luke, Christ prepares for ministry by visiting the wilderness. Following forty days and nights of fasting, Satan comes to tempt Jesus physically, emotionally, and spiritually. In each situation, Jesus responds by quoting Scripture and denying himself what Satan offered. In many respects, fasting is the spiritual discipline that launches Christ into his ministry.

As a culture, we struggle with the exercise of fasting because we often fail to find the value in it. When we talk about fasting, it is assumed that we are talking about food or observing Lent. As we see in Christ's experience, fasting provides insight into the fullness of his humanity, as well as the fullness of his divinity. If we believe God created us and made us good, as Genesis says, we should pay attention to the lessons from our bodies. Women's bodies are suggesting we fast each month from sexual activity and instead fill the space with an intentional focus on deepening emotional and spiritual intimacy. When in tune with our design, we are called to slow down and connect on more intimate levels than sex. Much like the feasts that Israel celebrates to commemorate God's presence and blessing, fasting from sexual activity during menstruation is an opportunity to become more in tune with the emotional and spiritual nuances of marriage, as well as an opportunity to submit even our healthy desires to the God we serve. Stewarding our sexuality means we allow the Holy Spirit to work out of us the assumptions and beliefs that a sexualized culture has worked in, even when we are mostly unaware of their influence.

The Scriptural Approach: Oxytocin

Last, we see the scriptural approach, which is intended to hold a healthy tension between pleasure, procreation, and pair-bonding. As our bodies clearly indicate, we were designed with the intent to experience pleasure and, often, the capacity for procreation; however, in our social neurobiology and from our earliest ages we are designed to exist in pair-bonding relationships. Throughout our lives, even while still in the womb, we connect and bond, beginning with parents or primary caregivers, transitioning in adolescence to our social peers and friends, and in young adulthood into romantic partnership. Oxytocin, a nine amino acid neuropeptide, is the primary catalyst for comfort, connection, trust, and safety in relationship. From the sense of fullness after suckling at the mother's breast to the opportunity for bonding found in the post-orgasmic window, oxytocin is the physical representation of God's design for human relationships. Pleasure and procreation, while good and important, can never have the same importance in the human experience as pair-bonding.

The attachment process beautifully depicted in the birth of a new baby highlights the importance of pair-bonding as human beings. One of the most precious photographs I have ever seen is of a friend's son seconds after his birth. Still attached via the umbilical cord, eyes not yet open, and before his first newborn scream, the child in this picture captures the essence of our capacity for faith. The child's little hands are open, and his arms are outstretched. Instinctively, he is reaching out for the one he knows will be there to hold, comfort, protect, and nurture him, even though he has not yet experienced the warmth of the skin or the sustenance of the breast. The picture reminds me of the birth of my middle son. As I heard his first healthy scream, I tried to soothe him by saying, "It's going to be okay, baby Graham." While I was too far away for his newborn eyes to distinguish me from anything else in the room, he turned his head to the sound of my voice and stopped crying. His eyes strained in search of me, seeking out the comfort and security he needed in that moment. The coldness and fear he experienced upon his arrival to the world were calmed by the presence of one he could not see, but whose voice he knew.

These examples demonstrate the profound link between our faith and our inborn desire to be known in relationship. We are created for connection, and this truth is both physical and spiritual. The scriptural model focuses on the innate capacity of spouses to attach healthily to one another. Two becoming one flesh is much more than a scriptural euphemism. It is an embodied process wherein we begin to think, feel, and act in harmony with one another on a level that transcends the capacities of other types of relationship. The corrective experience of faith is not merely a cognitive shift in how we think about ourselves and others; it is a transformation of our emotional selves that allows us to be fully felt and securely attached to one another. In the marriage covenant, healthy sexuality becomes an opportunity to experience one part of the fullness of God's design for our lives in the unique love shared between husband and wife.

When we operate with a model of sexuality that emphasizes healthy attachment, we refute the distortions of sexuality so readily apparent in our world. Sexual messages about objectification, power, and intensity are transformed into valuing, surrender, and connection when we live in the freedom of secure attachment. Similarly, the use of sex to find love and acceptance, beauty, and significance becomes unnecessary as the nonsexual aspects of interpersonal relationship communicate that we are chosen and prized far before and long after sexual gratification. Stewarding our sexuality equips us to respond to the distorted messages we receive about sex with sound scientific principles and biblically based truths.

Orgasm and offspring are tremendous blessings, but we may not all become parents, and our sexual responsiveness is subject to the same brokenness as other parts of the fallen world we live in. Our identity is not to be found in marital status, the frequency or intensity of sexual experience, or in earthly paternity, but rather in receiving the fullness of love from the Author of Love and reflecting this love in the mosaic relationships we are blessed to share with others. When our story does include marriage, we experience a glimpse of God's original design for sex when we participate in this gift in its appropriate context. As Bill Struthers states, "Our sexual longings can be about more than procreation; they can drive us toward intimacy with another human being and offer a taste of the transcendence found when we are in communion with God" (Struthers, 2009, 121).

REFERENCES

Bowman, T. (2013). *Angry Birds and Killer Bees: Talking to Your Kids About Sex*. Kansas City, MO: Beacon Hill.

John Paul II. 2006. *Man and Woman He Created Them: A Theology of the Body*. M. Waldstein, trans. Pauline Books and Media. Original work published 1986.

———. 1997. *The Theology of the Body: Human Love in the Divine Plan*. Pauline Books and Media.

———. 1979. March 4. *Redemptor Hominis*. https://www.vatican.va/content/john-paul-ii/en/encyclicals/documents/hf_jp-ii_enc_04031979_redemptor-hominis.html.

McDowell, J., and McDowell, D. 2012. *Straight Talk with Your Kids about Sex*. Eugene, OR: Harvest House Publishers.

Ratzinger, J. 1996. "Truth and Freedom". *Communio* 23, 16-35.

Robinson, M. 2009. *Cupid's Poisoned Arrow: From Habit to Harmony in Sexual Relationships*. Berkley, CA: North Atlantic Books.

Struthers, W. 2009. *Wired for Intimacy: How Pornography Hijacks the Male Brain*. Downers Grove, IL: InterVarsity Press.

CHAPTER 7

REDISCOVERING JOY:
Disempowering Shame through Vulnerability

Curt Thompson, MD

It had been twelve days since Sam had last viewed pornography. His habit had been years in the making, and the withdrawal lay like a lead weight upon his soul, its crushing mass rendering him virtually immobile—physically, cognitively, and in a more comprehensive way, spiritually. It was taking every ounce of energy at his disposal to get through his day at work. His thoughts moved like a clogged drain, and he felt the depth of his malaise and depression literally at the center of his solar plexus. Like so many, Sam's behavior had been discovered by his wife while she was scrolling through his cell phone. As he saw it, his choice at that point was simple and excruciating: lose the habit or lose his marriage. He chose to lose the former. And so, here he sat, his decision to move out of his deeply felt shame and inertia taking place one step, one day, and one relationship at a time.

Unsurprisingly, one thing he found particularly challenging was his sense of drowning in a despair that felt every bit as physical in its essence as it did emotional. The hallmark of his state of mind was the virtual absence of enjoyment at any level of engagement with life. Rather, he was mostly engulfed in shame. This was predictable, given the extent of his pornography activity and its abrupt discontinuation. I offered to Sam (along with his individual psychotherapy) an intervention that initially evoked in him the sense of feeling jolted—not exactly what he was looking for in his search for relief from pain. I suggested he consider joining a group of men who were meeting to receive help and healing from their addictive behaviors. I shared with him about how vulnerability in a safe, confident community in which we become deeply known can provide freedom from shame, along with courage to take proper risks and develop new, durable relationships—while changing the neural connections of the mind in the process.

Sam's approach to the group process was cautious and skeptical, wanting to make something new of his life but unsure if it was possible. But as I said to him, if joy was what he wanted to create and maintain in his life, both neuroscience and the biblical narrative were pointing a way forward—a way both simple and very hard.

This chapter will focus our attention on the place and role of vulnerability and joy in flourishing relationships. It will also cover the disintegrating force of shame in those relationships, especially as it functions in the experience of sexual brokenness, and the efficacy of vulnerability toward the healing of shame, the recommissioning of relationships, and the recovery of joy in that process. I frame the conversation by drawing on features of Christian anthropology and interpersonal neurobiology (IPNB). I invite the reader to imagine particular features of God's unfolding process of creation and how those features are crucially related to the topics of joy, shame, vulnerability, and healing. In addition, we briefly explore the various domains of the integration of the mind as described by Siegel. As we do, I invite the reader to entertain the notion that a commitment to living a vulnerable life in the ongoing presence of a safe, confidence-building community, while at first glance somewhat counterintuitive, is not merely a helpful option but a necessary ingredient for the acquisition of sexual wholeness. It is necessary for human flourishing in general, for it is how we have been created to live from the beginning. Indeed, it is vulnerability of the sort we will explore that provides the elements for growing in our experience of embodied, joyful living, moving us beyond theological platitudes into every domain of our relational encounters, not least our behaviors of disordered sexuality.

JOYFULLY CREATED FOR JOYFUL RELATIONSHIPS

We were created for joy. We were, if the biblical narrative is to be believed, made joyfully, and made to live joyfully. Within Genesis 1 we can infer the pleasure of the Holy Trinity in forming us. In those poetic verses, we find the rhythmic cadence of the words, "And God saw that it was good." The goodness to which the writer of the text draws our attention is the same to which God's attention was drawn: "And God *saw* . . ." He saw something and immediately found goodness in it. By the time we get to the end of the chapter, God is seeing goodness everywhere, in all he had made. One could easily imagine at the completion of each day hearing God say, "Wow, can you believe it? Just look at that!" One thing this reveals is what it is like for God to have made us. It was a pleasure for the Holy Trinity to make us. The words not only tell us about the goodness that God saw, but also what it was like for him to see it. This is not unlike when a baby comes into the world. We see the child and immediately are overwhelmed with joy that she has arrived. We lavish her with the delight we experience at her arrival, and as Jim Wilder and his colleagues have noted, essentially tell her, "We're so glad you're here!" (Wilder et al. 2013, 6–8).

Can you imagine for a moment what it must be like to hear someone say to you, "We're thrilled you're here! We're so happy to see you!"? This is what God is saying about his experience of his work of creation. Our desire to hear that begins at birth and never ends. Joy is what we experience primarily in the presence of others who are delighted that we are in the world and in their presence, and they in ours. We sense our being a pleasure to others, God not the least, and there is no substitute for that.

One could imagine that God's experience was a veritable dance of joy—but joy that emerged precisely because it is shared. The attuned reader becomes aware that Genesis 1 describes a relational God. "Let *us* make mankind . . ." (Gen. 1:26, emphasis mine) reminds us that from the very beginning, if there is any joyful dancing going on, it is a communal dance, not that of someone off by himself or herself with no one to witness his or her awkward moves. In fact, we might say that joy is only ever truly, sustainably realized as a function of something that happens as a shared encounter between people, not limited to or mostly within the privacy of a single person's experience. This echoes what we have learned in the field of attachment research: that the primary mission of newborns and infants is to establish joyfully connected human relationships that necessarily require the interaction between people (Schore 2003, 37–41). A baby simply can't sustain joy by herself in the privacy of her own mind. This is not to suggest that we cannot ever experience joy as individuals, but we do not first learn it there, and to whatever degree we can imagine and maintain it, it is to the degree that we are deeply connected to other people. Hence, our joy emerges in no small part as a reflection of God's trinitarian, relational nature. Joy is not a feature of the inner mind of a monad but rather that of a relational God that is differentiated in his nature (Father, Son, Spirit) while being linked in deep intimacy.

Returning to the story from above, Sam knew the ecstasy of orgasm and the heightened state of his sympathetic drive system as his arousal crescendoed. He didn't know joy. In fact, his addiction made it virtually impossible for his neural apparatus to fire in a way that would make joy available to him. Joy depended on Sam's being available to share life with other people in mutually giving relationships where hoarding was out of the question. But pornography had taken its toll such that when Sam first began work in the group, the possibility of knowing joy in a sustainable fashion seemed like a mountain too hard to climb and whose peak was covered in clouds. I assured him that joy was coming but that given the neuroplastic realities of his brain and where it had been, it would require practice over possibly a lengthy period of time for him to realize it—not unlike the long climb up the mountain whose summit he couldn't currently see.

VULNERABLY CREATED FOR
VULNERABLE RELATIONSHIPS

Continuing in Genesis 1, we discover that the writer also describes how every element of creation is functionally named to work in relationship with its respectively partnered element. On day one of creation, after calling forth light, God separated it from darkness. On day two, he separated the water above from that below; on day three, he separated the land from the sea.

On days four, five, and six he separated the moon and stars from the sun, and the fish of the sea from the birds of the air, and human beings into male and female—the pinnacle of creation reflecting not only God's image but also the pattern of creation of all that preceded us. Each dimension of creation is given meaning not merely in its own individual right, but always in dynamic relationship with something else. No element of creation has purpose apart from its relationship to that from which it has been separated.

In this way, we see that not only are we made in relationship to something else, but our very identity depends on the presence of the other. I only know that I am a male because females are also on the earth. My sense of myself is inextricably dependent on the presence of something other than me; I cannot fully know myself—I cannot experience the joy for which I was created—apart from my interrelatedness to someone else. I was made, intentionally, to need and to give myself to the other. To need is to be vulnerable. But it is in relationship to that which I need and to whom I can give myself—in my vulnerability—that I am enabled to create beauty and goodness the likes of which would never be possible were I to live on my own. Again, the trinitarian nature of the God of the Bible is put fully on display in the essence of how every feature of creation appears. Father, Son, and Holy Spirit are distinct, separate, unique, yet deeply connected in dynamic relationship with one another.

Addiction is an interpersonal neurobiological process that isolates neural networks within my brain from each other while simultaneously isolating me from other people. What happens physiologically inside is reflected relationally outside. When I am in the throes of sexual compulsivity for reasons addressed in previous chapters, I am caught in a riptide of events that is moving against the grain of how the entire creation is intended to function. Addiction becomes one of the ways evil disintegrates us by tearing at the seams of the multiple ways we were intended to live in rhythmically dynamic relationship with others, especially with those with whom we have great difference.

Notice as well that in the Genesis account no single element ever has dominance over the other: the land and sea, the birds and fish, night and day. Each plays its role in a rhythmic dance with the other without one devouring the other. But addiction? When in that state, I want to own, to clutch, to hoard, to have absolute power over whatever the experience is. And given the power of our sexual urges, we see how this becomes so much more destructive to human relationships. With sexual addiction, my attention is not focused on another embodied person; rather, my attention is fixed on my anticipation of the feeling of arousal and climax. I do not want to be with something or someone for the purpose of giving to it but rather taking, owning, clutching, and hoarding it as a means of regulating my emotional distress. As we will soon see, it is in this context that shame emerges as a function of our consumption of people (ourselves included), of our having acted, essentially cannibalistically. In Sam's story, he had been trapped in the whirlpool of isolation, using his addiction to protect himself from the vulnerability that is necessary to embody real relationships.

Transitioning to Genesis 2, our state of vulnerability is made even more explicit where we read at the chapter's conclusion that the man and the woman were "naked, and they felt no shame" (Gen. 2:25). But for the careful reader, these words do not just tell us about Adam and Eve. They bring God's nature into sharper focus. For the ancient writers of this text, to be naked was not merely about the first couple's absent wardrobe. The writer is drawing the reader's attention to the comprehensive state of vulnerability of their personhood—in particular, vulnerability in the absence of shame.

It is easy to remember that we are made in God's image. It is not that easy to imagine God being naked. Christians believe that God came into the world as a naked newborn and was cast naked on a cross three decades later, yet our imaginations remain underdeveloped when it comes to understanding God being inherently vulnerable. How is that possible for an omnipotent God? We do not have many relational experiences in which we encounter someone who is vital and strong as well as deeply vulnerable. We see that God has made us to be vulnerable. We don't as easily comprehend that he made us this way precisely because he is vulnerable as well. To be vulnerable is to be made in God's image.

Moreover, it was a vulnerable act for God to make us in the first place. A closer view of Genesis 1:26 hints at this. One would expect that when it came to making humanity, the text would have followed the usual pattern: "Let there be light," "Let there be a vault," "Let the water under the sky be gathered to one place," "Let the land produce vegetation," and so on. But in verse 26, we do not read, "Let there be mankind." We read, "Let us make mankind . . ." Almost as if God is reflecting on what he is about to do, perhaps taking into consideration all that it will cost him—and it will, as it would turn out, cost him greatly—to enter into this adventure. From the very beginning, then, we see a picture of a God who was taking a risk—not one that would overwhelm him, but certainly one that could and would hurt him. Again, we were made by a vulnerable God who created us to be like him in our vulnerability, with one minor difference: God has no lack or unmet need. Our needs are most fully and healthily met in the context of vulnerable, attuned, and trusting relationships, both with God and with others. Vulnerability, then, is not to be understood as a weakness or liability but the very foundation upon which the creation of relationships where goodness and beauty rests.

THE JOY AND VULNERABILITY OF INTEGRATION

This notion of God separating things to enable them to have deep, joyful, vulnerable relationship with each other while maintaining their unique differences is reflected in the research findings of interpersonal neurobiology (IPNB). This field of research describes the mind as an embodied and relational process that emerges from within and between brains that regulates the flow of energy and information. Others have written more extensively about this (Siegel 2007, 4–5), but for our purposes, it is enough to know that the mind—that which addiction targets—flourishes when it is, in the language of IPNB, *integrated*. This refers to any system in nature in which the subset parts of that system are both well developed (differentiated) and effectively connected to each other (linked), much like an orchestra in which the various musical sections (e.g., brass, woodwinds) need to know their respective parts well while at the same time paying close attention to the role of other parts, all being directed by the conductor. Using this metaphor, we experience the joy of the symphony when all of the differentiated parts—each of which is dependent on the others—are linked, vulnerably, together.

We speak of how the mind has several functional domains (Siegel 2010, 71–75), much like the parts of an orchestra, that when differentiated and linked enable us to flourish. Those domains are identified as follows:

- **Consciousness.** We are aware that we are aware, and all activity of the mind hinges on to what we at any given time are attuning our attention. The guiding question related to this function is, "How well are you paying attention to what you are paying attention to?" In addiction we often find ourselves on autopilot, with our attention drawn powerfully into anticipating what our behavior will provide for us, able to shift our attention to little else.

- **Vertical.** The central nervous system develops from the bottom up, ascending from the spinal cord to the brain stem and limbic system, eventually emerging with the cortex, the prefrontal cortex in particular being its culmination. This progression is highly correlated with our awareness of our bodies and what they are sensing, both internally as well as externally. It is often the case that the cravings we experience are driven by physical sensations that we experience at nonconscious levels. We often are unaware of how our bodies' sensations are driving our behavior.

- **Horizontal.** The brain is divided into a right and left hemisphere, each of which has unique functions. The right tends to develop first, with the left catching up soon thereafter. The right tends to be the place of visuo-spatial orientation; emotion; nonverbal communication and a sense of timelessness or being "in the moment." The left is the source of our language center, along with logical, linear, and literal thinking processes. One way to think of this is that first the right brain senses things, then the left brain makes sense of what we sense. It is the right hemisphere that houses so much of the neural networks that are involved in addiction. Attempting to override them by simply trying to apply logical information is therefore bound to meet resistance—we take in that logical data at the level of our left hemisphere, and so are less able to change our experience that is mostly taking place on the right side of the brain.

- **Memory.** There is nothing we do in which we do not employ our memory, from walking to considering where we put our keys. This domain includes implicit memory, which is largely nonconscious and involves emotion, sensation, and perception as well as behavior; and explicit memory, which involves the recall of facts and what we term autobiographical memory, or our ability to recall the emotional and relational elements of past events of our lives. It is memory that is so powerfully highjacked in addiction, the implicit form especially. I tell patients that we remember our future; in essence, we anticipate our future based on what we recall from our past. To treat addiction requires that we address the way our memory of so many things is in charge of our behavior.

- **Narrative.** We humans, unlike any other creatures, all tell stories. In the course of human development, we incorporate all of the domains of our minds' activity toward that end. Our narratives are highly influenced by our most important attachment relationships, which is why the development of healthy attachment is such a key element in treating addiction. To the degree that our narrative is missing deeply connected relationships in which we are fully known, our sexually driven behavior, especially in its isolated forms, steps in to make up for the joy that we so desperately long for and were created to experience.

- **State.** Neuroscientists consider "states of mind" to be actual phenomena that represent stable neural firing patterns highly correlated with our changing daily activities. For instance, I have a pattern that represents my morning routine from rising to shower to breakfast, a different pattern for when I am at work, and yet another for when I am at home with my family. Life at its best is realized when I can flexibly transition between states. Addiction, on the other hand, tends to keep us fixed in its state to the degree that we have great difficulty moving out of it.

- **Interpersonal.** No matter how much I would like to believe that my mind is mine and mine alone, the reality is that it is always responding to my real or perceived interactions with other people's minds. Human flourishing takes place when we are engaged in the rhythmic movement between solitude and community, just as there is movement between day and night, and between the tide of the ocean and the land. But we never exist as wholly isolated beings, no matter the direction of the current of culture. To the degree that we each pay attention to the other minds in our lives and intentionally enable connection with them in rhythm with opportunity for solitude (vis-à-vis isolation), we enable integration. Addiction tends to leave us more fully isolated and unable to imagine the meaningful relationships in our lives, let alone actively engage with them. Consequently, our brains have to work harder to manage the enhanced stress that ensues in the face of relational disconnection. It is therefore little wonder that sexual addiction is eventually so highly correlated with depression.

- **Temporal.** We are the only creatures who reflect on our past while being aware that we will die. Our awareness of temporality, then, significantly impacts our behavior, despite our largely being unreflective that this is actually taking place. Addictive behaviors tend to relieve us temporarily from the anxiety that we often feel in the face of our anticipation of our future.

Human flourishing and the joy inherent in it depend on the integration—the differentiation and linkage—of these domains. We long for this integration, this wholeness, just as the psalmist writes, "Teach me your way, LORD, that I may rely on your faithfulness; give me an undivided heart, that I may fear your name" (Ps. 86:11). Our hearts are made in divided, differentiated form, and it is their unity that enables us to live most truly, most joyfully. And just as the writer needs the help of the God to whom he prays, a mind other than himself, so also integration is only made possible in the context of growing, securely attached relationships. These very different domains that are correlated with distinct neural networks of the brain only come into functional maturity when we are living in relational contexts in which we are deeply known. Reflecting the pattern of the entire creation that has preceded it, we are intended to live in rhythmic cadence with others, not least those with whom we have great difference, with that engagement enabling the joyful expression of our minds.

This may all sound like so much neuroscience gobbledygook pasted over a cursory reading of Genesis 1 and 2. What does any of this have to do with addiction or its healing? It turns out that it made a difference for Sam. He discovered the role that shame plays in sexual addiction, disrupting as it does the entire process of integration. Despite the fact that we were created for joy and that joy was to be realized in the context of vulnerable, integrated, deeply connected relationships, why did that seem to be so difficult to realize? What was it that seemed to so easily corrupt the desire for meaningful relationship? In the context of the group, Sam and the others grappled with the reality that from the beginning of creation right up and through their own lives, evil has been in the business of using shame to actively disintegrate and devour all that is beautiful and good, including us. So it is to shame that we now turn to better understand its role in addiction and how vulnerability is the antidote to its poison.

SHAME AND THE DISINTEGRATION OF THE MIND

We have already alluded to shame as having a prominent, primal place in the biblical narrative of creation. If we examine the current literature about its nature, we will find several different aspects that are helpful in our understanding of its role in sexual addiction.

Shame is first and foremost a neuroaffective event (Thompson 2015, 62–65) that can emerge in a child's experience as early as fifteen to eighteen months of age (Lewis 1992, 91–94). We sense it as a felt, embodied phenomenon that we eventually make sense of through the telling of our story. One metaphor that has provided a helpful understanding of shame from a brain standpoint is that of a standard transmission automobile. In normal human development, the interchange between an adult and child is largely centered around helping the child learn how to balance his sympathetic (SNS) and parasympathetic (PNS) nervous systems. These two systems are involved in the regulatory process of emotional tone that is highly influenced by the relational exchanges between the adult and child. The sympathetic system is activated in states of arousal that include those instances in which the child is expressing interest in approaching something, be that a person or a plant. It supports the physiological responses necessary for that arousal to be maintained. In the metaphor of the automobile, this system acts as the accelerator.

The parasympathetic system functions more like a brake, slowing the child's behavior, from his heart rate to his physical movement. When Mom says, "No!" to a child, she activates the child's parasympathetic system, interrupting his sympathetic system's engagement that was acting on behalf of the child's interest in running toward the edge of the pool or any other behavior that is involved in the pursuit of a desired outcome. The key element involved any time this happens is the maintenance of an attuned relational connection between parent and child. This attunement comes out of the neural activity of the parent's prefrontal cortex, with the parent being deeply connected and curious about the state of the child's mind, even in the midst of having to apply the brake. It is this attuned connection to the child's mind that acts as the clutch. An attuned parent learns how to say "no" while maintaining connection to the child in her tone of voice and body language. Even in instances in which parents must be forceful in their "No!" a swift movement to physically and emotionally reconnect with the child serves the same purpose as using the clutch so as to not lose the relational connection. In this way the child learns how to balance the overall tone of emotional energy of his own body with the help of attuned communication with his parent (Siegel and Hartzell 2003, 215).

Although this process begins in early childhood, it never ends. Even as adults, we are often in the accelerator mode of operation that supports our interest in any adventure, no matter how large or small. Our desire to make connection and create things, supported by our SNS, is inherent as part of our reflecting God's image in and to the world. As well, our PNS supports the action of restraint, which is of equal necessity for human flourishing. Be it in the board room, the classroom, our marriages, our friendships, our leisure activities or casual conversations, we are attempting to enter into the life that God has placed before us. When done well, we do so with joy and with vulnerability. And it is the meaningful attuned relationships in our lives that act as the clutch and make all of this possible.

But evil is having nothing of the creation of a world of goodness and beauty and wields shame as its vector of disintegration. Shame is the neurophysiologic result of what happens when the brake is applied and no clutch is engaged.

Any time "no" is communicated in the absence of an attuned relationship, shame is likely to be the result. A child can experience it as early as fifteen to eighteen months of age, incorporating it largely via the nonverbal cues she receives from her caregivers, long before she has language to make any sense of it. Again, this process can be mediated by events both large or small, loud and harsh, or barely noticeable in its silence. The tone of voice. The glance. The sigh.

In Sam's case of addiction, it was not hard to connect the dots of how shame had become so powerful in his life. The natural arousal and interest in sex, especially as it presented itself in pornography, had become deeply spliced together with the shame that would immediately follow his actions when he considered the possibility that another person would come to know this part of him. In the case of this behavior, we have a clear example of the accelerator being tied to the experience of shame and then repeated over and over again. Given the neuroplastic pattern Sam had established, the price he paid for the exhilaration of arousal was the interpersonally neurobiological entrenchment of shame, for no attuned relationship was present to mitigate his experience, nor would that ever be possible given the fundamental nature of pornography, dependent as it is on relational isolation.

Disintegration

All of this leads to other common features of shame. The first is the disintegration of the mind. It is virtually impossible to think clearly, to make sense of what you feel emotionally, or to be creative when experiencing shame. It disconnects neural networks from each other that otherwise are intended to provide for an integrated mind. Moreover, the disintegration continues in the form of relational distancing. With sexual addiction, we spend a great deal of energy managing our shame, so much so that we then have little to generate movement toward bonding vulnerably with others. To the degree that the networks of our brain are less integrated, our relationships reflect the same.

The domains of integration that we explored above are the primary target areas of shame as it disconnects our consciousness from our body, memory, narrative, and so on. The neurophysiologic effect of shame makes it virtually impossible for us to maintain connection between the various functional aspects of the mind, necessarily shearing off any ability to be imaginative or creative. In this way, the disintegrating effects of shame do not simply disable my mind from working well or make me feel bad, it truncates my ability to make new things by paralyzing my ability to engage the world creatively. And this is one of evil's most important missions: not just to use shame to create feelings of dis-ease within us or to separate us from God and others, but to truncate our capacity to create. Shame ruins God's intended purpose for us to reflect his image by making things as he does.

Hiding

This disintegration is accompanied by an active form of hiding. Just as a dog lowers its head and averts its gaze—shame emerges from neural networks in lower parts of our brain, just as it does in lower mammals—we turn away physically in a similar fashion and turn away relationally by burying our shame in the crevasses of memory we wish we could delete from our minds. We are loathe to invite others into the center of our private anguish. We are too fearful of being found— and found to be disgusting. With sexual addiction, it is but a short step from the disintegration described above to the isolation and hiding.

Stasis

This isolation eventually leads to a posture of mental stasis. One of the features that indicates the presence of biological life is movement, be that the cilia of a bacteria or the pulse of the cardiovascular system. With shame, our mental and physical processes can feel as if they are mired in clay, disabled from taking proper risks, be that thinking creatively or moving toward someone in order to be found and be healed. It is here that a crucial element of shame should be mentioned: the stasis that accompanies it—our inability to move, especially toward someone— makes it difficult for us to seek help when buried under our shame. In this sense, we are seldom reluctant to seek help with our sexual addictions simply because we don't want it, nor because we are too weak or obstinate. Rather, the profound sense of shame that we carry prevents our movement toward those relationships in which our healing awaits—precisely because of our anticipation of feeling shame, from which we sense there would be no escape.

Disintegration, hiding, and stasis were all part of Sam's landscape. The depressed state he felt in the wake of his sobriety was only a more distilled version of what he had been experiencing before he shut off his pornography viewing. He had become more listless and stagnant in his work, distant emotionally at home, and his friends had begun to notice over a long period of time a dampening of what had at one point been a more engaged person. But there was more that shame was up to.

CRITICISM, CONDEMNATION, AND FEELINGS OF ABANDONMENT

I remind patients that although shame is unsurprisingly felt as a result of major life traumas, the vast majority of its power lies in the multiple micro-moments of our days in which we hear the voice of our inner shame attendant whisper, "I should not have done that." Or "How stupid could I have been?" Or "I'm not going to be okay." Or some other version of a death of a thousand cuts. This is how evil wields shame so well—by its silence and subtlety and the frequency of small insults that we utter to ourselves, and often without words, in the privacy of our own minds. Sam's shame was not restricted to the times he viewed pornography. The greater volume of his encounters with it were at other times when he would imagine his friends finding out about his habit or be reminded "what a hypocrite I am" by the felt sense of his own voice, even if it didn't require words. In this way, the shame associated with addiction spreads with easy access across time and space to enter every aspect of our lives, far beyond the boundary of our actual encounter with our particular disordered sexual behavior. This, as we will see shortly, is why healing from sexual addiction (like that of any other) requires so much more than sobriety from the addictive behavior. Shame will continue to attempt to work its dark magic, providing a felt sense within us that we will not be okay without sex in the way we have come to misuse it.

Another important reality about shame is that although it is primarily a neuroaffective event, given that we are storytellers at heart, eventually our experience of it emerges into some cognitive version of "I'm not enough" or "I'm not okay." Put bluntly, the primary message of shame is condemnation. Whether the engine of our analogical standard transmission automobile decelerates because of the brake, or merely because we take our foot off the gas, the absence of the clutch leads to the same end: the violent stopping of the motor. You could be publicly humiliated by the words of someone else, or the comment you casually offered at a dinner party could be summarily ignored or passed over. In both cases, the same interpersonal neurobiological mechanics are put in play, and the message is the same: You don't matter. You are not important. You are unworthy. Eventually we get to the point where words are not even necessary. The condemnation is sensed physically and perceived emotionally as much as it is cognitively interpreted.

This condemnation lay heavy upon Sam. He not only condemned himself; he lived in a narrative in which he assumed himself to be condemned by others, any others who would come to know *not just that he had a sexual addiction, but that because of this, and beyond this, he was irreparably beyond reach or repair. He was beyond hope.* As much as he wished that he could simply "change his mind" about what he believed to be true, his brain was not so easily ready to cooperate due to the hours and days and years he had spent making quite permanent those neural networks that so tightly correlated with the condemnation he had come to know. And the incessant condemnation was merely the harbinger of the final aspect of shame that we humans fear more than anything—the specter of abandonment.

Ultimately, shame is the herald of abandonment. The foundational anthropologic statement that it is not good for the man to be alone is not a one-off from God, his having casually noticed something minor in the creation that needed a slight adjustment. There is no greater fear we carry as humans than the anticipation that others want nothing to do with us. Shame tells us not only that something is wrong with us and we are not enough, but that because of this, no one will be looking for us when we are lost. This cuts directly against the grain of every baby's experience who comes into the world looking for someone looking for him or her.

Although Sam was able to live most days presenting to others a picture of at least an adequate life, his entire internal state of awareness was an elaborate defense against his deep conviction that he was alone. Should anyone discover the truth about him and his addiction, people would leave him as fast as their feet could carry them. With all of these different features of shame disrupting Sam's capacity to flourish, what was he to do? How would it be possible to move from where he was to where he thought he wanted to be but found so challenging to imagine? As we have hinted at earlier, it is again to biblical anthropology and IPNB that we turn for helpful answers.

THE REPAIR OF RUPTURES AND THE RECOMMISSIONING OF VOCATION

Sexual addiction embodies relational rupture in an almost endless number of ways. Healing sexual addiction involves the deep repair of ruptures both intra- and interpersonally as well as neurobiologically. Many aspects of intervention for sexual addiction are covered elsewhere in this volume. One element that threads its way throughout the process that leads to the repair of ruptures is the intentional vulnerability that a patient necessarily offers in exposing to others the reality of his or her life. As I have pointed out, to be vulnerable is not something we have to conjure; it is something we are. We were made to live naked and unashamed. Our terror of being vulnerable lies in the presence and activity of shame as it plies its way through our memory and anticipated future, ultimately ruining our ability to create as the Holy Trinity intended. But it is the only way we can ultimately be free of shame. Revealing the verities of our lives to other minds willing to receive them with grace and appropriate boundaries disarms shame in interpersonal and neurobiological fashions, as Sam discovered in the group, despite his initial trepidation.

Sam initially felt intimidated upon entering the group I facilitated and had invited him to join. As he initiated the process of telling his story and listening to others', he slowly began to recover joy in his life when it seemed his sexual addiction had stolen all of it—but courageous vulnerability was required.

For instance, initially when he disclosed to the other members what it had been like for him in his early years in his family, he revealed that he had grown up "in a loving Christian home." When asked to provide more details about what that meant, he eventually divulged that in fact his father had been emotionally and physically abusive, especially to his younger brother. By happenstance, he had his first encounter with internet pornography at thirteen years old. As much as it was a problem about sex, even more so it served as an anxiolytic, calming his distress about his father's anger and the family's general suffering. As Sam offered this truer version of his remembered life, other group members noticed how his body language, facial expression, and tone of voice changed. Sam was telling a more detailed, complex version of his story that involved all of the domains of integration of his mind. In this version of his story, the shame of his pornography habit was neurally spliced together with his anger and shame about his father's behavior. I inquired what he felt as he revealed these details. He replied, "I just feel really embarrassed." I attempted to gently press further in and wondered what he sensed in his body and where. He was able to describe the tightening in his chest and throat, aware that he did not want to look at anyone.

I paused the group process and invited Sam to slowly take two deep breaths at first, then proceed to breathe slowly and deeply, closing his eyes, and in his mind's eye visualize his lungs as he inhaled and exhaled. He did this for only about thirty to forty seconds, opening his eyes afterward. I then asked the group members to express what they were feeling. To a person, each reported their felt sense of empathy, sadness, and compassion for Sam. Some went further to state their anger on his behalf, noting feeling protective of him when considering his life as a young boy in his home. When I asked Sam what it was like for him to hear their words, he spoke of the relief, connection, and surprise he felt as his tears welled and streamed. It was an example of how his vulnerability—his telling increasingly more of his story more truly despite the acutely anticipated fear of a threatening outcome—was expressed by drawing his attention to his emotions, physical sensations, memory, narrative, and the interpersonal domains of his mind as he allowed himself to receive the presence of others through their words and nonverbal cues as a means of healing his shame.

I then gave Sam the homework of journaling about and practicing at least twice a day his remembered experience of being in the room as others offered him the embodied response of acceptance when he was anticipating rejection. Moreover, he was also tasked with practicing restraining his mind's attention from wandering down into shame-laden rabbit holes of "Perhaps I made my dad look worse than he was. I shouldn't be talking about my father like that. I'm sure there are things about me that will make the group members want to have nothing more to do with me when they find out the truth." This habit of practicing paying attention to his embodied experience—remembering it—was necessary in the neuroplastic rewiring of his mind. His encounter with the group members made possible the formation of new neural networks that heretofore could not have existed apart from his willingness to be vulnerable with others who welcomed his story into their community.

All of this is exemplary of how Sam used what he was learning at the intersection of IPNB and Christian spiritual formation, and how intentional acts of vulnerability in the context of a safe, limit-setting community enabled new creation. He learned what it meant to pay attention to what he was paying attention to; to become increasingly aware of the role his body played in driving his thoughts and emotions; to discover the nonverbal ways he communicated to others and himself that often overpowered the words coming out of his or others' mouths; to become aware of how his implicit memory was so cut off from his conscious awareness and the power it had to dictate his cravings in response to environmental cues, both inside and outside his head; to tell his story more truly, more fully, in the context of people who refused to leave the room, no matter how messy it was; to grow in awareness of his transitions from one state of mind to another and the work involved to disallow those transitions from becoming a place where his addiction tendencies could regain momentum to disintegrate his life; to pay attention to the deep presence of others in his mind's activity and to call upon them as a way for him to regain his emotional balance at times when he was feeling overwhelmed; and to work to remain as much in the present moment as he could instead of allowing his attention to wander to regrets of the past or anxiety about the future. And in the process, his relationship and engagement with God changed in substantive, permanent ways.

As he did so, Sam reported how he slowly began to regain a deeper, more sustained sense of joy that emerged as a function of his awareness of the people in his group being genuinely thrilled to see him each week, as he was them. That facilitated the integration of the multiple domains of his mind that the group was learning about and incorporating in concrete ways into their daily lives. Indeed, these domains of integration became more than just abstract notions of neuroscience; rather, they transcended the world of ideas to become active, embodied events that took place within the group sessions that they remembered and took with them into their families, work, and church lives. In this way, Sam was not only dealing with his addiction, but also learning to love God with all of his mind—not just his thinking brain, but every additional aspect of it to which the group had been introduced from the field of IPNB.

REFERENCES

Lewis, M. 1992. *Shame: The Exposed Self.* New York: Simon & Schuster.

Schore, A. 2003. *Affect Regulation and the Repair of the Self.* New York: W. W. Norton & Company.

Siegel, D. J. 2007. *The Mindful Brain: The Neurobiology of Well-Being.* New York: W. W. Norton & Company.

———. 2010. *Mindsight: The New Science of Personal Transformation.* New York: Bantam Books.

Siegel, D. J., and M. Hartzell. 2003. *Parenting from the Inside Out.* New York: Penguin.

Thompson, C. 2015. *The Soul of Shame: Retelling the Stories We Tell about Ourselves.* Downers Grove, IL: InterVarsity.

Wilder, E. J., E. Khouri, C. Coursey, and S. D. Sutton. 2013. *Joy Starts Here.* East Peoria, IL: Shepherd's House.

PART 2

——————

TREATMENT STRATEGIES

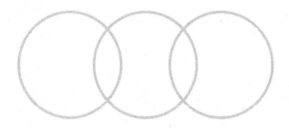

CHAPTER 8

ASSESSING COMPULSIVE SEXUAL BEHAVIORS:

Evidence Based Recommendations

JOSHUA B. GRUBBS, PhD, AND JOSHUA N. HOOK, PhD

The foundation of useful counseling or psychotherapy is careful and comprehensive assessment of the problems at hand (Hunsley and Meyer 2003; Meyer et al. 2001). Psychological and counseling literatures are filled with examples of why careful assessment—using a combination of clinical interviews, structured questions, and self-report inventories—is often necessary to gain a proper understanding of the scope of a psychological problem, the specific nuances of that problem, and the best path forward for treatment (Grubbs et al. 2017; Meehl 1954). This is particularly important for controversial or complex diagnoses, such as the diagnosis of compulsive sexual behavior (Grubbs et al. 2017). In this chapter, we will review the history of diagnoses related to compulsive sexual behavior, discuss the necessary domains relevant to assessing compulsive sexual behavior, and review free, open-access assessment instruments that can aid in understanding such behavior. This chapter will focus on compulsive sexual behaviors but not paraphilic, pedophilic, or other forms of aberrant or illegal sexual engagements—that extends beyond the scope of standard assessment procedures (often involving complex risk assessments) and the treatment expertise of both authors of this chapter.

DEFINING AND DIAGNOSING
COMPULSIVE SEXUAL BEHAVIOR

Over the years, Compulsive Sexual Behavior (CSB) has been known by many names (Black 1998; Coleman 1991, 1992). Historically, terms like *nymphomania, hyperlibido*, and *erotomania* were used to identify people experiencing excessive or compulsive engagement in sexual behaviors (Coleman 1992). More recently, CSB has been referred to as "sex addiction" (Gold and Heffner 1998). Regardless of the name by which it is known, CSB has long been a focus of therapists and counselors, but formal recognition of this disorder by the mental health community at large had been elusive until recently.

Hypersexual Disorder

Prior to 2018, the most substantive attempt to have CSB recognized as a discrete disorder was during the development of the American Psychiatric Association's *Diagnostic and Statistical Manual of Mental Disorders Fifth Edition* (DSM-5). Although some authors had speculated about CSB for decades (for a review of early work, see Gold and Heffner 1998), it was only during the development of this manual that some of the more rigorous and systematic research emerged. Specifically, this research was related to the proposed diagnosis of hypersexual disorder (Kafka 2010; 2014; Reid and Kafka 2014). Given many decades of prior work noting that CSB seemed to be a real and persistent problem for some clients, the diagnostic proposal for Hypersexual Disorder (HD) provides a framework by which these behaviors might be understood as a discrete psychiatric diagnosis. These proposed diagnostic criteria are available in Table 8.1.

Table 8.1: Proposed Diagnostic Criteria for Hypersexual Disorder

A. Over a period of at least 6 months, recurrent or intense sexual fantasies, sexual urges, or sexual behaviors in association with three or more of the following five criteria:
1. Time consumed by sexual fantasies, urges, or behaviors repetitively interferes with other important (nonsexual) goals, activities, and obligations.
2. Repetitively engaging in sexual fantasies, urges, or behaviors in response to dysphoric mood states (e.g., anxiety, depression, boredom, irritability).
3. Repetitively engaging in sexual fantasies, urges, or behaviors in response to stressful life events.
4. Repetitive but unsuccessful efforts to control or significantly reduce these sexual fantasies, urges, or behaviors.
5. Repetitively engaging in sexual behaviors while disregarding the risk for physical or emotional harm to self or others.
B. There is clinically significant personal distress or impairment in social, occupational, or other important areas of functioning associated with the frequency and intensity of these sexual fantasies, urges, or behaviors.

C. These sexual fantasies, urges, or behaviors are not due to the direct physiological effect of an exogenous substance (e.g., a drug of abuse or a medication).

Specify if:
- Masturbation
- Pornography
- Sexual Behavior with Consenting Adults
- Cybersex
- Telephone Sex
- Strip Clubs
- Other: (e.g., prostitutes, adult massage parlors, strip clubs/adult bookstores)

(Kafka 2010; 2014; Reid et al. 2012)

In many ways, the proposed diagnostic criteria are similar to the only other behavioral addiction recognized in the DSM-5, Gambling Disorder. That is, HD requires that the client or patient (1) be spending excessive time engaged in the behavior, (2) be using such behaviors to cope with or avoid dysphoric states, (3) have experienced numerous failed attempts to regulate the behavior, and (4) engage in those behaviors to the detriment of themselves or others.

The original testing of the diagnosis of HD and the aforementioned criteria was largely successful (Reid et al. 2012). Clinicians who used these criteria found them to be useful and reliable. Data from the initial field trial noted that compulsive use of pornography was the most commonly encountered behavior that met criteria for this disorder. Moreover, initial testing of this diagnosis found that compulsive pornography use was the most commonly reported problem in clinical settings. Even so, however, when the DSM-5 was published, HD was not included in any part (Kafka 2014). Despite its exclusion, continued research points to the reality of suffering among individuals reporting problematic sexual behaviors, and future editions of the DSM hold the potential for eventual inclusion.

Compulsive Sexual Behavior Disorder

Despite the failure of HD to be included in the DSM-5, research into the topic has flourished in the years since its publication. This research has recently culminated in the inclusion of the diagnosis Compulsive Sexual Behavior Disorder (CSBD) in the forthcoming eleventh edition of the World Health Organization's *International Classification of Diseases* (ICD-11; Kraus et al. 2018). This inclusion represents a monumental shift in scientific and medical opinion regarding the treatment of compulsive sexuality, as it is the first official diagnosis in any respected diagnostic system that can be used to directly diagnose, treat, and bill insurance providers for issues related to sexual compulsivity. These diagnostic criteria are available in Table 8.2.

Table 8.2: Compulsive Sexual Behavior Disorder

Compulsive sexual behaviour disorder is characterized by a persistent pattern of failure to control intense, repetitive sexual impulses or urges resulting in repetitive sexual behaviour.

Symptoms may include:
- Repetitive sexual activities becoming a central focus of the person's life to the point of neglecting health and personal care or other interests, activities and responsibilities;
- numerous unsuccessful efforts to significantly reduce repetitive sexual behaviour;
- and continued repetitive sexual behaviour despite adverse consequences or deriving little or no satisfaction from it.
- The pattern of failure to control intense, sexual impulses or urges and resulting repetitive sexual behaviour is manifested over an extended period of time (e.g., 6 months or more), and
- causes marked distress or significant impairment in personal, family, social, educational, occupational, or other important areas of functioning.

Distress that is entirely related to moral judgments and disapproval about sexual impulses, urges, or behaviours is not sufficient to meet this requirement.

(Kraus et al. 2018; World Health Organization 2018)

As is obvious from comparisons of Tables 8.1 and 8.2, HD and CSBD share some similar features. Both require repetitive engagement in sexual behaviors, to the point of experiencing significant consequences or impairment in various life domains. Both require that CSB be resistant to prior attempts to change (i.e., the person has previously attempted and failed to restrict behaviors in question). Both require patterns of behavior extending for at least six months. Yet these diagnoses are not identical. For example, HD also notes that many individuals use CSB as a means of relieving intense negative emotion, whereas CSBD does not mention such a possibility. That is, the use of CSB to cope with negative emotions is not part of the CSBD diagnosis. Additionally, CSBD specifically notes that distress related entirely to moral judgments or disapproval of sexual behaviors is not sufficient to warrant a diagnosis. (This rule-out criteria will be discussed in more depth in subsequent sections of this chapter.)

Despite the utility of the CSBD diagnosis, it is worth noting that the diagnosis is still nascent and should not be considered official recognition of sexual addiction. That is, in the development of the diagnostic criteria for CSBD, it was noted that the mechanisms underlying the disorder are still poorly understood (Kraus et al. 2018). Whether or not the specific underpinnings of CSBD are addictive in nature, like gambling or substance abuse disorders, is still unclear (Kowalewska et al. 2018). As such, the diagnosis is included in the ICD-11 as an Impulse Control Disorder, alongside Pyromania, Kleptomania, and Intermittent Explosive Disorder. Such a categorization does not necessarily imply that CSBD is not addictive, but rather that there is not sufficient information at present to definitively state that CSBD is an addiction. This is consistent with Gambling Disorder's original inclusion in the ICD, as it was first included as an impulse control disorder and later recategorized as an addictive disorder. Future research will be needed to clarify whether CSBD is truly addictive and whether it warrants re-categorization as an addictive disorder.

THE ROLE OF MORAL INCONGRUENCE

Importantly, despite the promising results put forth by field trials for HD and the recent recognition of CSBD, the correct understanding and diagnosis of sexual addiction is still a domain filled with controversy and conflict. The ICD-11 diagnosis of CSBD requires that the symptoms of impairment and distress be independent of morally or religiously based distress. That is, to receive a diagnosis of CSBD, the client must be dealing with problems that are not solely the result of feeling morally incongruent about their sexual behaviors. This distinction is important, as recent works have repeatedly highlighted the role of moral incongruence in driving perceptions of addiction, compulsivity, and distress in reaction to sexual behavior (Grubbs and Perry 2019; Grubbs et al. 2019; Perry 2018; Walton 2019).

In recent years, numerous therapists, researchers, and authors have posited that sexual addiction is a false construct propagated by financially or morally motivated therapists and researchers (Ley 2012; 2018). Indeed, the moral controversies around sexuality in general and around excessive sexual activity specifically have been well documented in academic literature (Monge et al. 2016; Reid and Kafka 2014; Wakefield 2012). Many of these debates have focused on the nature of pornography use (Droubay, Butters, and Shafer 2018; Fisher, Montgomery-Graham, and Kohut 2019), which is unsurprising, given that pornography use is common, and self-reported dysregulation as a result of such use is a frequently endorsed clinical presentation with excessive sexual behavior (Reid et al. 2012; Short et al. 2016).

Much of the controversy around the morally charged nature of sexual behavior in general, and pornography use specifically, stems from the large body of literature now documenting that many individuals interpret their own sexual behaviors in ways that may be distressing, even when such behaviors may not be objectively dysregulated (Efrati 2018; Hook et al. 2015; Kraus and Sweeney 2019; Walton 2019). That is, there is now considerable evidence that many people experience moral incongruence—a misalignment of their beliefs and their behaviors—in their sexual behaviors (Grubbs and Perry 2019; Hook et al. 2015; Perry 2018). For such individuals, incongruence between beliefs and behavior may be a major contributing factor in self-reports of addiction or compulsivity (Grubbs, Kraus, and Perry 2019; Perry 2019).

Sexual behavior generally and pornography use specifically are controversial topics about which people—particularly religious people—tend to have strong, morally based opinions (Ahrold and Meston 2010; Efrati 2018; Grubbs and Hook 2016). Religious people are more likely to disapprove of pornography use in general (Grubbs, Kraus, and Perry 2019), support the censorship of pornography (Droubay, Butters, and Shafer 2018), and report restrictive views of sexual behavior and fantasy (Ahrold and Meston 2010). Not surprisingly, then, religious people are also more likely to report that they use less pornography and engage in less CSB than their nonreligious counterparts (Hagen, Thompson, and Williams 2018; Karaga et al. 2016; Rasmussen and Bierman 2017). However, the relationships between religiousness, morality, and CSB are complex.

There is now a body of research demonstrating that, in the general population (i.e., not among treatment-seeking individuals), religiousness and moral incongruence (i.e., engaging in a behavior one finds to be morally wrong) are often the most powerful predictors of self-reported issues with CSB (Grubbs, Grant, and Engelman 2019; Grubbs, Kraus, and Perry 2019). Indeed, recent meta-analyses have demonstrated that, across a number of studies and a variety of cultural settings, the best predictor of self-reported feelings of addiction to pornography are feelings of moral incongruence about pornography use (Grubbs et al. 2019).

However, even according to the most current and comprehensive accounts of the nature of moral controversies around pornography use (Grubbs and Perry 2019; Grubbs et al. 2019), such controversies are not described as invalidating or decrementing current understandings of CSBD. Moreover, although these controversies certainly bear consideration in the proper assessment and diagnosis of CSBD (Kraus et al. 2018), such moral controversies in no way refute the recognition and diagnosis of CSBD. Rather, they provide needed nuance. By providing an account of how moral distress and related emotions may, in fact, cause someone to experience problems associated with sexual behavior, the apparent controversies around moral incongruence as a predictor of self-reported addiction actually help establish guidelines for professionals assessing CSB.

Given these factors, any assessment of problematic sexual behavior must account for the roles of a client's religiousness and morality in the client's experiences of their own sexual behaviors. By assessing how sexual behaviors are integrated into the larger context of an individual's beliefs and values, the therapist can more accurately determine the foci and goals of treatment.

ASSESSING COMPULSIVE SEXUAL BEHAVIOR

Building on the above reviewed literature, the primary purpose of this chapter is to provide guidance on how to accurately assess CSB. At a minimum, the assessment of compulsive sexual behavior is simply an attempt to determine if a patient or client meets the above diagnostic criteria for CSB. However, such criteria are not meant to stand alone as comprehensive assessments of a condition or problem. Rather, they represent the necessary and sufficient conditions for diagnosing a person with a disorder. A comprehensive assessment of CSB will extend far beyond diagnostic criteria and must assess (1) the reported symptoms, (2) the objective behaviors, (3) the social consequences, and (4) the cultural context in which the person is reporting symptoms.

Reported Symptoms

Primarily, when assessing CSB, it is important to get an accurate and comprehensive account of the symptoms being reported. This part of the assessment is relevant to diagnostic criteria mentioned above, as most of the criteria are based on client reports of their symptoms. It is imperative to understand if clients experience their behaviors as being dysregulated or out of control, if they feel they cannot stop their behaviors, if they think those behaviors are controlling or ruining their lives, and if they believe those behaviors have harmed themselves or others.

Objective Behaviors

In addition to assessing the client's reported symptoms, the actual behaviors of the client are also important. That is, it is the therapist's, counselor's, or clinician's job to construct an accurate account of the behaviors causing the client trouble. This means asking detailed questions about the frequency, variety, and dangers or risks of the behaviors in question. This typically involves asking questions like, "How many times per week do you engage in behavior X?" and "When was the last time you engaged in behavior X?" or "In the past 24 hours, have you done X?" Such specificity may seem unnecessary, but as previously mentioned, there is often a disconnect between client self-report of their behaviors and their actual behaviors, particularly if their behaviors are incongruent with their values or morals. Gaining clarity about types and frequencies of problematic behaviors will allow the counselor to more accurately identify and highlight discrepancies between the client's behavior and their reported symptoms. These efforts can be enhanced by incorporating daily tracking activities between sessions to understand the frequency and patterns that characterize the problematic behavior.

Social Consequences

It is also imperative that counselors perform an accurate and comprehensive assessment of the social costs of the client's behaviors. CSB is likely to impact close personal relationships, particularly with romantic partners, as well as a person's roles as a parent or family member. Additionally, CSB may inhibit someone's work or educational performance (e.g., engaging in pornography use and masturbation at work, leading to lost productivity and/or potential conflicts with employers). In more extreme cases, CSB may be associated with legal problems as well (Ley, Brovko, and Reid 2015). These domains of consequences are important for understanding the scope of the client's problem, as well as for understanding the factors that might be motivating their pursuit of treatment.

Cultural Context

Finally, an adequate assessment of CSB will account for the role that cultural context plays in the experience of compulsive sexual behavior. Often, this means a focus on the role of personal beliefs, values, and morals contributing to, exacerbating, or (in some cases) ameliorating symptoms. As noted above, feelings of moral incongruence about sexual behavior often lead to pathological interpretations of that behavior. Men and women alike who use pornography, even infrequently, often report feelings of addiction based on moral incongruence, as such use violates their personal or religious beliefs. Moreover, some work suggests that people with extremely strict religious standards for sexual behavior may experience such distress over normal sexual urges that they develop anxious obsessions with sexual behavior (Efrati 2018). As such, there is a need to understand how the person's sexual behaviors correspond to their beliefs and how their beliefs inform their interpretations of their behaviors.

Undoubtedly, assessing the above listed domains requires careful attention and a great deal of time. However, accurate assessment of the problem at hand is the foundation of good counseling and psychotherapy (Hunsley and Meyer 2003; Meyer et al. 2001). To an inexperienced or time-pressed therapist, performing such an assessment may seem daunting, if not impossible. Fortunately, there are several existing measures that may simplify this process.

USEFUL MEASURES

Building on the above research and general guidelines, we will now discuss the various measures that may aid in the assessment process. Although a plethora of assessments exist (Hook et al. 2010; Womack et al. 2013), we only describe instruments that are freely available to researchers, clinicians, and lay counselors. That is, we have only reviewed instruments that can be obtained and administered at no cost to either the therapist/counselor or the client/patient. Although some proprietary assessments do exist, we believe CSBD can be accurately assessed using wholly free instruments that are easy to administer and interpret.

Hypersexual Behavior Inventory 19 (Gold Standard)

One of the most widely used measures of CSB is the Hypersexual Behavior Inventory (HBI-19; Reid, Garos, and Carpenter 2011). This measure was initially developed in clinical samples of men seeking treatment for compulsive sexual behavior. That is, it was not only developed as a research instrument (as many of the other measures we discuss later were). The purpose of this inventory, since its inception, has been to inform clinical care. For this reason, it is extremely easy to use, administer, score, and interpret.

The HBI-19 consists of nineteen items that measure the individual's experience of CSB symptoms in three domains: Control, Consequences, and Coping (Reid, Garos, and Carpenter 2011). Items assessing Control tend to examine the extent to which users feel like they have lost the ability to regulate their sexual behaviors (e.g., "My attempts to change my sexual behavior fail," or "My sexual behavior controls my life"). Items assessing Consequences examine how individuals feel their sexual behaviors are impacting their lives (e.g., "My sexual activities interfere with aspects of my life, such as work or school," or "I sacrifice things I really want in life in order to be sexual"). Items assessing Coping examine the extent to which individuals feel that their sexual behaviors are being used as a means to alleviate or soothe unpleasant emotions or experiences (e.g., "Sex provides a way for me to deal with emotional pain I feel," or "I use sex as a way to try and help myself deal with my problems"). All nineteen items of the HBI-19 are scored on a scale of 1 (*never*) to 5 (*very often*). The scale has a potential range of 19–95. Scores exceeding 53 are indicative of problems with CSB (Reid, Garos, and Carpenter 2011).

Alongside the HBI-19, Reid and colleagues have developed an independent measure of hypersexual behavior consequences, the Hypersexual Behavior Consequences Scale (Reid, Garos, and Fong 2012). This measure was developed and tested in a sample of patients who were seeking help for self-reported symptoms of CSB. This 22-item inventory requires individuals to report on a diverse range of potential consequences associated with hypersexual behavior (e.g., "My spiritual well-being has suffered because of my sexual activities," or "I have been humiliated or disgraced because of my sexual activities"). Although this measure does not provide a cutoff score, it is useful for establishing a comprehensive assessment of the various ways in which CSB has affected the patient's life.

Taken together, the HBI-19 and the HBCS are quickly administered and easily scored measures of the symptoms and consequences associated with CSB. When administered alongside a careful clinical interview that examines the previously discussed domains (reported symptoms, objective behaviors, social consequences, and cultural context), these measures provide additional data that clearly point toward diagnostic conclusions. That is, these inventories allow the counselor or therapist to confirm a diagnosis of CSBD more easily.

Compulsive Sexual Behavior Inventory

Another widely used and freely available measure of CSB is the Compulsive Sexual Behavior Inventory (CSBI; Coleman, Miner, and Ohlerk 2001; McBride, Reece, and Sanders 2008; Miner et al. 2007). Originally developed in samples of men who have sex with men (Coleman, Miner, and Ohlerk 2001), a number of studies have demonstrated that the CSBI is useful in both men and women, regardless of sexual orientation (Dickenson et al. 2018; McBride, Reece, and Sanders 2008).

The 22-item CSBI requires participants to report the frequency with which they have had certain experiences related to their sexuality on a scale of 1 (*never*) to 5 (*very frequently*). Responses are summed. The measure contains two subscales: Control (13 items, e.g., "How often have you made pledges or promises to change or alter your sexual behavior?") and Violence (9 items, e.g., "Have you given others physical pain for sexual pleasure?"). Importantly, recent analyses of the measure suggest that only the Control subscale is relevant for use in assessing issues with CSB (Dickenson et al. 2018; Miner et al. 2017). In this regard, investigations using this measure in men have demonstrated that a sum score of 30 on the Control subscale (range 13–65) of the CSBI is sufficient to warrant further examination for CSBD (Miner et al. 2017). That is, a cut score of 30 is useful as a general screener for problematic sexual behavior.

Measures in Development

As previously mentioned, the inclusion of CSBD in the ICD-11 has already started to revolutionize the literature related to the assessment, understanding, and treatment of compulsive sexual behaviors. A key part of this has been the development of novel assessment instruments that accurately capture the diagnostic criteria that were established for the CSBD diagnosis. At present, these novel assessments have not been publicly released, though they are being actively tested in multinational studies (e.g., Poland, Israel, Hungary, Germany, and the US). It is likely that, upon their release, these measures will be publicly available for free and will quickly become the established international standards for assessing compulsive sexual behaviors.

SPECIFIC MEASURES OF COMPULSIVE SEXUAL BEHAVIOR

Since the advent of the internet, problematic use of the internet for sexual purposes—most often compulsive pornography viewing—has been a popular topic of research and clinical interest (for reviews on this topic, see Grubbs and Perry 2019; Peter and Valkenburg 2016; Rasmussen 2016; Short et al. 2012). Due to the widespread nature of internet pornography use (in the US, approximately 16–17% of women and 45% of men using monthly or weekly; Grubbs et al. 2019; Regnerus, Gordon, and Price 2016), there has been a proliferation of measures that purport to assess problematic internet pornography consumption. Taken alongside the documented fact that most people seeking treatment for CSB are dealing with excessive use of pornography (Reid et al. 2012), it is likely that most counselors and therapists who encounter CSB in their practices will encounter pornography-related problems as well (Short et al. 2016). For this reason, we will also consider a number of measures that assess problematic pornography use.

Brief Pornography Screener

Currently, the most extensively and carefully developed measure of problematic or excessive pornography use is the Brief Pornography Screener. This measure was developed and validated using clinical samples of men seeking treatment for excessive pornography use, cross-validated in treatment-seeking people in Poland, and standardized in US nationally representative samples (Kraus et al. 2019). This robust body of evidence has shown that this five-item measure is extraordinarily easy to administer, score, and interpret. Participants respond to key items ("You find yourself using pornography more than you want to") focused on the past six months on a scale of 0 (*never*) to 3 (*very often*). A sum score of 4 is indicative of possible pornography-related problems that warrant further assessment and consideration.

Cyber Pornography Use Inventory (Including Brief Versions)

At present, two of the most widely used measures of problematic pornography use are the Cyber Pornography Use Inventory (CPUI; Grubbs et al. 2010) and its short version, the Cyber Pornography Use Inventory 9 (CPUI-9; Grubbs et al. 2015). In its original, long form, the CPUI was developed as a pornography-specific version of the more general Internet Sex Screening Test (Delmonico and Miller 2003), which attempted to measure various ways in which an individual might report dysregulation or distress related to online pornography consumption. However, the original version of this inventory was inconsistent with regards to factor structure and psychometric reliability (Egan and Parmar 2013; Grubbs et al. 2015). In response to this, the shorter CPUI-9 was developed.

The CPUI-9 is a brief (nine-item) measure of problems related to internet pornography use. This measure assesses such problems in three subscales: Perceived Compulsivity (e.g., "I am addicted to pornography"), Access Efforts (e.g., "I have put off things I needed to do to view pornography"), and Emotional Distress (e.g., "I feel depressed after viewing pornography"). In its original development, the CPUI-9 demonstrated good psychometric qualities in both clinical and non-clinical samples (Grubbs et al. 2015). More recently, longitudinal studies have demonstrated that CPUI-9 scores are relatively stable over time as well (Grubbs et al. 2018). This body of evidence suggests the instrument is useful for assessing the cognitive aspects of dysregulated pornography use (e.g., feeling out of control, as measured by the Perceived Compulsivity subscale), the emotional aspects of dysregulated use (e.g., feeling distressed over use, as measured by the Emotional Distress subscale), and the behavioral aspects of problematic use (e.g., pornography behaviors interfering in daily life, as measured by the Access Efforts subscale). Moreover, at present, this is the only measure that distinguishes between the cognitive, emotional, and behavioral elements of self-reported problems.

Pornography Craving Questionnaire

Moving beyond assessments of problematic use directly, there are a number of inventories that measure aspects of pornography use that may be important to understanding a person's struggles with it. One such instrument is the Pornography Craving Questionnaire (PCQ; Kraus and Rosenberg 2014). The PCQ is a twelve-item measure that assesses the extent to which a person is actively experiencing craving for pornography. Given that craving is an essential aspect of almost all addictive disorders (Albein-Urios et al. 2014; Allen, Kannis-Dymand, and Katsikitis 2017; Young and Wohl 2009), it is also likely a part of compulsive use of pornography. This measure requires a person to answer statements such as "I want to watch porn right now" on a scale of 1 (*disagree completely*) to 7 (*agree completely*). Although a precise cutoff for this inventory has not yet been established, higher scores indicate greater struggles with craving. As is the case with other addictive disorders, higher levels of craving are likely to be associated with greater compulsivity and greater risk of relapse during treatment.

Pornography Consumption Inventory

In addition to understanding whether a client is experiencing cravings for pornography, it can also be useful to understand the motivations that guide pornography use. The Pornography Consumption Inventory (PCI; Reid et al. 2011) accomplishes just that. Specifically, the fifteen-item PCI assesses motivations for pornography use in multiple domains, using a scale of 1 (*never like me*) to 5 (*very often like me*). Reasons for use are grouped into four domains: Emotional Avoidance (e.g., "I use it to avoid feeling uncomfortable or unpleasant emotions"), Excitement Seeking (e.g., "It gives me a sense of excitement"), Sexual Curiosity (e.g., "I use it to expand my knowledge about sexual possibilities"), and Sexual Pleasure (e.g., "I use it to sexually arouse myself"). Assessing such motivation is particularly useful when assessing problematic pornography use, as the use of sexual behavior to avoid negative emotion is a hallmark of CSB (Reid et al. 2012).

Ultra-Brief Measures

In addition to the above measures, in recent research, other ultra-brief measures of problematic pornography use have been examined. For example, in a one-year longitudinal study of men, the CPUI-9 was reduced to four items and titled the Cyber Pornography Use Inventory-4 (CPUI-4; see Table 8.3), which demonstrated excellent psychometric qualities and a high degree of test-retest reliability, even over a year (Grubbs and Gola 2019).

Table 8.3: Cyber-Pornography Use Inventory—4

	Strongly Disagree	Disagree	Somewhat Disagree	Neither Agree nor Disagree	Somewhat Agree	Agree	Strongly Agree
I believe I am addicted to Internet pornography	1	2	3	4	5	6	7
I feel unable to stop my use of online pornography	1	2	3	4	5	6	7
Even when I do not want to view pornography online, I feel drawn to it	1	2	3	4	5	6	7
I have put off things I needed to do in order to view pornography	1	2	3	4	5	6	7

In-progress works also suggest this measure is useful in distinguishing between individuals who are seeking treatment for compulsive pornography use and those who are not (Grubbs and Gola 2019). Additionally, recent works have found that simple, binary-response statements (e.g., a true/false response to a statement such as "I believe I am addicted to Internet pornography") are useful for identifying individuals with a high level of pornography use and associated problems (Grubbs, Grant, and Engelman 2019). Although we recommend using comprehensive measurements of problematic pornography use such as those mentioned above, these findings strongly suggest that problematic pornography use may be measured quickly and efficiently with very brief measures when time is limited (such as in initial paperwork a client might complete at the start of therapy or counseling).

THE LIMITATIONS OF DIAGNOSIS AND ASSESSMENT

Ultimately, assessment is a holistic and ongoing aspect of therapy or treatment for any disorder. Although the above recommendations and instruments might be of use in conducting a formal, comprehensive assessment of CSB, all assessments are limited by both time and the client's willingness to self-disclose. Often, clients might find it especially threatening or difficult to discuss painful or embarrassing aspects of their current behavior patterns, particularly at the outset of treatment. This may lead to the client progressively revealing the true severity of symptoms after the initial session has passed (e.g., a client reporting mild problems with pornography use, who, after several weeks, reveals much more severe problems and impairment). This type of gradual disclosure often happens in therapeutic settings and necessitates careful and ongoing assessment by the therapist or counselor. Such ongoing assessment can involve the re-administration of the aforementioned inventories in regular intervals (e.g., biweekly or monthly), or it may simply involve targeted, explicit questions about the behaviors being treated (e.g., "How many times in the past seven days have you engaged in _____?" or "Have you engaged in _____ in the past twenty-four hours?"). Although these types of questions may be uncomfortable for both the counselor and the client, they are essential to maintaining an accurate record of the client's progress and difficulties, which inform future treatment planning. As such, careful, ongoing reassessment of CSB is necessary throughout the duration of treatment.

CONCLUSIONS

Compulsive sexual behavior is, and will likely continue to be, a controversial domain of research and treatment in the mental health community more broadly.

Despite these controversies, however, counselors, therapists, and clinicians are likely to encounter such behavior in their clientele, so accurate and efficient assessment of such behaviors is crucial for all practicing clinicians. Although establishing a diagnosis is an important aspect of assessing compulsive sexual behaviors, quality assessment means examining much more than a checklist of symptoms. Diligent counselors and therapists must assess the objective behaviors of the client, the subjective distress of the client, the symptoms reported by the client, and the cultural context of the client. Such comprehensive assessments provide needed nuance in understanding and treating problematic sexual behavior. Fortunately, at present, there are a number of well-validated, freely accessible measures that are ideal for such assessment purposes. These measures, taken alongside a careful clinical assessment by a thoughtful counselor or therapist, can provide the necessary foundation for treating these problems experienced by many people.

REFERENCES

Ahrold, T. K., and C. M. Meston. 2010. "Ethnic Differences in Sexual Attitudes of U.S. College Students: Gender, Acculturation, and Religiosity Factors." *Archives of Sexual Behavior* 39, no. 1: 190–202.

Albein-Urios, N., A. Pilatti, Ó. Lozano, J. M. Martínez-González, and A. Verdejo-García. 2014. "The Value of Impulsivity to Define Subgroups of Addicted Individuals Differing in Personality Dysfunction, Craving, Psychosocial Adjustment, and Wellbeing: A Latent Class Analysis." *Archives of Clinical Neuropsychology* 29, no. 1: 38–46. https://doi .org/10.1093/arclin/act072.

Allen, A., L. Kannis-Dymand, and M. Katsikitis. 2017. "Problematic Internet Pornography Use: The Role of Craving, Desire Thinking, and Metacognition." *Addictive Behaviors* 70: 65–71. https://doi.org/10.1016/j.addbeh.2017.02.001.

Black, D. W. 1998. "Compulsive Sexual Behavior: A Review." *Journal of Psychiatric Practice* 4, no. 4: 219.

Coleman, E. 1991. "Compulsive Sexual Behavior." *Journal of Psychology & Human Sexuality*, 4: 37–52. https://doi.org/10.1300/J056v04n02_04.

Coleman, E. 1992. "Is Your Patient Suffering from Compulsive Sexual Behavior?" *Psychiatric Annals* 22: 320–325.

Coleman, E., M. H. Miner, and F. Ohlerk. 2001. "Compulsive Sexual Behavior Inventory: A Preliminary Study of Reliability and Validity." *Journal of Sex & Marital Therapy* 27, no. 4: 325–332. https://doi.org/10.1080/009262301317081070.

Delmonico, D. L., and J. Miller. 2003. "The Internet Sex Screening Test: A Comparison of Sexual Compulsives versus Non-sexual Compulsives." *Sexual and Relationship Therapy* 18, no. 3: 261–276. https://doi.org/10.1080/1468199031000153900.

Dickenson, J. A., N. Gleason, E. Coleman, and M. H. Miner. 2018. "Prevalence of Distress Associated with Difficulty Controlling Sexual Urges, Feelings, and Behaviors in the United States." *JAMA Network Open* 1, no. 7: e184468. https://doi.org/10.1001/jama networkopen.2018.4468.

Droubay, B. A., R. P. Butters, and K. Shafer. 2018. "The Pornography Debate: Religiosity and Support for Censorship." *Journal of Religion and Health* 60: 1652–1667. https://doi .org/10.1007/s10943-018-0732-x.

Efrati, Y. 2018. "God, I Can't Stop Thinking about Sex! The Rebound Effect in Unsuccessful Suppression of Sexual Thoughts among Religious Adolescents." *The Journal of Sex Research* 56, no. 2: 1–10. https://doi.org/10.1080/00224499.2018.1461796.

Egan, V., and R. Parmar. 2013. "Dirty Habits? Online Pornography Use, Personality, Obsessionality, and Compulsivity. *Journal of Sex & Marital Therapy* 39, no. 5: 394–409. https://doi.org/10.1080/0092623X.2012.710182.

Fisher, W. A., S. Montgomery-Graham, and T. Kohut. 2019. "Pornography Problems Due to Moral Incongruence." *Archives of Sexual Behavior* 48, no. 2: 425–429.

Gold, S. N., and C. L. Heffner. 1998. "Sexual Addiction: Many Conceptions, Minimal Data." *Clinical Psychology Review* 18, no. 3: 367–381.

Grubbs, J. B., and M. Gola. 2019. "Is Pornography Use Related to Erectile Functioning? Results from Cross-sectional and Latent Growth Curve Analyses." *The Journal of Sexual Medicine* 16, no. 1: 111–125. https://doi.org/10.1016/j.jsxm.2018.11.004.

Grubbs, J. B., J. T. Grant, and J. Engelman. 2019. "Self-identification as a Pornography Addict: Examining the Roles of Pornography Use, Religiousness, and Moral Incongruence." *Sexual Addiction and Compulsivity* 24, no. 4: 269–92. https://doi.org /10.1080/10720162.2019.1565848.

Grubbs, J. B., and J. N. Hook. 2016. "Religion, Spirituality, and Sexual Addiction: A Critical Evaluation of Converging Fields." *Sexual Addiction and Compulsivity* 23, no. 2–3: 155–66. https://doi.org/10.1080/10720162.2016.1150925.

Grubbs, J. B., J. N. Hook, B. J. Griffin, J. K. Penberthy, and S. W. Kraus. 2017. "Clinical Assessment and Diagnosis of Sexual Addiction." In *Routledge International Handbook of Sexual Addiction*, 1st ed., edited by T. Birchard and J. Benfield, 167–80. Abingdon, Oxon: Routledge.

Grubbs, J. B., S. W. Kraus, and S. L. Perry. 2019. "Self-Reported Addiction to Pornography in a Nationally Representative Sample: The Roles of Use Habits, Religiousness, and Moral Incongruence." *Journal of Behavioral Addictions* 8, no. 1: 1–6. https://doi.org/10 .1556/2006.7.2018.134.

Grubbs, J. B., and S. L. Perry. 2019. "Moral Incongruence and Pornography Use: A Critical Review and Integration." *The Journal of Sex Research* 56, no. 1: 29–37. https://doi.org/10 .1080/00224499.2018.1427204.

Grubbs, J. B., S. L. Perry, J. A. Wilt, and R. C. Reid. 2019. "Pornography Problems Due to Moral Incongruence: An Integrative Model with a Systematic Review and Meta-Analysis." *Archives of Sexual Behavior* 48: 397–415. https://doi.org/10.1007/s10508-018-1248-x.

Grubbs, J. B., J. Sessoms, D. M. Wheeler, and F. Volk. 2010. "The Cyber-Pornography Use Inventory: The Development of a New Assessment Instrument." *Sexual Addiction and Compulsivity* 17, no. 2: 106–126. https://doi.org/10.1080/10720161003776166.

Grubbs, J. B., F. Volk, J. J. Exline, and K. I. Pargament. 2015. "Internet Pornography Use: Perceived Addiction, Psychological Distress, and the Validation of a Brief Measure." *Journal of Sex & Marital Therapy* 41, no. 1: 83–106. https://doi.org/10.1080/0092623X.2013.842192.

Grubbs, J. B., J. A. Wilt, J. J., Exline, K. I. Pargament, and S. W. Kraus. 2018. "Moral Disapproval and Perceived Addiction to Internet Pornography: A Longitudinal Examination." *Addiction*, 113, no. 3: 496–506. https://doi.org/10.1111/add.14007.

Hagen, T., M. P. Thompson, and J. Williams. 2018. "Religiosity Reduces Sexual Aggression and Coercion in a Longitudinal Cohort of College Men: Mediating Roles of Peer Norms, Promiscuity, and Pornography; Religiosity Reduces Sexual Aggression and Coercion." *Journal for the Scientific Study of Religion* 57, no. 1: 95–108. https://doi.org/10.1111/jssr.12496.

Hook, J. N., J. E. Farrell, M. J. Ramos, D. E. Davis, S. Karaga, D. R. V. Tongeren, and J. B. Grubbs. 2015. "Religiousness and Congruence between Sexual Values and Behavior." *Journal of Psychology and Christianity* 34: 179–189.

Hook, J. N., J. P. Hook, D. E. Davis, E. L. Worthington Jr, and J. K. Penberthy. 2010. "Measuring Sexual Addiction and Compulsivity: A Critical Review of Instruments." *Journal of Sex & Marital Therapy* 36, no. 3: 227–260.

Hunsley, J., and G. J. Meyer. 2003. "The Incremental Validity of Psychological Testing and Assessment: Conceptual, Methodological, and Statistical Issues." *Psychological Assessment* 15, no. 4: 446.

Kafka, M. P. 2010. "Hypersexual Disorder: A Proposed Diagnosis for DSM-V." *Archives of Sexual Behavior* 39, no. 2: 377–400.

———. 2014. "What Happened to Hypersexual Disorder?" *Archives of Sexual Behavior* 43, no. 7: 1259–1261.

Karaga, S., D. E. Davis, E. Choe, and J. N. Hook. 2016. "Hypersexuality and Religion/Spirituality: A Qualitative Review." *Sexual Addiction and Compulsivity* 23, no. 2–3: 167–181. https://doi.org/10.1080/10720162.2016.1144116.

Kowalewska, E., J. B. Grubbs, M. N. Potenza, M. Gola, M. Draps, and S. W. Kraus. 2018. "Neurocognitive Mechanisms in Compulsive Sexual Behavior Disorder." *Current Sexual Health Reports* 10: 255–264. https://doi.org/10.1007/s11930-018-0176-z.

Kraus, S. W., M. Gola, J. B. Grubbs, E. Kowalewska, R. A. Hoff, M. Lew-Starowicz, S. Martino, S. D. Shirk, and M. N. Potenza. 2019. "Validation of a Brief Pornography Screener across Multiple Samples." Unpublished manuscript.

Kraus, S. W., R. B. Krueger, P. Briken, M. B. First, D. J. Stein, M. S. Kaplan, V, Voon, C. H. N. Abdo, J. E. Grant, E. Atalla, and G. M. Reed. 2018. "Compulsive Sexual Behaviour Disorder in the ICD-11." *World Psychiatry* 17, no. 1: 109–10. https://doi.org/10.1002/wps.20499.

Kraus, S. W., and H. Rosenberg. 2014. "The Pornography Craving Questionnaire: Psychometric Properties." *Archives of Sexual Behavior* 43, no. 3: 451–462.

Kraus, S. W., and P. J. Sweeney. 2019. "Hitting the Target: Considerations for Differential Diagnosis When Treating Individuals for Problematic Use of Pornography." *Archives of Sexual Behavior* 48, no. 2: 431–435.

Ley, D. J. 2012. *The Myth of Sex Addiction*. Lanham, MD: Rowman & Littlefield.

———. 2018. "The Pseudoscience behind Public Health Crisis Legislation." *Porn Studies* 5, no. 2: 208–212. https://doi.org/10.1080/23268743.2018.1435400.

Ley, D., J. M. Brovko, and R. C. Reid. 2015. "Forensic Applications of 'Sex Addiction' in US Legal Proceedings." *Current Sexual Health Reports* 7, no. 2: 108–116.

McBride, K. R., M. Reece, and S. A. Sanders. 2008. "Predicting Negative Outcomes of Sexuality Using the Compulsive Sexual Behavior Inventory." *International Journal of Sexual Health* 19, no. 4: 51–62. https://doi.org/10.1300/J514v19n04_06.

Meehl, P. E. 1954. *Clinical Versus Statistical Prediction: A Theoretical Analysis and a Review of the Evidence*. Minneapolis: University of Minnesota Press.

Meyer, G. J., S. E. Finn, L. D. Eyde, G. G. Kay, K. L. Moreland, R. R. Dies, E. J. Eisman, T. W. Kubiszyn, and G. M. Reed. 2001. "Psychological Testing and Psychological Assessment: A Review of Evidence and Issues." *American Psychologist 56*, no. 2: 128.

Miner, M. H., E. Coleman, B. A. Center, M. Ross, and B. R. S. Rosser. 2007. "The Compulsive Sexual Behavior Inventory: Psychometric Properties." *Archives of Sexual Behavior 36*, no. 4: 579–87.

Miner, M. H., N. Raymond, E. Coleman, and R. S. Romine. 2017. "Investigating Clinically and Scientifically Useful Cut Points on the Compulsive Sexual Behavior Inventory." *The Journal of Sexual Medicine 14*, no. 5: 715–720.

Monge, M. P., G. M. David, D. D. Arántzazu, D. C. Sandra, T. G. M. Fernanda, S. D. L. P. Silvia, A. L. M. Fernanda, and O. B. Rubén. 2016. "Controversy Diagnosing Sex Addition." *European Psychiatry 33*, no. S1: S591–S592. https://doi.org/10.1016/j.eurpsy .2016.01.2204.

Perry, S. L. 2018. "Not Practicing What You Preach: Religion and Incongruence between Pornography Beliefs and Usage." *Journal of Sex Research 55*, no. 3: 369–380. https://doi .org/10.1080/00224499.2017.1333569.

———. 2019. "Pornography Use and Marital Quality: Testing the Moral Incongruence Hypothesis." *Personal Relationships* (forthcoming). https://doi.org/10.17605/OSF.IO /XM2TP.

Peter, J., and P. M. Valkenburg. 2016. "Adolescents and Pornography: A Review of 20 Years of Research." *The Journal of Sex Research 53*, no. 4–5: 509–531. https://doi.org/10.1080 /00224499.2016.1143441.

Rasmussen, K. R. 2016. "A Historical and Empirical Review of Pornography and Romantic Relationships: Implications for Family Researchers; Pornography and Romantic Relationships." *Journal of Family Theory & Review 8*, no. 2: 173–191. https://doi .org/10.1111/jftr.12141.

Rasmussen, K. R., and A. Bierman. 2017. "Religious and Community Hurdles to Pornography Consumption: A National Study of Emerging Adults." *Emerging Adulthood 5*, no. 6: 431–442.

Regnerus, M., D. Gordon, and J. Price. 2016. "Documenting Pornography Use in America: A Comparative Analysis of Methodological Approaches." *The Journal of Sex Research 53*, no. 7: 873–81.

Reid, R. C., B. N. Carpenter, N. N. Hook, S. Garos, J. C. Manning, R. Gilliland, E. B. Cooper, H. McKittrick, M. Davtian, and T. Fong. 2012. "Report of Findings in a DSM-5 Field Trial for Hypersexual Disorder." *The Journal of Sexual Medicine 9*, no. 11: 2868–77.

Reid, R. C., S. Garos, and B. N. Carpenter. 2011. "Reliability, Validity, and Psychometric Development of the Hypersexual Behavior Inventory in an Outpatient Sample of Men." *Sexual Addiction and Compulsivity 18*, no. 1: 30–51. https://doi.org/10.1080/1072016 2.2011.555709.

Reid, R. C., S. Garos, and T. Fong. 2012. "Psychometric Development of the Hypersexual Behavior Consequences Scale." *Journal of Behavioral Addictions 1*, no. 3: 115–22. https:// doi.org/10.1556/JBA.1.2012.001.

Reid, R. C., and M. P. Kafka. 2014. "Controversies about Hypersexual Disorder and the DSM-5." *Current Sexual Health Reports 6*, no. 4: 259–64.

Reid, R. C., D. S. Li, R. Gilliland, J. A. Stein, and T. Fong. 2011. "Reliability, Validity, and Psychometric Development of the Pornography Consumption Inventory in a Sample of

Hypersexual Men." *Journal of Sex & Marital Therapy 37*, no. 5: 359–85. https://doi.org/10.1080/0092623X.2011.607047.

Short, M. B., L. Black, A. H. Smith, C. T. Wetterneck, and D. E. Wells. 2012. "A Review of Internet Pornography Use Research: Methodology and Content from the Past 10 Years." *Cyberpsychology, Behavior, and Social Networking 15*, no.1: 13–23. https://doi.org/10.1089/cyber.2010.0477.

Short, M. B., C. T. Wetterneck, S. L. Bistricky, T. Shutter, and T. E. Chase. 2016. "Clinicians' Beliefs, Observations, and Treatment Effectiveness Regarding Clients' Sexual Addiction and Internet Pornography Use." *Community Mental Health Journal 52*, no. 8: 1070–81.

Wakefield, J. C. 2012. "The DSM-5's Proposed New Categories of Sexual Disorder: The Problem of False Positives in Sexual Diagnosis." *Clinical Social Work Journal 40*: 213–23.

Walton, M. T. 2019. "Incongruence as a Variable Feature of Problematic Sexual Behaviors in an Online Sample of Self-Reported 'Sex Addiction.'" *Archives of Sexual Behavior 48*, no. 2: 443–47.

Womack, S. D., J. N. Hook, M. Ramos, D. E. Davis, and J. K. Penberthy. 2013. "Measuring Hypersexual Behavior." *Sexual Addiction and Compulsivity 20*, no. 1–2: 65–78.

World Health Organization. 2018. "ICD-11." World Health Organization. Accessed June 29, 2018. https://icd.who.int/.

Young, M. M., and M. J. A. Wohl. 2009. "The Gambling Craving Scale: Psychometric Validation and Behavioral Outcomes." *Psychology of Addictive Behaviors 23*, no. 3: 512–22. https://doi.org/10.1037/a0015043.

CHAPTER 9

GROUP STRATEGIES FOR TREATING PROBLEMATIC SEXUAL BEHAVIOR

Forest Benedict, LMFT, SATP

Group therapy is a powerful modality for treating sexual addiction. As a sex addiction therapist who leads hundreds of recovery group sessions per year, I have witnessed many lives transformed. I have led sex addiction recovery groups for female addicts, male addicts, and adolescents. Because of these experiences, I believe all therapists treating sexually addicted populations should learn to lead therapeutic recovery groups.

Despite the usefulness of groups, often sex addicts resist participating in them. There are many reasons why they are terrified to join a group, and they will often only agree when told recovery will not come any other way. Many cannot heal from addiction at the necessary depth without the group experience. As Laaser writes, "I have never known a person to heal from sexual addiction alone. All of us need an army of support around us on the healing journey" (2004, 127). This is the great paradox of sexual addiction: what the client fears most will heal them (Benedict 2017).

BENEFITS OF THERAPEUTIC GROUPS

There are several reasons why group therapy is so effective when treating sexual addiction, and clients will likely draw different positives from participating in a group, depending on their personal narrative. While there are many potential helpful experiences that an individual in recovery may find within a therapeutic group, there are also more universal dynamics that help propel their healing process forward. Below, you will find six significant benefits of therapeutic groups, many of which emerge from Bowman's Four Cs of recovery in chapter 3.

Connection

For many sex addicts, their addictive behavior is rooted in an attachment disorder (Flores 2004) originating in their childhood. Many of them learned about human relationships through the lenses of abuse, emotional neglect, or trauma (Carnes 1998). With this historical backdrop, sex addicts "were taught not to trust relational comfort, learning instead to self-soothe in sexually addictive ways" (SaaviAccountability 2010 as cited in Benedict 2017, 146). Their addiction progressed as they became increasingly reliant on a mood-altering experience for relief. To release their attachment to the addictive behavior, addicts must replace it with healthy attachments (SaaviAccountability 2010) to themselves and others. For this reason, I call group therapy the "connection classroom." In group therapy, the therapist teaches recovering addicts how to connect, confront, and care for one another. Addicts learn how to respond to the emotions of others. These skills can be transferred to other relationships but are also valuable in their own right as new friendships develop.

The sacred camaraderie in a group cannot be duplicated in individual therapy alone. According to Flores, "Giving and receiving empathy, reassurance, understanding, and self-assertion in group leads to freeing of impulses, and the capacity for greater closeness emerges" (2004, 226). Relationships were once a source of pain for addicts, but in groups they become a source of comfort. The core belief of sex addicts that "no one will love me as I am" (Carnes 2001) is challenged in groups, as individuals open up and experience acceptance. Groups are like a new family system, providing corrective emotional experiences and producing the hormone oxytocin in members' brains (Katehakis 2016). Many addicts grew up in closed-family systems where feelings were not seen, cherished, and responded to, and the group provides the opposite environment. It offers a safe haven where buried feelings resurrect. In group, feelings matter and the true self emerges (Flores 2004). It is the therapist's role to foster such a community in the group room.

Katehakis writes about the effectiveness of groups:

> Addicts of all stripes get better faster in group therapy because the brain is a social organ requiring community to grow, heal, and change biologically and psychologically. Nothing reduces shame—the faulty sense of self—like hearing a peer share about an activity the patient experienced in solitude and secrecy. As all group members fight the same fight and show the same vulnerable selves, fellowship grows and gradually bursts the isolation of addiction. (2016, 225)

In other words, learning to truly connect is the solution that satisfies like sex addiction never could (Benedict 2017, 37).

Confession

A therapeutic group provides an atmosphere of honesty. In the Bible, we are told that confession and mutual prayer lead to healing (James 5:16). In the group setting, where confidentiality is crucial, secrets are brought into the light of day and new life emerges. Addicts are invited to wrap words around what brings them shame. Confession, when responded to with compassion, is a catalyst for change, leading to deeper healing; when addicts share their secrets with others, their chains of shame fall away. Here's another way I've described the power of confession in groups:

> Nothing fuels addiction like secrecy and shame. Active in their addiction, addicts believe they are innately broken and unworthy of love. Unless they learn to give voice to their inadequacies and hidden transgressions amongst those who support them, their addiction will thrive. Groups provide a safe and confidential setting where they can share their shame-saturated secrets. As frightening as it may be initially, when they allow safe people to see inside of them, their shame is stunted and they develop a sense of belonging. While they once lived shackled by secrets, they experience how living in the truth sets them free. (Benedict 2017, 95)

Accountability

Therapy groups are a steady source of accountability. Laaser states, "Everybody in recovery needs to be in a support group. They need to be in a fellowship of men or women that are all committed to sobriety. The purpose of a support group is accountability" (M. Laaser, pers. comm., 2015). The therapist develops a community of accountability through communicating clear expectations. If certain behaviors are expected, such as doing homework or practicing specific recovery habits, there must be a system of accountability in place. I have found that check-ins at the beginning of the session are ideal places to report progress or lack thereof.

A therapist who teaches clients to respond to setbacks in sobriety and program progress with self-compassion does them a great service in their recovery from addiction: "When we do experience setbacks—which we will—we need to forgive those failures, and not use them as an excuse to give in or give up. When it comes to increasing self-control, self-compassion is a far better strategy than beating ourselves up" (McGonigal 2013, p. 154). The therapist should encourage clients to forgive themselves for mistakes and help them learn from what went wrong so they can strengthen their recovery plan. This process builds greater self-awareness for the individual in recovery, as well as helping them learn to receive support and encouragement from the group. By doing this, the therapist weaves accountability into the structure of the group.

Education

In therapeutic recovery groups, there is a high need for psychoeducation. This can be done in two ways. First, the therapist can engage in a "teacher role" (Nerenberg 2002, 186). Some of the ways necessary information can be communicated include showing a video, playing an audio, reading a book chapter, talking through a PowerPoint presentation, or telling a story. Clients need to understand addiction and the recovery process. Essential topics include attachment as it relates to addiction, the neuroscience of sexual addiction and recovery, the cycle of addiction, triggers, shame, family of origin, rebuilding trust with partners, recovery habits, and trauma. Workbooks are another great source of necessary information and can be used inside and outside of group.

The second source of information in group therapy is other members. While not everyone in group will have equal talking time, they all have equal learning time. Moses writes that "anyone does everyone's work" (1994, 4). The clients should be prepared to learn deeply about themselves as they observe others doing their own work in the group. The therapist helps clients understand the value of learning to listen while asking themselves, "How does this apply to me?" (S. Thacker, pers. comm. [2017]). After processing an issue with one client, the wise therapist will then turn to the group and ask them, "What feelings came up for you?" or "How did you relate to what you heard?" Clients can learn much about themselves and their history not only from listening to the experiences of others but also from observing their responses to others. What they notice triggered in themselves when interacting with the group can provide rich content for individual therapy. This is true of both sexual triggers and trauma triggers activated while interacting with other clients and with the therapist.

Experience

While increasing the client's knowledge is important in recovery, experience is the true catalyst of change (Flores 2004). Therapeutic groups provide life-altering experiences. Healing happens in the room. Part of the therapist's role will be to facilitate experiential exercises and interventions at the right times. Clients' brains are changed through emotional engagement (Flores 2004), an expected result of experiential exercises.

Power

The writer of Ecclesiastes knew that the strength of a few was greater than the strength of one: "Though one may be overpowered, two can defend themselves. A cord of three strands is not quickly broken" (Eccl. 4:12). This is a powerful benefit of group participation. In groups, "We can do what I couldn't" do alone (Duffy 2006). Nonreligious clients may see the group as their "higher power" (Elements Behavioral Health 2015). Clients can experience this strength within the group setting as well as between group sessions. Laaser writes that "we need groups of people to be accountable to, lists of names and phone numbers to call when we are vulnerable" (2004, 128). Many addicts do not trust easily and will remain resistant to the idea of reaching out to others, perceiving it as weakness. Uncompromising independence can have cultural roots as well. To progress, they must realize that the humility and courage to reach out is a strength and a necessary recovery skill. The client's group becomes their team working for the good of each player. They are no longer alone. They are stronger together (Benedict 2017).

THE THERAPIST

There are benefits to having two therapists co-facilitate a sex addiction recovery group (Nerenberg 2002), but this may not be possible. Qualities of an effective sex addiction group therapist include warmth, attentiveness, intuition, empathy, creativity, playfulness, and emotional presence. Nerenberg writes that "it is necessary for the therapist to be encouraging and reassuring to group members, as well as direct and confrontative when necessary" (2002, 197). It is important for the therapist to balance having a plan with being led by the Spirit, according to the needs of the group. The therapist's role is to create a safe, structured environment with consistent boundaries. The therapist models connection skills, which may include receiving feedback and repairing relationships with clients when needed. The therapist guides clients into new experiences, such as learning to vocalize emotional responses to others, reconciling with others, and receiving feedback. According to Corley et al., "The leader must be fairly directive and interactive with the clients" and "demonstrate that [they're] the most consistent and reliable member of the group" (2012, 132). Leading from these qualities, the skilled sex addiction therapist turns group work into an art.

Many therapists are drawn to this work as a result of their own recovery. If this is true of the therapist, it is essential that they are actively working their recovery. As Laaser points out, "We are our own best examples of the principles we teach" (M. Laaser, pers. comm., 2015). A therapist in active addiction cannot offer the necessary emotional availability to clients, and their shame could limit their willingness to confront their client's behavior. Inauthenticity in the therapist will be sensed by the client (Bauman 2018). Clients don't need a perfect therapist, but they do need a present therapist. Bauman's perspective is that the presence one embodies in the counseling relationship is what will likely hold the most impact; a lack of attuned presence or attempts to control the clients' behaviors or fix them do not work as the primary need for many in recovery is the need to be seen and known right where they are (2018).

In preparation for group, the therapist can find or create a ritual that connects them with both their heart and with the heart of God. I personally use an Internal Family Systems (IFS) practice called *Unblending* (See Riemersma 2020), where I mindfully connect with parts of me that I feel present before the group session. I may feel parts of me wanting to perform, perfect, please, rescue, impress, critique, or control. I listen to them then ask them to step back a bit so that I can embody an open-hearted, compassionate, curious, calm, and confident presence that will help me serve my clients. In that state, I can connect with God's love and compassion for both myself and my clients.

Therapists in this field must do their own work; they can only lead others as far as they have gone themselves (Bauman 2018). This is true of pastors and other helpers, as well, even if they have never struggled with problematic sexual behavior. The good news about recovering therapists is that "transformed people transform people. When you can be healed yourself and not just talk about healing, you are, as Henri Nouwen said, a 'wounded healer'—which is probably the only kind of healer!" (Rohr 2016).

While therapist self-disclosure is commonly discouraged in regular psychotherapy settings, recovering addicts benefit deeply from self-disclosure done right. I have found it useful in groups to share appropriately about the process of healing personal trauma, using my story to model or teach a relevant concept. Katehakis writes that cognitive disclosure "decreases patients' isolation and shame by letting them know the therapist relates directly to their challenges" (2016, 230). Still, the wise therapist uses self-disclosure according to good clinical judgment, for the benefit of the client, at the right time and depth, providing clients with the opportunity to process their reaction to the shared information (Katehakis 2016).

Affective self-disclosure by the therapist is an intervention that regulates the client, provides safety, and strengthens the client/therapist attachment bond (Katehakis 2016). It "is a right-to-right brain communication that deepens connections as the therapist details her or his personal (that is, physical) and immediate affective experience" (Katehakis 2016, 231). Right hemisphere to right hemisphere connection between therapist and client not only regulates emotions but, in doing so, allows "the client to go deeper into their attachment stories" (Frye, n.d.). This connection begins with the therapist sharing their somatic and emotional responses to the client as they occur (Katehakis 2016). Saying something like, "I feel sad when I hear you talk about your mother's death," is one example of affective self-disclosure. These words, paired with a facial expression of sadness, communicate that a connection is being made. After using affective self-disclosure, the therapist should then process the client's experience of feeling felt (Katehakis 2016). It should be noted that attunement to the experience of another cannot be faked (Flores 2004). Even when we cannot fully understand the depth of emotion the other might be feeling in the moment, empathic attunement indicates that we allow ourselves to meet the client with whatever capacity for emotional connection we have at that point in time. Stories where sexual addiction is present almost always involve deep points of pain and suffering, and the work can be overwhelming even for the most seasoned clinician or pastor. The goal is not to operate perfectly as a helper, as every pastor and therapist have days where the emotions they are carrying themselves will impede their ability to operate at full capacity. Also, the goal here is not to take on the entire weight of the story *for* the client, but rather to *join with* them in the process of feeling and healing their pain. The goal is to offer whatever depth of authentic empathy and attunement we have in that moment, for in doing so we embody the bearing of another's burdens we are called to (Gal. 6:2).

Lastly, due to the complexities of sex addiction treatment, it is highly recommended that therapists doing this work pursue reputable sex addiction certification of some kind (e.g. CSAT, SATP). Also, trauma training such as IFS and/or EMDR will make a significant difference in this work. IFS is my preferred modality for treating sex addiction and its underlying trauma and shame. IFS is powerfully effective with both individual and group therapy.

GROUP RULES

Therapeutic sexual addiction recovery groups require clearly communicated rules that all participants agree to follow. The therapist can create these rules or allow the clients to collaborate on them to create buy-in. These rules can be presented in contract form and signed by the clients (Corley et al. 2012). At the minimum, group rules should be written down and followed by a verbal agreement. In an open group, all rules should be explained and agreed upon each time a new person joins the group. Here are seven recommended rules:

Be On Time and Ready

Clients must understand the importance of arriving on time, prepared to participate. Their readiness may include doing homework during the week, preparing for check-ins, and setting their intentions for meaningful participation in the group session. Group leaders often establish boundaries for timely arrival, and the group can recommend reasonable consequences for tardiness. Timeliness and preparedness are two primary indicators of psychological readiness and willingness to change.

Maintain Confidentiality

Confidentiality is essential for trust to grow. This is true of any therapy group, but it is especially important for sex addicts due to the depth of shame they experience. The group walls will witness secrets and stories that have never been spoken before. So, when the first session begins, confidentiality should be explained in detail. Anonymity of members must be honored, and content shared by others must not be repeated outside of the room. Clients are allowed to talk about anything they learn in group that does not pertain to others and anything regarding their own recovery if they wish (S. Thacker, pers. comm., [2017?]). Sharing this type of information with a partner is one way to begin rebuilding trust (Covenant Eyes, 2015). But clients should know that breaching confidentiality could lead to disciplinary action in group and could even become a legal matter between members (S. Thacker, pers. comm., [2017?]).

Avoid Unnecessary Details

In a sex addiction recovery group, it is likely that group members will get triggered at times by what other members say. This is not necessarily a negative dynamic if the trigger is voiced and processed within the group (T. Love, pers. comm., [2017?]), but minimizing triggers when possible makes the group a safer environment for participants. This begins by asking clients not to say names of movies, websites, pornography performers, acting out partners, or sharing ideas about other avenues of acting out. It will also be important that clients not share graphic descriptions of how they have acted out. In S Fellowship meetings (e.g. SA, SAA), a member can quietly raise their hand if the content of a share is triggering them, which cues the speaker to use less detail in their language. In a therapeutic group, there is an opportunity to help raise self-awareness within the individual by processing the impact that the graphic content had on the other members and explore the potential for euphoric recall, where past sexual content or experiences are being reflected upon as a type of edging or foraging, given the anticipatory high that coincides with this process. Boundaries for healthy participation should be outlined as members are prescreened for the therapy group, and one of these boundaries should include the protocol for navigating the nature of graphic content in shares and the process for maintaining group membership for participants who are unwilling to abide by the group norms.

Be Mindful of Others

Everyone has the right to speak in a group and talking time should not be monopolized by one member. Since one purpose of the group is teaching social skills, clients can practice being courteous and listening to others. Therapists are ultimately responsible for guiding the flow of the group discussion. Redirecting a rogue conversation may require subtle or direct confrontations.

Don't Compare

In any group setting, it is inevitable that members will come from different backgrounds and act out in diverse ways. When clients compare themselves to others, there could be two detrimental outcomes. First, they may look at those who have what appear to be worse behavior and minimize their own choices, leading to a decrease in their drive to recover. Second, they may look at those who have what appear to be less serious behaviors and catastrophize their own situation, experiencing increased shame and hopelessness. Rather than comparing, it is more helpful for clients to ask themselves, "What do we have in common?" and "What can I learn about myself from their story?" Regardless of backstory, every addict's situation is serious and requires help.

Reach Out Appropriately

It is important to communicate expectations for communication and interaction between group sessions. I have always encouraged outside interaction, recommending that group members pair up as accountability partners (or find someone else to hold them accountable) and teaching them how to make emergency calls when they are feeling the urge to act out. I have found that a group text including the therapist can be a helpful medium for teaching clients how to reach out for help. As the therapist, I use the group text to share articles and last-minute changes. If a group text is used, confidentiality must be emphasized. It is best used as a springboard into connection. Due to the heightened risk of someone outside the group viewing a text message, rather than venting via text, clients can use it to ask who is available for a phone call. In this way, they can learn how to reach out in times of need, increasing attachment skills.

Roleplaying ways to effectively reach out through calling others and how to respond when a call is received is a great use of group time in the first weeks of the group. Another rule to consider for outside-of-group interaction could be to not discuss what is done or talked about in group and not hooking up with group members sexually. Hooking up with another group member is known as "13th stepping" in recovery communities and is a violation of the trust and equality that is intended to exist between members of that community. In a therapy group context, the boundaries are able to be drawn more clearly by the group facilitator and this phenomenon can be processed more directly than it is in S Fellowships. Regardless of group type or context, there is a violation of community that occurs when members of a group hook up with one another, and the impact on the group itself will depend on the type of group the members were a part of (ie SLAA, therapy group, etc). With the right coaching, outside connection can increase the effectiveness of treatment as friendships are developed. The downside of outside group interaction is that it is beyond the therapist's influence and could go poorly. But, like all things, a negative interaction outside of group could be "grits for the mill" in therapy, an opportunity to learn conflict resolution skills and process whatever was triggered.

Do the Work

Recovery works when the process is worked. While the individual in recovery is responsible for the day-to-day aspects of this work, whoever is helping them is providing the roadmap for recovery. This roadmap for recovery, with very few exceptions, involves group participation. The therapist should communicate all group requirements, which may include practicing daily recovery habits (e.g., prayer, reading, journaling, self-care), attending meetings, calling a sponsor and accountability partners, and progressing in program homework. These daily activities are the driver of recovery, fostering a sense of self-awareness, surrender, mindfulness, humility, and all the internal growth that happens when recovery is authentic.

GROUP FORMAT

It is recommended that the group have a consistent format, divided into the three components of opening ritual, middle section, and closing ritual. Let's examine each of those three components in more detail.

Opening Ritual

When clients arrive, welcome them with warmth, and then begin on time. The group session can start with a few moments of quietness to connect with God (Corley et al. 2012) and set the clients' intentions for their upcoming time together. This can be followed with a structured check-in process, which should be consistent in every group session. The check-in process "is one thing that differentiates a sex addiction treatment group from a generic therapy group, because it creates a forum for assertion and accountability from the moment group begins" (Corley et al. 2012, 130). Check-ins provide a detailed view of the clients' recovery progress (Nerenberg 2002) and show how they are feeling in the moment. The therapist can determine beforehand what components will make up their group's check-in process.

Check-ins can include how the client is feeling in the moment physically, emotionally, and spiritually. I do not allow my clients to use words such as good, bad, better, or fine to describe how they are feeling but often refer them to the feeling charts they are given, teaching them how to become emotionally literate and attuned to themselves as they name how they feel in each area. This is an especially important skill to develop for clients with alexithymia, which is "a characteristic pattern indicating an inability to name and use one's emotions" in which the addict is "confronted with sensations rather than feelings" (Flores 2004, 179). The therapist can expect to redirect the client repeatedly in group, helping them understand how they are truly feeling in a given moment, not just what they are thinking. Some additional parts of the check-ins I have used in groups include the following:

- Level of connection to God, self, and others
- Slips, relapses, unhealthy coping, or numbing behavior this week
- Recovery-habits progress
- Homework progress, voicing "I am ready to present _____," or "I am working on _____," or "I did not make time to work on my program this week."
- Sobriety date
- Read an affirmation
- Level of commitment to recovery (on a scale of 0 to 10)

In order to leave time for the group processing and activities, it is recommended that clients be prepared to check in and not be allowed to go on tangents. Check-ins are an opportunity to learn the social skill of being considerate of the time of others. I recommend total check-in time not exceed the first third of the group. Limiting check-ins to three minutes, using a stopwatch, has proven to be an effective way of teaching clients to maintain this time boundary. Also, check-in is an opportunity for the therapist to listen for patterns (S. Thacker, pers. comm. [2017?]) that can be addressed or processed afterward. These patterns provide golden opportunities to respond with spontaneous interventions (see "In-Group

Interventions") as well. Therapists can also split the group into dyads or triads for check-ins at their discretion.

Middle Section

This part of the group is dedicated to going deeper with clients. The therapist will guide this process. There are a number of activities the therapist could focus on. A prepared lesson can be presented. Group members can share completed homework or ask questions. The therapist can lead a spontaneous or planned experiential exercise. A video or song that relates to recovery can be played. This is also the time to do deeper group processing, picking a theme to follow from check-ins, focusing on a specific challenge one member is experiencing, or exploring relational dynamics within the group.

Yalom asserts the following:

Group members learn most effectively by studying the very interactional network in which they are enmeshed. . . . They profit enormously by being confronted, in an objective manner, with on-the-spot observations of their own behavior and its effects on others: they may learn about their interpersonal styles, the responses of others to them, and about group behavior in general (1995, 487).

Remarkable growth and increased awareness can occur in the middle section of the group. Specific activities that can be used in this section are explained in detail later in this chapter. It must be noted that after any emotionally triggering experiences in group, an adequate time of cognitive processing should follow, helping the client re-engage their prefrontal cortex to ground them (F. Godfrey, pers. comm., 2016) so they are prepared to leave when the group session concludes. Failing to ground clients at the end of group could lead to compromised sobriety (F. Godfrey, pers. comm., 2016).

Closing Ritual

A closing ritual allows a short time of self-reflection. The therapist could ask the group to share their highlight from the group session and why it was significant (Yalom, 1995). Exercises such as these increase self-awareness, understanding of what occurred in group, insight from hearing the experiences of others, and intentionality with how to proceed. These closing rituals could be practiced sitting or standing in a circle or using a huddle formation with arms around the shoulders of the person next to them (F. Godfrey, pers. comm., [2017?]), including the therapist. Looking at each other as they speak makes this a vulnerable exercise, but it is also a powerful source of healthy touch and

188 • *Treatment Strategies*

connection. A variation of the huddle called "The Well" (Corley et al. 2012) is a closing ritual recommended for a female therapeutic group.

GROUP STRUCTURE

There is no specific formula for creating a group, but there are a few specific structural aspects to consider.

Size

In my experience, the ideal group size is five to eight people. I would not recommend exceeding ten group participants. One challenge of working with a large group is allowing time for everyone to share and feel heard. One way I have managed a larger group is by splitting the group into smaller groups for check-ins (for example, a ten-person group could be divided into two groups of five or three groups of three, three, and four) (Love 2015). When I know a client has a time-consuming project to present (like their Inventory or Trauma Egg) or an experiential activity is planned that will take extensive group time, I often ask group members to check in in dyads to expedite the check-in process.

Open versus Closed

In open groups, new participants are allowed to join until the group reaches maximum capacity, and when clients drop out the spaces are filled with new members (Yalom 1995). A closed group means no new members are allowed to join, which can be problematic in longer-term groups due to natural member attrition (Yalom 1995). An open group is more likely to remain full, and members will be at different stages of recovery. A closed group will have greater cohesiveness and consistency without the disruption of integrating new members. Each therapist should decide which format is best for their group before it begins.

Content

To maximize the potential of group therapy, it is highly recommended that the therapist assign some form of homework to accomplish during each week. This content can be workbooks, book reports, writing assignments, and other prepared activities. Additionally, sobriety is supported through effective daily recovery habits. To help the clients experience a strong recovery, the therapist can create a list of potential recovery activities and a system to track progress, which can be reported at group check-ins. In the chapter, "The Neuroscience of Self-Care" in *Life after Lust* (Benedict 2017), I emphasized the importance of sleep, exercise, mindful breathing, and healthy eating for increasing self-control

(McGonigal 2012). Other daily recovery habits could include journaling, accountability calls, tracking sobriety, prayer, relaxation, attending a twelve-step meeting, and recovery reading. The daily habit I prioritize with my clients is an IFS-based parts check-in in which they connect with and listen to their "parts"/ emotions, responding with care and compassion. There is not a prescriptive recovery formula that everyone must follow; recovery habits vary on a case-by-case basis. The point is to create a recovery structure for clients to follow outside of the group, helping them create healthy habits that will daily rewire their brains.

Depending on the format of the group (open or closed), clients will either work through the same content simultaneously or according to their individual track. An example of the individual track is how twelve-step programs are formatted. Each person begins working the twelve steps at step 1, regardless of what step the other members are on and continues working through the course of the steps at their own pace. When organized well, I have found this rotating group format to be highly effective, and it allows groups to remain open to new participants until full. Another advantage of a rotating group is that everyone benefits from hearing what is shared by other members, even if it is a reminder of something they learned in the past. But even rotating groups need some activities that everyone can do together (such as specific lessons and experiential exercises). Each time a new member joins, introductions should be shared again, with the new person sharing last.

Length

Length refers to both hours of a group session and months before the group ends. The ideal length a group session should run is seventy-five to ninety minutes, depending on the number of members present. While recovery from sexual addiction can take three to five years (Carnes 2015), a therapy group is not needed through that entire duration. Clients could be led through a short intensive group experience lasting a few long days, a six-week-long group, a one- to two-year program, or an ongoing (never-ending until each client is ready) group. Since much of the recovery work is related to healing attachment and trauma, a longer group is recommended because it allows time to connect and build trust. Groups should meet weekly. When clients have planned absences, the therapist can video conference them into the session to promote consistent attendance.

DEMOGRAPHICS

There are specific recommendations regarding the demographics of participants in sexual addiction recovery groups. While many S Fellowships (e.g., SA, SAA) have open meetings where anyone is welcome, mixed-gender therapy groups are discouraged because they can be triggering to those present, as well as their partners. Being in a healthy group where they can feel accepted and loved, clients can experience increased connection and decreased shame (Love 2016).

Diversity among faith backgrounds, economic statuses, ethnicities, sexual orientations, gender identities, and ages (not mixing minors and adults) can be beneficial in a group as long as there is mutual respect and acceptance. Mixing recovery newbies with veterans can naturally facilitate a mentoring dynamic. Clients with varying acting out experiences can be combined. It has worked well for me to put clients who have had affairs with sexual addicts, finding treatment similarities such as the need to heal attachment wounds, mourn the loss of the fantasy, and rebuild trust. Clients recovering from infidelity who are not sexually addicted should have program modifications (Weiss and Ferree 2018).

There are some populations that are not a good fit for group therapy, so pre-screening is essential. Clients who have extreme character pathology such as a personality disorder or psychotic symptoms (including delusions and paranoia), those who are unwilling to participate or have schedules that do not allow regular participation, those who are severely anxious in groups, and those who are unable to keep the commitments of the group likely will not be appropriate for group therapy (Center for Substance Abuse Treatment 2005). When adding a new member to an existing group, the therapist must be mindful of the best fit for both the new client as well as for the group.

Adolescents

There is a growing need for therapy groups and programs treating adolescent pornography addicts. Adolescents in our day are exposed to pornography in unprecedented numbers, and the need for quality treatment will only increase. A therapist wanting to lead groups for adolescents can create a structured, age-appropriate program that helps young people while also educating their parents. Under the guidance of therapist Floyd Godfrey, PhD, CSAT-S, I once created a therapeutic program for adolescent males, which included education, games, food, connecting opportunities, homework, a ranking system, and a parent education component. After years of work with adolescents, Dr. Godfrey and his colleague Matt Wheeler, LPC, CSAT, published their program as the *Band of Brothers* in 2017, making it available to the public. This is a helpful and practical resource for therapists working with adolescent clients.

As with all the work we do, we cannot forget that pornography addiction is not just a male issue. On that note, if a sexually addicted client identifies with a gender or sexual orientation that the therapist is not competent to treat or is uncomfortable with due to personal convictions, it is in the client's best interest to receive an appropriate referral to a sex addiction therapist who is. In doing so, the Christian clinician models the humility and love of Jesus. Additionally, sex addiction therapists focus on treating compulsive behavior, relational problems, and trauma. It is unethical and harmful to attempt to treat or change a client's sexual orientation or gender.

While adolescent pornography use may be problematic for religious reasons, it does not necessitate addiction. This applies to people of all ages. Harm can be done by the therapist who accepts a client's self-diagnosis of pornography addiction alone or assumes they are addicted simply on the basis that their pornography use goes against the client's or their parents' religious and moral values. As with all the work we do, proper clinical assessment is warranted. Those who struggle to stop unwanted pornography use but do not meet the criteria for addiction, especially those who are younger, are in need of having their sexual desires, interests, and behaviors explored in the context of caring conversation. Their curiosity in this important aspect of their humanity must be normalized to decrease shame, and guidance can be provided on how to create personal boundaries, get compassionate support, and stop unwanted pornography use.

Young Adults

Many young adult pornography addicts do not meet the criteria for classic sex addiction (R. Weiss, pers. comm., October 16, 2018). Laaser shares that "the internet has been the major league escalator; it's drawn a lot of people into addiction that don't necessarily have all the same family system dynamics that we used to see" (M. Laaser, pers. comm., 2015). From a treatment perspective, this is important because some young adult addicts will not need treatment for trauma and emotional neglect and others will require it. Research is needed in this emerging area (R. Weiss, pers. comm., October 16, 2018). In my experience leading a young adult recovery group, this population strongly benefits from mutual support and encouragement. I've also found that this age group has difficulty achieving sobriety. I believe one reason young people are less motivated to do the work necessary to change is they often aren't facing the significant life consequences of their addiction yet. Unlike addicts facing divorce or job loss, young single adults must muster their motivation to recover based on obvious present consequences, personal values, and a deepening understanding of their possible future trajectory. It is my hope that more resources for young adults will be created soon for this struggling demographic.

Women

Groups for male and female sex addicts will be different in some significant ways. When considering how to treat female sex and love addicts, we must remember that "men and women have different brains. Clinicians have long recognized that therapeutic interventions that work with one gender don't necessarily translate to the opposite gender. The same is true when treating sex and love addiction" (Ferree et al. 2012, 97). Therapist Staci Sprout, CSAT, a leading expert in female sex and love addiction treatment, emphasizes that while men may do well with a more cognitive-behavioral and firm approach, women respond better to a caring, attuned, and softer approach (S. Sprout, pers. comm., September 29, 2018). Sprout shares that since their "relational betrayal is so acute, [women's groups] bond much more slowly than men's groups, not like a sports team but more like a soufflé, delicate recipe mixing carefully together and hope the bonding 'rises.'" Like their male counterparts, she says female addicts "need people, not programs" to heal.

Another challenge unique to working with female addicts is their distrust toward each other, rooted in attachment wounds (Corley et al. 2012). Within the group, there may be cliques and scapegoating (S. Sprout, pers. comm., September 29, 2018), jealousy and attention-seeking (Corley et al. 2012). As the therapist navigates these challenges, they "can emphasize to all members that group therapy often surfaces long-buried coping mechanisms, and that the group offers a place to learn healthier ways of behaving and communicating" (Corley et al. 2012, 141). While other women may at first be seen by addicts as the enemy (Corley et al. 2012), in groups they become a source of deep healing.

For female groups, the gender of the therapist is less important than their emotional health and skills (Corley et al. 2012). As a male therapist, I have facilitated a female sex and love addiction group and found the experience both effective and meaningful. The women benefit from learning to interact with a man in new, healthy ways. The therapist's competence with sexual addiction treatment and care are the most important variables in the success of these groups.

Therapists treating female sex and love addicts are encouraged to study the "Best Practices for Group Therapy" chapter in *Making Advances: A Comprehensive Guide for Treating Female Sex and Love Addicts* to more deeply understand the nuances and intricacies of working with this population (Corley, Ferree, Hudson, Katehakis, Vermeire, and Weeden 2012). Both Marnie Ferree and Staci Sprout provide training for therapists who want to work with female sex and love addicts.

Telehealth

An emerging treatment platform is online therapy. Weiss agrees that the internet is the next frontier for all treatment, including sex addiction treatment (R. Weiss, pers. comm., October 16, 2018). Some research shows that online therapy can be more effective than in-person therapy (Wagner, Horn, and Maercker 2013). Due to the shameful nature of sexual addiction, some addicts may prefer therapy through this more private modality. Providing online treatment also expands the reach of sex addiction therapy. For the past three years, I have run recovery groups solely online and I have found this incredibly effective for both treatment and connection. Therapists choosing to provide online groups should get additional training, ensuring that all treatment is ethical, legal, and effective.

INTERVENTIONS

There are countless exercises that can be used in the middle section of the group session. Some interventions are simple and can be used spontaneously, while others are complex, requiring extensive preparation. Remember, a "group leader should not use techniques for which they have not been trained or for which they are not under supervision by a counselor familiar with the intervention" (Corey et al. 2004, 37). The following section is an introduction to group interventions, not a complete explanation. All interventions should be researched by the therapist and used according to client readiness to minimize harm and maximize growth.

In-Group Interventions

It is advantageous for the therapist to be prepared with many potential therapeutic tools. Several interventions can be preplanned by the therapist or used spontaneously as the need arises. Some written interventions include The Self-Compassion Letter (McGonigal 2012), the Prelapse Self-Evaluation (Benedict 2017, 55–58), the Letter from Your Future Self (Benedict 2017, 133), the Responsibility Self-Evaluation (Benedict 2017, 30–31), the Failure Response Worksheet (Benedict 2017, 123–125), the Secret Exercise (Yalom 1995, 7), and The Amends Matrix (Arterburn and Martinkus 2014, 145–166). Guided visualizations include Practicing Being Known (Thompson 2010, 143), Feeling God's Delight (Thompson 2010, 107), Future Self Visualization (Benedict 2017, 134), and Surfing the Urge (McGonigal 2011). Audio meditations include The Self-Compassion Break (Neff n.d.), Connecting to Your Source of Compassion (McGonigal 2012), and IFS meditations (Schwartz 2018).

Once in a young adult recovery group I led, check-ins revealed that numerous members had slipped with sobriety that week. My response to this was guiding the entire group through the "Recovering from Relapse" chapter in *Life after Lust* (Benedict 2017), including their completion of the Failure Response Worksheet. The Failure Response Worksheet allows the client to examine their triggers, practice responding compassionately to themselves, reconnect with their accountability network and God, and work toward creating different future outcomes. After the exercise, we processed the experience as a group. I encouraged them to practice this tool immediately after a future slip. Using this intervention, I maximized a teachable moment, modeled non-shaming responsiveness to their present issues, and equipped them for the future.

Prepared Interventions

There are many interventions that require preparation by the client. The following are some exercises that can be used in a group. Interventions can be led differently than how they are described here.

The Farewell Letter

In this exercise, the client writes a goodbye letter to their addiction. An example is provided by Katehakis (2016, 233). Once completed, this letter can be read to the group and processed. In my perspective, an adversarial stance toward the addiction is not an effective long-term strategy and will back-fire. Thanking the addiction for helping one cope with pain and creating a new relationship with the addiction deepens one's sense of gratitude and can help build sustained sobriety.

The Inventory

In the First Step Inventory of Sexaholics Anonymous, the addict writes an account of every acting out behavior in their history (Sexaholics Anonymous, n.d.). If a client writes this inventory, they can read it in group. Another option is asking them to use a modified version similar to one I have created. In this version, the client writes out a narrative in chronological order of every acting out behavior in their history and includes the context in which those behaviors occurred, sparing triggering details. The context is what was happening in their life when they acted out (including traumas, abuse, family dynamics, loss, and more). Writing this assignment in this way helps the client understand why they turned to their addiction to cope with pain when they did, increasing self-understanding and self-compassion. Once completed, they can read this to the group, then feelings and responses are processed. Sharing an honest, self-reflective inventory amongst caring peers is the foundation upon which the client's new life can be built.

Disclosure

If a client in the group is doing a formal disclosure to their partner with a trained therapist, I have found it beneficial for them to read it to their group in preparation. The formal disclosure is the sharing of a prepared document chronicling the individual's sexual development, sexual acting out, and lying history with their partner and therapist present. Sharing this content beforehand in the group setting provides a dress rehearsal for the difficult, shame-inducing, and emotionally charged experience to come. Clients can also schedule their disclosure on the same day as their group for added support afterwards. Fellow group members could also be at a pre-arranged location to meet with the client and offer support after the disclosure takes place (G. Steurer, pers. comm., 2016). Having the support of the group before and after the disclosure can decrease shame and deepen attachment bonds.

Egg Work

Two advanced exercises used in group therapy are the Trauma Egg and the Angel Egg. These tools are a type of artistic rendering to capture various moments of an individual's life story that have had significant influence in shaping their life and development. They are more about using colors and pictures or symbols to capture and communicate these events rather than words in an attempt to tap into the emotion buried underneath each event. These exercises should be used later in treatment, once trust in the group is developed and the client has a deepened understanding of their family of origin and trauma. I prepare clients for Egg work using the books *Running on Empty* (Webb 2012) and *Finding Peace* (Love 2017). Egg work is also a great way for a client to understand what trauma can be treated in their individual therapy.

Kotry (2009) identifies these four purposes of the Trauma Egg:

1. Understanding the client's trauma history
2. Identifying life patterns
3. Determining core beliefs and defining methods of coping
4. Creating a mission statement that explains why the client returned to addictive patterns

There are many variations of the Trauma Egg exercise. Each therapist is encouraged to find their preferred variation that fits the population they are working with (See Campling et al. 2012; Machen 2016; Center for Healthy Sex 2014). Some therapists do the Trauma Egg as a psychodrama, enlisting group members to participate (F. Godfrey, pers. comm., 2016). The client prepares their Trauma Egg based on instructions given then presents it to the group. The Trauma Egg presentation can be lengthy, extending through one to two entire group sessions. Healing occurs as the client shares their most painful and shame-filled memories in the presence of their caring and compassionate therapist and peers. The group provides comfort that was unavailable to the client at the moment the trauma occurred, providing a corrective emotional experience. According to Sprout, "Buried truths, when compassionately understood, become treasures" (2015, 2).

The Angel Egg is recommended as a follow-up exercise to the Trauma Egg. In this exercise, angels are the nurturing and positive people and experiences that impacted the client's life (Kotry 2009). After preparing this Egg, it is presented similarly to the Trauma Egg, examining patterns, core beliefs developed, and a new mission statement. This exercise brings a more balanced and optimistic perspective to the client's life.

Autobiography

I created this exercise as a culmination of the First Step Inventory, the Eggs, and the previous work accomplished in group. The autobiography helps the client understand their entire story from a new perspective. I ask the client to write a ten-page autobiography, with the first two pages about their family history; the middle six pages about their life, addiction, and recovery; and the last two pages about their visions for the future. Once completed, they read their story to their group. Then the emotions and experiences are processed, first with the client presenting, then with the other group members who offered compassionate witness. This exercise fits well near the end of the group therapy experience, providing a sense of self-understanding, closure, and hope for the future. A similar autobiographical narrative activity that integrates the participant's prefrontal cortex and deepens connection is explained in Thompson's book *Anatomy of the Soul* (2010, 173).

Psychodrama

Psychodrama is an effective treatment of addictions and trauma (Arnold, n.d.). Since "trauma is connected to the mind and body . . . a well-rounded treatment plan should also take a body-mind approach, which is precisely the goal of psychodrama counselors" (Clark and Davis-Gage 2010). Therapist Floyd Godfrey, PhD, CSAT, uses psychodrama in his groups for sex addicts and for partners. Psychodrama is an intensive and interactive group activity that allows clients to be in the present, expressing and processing emotion (F. Godfrey, pers. comm., 2016). This includes the use of role-play and reenactments.

Since psychodrama is an advanced modality, sexual addicts should not participate in it until they have done enough recovery work (F. Godfrey, pers. comm., 2016). They should have a network system in place, be able to reach out to others, know how to be transparent and authentic, be able to resource themselves when trauma is triggered, have control of mental health issues, and experience an increased ability to maintain sobriety (F. Godfrey, pers. comm., 2016).

Dr. Godfrey reports phenomenal results with recovering sex addicts in his psychodrama groups. His clients report a decreased drive to act out. Dr. Godfrey believes psychodrama helps his clients develop emotional tolerance, which is protective against emotional triggers (2016). It is highly recommended that therapists who want to utilize psychodrama techniques in their treatment get trained in this area.

GRADUATION

As a client prepares to end their group experience, "closure is extremely important, as most sex addicts have not had successful endings to any relationships" (Nerenberg 2002, 197). Recovering clients benefit from learning to say goodbye well. Saying goodbye to the group does not necessarily mean they will lose contact with one another, but it honors the experience they had together, acknowledging that it has come to an end. If a group member leaves a group prematurely, I ask them to come back one last time to say goodbye to the group, giving everyone the gift of closure. Sadly, some clients choose not to do so.

Graduation is an opportunity to celebrate the life-changing experience a group had together. When an individual or group completes their program, a party is warranted. In my groups, this means a potluck, one last check-in, and then a goodbye ritual that affirms all parting members. Group members could sign a card or a book for the graduate or each bring a small parting gift that is symbolic of recovery (Corley et al. 2012). The therapist could have the graduate prepare and share their long-term recovery plan with the group. One graduation exercise that can be done is to have each group member, including the parting member, write down qualities they see in the graduate (such as brave, strong, lovable). Once finished, each person takes a turn sharing the qualities, giving examples if they wish, then giving the sticky note to the graduate to keep. The graduate shares the qualities they see in themselves as well. This is a powerfully affirming exercise to conclude the group's time together. Emotions can be processed afterward. If time permits, the graduate may want to address each of the other members and the therapist directly. For additional ideas for graduation rituals, the reader is directed to *Making Advances* (Ferree 2012, 151–52).

Graduation is bittersweet. As the group therapist, it is one of the most reward-ing experiences we will have. It reminds us that this lengthy and difficult work we do leads to changed lives and transformed hearts.

CONCLUSION

Group therapy is wonderful work that supports long-term recovery. Many addicts have experienced firsthand how groups helped them connect, grow, and create new lives. In groups, sacred experiences of mourning and laughing together become the foundation of lifelong relationships. Clients learn how to know, love, and be themselves. They become part of something greater. We witness the resurrection power of Christ in community. Group work changes our clients and it changes us.

REFERENCES

Arnold, M. (n.d.). Psychodrama Therapy: What Is It? www.crchealth.com/types-of-therapy/what-is-psychodrama/.

Arterburn, S., and J. B. Martinkus. 2014. *Worthy of Her Trust: What You Need to Do to Rebuild Sexual Integrity and Win Her Back*. Colorado Springs: WaterBrook.

Bauman, A. 2018. "Benedict Bauman SATP Interview." Forest Benedict, LMFT, SATP's Channel. March 14. YouTube. www.youtube.com/watch?v=qQGABt7hvIA&t=276s.

Benedict, F. 2015. "My One Thing: Forest Benedict." Belt of Truth Ministries. July 11, 2015. YouTube. www.beltoftruth.com/my-one-thing-forest-benedict/.

Benedict, F. 2017. *Life after Lust: Stories and Strategies for Sex and Pornography Addiction Recovery*. Fresno, CA: Visionary Books.

Campling, S., D. Corley, M. Ferree, and L. Hudson. 2012. "Best Practices for Arresting Acting Out." In *Making Advances: A Comprehensive Guide for Treating Female Sex and Love Addicts*, edited by M. Ferree, 119–155. Royston, GA: SASH.

Carnes, P. 1998. The Making of a Sex Addict. www.yumpu.com/en/document/read/1124 2970/the-making-of-a-sex-addict-iitap.

_____. 2001. *Out of the Shadows: Understanding Sexual Addiction*. Center City, MN: Hazelden.

_____. 2015. "Dr Patrick Carnes, Leading Sex Addiction Expert, Video Interview." Joe Polish YouTube Channel. www.youtube.com/watch?v=i1pQfGD_MQI.

Center for Healthy Sex. 2014. "Using the Trauma Egg to Reveal and Heal Your Past: Shereen Hariri Lecture at CHS." YouTube. www.youtube.com/watch?v=ruAGHKzXuzQ.

Center for Substance Abuse Treatment. 2005. "Criteria for the Placement of Clients in Groups." In Substance Abuse Treatment: Group Therapy, Treatment Improvement Protocol (TIP) Series, No. 41. Rockville, MD: Substance Abuse and Mental Health Services Administration. PDF. https://www.ncbi.nlm.nih.gov/books/NBK64220/pdf/Bookshelf_NBK64220.pdf.

Clark, T. L., and D. Davis-Gage. 2010. "Treating Trauma: Using Psychodrama in Groups." https://www.counseling.org/docs/disaster-and-trauma_sexual-abuse/treating-trauma _psychodrama-in-groups.pdf?sfvrsn=2.

Corey, G., M. S. Corey, P. Callanan, and J. M. Russell. 2004. *Group Techniques*. 3rd ed. Pacific Grove, CA: Thomson Brooks/Cole.

Corley, D., M. Ferree, L. Hudson, A. Katehakis, J. Vermeire, and S. Weeden. 2012. "Best Practices for Group Therapy." In *Making Advances: A Comprehensive Guide for Treating Female Sex and Love Addicts*. Edited by M. C. Ferree, 119–55. Royston, GA: SASH.

Covenant Eyes. 2015. "8 Ways to Rebuild Trust with Your Wife." YouTube. www.youtube .com/watch?v=JLa7Fu-ixdY&t=1s.

Duffy, B. 2006. "Aa and Cbt: One in the Same?" HMP Global Learning Network. www .hmpgloballearningnetwork.com/site/addiction/article/aa-and-cbt-one-same.

Elements Behavioral Health. 2015. "Defining Your Own Higher Power in Addiction Recovery." www.recoveryplace.com/blog/defining-your-own-higher-power-in-addiction-recovery/.

Engel, B. 2013, July 14. "How Compassion Can Heal Shame from Childhood." Psychology Today. www.psychologytoday.com/blog/the-compassion-chronicles/201307 /how -compassion-can-heal-shame-childhood.

Ferree, M., A. Katehakis, K. McDaniel, A. Valenti-Anderson, and J. Vermeire. 2012. "Therapeutic Considerations and Settings." In *Making Advances: A Comprehensive Guide for Treating Female Sex and Love Addicts*. Edited by M. C. Ferree, 119–55. Royston, GA: SASH.

Flores, P. J. 2004. *Addiction as an Attachment Disorder*. Lanham, MD: Jason Aronson.

Frye, T. (n.d.). Counseling Sexual Addictions. Fresno, CA: Class at Fresno Pacific Biblical Seminary.

Germer, C. K., and K. D. Neff. 2013. "Self-compassion in Clinical Practice." Journal of Clinical Psychology 69, no. 8: 856–867. DOI:10.1002/jclp.22021.

Godfrey, F., and M. Wheeler. 2017. *Workbook 1: Guardian (Band of Brothers)*. Mesa, AZ: CreateSpace.

Katehakis, A. 2016. *Sex Addiction as Affect Dysregulation: A Neurobiologically Informed Holistic Treatment*. New York: W. W. Norton & Company.

Kotry, J. 2009. "An Introduction to the Trauma and Angel Egg." Presentation. Ontario, Canada.

Laaser, M. R. 2004. *Healing the Wounds of Sexual Addiction*. Grand Rapids: Zondervan.

Love, T. 2015. "Experiential Exercises for Phase 2." Conference presentation. LifeSTAR Conference, Salt Lake City, UT.

———. 2016. "Treating Gay Clients with Compulsive Sexual and Addictive Behaviors." Conference presentation. LifeSTAR Conference, Salt Lake City, UT.

———. 2017. *Finding Peace: A Workbook on Healing from Loss, Rejection, Neglect, Abandonment, Betrayal, and Abuse*. Yuma, AZ: CreateSpace.

Machen, E. 2016. "Understanding How to Use the Trauma Egg." YouTube. https://www .youtube.com/watch?v=D2xU1O18ZnY.

McGonigal, K. 2011, November 27. "How Mindfulness Makes the Brain Immune to Temptation: Paying Attention to Cravings Takes Away Their Power." Psychology Today. www.psychologytoday.com/us/blog/the-science-willpower/201111 /how-mindfulness -makes-the-brain-immune-temptation.

McGonigal, K. 2012. *The Neuroscience of Change: A Compassion-based Program for Personal Transformation*. Audiobook. Louisville, CO: Sounds True.

———. 2013. *The Willpower Instinct: How Self-Control Works, Why It Matters and What you Can Do to Get More of It*. New York: Avery.

Moses, K. 2015. "Grief Groups: Rekindling Hope." The Journal of the American Academy of Psychotherapists 51, no. 2: 83-89.

Neff, K. (n.d.). The Self-Compassion Break. https://self-compassion.org/wp-content /uploads/2020/08/self-compassion.break__01-cleanedbydan.mp3.

Nerenberg, A. 2002. "The Value of Group Psychotherapy for Sexual Addicts." In *Clinical Management of Sex Addiction*. Edited by P. J. Carnes and K. M. Adams, 183–98. New York: Brunner-Routledge.

Riemersma, J. 2020. *Altogether You: Experiencing Personal and Spiritual Transformation with Internal Family Systems Therapy*. Marietta, GA: Pivotal Press.

Rohr, R. 2016. "Wounded Healers." Adapted from *A Spring within Us: A Book of Daily Meditations*. Sheridan, WY: CAC Publishing, 123. https://cac.org/wounded-healers -2018-10-26/.

SaaviAccountability. 2010, September 27. "Intimacy Disorder and Sexual Addiction." YouTube. www.youtube.com/watch?v=KeXfs2A84Hs&t=137s.

Schwartz, D. (2018). *Greater Than the Sum of Our Parts*. Audiobook. Louisville, CO: Sounds True.

Sexaholics Anonymous. (n.d.). "First Step Written Guide." PDF. www.saiecv.org/documents /1st%20Step%20Guide.pdf.

Sprout, S. 2015. *Naked in Public: A Memoir of Recovery from Sex Addiction and Other Temporary Insanities*. Seattle: Recontext Media.

Talks at Google. 2012, February 1. "The Willpower Instinct: Kelly McGonigal." YouTube. www.youtube.com/watch?v=V5BXuZL1HAg&t=1s.

Thompson, C. 2010. *Anatomy of the Soul: Surprising Connections between Neuroscience and Spiritual Practices That Can Transform Your Life and Relationships*. Carol Stream, IL: Tyndale.

Wagner, B., A. B. Horn, and A. Maercker. 2013. "Internet-based versus Face-to-Face Cognitive-Behavioral Intervention for Depression: A Randomized Controlled Non-inferiority Trial." Journal of Affective Disorders 152–54: 113–21.

Webb, J. 2012. *Running on Empty: Overcome Your Childhood Emotional Neglect*. New York: Morgan James.

Weiss, R., and M. Ferree. 2018. *Out of the Doghouse for Christian Men: A Redemptive Guide for Men Caught Cheating*. Palm Springs, CA: Three iii Publishing.

Yalom, I. D. 1995. *The Theory and Practice of Group Psychotherapy*. 4th ed. New York: Basic Books.

CHAPTER 10

UNDERSTANDING AND ADDRESSING BETRAYAL TRAUMA

Dr. Kevin B. Skinner, LMFT, CSAT

I can't concentrate on anything," Lisa said during our intake therapy session. For the past six months, she reported that she could not think of much else besides the affair of her husband, Tom. To make matters worse, during the past few months, Tom had revealed that it was not just one affair. He admitted to having three other affairs during their twelve-year marriage.

Since these surprising disclosures, Lisa had been reviewing the past twelve years of their marriage over and over in her mind. She was trying to make sense of her world but couldn't. It was like putting a puzzle together without all the pieces. She began barraging Tom with questions about where, when, and with whom he had these affairs. In the beginning, he answered many of her questions, but eventually he got tired of her relentless questioning. He told her he would never do it again, but that did not help her.

She had not been sleeping well. She was angrier than she could ever remember and had outbursts that surprised even her at times. She was monitoring Tom's behaviors like a hawk. She had obsessive thoughts about what he had done, and it was consuming her life. She finally decided to reach out for professional help.

Before we met, I had Lisa complete a battery of online assessments. These assessments help me understand more about my clients and their responses to sexual betrayal. By having Lisa complete the assessments, I knew her level of depression, anxiety, and stress. In addition, she completed the Trauma Inventory for Partners of Sex Addicts (TIPSA), which is designed to evaluate

201

clients for posttraumatic stress disorder (PTSD) brought on by a partner's sexual betrayal. When she came in, she said, "That assessment you gave me described a lot of things I have been feeling over the past few months. Do you think I have PTSD?"

<h2 style="text-align:center">RECOGNIZING TRAUMA FROM
SEXUAL BETRAYAL</h2>

I began by letting her know that over the past few years, researchers have found that PTSD is common after discovering sexual betrayal. When I told Lisa this and reviewed her scores with her, she was surprised. Before taking the assessments, she had simply thought that she was losing her mind.

"So what did my results tell you about me?" Lisa wanted to know.

I told her that before I gave her the results, I needed to explain PTSD and the five core ways it manifests itself. The five criteria are as follows:

Criterion A: Threat to Life

While most people do not consider an affair to be a threat to life, many do fear getting an STD or have actually received an STD from their partner. I learned that Lisa had considered being tested for an STD, but she hadn't been to the doctor yet. I told her that when I first started administering the TIPSA to my clients and others, I didn't anticipate that many would qualify for Criterion A: Threat to Life. However, to my surprise, 60% of individuals who have experienced sexual betrayal report that they are worried about getting an STD from their partner after discovery.

Under Criterion A, there are other questions that involve potential for abuse or physical harm. Specifically, this criterion for PTSD involves exposure to death, threatened death, actual or threatened serious injury or actual or threatened sexual violence via direct exposure, witnessing the trauma, learning that a close loved one was exposed to a trauma, or indirect, vicarious exposure to the trauma, which can include pastors and therapists. Lisa did not report experiencing any form of abuse on her assessment or in our discussion.

Criterion B: Reliving the Event

The next area, I explained, is one of the most common ways people respond to sexual betrayal. Symptoms include nightmares, flashbacks, and triggers that remind you of what happened. When I listed off those symptoms, Lisa said, "I have them all." Her affirmation validated the test results, which showed she was experiencing elevated symptoms in this area.

Criterion C: Avoidance

After discovery, many individuals report that they do not know whom to trust. As a result, it is common for them to avoid people and places they used to enjoy. They begin to feel lonely and isolated and report feeling like nobody understands them or that they are afraid of being judged by others. When I talked about this with Lisa, she said, "The past six months, I have had a hard time going to church. I feel like everyone is watching me." We discussed events she was avoiding and the places she used to enjoy visiting, but they were too triggering to her. Then we talked about some of the people she was avoiding. She said, "I'm not talking with my family as much. I don't want them to know what Tom did and judge him. I feel like there is no one I can talk to." I suggested to Lisa that this was a common response that we would need to address soon because isolation prevents healing and, in many cases, makes things much worse.

I then followed up on a question from the assessment that read, "How often do you attempt to push away memories, thoughts, or feelings related to your partner's sexual behaviors?" She said, "I try to push away the memories, but they keep coming back. It doesn't matter how hard I try to get rid of the thoughts, I can't get my mind to stop thinking about them." After discovering how much she was avoiding her own thoughts, I said, "The issue of avoidance is something that we will want to focus on in your healing." To this she said, "Please help me stop thinking about these things. I can't keep doing this."

Criterion D: Mood and Negative Cognitions

The fourth symptom of PTSD manifests in experiences with depression, feeling unsafe in society (e.g., believing, "The world is completely dangerous"), and feeling like what happened is your fault (e.g., thinking, "I am bad" or "I am to blame"). Those who qualify for this criterion also report negative emotional states like fear, anger, and shame. In addition, they report little interest in participating in activities they used to enjoy.

After I described these symptoms to Lisa, she said, "I just thought there was something wrong with me. I haven't felt like doing things I used to do, and I have questioned whether the world is a safe place anymore. I have lost my trust in almost everyone." It was relieving for her to know these are common symptoms.

Criterion E: Arousal and Emotional Reactivity

The fifth criterion associated with PTSD is usually manifest through a racing mind. The racing mind usually wears individuals down and can contribute to outbursts of anger, difficulty concentrating, a need to monitor a partner's behaviors called hypervigilance, poor sleeping patterns, and self-destructive behaviors.

As I outlined these symptoms, Lisa confirmed, "I haven't been sleeping, I am constantly monitoring Tom's behaviors, and over the past six months, I have lost my car keys on more occasions than I would like to admit."

Once we finished this conversation, I showed Lisa her test results, which you can see below in Chart 1. Based on these results, she was experiencing significantly elevated trauma for Criteria B, D, and E. Criterion C was also significant, as she scored in the mid-high range. Finally, while she reported the lowest scores on Criterion A, her response was still significant because she reported that she worried about contracting an STD. Clearly, Lisa was experiencing many symptoms associated with PTSD. Seeing her results validated what she had been going through and helped her realize that it wasn't just in her mind. Based on her results and areas where she scored highest, we developed her treatment plan.

Chart 10.1: TIPSA Results

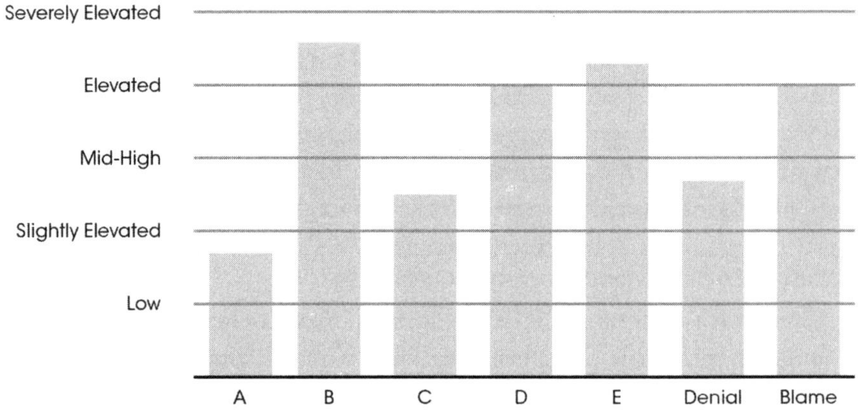

WHY PTSD?

After reviewing the symptoms associated with PTSD and showing her the results, Lisa said, "Why am I responding this way? What's wrong with me?"

To this I responded, "There's nothing wrong with you. You're responding the way 70 to 80% of people do after discovering sexual betrayal in their relationship." She was surprised at how many others were experiencing the same symptoms as she.

Why do so many people experience PTSD symptoms after discovery of sexual betrayal? One answer comes from the work of Stephen Porges, who found that when we choose to socially bond or connect with others, we have to first determine two things. He wrote, "What allows engagement behaviors to occur, while disabling the mechanisms of defense? To switch effectively from defensive to social engagement strategies, the nervous system must do two things: (1) assess risk, and (2) if the environment looks safe, inhibit the primitive defensive reactions to fight, flee, or freeze" (Porges 2011, 12). In other words, when we connect with others, we first assess whether they are safe, and if we determine they are, then and only then do we override our natural defense responses and socially bond.

Based on this information, imagine what happens in a committed relationship when one spouse believes their partner is one way (e.g., faithful and committed to them) and then discovers that they are not. Using Porges's model, we would expect that their nervous system would re-evaluate for risks (e.g., "Am I safe with you?" or "Are you who I thought you were?") and then determine whether they should protect themselves or re-attempt to connect. Based on my research, a majority feel compelled to protect themselves by fighting, fleeing, or freezing.

After discovering a partner's sexual betrayal, many people begin to question themselves, others, and society. Many people have told me they feel stupid for not knowing what was happening. Others report having more intense emotions, such as high anxiety. For example, one client told me her angry outbursts were so strong that she was surprised. She had never felt so much rage. These new thoughts, emotions, and behaviors often make betrayed individuals question themselves, asking, "Who am I?"

In social situations with family and friends, many report feeling confused. They wonder if they should share what is happening or if they should keep things to themselves to avoid embarrassment. It has been my experience that many people are afraid to open up about what is happening in their relationships because they don't want to be judged.

Some individuals do reach out but receive feedback that adds to their pain. One person's husband was looking at pornography, lusting after other women in public when she was present, and engaging in other sexual fetishes. She said, "I asked my mother her opinion on what I should do. She told me I was overreacting." When a person's social support reacts differently from how they react, they often question themselves by asking questions like, "What is wrong with me?"

When social support falters, individuals turn silent and pull back not only from close friends and family, but from all of society. They frequently stop attending activities or events in which they used to participate. When they attend activities, their family and friends can tell something is wrong, but they brush off the questions. They may use excuses like, "We've been so busy," or "I haven't been feeling well." The inability to be open then creates two worlds for the individual: what is really happening inside is opposed to the image they give to others. This dual identity creates internal stress.

When we can't be open and honest with the people closest to us, we are prone to becoming depressed and anxious. Our fears and worries grow while isolation increases. Then it is natural to fear others and worry about how they perceive you. There are many other challenges associated with betrayal, such as sleep problems, inability to concentrate, and poor functioning in important tasks (e.g., work, parenting). Attempting to hide internal pain is torture.

The consequence of social isolation and/or hiding what is really happening often triggers individuals to question themselves. They think things like, *Maybe I'm not who I thought I was*, or *I thought I was a good spouse. Now I wonder if I was ever enough for him/her?* Sometimes they even question their parenting: *I thought I was a good mom, but now I am angry and upset all the time when I am around my kids.* In essence, they question every aspect of how they see themselves. Their identity is being lost.

After I explained all of this to Lisa, she said, "I had no idea. I thought it was just me. It is relieving to know that what I have been experiencing has a name and that others respond just like me. So what do I do about it?"

TREATING THE SYMPTOMS OF PTSD

My response to Lisa and to the many others I have worked with who are dealing with sexual betrayal is this: If PTSD is the accurate diagnosis for individuals experiencing sexual betrayal, then the proper treatment should be a PTSD treatment—help those suffering reduce and, if possible, eliminate their PTSD symptoms.

Giving a client the diagnosis of PTSD is not something I take lightly as a clinician because it has historically been tied to war veterans who have witnessed and experienced horrendous things. However, based on my findings and along with other professional researchers who have studied how people respond to sexual betrayal, it is clear that PTSD is an accurate diagnosis in many cases.

In 2002, the founder of Emotionally Focused Therapy, Susan Johnson indicated that relational trauma between partners may exhibit the classic symptoms characteristic of PTSD, such as re-experiencing numbness, and hypervigilance (Johnson 2002). Then in 2006, the first study of betrayed partners assessing for PTSD found that around 70% of those surveyed would qualify for PTSD. In their research, Steffens and Rennie discovered that a majority of women will experience significant trauma-related distress with discovery or disclosure of their sexually addicted spouse's behavior (Steffens & Rennie, 2006). In my own research with more than 5,000 participants, I discovered that perhaps up to 80% of individuals experiencing sexual betrayal manifest many of these symptoms.

Based on these findings, it is critical that professional therapists treat betrayed spouses using a trauma model. Historically, when working with partners of addicts, clinicians have used a codependency model. However, given the growing body of evidence that sexually betrayed spouses are experiencing PTSD, a trauma-based treatment model is essential for long-term healing.

UNDERSTANDING THE DEPTH OF TRAUMA

Treating trauma from sexual betrayal is not easy and is often complicated by the fact that many individuals who are experiencing current relationship betrayal have also had other traumatic life experiences. As a result, it is important for betrayed individuals and those who help them to understand that other life traumas may be adding to their current level of trauma. This is what professional researchers and clinicians refer to as complex trauma.

There are multiple ways that trauma can occur. For example, Terr distinguished between Type I, single-incident trauma (i.e., an event that is "out of the blue" and thus unexpected, such as witnessing violence, a traumatic accident or a natural disaster, a terrorist attack, or a single episode of abuse or assault), and Type II, complex or repetitive trauma (e.g., ongoing abuse, domestic violence, community violence, war, or genocide) (Terr 1991). Type II trauma is more prevalent than typically recognized, affecting as many as one in seven to one in ten children; more often occurs in combination or cumulatively (i.e., "polyvictimization") (Finkelhor, Ormrod, and Turner 2007); and usually involves a fundamental betrayal of trust in primary relationships because it is often perpetrated by someone known by or related to the victim (Courtois 2000). Finally, Type II trauma is associated with a much higher risk for the development of PTSD than is Type I trauma (e.g., 33–75+% risk vs. 10–20%) (Copeland, Keeler, Angold, and Costello 1999).

In one case that illustrates Type II trauma, I had a client report that she couldn't make sense of why she was so upset at her husband's use of pornography. She said, "I don't like it when he views it, but even with him trying to stop, I still yell at him and criticize him all the time." As we explored other relationships in her life, she revealed that her mother had left her father for another man. As we discussed her emotions, she reported feeling a fear of being abandoned. Upon gaining this insight, she had an "aha" moment when she realized that what she was feeling with her husband's porn use was similar to how she felt as a girl when she discovered her mom's behaviors.

She realized that her mom's sexual betrayal of her dad triggered fears of abandonment in her, and then after discovering her husband's hidden use of pornography, she was having strong feelings that he was going to abandon her too. While this awareness didn't change how she felt about him viewing pornography—she didn't like it at all—it allowed her to look more accurately at her husband's use of pornography. She realized he wasn't acting like her mother when she left. In fact, he was quite the opposite in that he felt bad that it hurt her, and he was seeking treatment to stop his behaviors.

EARLY CHILDHOOD TRAUMA

Over the years, many people have asked me how early childhood trauma influences an individual's response to sexual betrayal. To respond to their questions, I began researching this topic in 2016. What I discovered is that individuals who have experienced significant traumatic experiences in their childhoods (meaning a 4 or more on the adverse childhood experiences [ACE] scale) have elevated symptoms of PTSD after discovery of sexual betrayal. However, more than 60% of individuals whose ACE score was less than 3 still reported having symptoms of PTSD. This preliminary research suggests that regardless of the number of adverse childhood experiences someone has experienced, most are still experiencing PTSD symptoms from sexual betrayal (Unpublished Research, Skinner 2018). Now let's turn our attention to solutions for treating betrayal trauma.

TREATING TRAUMA FROM SEXUAL BETRAYAL

Early in my work with Lisa, we frequently reviewed her results from her assessment, as it was our guide to what areas we needed to focus on in her healing. The rest of this chapter will provide ideas that I used with Lisa and many others as we focused on treating PTSD.

Treatment for Criterion A: Threat to Life

In review, Criterion A focuses on issues related to being exposed to something: death, threatened death, actual or threatened serious injury, or actual or threatened sexual violence. In Lisa's case, she periodically feared that she could get an STD from her husband and reported that she felt violated in her relationship with her husband. She worried that his affairs could have been with people who had STDs.

This was a difficult subject for her to discuss, but as she opened up about her concerns, it became apparent that it would be important in her healing. As we discussed her fears, she decided she would be proactive and get tested. She said, "At least I will know, rather than fear the unknown." Initially she was hesitant to take this step because she feared being judged by the doctor and nurse for simply asking. She ultimately decided her life was more important to her than worrying about their opinions.

The next challenge was to create boundaries that would help her feel safe with her husband. Since the disclosure by Tom, Lisa had tried to forgive him, but she was finding it more difficult than she anticipated. He seemed ready to move on and had repeatedly asked for her forgiveness. While Lisa too wanted to move on, she still had concerns about some of his behaviors, especially related to their sexual relationship. He wanted to re-engage sexually, but she wasn't ready. This was partially due to her worries about getting an STD and partially due to her worry that he was still lying to her.

Because of her concerns, she decided to create a few boundaries around their sexual interactions. First, she decided she would ask him to also be tested for an STD. She emphasized to him that this was important for her to feel safe being sexual with him again. Second, she asked him if he would be willing to take a polygraph test. She had read online about others who had been sexually betrayed and had heard how a polygraph brought more assurance that what they were being told was validated. She was afraid he was not telling her the truth about his current behaviors and that there was more that he had not revealed. A third boundary she established wasn't related to their sexual relationship but to the ways that he had sexually betrayed her over the years: She asked him to do a more formal disclosure with their therapists.

It is important to note that these were Lisa's boundaries. They are what she felt she needed to feel safe in their relationship and were the beginning steps to helping their relationship heal. It may be helpful to note some of the other boundaries she considered. She thought about asking for a separation but in the end decided that was not what she wanted. She also considered having him tell his family about his affairs but decided to let him make that decision. Other boundaries she considered included having him attend a twelve-step group, get a sponsor, and do weekly counseling. But she didn't want to force him into recovery and decided she would wait and see how he approached his recovery. After identifying her three boundaries, she told me that for the first time in a while she felt more in control of herself.

The next, and perhaps most difficult, part for her was to discuss these boundaries with her husband. We role-played what she was going to say and how she would say it. She needed to practice what to say and how to say it because throughout their marriage she had avoided conflict as much as possible. She began realizing that was a problem.

Initially, Tom was hesitant to do what she wanted. He too was embarrassed to be tested for an STD, but he realized Lisa was firm in her boundaries. The polygraph was something he absolutely did not want to do, but again she held her ground. Her third request of doing a full disclosure was something he was willing to do, but he didn't know how to go about the process. Lisa and I had discussed the process and how a therapist could prepare him to do that.

While these boundaries ended up working for Lisa, it is important to note that not all spouses respond like Tom did. He was consistent in saying he wanted their marriage and that he would do whatever it took to keep it. This enabled Lisa to be bolder than she had been in their entire marriage. I have met with individuals whose spouses were unwilling to seek help. In cases like that, establishing boundaries is still important, but the outcome may be separation and possibly divorce.

Treatment for Criterion B: Reliving the Event

The next area of focus for Lisa was related to the intrusive memories and involuntary thoughts that came to her mind. As we reviewed this section of her assessment results, the symptoms were higher than any of the other categories. She reported having the following symptoms:

- Painful memories related to the sexual betrayal (*always*)
- Disturbing dreams associated with affairs (*more often than not*)
- Physically ill or nauseous when thinking about the affairs (*more often than not*)
- Reliving the event in her mind (*more often than not*)
- Difficulty thinking about anything else besides the sexual betrayal (*always*)

Since these symptoms were so frequent and disturbing for Lisa, the focus of the next few sessions was to provide her with ideas on how to respond to them. The process of reducing the frequency of intrusive memories is not simple because they often come without individuals recognizing their frequency. By increasing awareness of their presence and then providing ideas on how to respond when they do come, clients begin making steps toward healing. When individuals learn how to respond to these symptoms, they generally feel better because they understand what is happening to them. Knowing how to respond is a part of the healing process.

I began by having Lisa talk me through the intrusive dreams she was having. She described a vivid dream of seeing Tom with another woman. She didn't have an exact image of the woman, but she reported waking up feeling physically anxious and with a sick feeling in her stomach each time the dream occurred.

To help her respond to her dreams, we tried a couple of things. The first thing we did was focus on the disclosure process with Tom. Disclosures often help the betrayed partner make more sense of what happened, when things were happening, and with whom their spouse was acting out. There are times when the disclosure process alone seems to reduce or eliminate the nightmares.

Additional ideas that I gave to Lisa with her recurring memories and the physical way her body was responding to Tom's affairs included the following:

- **Mindfulness.** This approach helps individuals pay closer attention to their thoughts as they come. Often by paying attention in a nonjudgmental way, the individual can see what is happening to their thoughts, emotions, and physical sensations and simply be with them rather than feel threatened by them. This process helps individuals remain aware as they are going through the triggering process.
- **Identifying the core self-belief associated with the memories** (e.g., I must not be enough). The process of identifying the beliefs an individual forms about themselves as a result of the sexual betrayal is an important component of healing and has been helpful in reducing powerful triggers.
- **Understanding how past memories of betrayal and hurt may be influencing current memories.** In some cases, current triggers from sexual betrayal are linked with previous memories (e.g., one parent cheating, being cheated on in other relationships).

In our work together, Lisa was able to significantly reduce her nightmares and the intrusive memories she had during the day by doing the things listed above. Perhaps the most important event for Lisa was Tom's disclosure. That seemed to be a turning point for her because she finally felt that Tom was being honest with her.

Treatment for Criterion C: Avoidance

Another area we worked on was Lisa's avoidance of stimuli that would remind her of Tom's behaviors. She reported that when triggers came reminding her of what Tom had done, she tried to push the thoughts out of her mind as quickly as possible. She found that she was avoiding any situation that would remind her of what Tom had done. She found that she had a hard time being in public because other women felt threatening to her, especially when she was with Tom.

She found that malls and shopping centers were triggers for her. She couldn't stand swimming pools or locations where people would be dressed in swimming apparel. Her triggers, however, were not limited to public places. She began avoiding her friends' invitations to do things together. This was confusing for her because she loved her friends, but she started feeling overwhelmed by their "perfect" lives. She reported that her life was falling apart while everyone else seemed to have things together and their husbands were being faithful to them.

The past few months had dramatically altered her life. In Lisa's assessment results, she reported the following symptoms that are associated with Criterion C:

- Pushing away memories, thoughts, or feelings related to Tom's behaviors (*more often than not*)
- Finding it difficult to participate in things that she previously enjoyed (*more often than not*)
- Avoiding people, places, or activities that reminded her of Tom's behaviors (*always*)

These symptoms were preventing her from doing things she previously enjoyed. When she began avoiding friends she used to enjoy being with, she felt guilty. They hadn't done anything to her, but she couldn't hide her pain from them, and she was too afraid to tell them because she didn't want them to judge Tom. She was afraid she couldn't hide her pain and hurt from them, which would prevent her from being her "real" self with them.

In my experience, this form of isolation adds to an individual's trauma. Since discovery, Lisa had been overwhelmed by her own pain, but it was made worse because she hadn't felt comfortable sharing what had happened with anyone. Her fears had spread from not trusting Tom to not knowing if she could trust anyone. This generalization is common in my research. I found that over 95% of those who completed my survey reported that they at least "sometimes" found it hard to trust anyone after discovering their partner's sexual betrayal. (See Chart 10.2 below.)

Chart 10.2: Trust After Sexual Betrayal

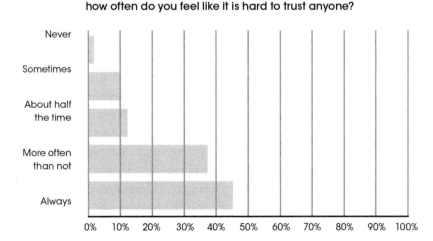

Lisa was surprised that so many people were experiencing the same symptoms she was. "Strangely," she said, "this brings me a little more comfort knowing others feel this way too." Then she wisely asked, "What can I do to overcome this? I miss my friends, and I can't live my life avoiding everything." We began discussing alternative options that would help her overcome isolation but not put her at risk of being too vulnerable with people who wouldn't understand.

My first suggestion for Lisa was to join a group of women who were experiencing these same symptoms. I explained to her that a group is designed to help her give voice to the pain she was feeling with others who would understand her hurts and pains. Initially, she was hesitant to participate in a group like this because of the unknown. I reassured her that these groups were designed to provide emotional support in nonjudgmental ways.

The group she joined was perfect for her. There were six other women in the group, and over the next few months, Lisa developed relationships with these women. They began meeting outside of the group for lunch dates. When one of them was struggling, they could reach out for support.

On one occasion, Lisa was having an especially hard day, so she called Rachel, one of her new friends from the group. Lisa had been triggered by Tom when he had forgotten to turn his phone back on after a business meeting and had not returned her phone call. She was ready to "rip his head off," she explained to Rachel. Fortunately, instead of attacking Tom like she had been doing over the past few months, she called Rachel. Rachel asked her to take a few breaths and explain what had happened. As Lisa shared the story, Rachel listened carefully and then gave her some solid advice. She said, "Lisa, it makes a lot of sense that this has triggered you. I get it. I have been there with my husband too. I want you to use the 'zoom in, zoom out' idea we have been discussing in group."

Rachel asked her to zoom in on her own pain instead of focusing on Tom's behaviors. As she continued zooming in, she reported that she felt like Tom didn't love her anymore, otherwise he would have remembered to check his phone. Because of his lies over the years, how would she know he wasn't lying again? She said, "I am just so angry that he cheated on me. I don't feel like I am loveable anymore." She began crying, and Rachel gently listened and validated the pain. Then she said, "Lisa, I know you may not feel loveable to Tom, but I want you to know you are an amazing woman. I am so glad you are a part of my life." This loving kindness did it for Lisa. She felt loved in her pain. It was one of the first times she felt like someone genuinely cared about her. Lisa would report to me that this was a major turning point for her healing.

A few minutes later in the conversation, Lisa said, "I guess I have to try to zoom out now." Zooming out is the process of identifying what the other person may have been feeling or thinking. As she zoomed out, she thought it was possible that Tom really did forget to turn his phone back on. After all, he had called as soon as he realized it had been off. She had left him a voicemail and a few text messages, but he hadn't been defensive like he had been before. He had listened to her fears and said, "I am sorry. I really did forget."

As Lisa zoomed out, she also identified that Tom had been working on his own recovery. He had been going to meetings, he had a sponsor, and he was talking with his own counselor. In addition, he had given her a full disclosure of his behaviors over the years and had listened to her share how his behavior had hurt her. She realized he was trying. In this process of zooming in and zooming out, Lisa gained a deeper insight into herself and Tom. Rachel had simply reminded her of this tool, because in the moment of being overwhelmed, Lisa hadn't been able to do it on her own.

There is great power in having a support team around you in the healing process. Lisa and Rachel's interaction is just one example of the power of social support in recovery. Over the years, I have seen additional support come from family, friends, religious leaders, and support coworkers. One of the most important parts of finding meaningful support is to determine who is safe and who is not safe to share this personal information with. Sometimes this takes time and effort. Over the years, I have found that some people who my clients think will be supportive actually aren't able to provide the emotional support they need. Others who people thought wouldn't understand rise up and provide the best support to those experiencing betrayal.

Here are a couple of things I have found to be true of effective supporters:

1. They listen more than they give advice.
2. They don't push their agenda; instead they help you talk through your thoughts and emotions and come to your own conclusions.
3. They don't judge.
4. They can listen to your deepest of pains and still be available. In other words, your emotions do not overwhelm them.
5. They are not overly critical of your spouse. This is important to many of my clients. Many report that they sometimes feel like they have to defend their choice to stay in the relationship.
6. They make you feel like you are loved even when they see you in your darkest moments (e.g., in your anger and rage).

As Lisa developed her support team, she found that she was feeling better about herself and others. This pulled her out of her isolation. That in turn helped her find her voice to express her hurts and pains. The end result was that Lisa no longer felt like she couldn't trust others. In fact, she found that in sharing what she was going through with the right people, she developed new friendships and deepened others.

Treatment for Criterion D: Mood and Negative Cognitions

One of the common negative outcomes of betrayal trauma is the internalized thoughts that are felt after the discovery experience. It is normal for betrayal to trigger thoughts like Lisa shared with Rachel when she said, "I feel like I'm unlovable." These negative self-beliefs trigger a cascade of self-talk that, if not corrected, can lead to years of unhealthy thoughts.

As I looked over Lisa's answers to the questions in this category, I found the following responses:

- Do you feel like your partner acts out because you are not good enough? (*always*)
- Do you feel like you are a bad person because of what your partner did? (*always*)
- How often do you feel like you are different than everyone else due to your partner's sexual behaviors? (*always*)
- How often do you feel like you are stupid for not discovering your partner's behaviors earlier than you did? (*always*)
- Since discovering your partner's behaviors how often do you feel unlovable? (*always*)

Clearly, when Lisa took this assessment, she had a significant number of negative thoughts about herself and how she fit into society. When clients are experiencing these types of thoughts and emotions, I often spend time helping them identify when the thoughts and memories that accompany them first started. In some cases, they are new thoughts that come from betrayal, but in other cases, they have been part of their lives for many years.

In Lisa's case, she had fought against feelings of not being good enough since she was a teenager. In our work together, she shared an experience when her friends made her feel like she was too rigid with her sexuality. They encouraged her to loosen up a little bit because the guys wouldn't like her if she was too straight. This experience began a long self-worth battle inside of her. She wanted friends, but those friends made her feel like there was something wrong with her because of her moral values. Eventually, she pulled away from those friends, but this experience left a mark on her. She reported that that experience with her friends was one of the first times she remembered feeling like she wasn't enough.

When I observe clients whose negative thoughts are as consistent as Lisa's, I know that if they are going to heal, we will need to address those thoughts and help alter them. Fortunately, those disturbing memories and experiences can be worked through with treatments such as Eye Movement Desensitization and Reprocessing (EMDR), Cognitive Behavioral Therapy (CBT), and mindfulness-based approaches.

In Lisa's case, she responded well to EMDR. This treatment specialization has helped millions of clients desensitize painful memories and reprocess them. As they are reprocessed, the negative thoughts change. In Lisa's case, she had a few other negative memories from her social interactions that she had acquired over the years regarding relationships with others, but that first memory with her friends was still the most disturbing to her. She had felt inadequate in social settings and around other women because of her experiences.

After completing a few sessions of EMDR, her self-perception altered, and she no longer felt like she was unlovable. In fact, she remembered that she had some friends from junior high who made her feel special. By helping her address her negative self-beliefs, she began making good progress. This treatment approach was especially valuable because, as her beliefs were changing, she started to gain more trusting relationships in her therapy group and with other developing friendships. Her beliefs of not being lovable and not fitting in socially were rapidly changing.

For a more in-depth discussion of how EMDR can help in treatment trauma, I recommend Francine Shapiro's book *Getting Past Your Past*, and for individuals who have more complex trauma, I suggest Bessel van der Kolk's book *The Body Keeps the Score*.

Treatment for Criterion E: Arousal and Emotional Reactivity

As Lisa continued to make progress, she reported that she still struggled with some of her emotions. She reported that throughout the past few months, she had been angrier than she could ever remember. I reviewed her scores on Criterion E with her. Of the five categories for diagnosing PTSD, her scores were severely elevated on Alterations in Arousal and Reactivity.

As we reviewed her responses, here's how she answered:

- How often do you struggle with sleep since discovering your partner's behaviors? (*more often than not*)
- To what extent do you feel emotionally on edge since discovering your partner's behaviors? (*always*)

- How often do you find that you are critical of your partner since discovering his/her sexual behaviors? (*always*)
- How often do you monitor your partner's behaviors since discovery? (*always*)
- Since discovering your partner's sexual behaviors how often have you had suicidal thoughts? (*about half the time*)

Lisa's answers to these questions, especially the final one about suicidal thoughts, were important for me to understand. Early in the treatment process, we addressed those thoughts, and she told me she wasn't suicidal but had had thoughts about it since discovery. As we talked about suicidal thoughts, I shared with her that roughly six out of every ten people experiencing betrayal have those thoughts. She was surprised that even in this area, what she felt was common. We created a safety plan to help her work through times when she was in so much pain. (Please note: If you are feeling suicidal, please reach out for support and help. Your feelings are normal, and people can help.)

One thing that stands out in this category is how much those dealing with arousal and emotional reactivity report that their mind is racing. It is as if their mind is stuck in fight or flight mode. The manifestation of arousal and reactivity is often anger, difficulty sleeping, intense focus on a partner's behaviors (e.g., tracking them via their phone, looking at phone messages and emails). When the mind is stuck in fear mode, it doesn't get a break. As a result, one of the key areas of focus from the beginning of therapy was to provide Lisa with ideas on how to regulate these difficult and overwhelming emotions.

Some of the best solutions for a racing mind include the following:

- **Mindfulness.** This treatment strategy has been proven to provide a greater sense of personal awareness. The insight it provides can help individuals regulate anxiety, fears, and anger (Wright, Day, and Howells 2009).
- **Trauma centered yoga.** People who practice yoga begin to experiment with changing the way they feel. Bessel van der Kolk suggests that "simply noticing what you feel fosters emotional regulation, and it helps you stop trying to ignore what is going on inside you" (van der Kolk 2014, 275).
- **Getting to the root beliefs (e.g., I am unlovable) and reprocessing them.** This process is incorporated into the EMDR protocol. One of the first steps of EMDR is to help clients find a safe/calm place to help them deal with difficult and painful memories as they work through painful or traumatic memories.

As I shared the importance of learning how to regulate these difficult emotions, I did a simple breathing exercise with Lisa to help her experience what it is like to pay closer attention to your breathing and body sensations. As we talked through this process and how it could help during the day and with her sleeping patterns at night, she realized how out of touch she had been with her body. We enrolled her in our yoga course. A few weeks into her yoga class, I observed that Lisa was calmer and more relaxed in our sessions. She reported that she had felt better progress with anger, and her monitoring of Tom's behaviors had nearly stopped.

Next, we continued working on her negative self-beliefs by using EMDR. In one of our more powerful sessions, she worked through her first experience with her friends and realized her true worth and value. This was an "aha" moment for her because she had formed the negative belief as a teenager. Since then, she had simply become used to feeling like something was wrong with her. That change provided additional strength to her when she was confronted with difficult emotions that had controlled her in the past.

CONCLUSION

As I have taken you through Lisa's journey, it may seem overly simplistic. However, what I haven't described in this write-up are the difficult sessions filled with tears and heartbreak, the painful yet healing process of doing a full disclosure with Tom, and the consistent effort Lisa put into her own recovery (e.g., yoga, participating in group therapy, and regular counseling). In addition, she learned to reach out for support, she dealt with the early negative beliefs she had formed about herself, and she and Tom did a significant amount of marital work to address unhealthy patterns they had developed over the years of their marriage.

The steps outlined in this chapter have focused on treating the symptoms associated with PTSD because I have found that this is the most effective way to help those who are suffering from betrayal trauma. Treating trauma from sexual betrayal is not easy. However, over my years of clinical work, I have observed many individuals reclaim their identities and live fuller and more complete lives. Some have done so with their spouses, and others have had to move on. Regardless of the outcome in the relationship, I have discovered that healing is possible.

REFERENCES

Copeland, W., G. Keeler, A. Angold, and E. J. Costello. 2007. "Traumatic Events and Posttraumatic Stress in Childhood." *Archives of General Psychiatry* 64: 577–584.

Courtois, C. 2000. "The Sexual After-effects of Incest/Child Sexual Abuse." *SIECUS Report; New York* 29, no 1: 11–16.

Finkelhor, D., R. Ormrod, and H. Turner. 2007. "Poly-victimization: A Neglected Component in Child Victimization." *Child Abuse and Neglect* 31, no. 1: 7–26.

Johnson, S. 2002. *Emotionally Focused Couple Therapy with Trauma Survivors*. New York: Guilford.

Steffens, B A., and R. L. Rennie. 2006. "The Traumatic Nature of Disclosure for Wives of Sexual Addicts." *Sexual Addiction and Compulsivity* 1, no. 2–3: 247–67.

Porges, S. W. 2011. *The Polyvagal Theory: Neurophysiological Foundations of Emotions, Attachment, Communication, and Self-Regulation*. Norton Series on Interpersonal Neurobiology. New York: W. W. Norton & Company.

Terr, L. 1991. "Childhood Traumas." *American Journal of Psychiatry* 148: 10–20.

Wright, S., A. Day, and K. Howells. 2009. "Mindfulness and the Treatment of Anger Problems." *Aggression and Violent Behavior* 14 no. 5: 396–401.

van der Kolk, B. A. 2014. *The Body Keeps the Score: Brain, Mind, and Body in the Healing of Trauma*. New York: Penguin Group.

CHAPTER 11

FROM TRAUMA TO TRANSFORMATION:

Posttraumatic Growth for Women Who Have Been Relationally Betrayed

By Debbie Laaser, M.A., LMFT

I was home with a friend and our children when my husband and two of his colleagues came home unannounced. Someone in that group said they needed to talk to me. The air was heavy and unwelcoming. I knew something was wrong. We proceeded silently to the living room and awkwardly took our seats. My friend quickly left with our little ones. And then in only a few minutes, the Christian doctor and therapist with whom my husband worked informed me that they found evidence that he was a sexual pervert and that he was being fired from his position in their clinic. They asked if I had any questions.

I was probably already in shock because I had a million questions. But I said no and asked them to leave. Alone in that moment and looking across at Mark in his chair, I saw a broken man. I was led by something greater than myself, I believe, to go to him and say something like, "I don't know what is happening, but I want to get help." Today I know that the Holy Spirit led me over to Mark to say those things. I believe God may have planted the seeds for writing about posttraumatic growth long ago. I was beginning to live my chapter on trauma. Would there be one about growth?

I was thirty-seven and stayed at home with our three little children, ages ten, seven, and four. As my husband and I now say, the world as I knew it "crashed and burned." It was the most traumatic experience of my life to date. This new information absolutely shattered my beliefs about myself, Mark, and our future.

My head was bursting with thoughts and questions: *I must have not been enough for him to have done these things. I don't even know this man I've been married to for almost fifteen years. How can he have been such a respected, successful, smart man and have betrayed me in this way? How can I ever trust him again? How will we provide for our family? Who can I even talk to about this? Nothing in my life has been true. My life has been wasted. Why would God allow this to happen to me when I've only tried to be a good person?*

I was in so much pain. Having the kids to attend to helped me keep going; I had to keep going for their sake. And thankfully, a recovering alcoholic at Mark's firing offered to find help for him. Just as we longingly wait for an ambulance in medical crisis, the "paramedics" arrived in our situation in the form of a treatment center. Mark was interviewed and accepted into the first in-patient program offered for sexual addiction, founded by Patrick Carnes. Within three days, Mark was traveling to Minnesota. For thirty days he would focus on the unmanageability and double-mindedness of sexual addiction. He would begin the journey of finding the pain behind the behavior. I was relieved, scared, and sad—relieved that he was being taken care of, scared about the future, and sad to be facing the devastation and losses in my life.

I was invited to Family Week about midway through Mark's program. It was the first time we spent much time talking since "the crash." As hard as the conversations were, the honesty between us was refreshing. It was new to feel included in the depths of Mark's thoughts and feelings—and to share mine. Therapists and psychiatrists were there to guide some of this process and to introduce me to Mark's group therapy. The counseling experience was all so new and brought an intimacy to our relationship that resided right alongside the pain.

When I returned to join Mark at the end of his month at treatment, I was surprised that we both received direction for our forthcoming counseling at home. I was glad to know that aftercare was being planned for Mark, but why me? *He's your guy! He's the one who needs help here,* I was thinking. *If he can get better, then everything will be fine.* But there were sessions scheduled for me. Dutifully I went, not wanting to look oppositional. And surprisingly, after my first individual and group therapy sessions, I was hooked. It is hard to find words to describe the passion that was ignited in me even early on—that I could learn more about myself and somehow grow through this pain. I had a gifted therapist who was able to hear my hurt and still hold hope for growth.

Thankfully, the resources of excellent therapy, a community of caring women who invested in therapy, a deepening of my spirituality, and practical steps to live authentically with Mark and myself birthed great changes in my life. I believe I am a better wife, mother, sister, friend, counselor, employer, and child of God than I would have been without a journey through adversity. Eventually my story led me back to graduate school to prepare for a second career in marriage and family therapy, where I have been able to walk with women who share similar stories. I have been transformed through this journey. I am not the person I would have been had I not faced the depths of my pain.

PAIN IS A PAIN

I never like being in pain. I don't know anyone who does. I hate the unknown nature of problems: *Why did this happen to me? How long will this take to fix? What can I do to get over this? How can I get out of pain?* It is unsettling to not know.

We all have learned things about problems and pain in our growing up years, and we have watched how others have tried to manage it. Is it a good thing? Do you try to avoid it at all costs? Is there anything good that comes from problems and pain? One of the life lessons from my family was that in time, pain would get better. Also, getting busy or working was helpful. Not talking about it was another strategy. Other people use drugs or alcohol, buy things, watch endless TV, overfocus on helping others, get busy, exercise excessively, hang out on social media, emotionally eat, withdraw, or use sex to cope. The list is endless. You can use virtually anything to manage problems and pain and to comfort yourself. And sometimes the use turns into a compulsion or addiction. Everyone carries messages inside about emotional pain and have developed strategies for how to handle it. Sometimes you're not conscious about these lessons, but they still direct your beliefs and behaviors.

Most of us do not by nature consider pain and suffering a privilege. Yet we admire books, songs, and stories that tell us that maybe pain can be a good thing because it can lead to something better. *What Doesn't Kill Us* (Joseph 2011) sits on my shelf reminding me that I can grow from adversity. Stories of underdogs and overcomers tug at the heartstrings of many of us too. I'm always rooting for them! I love the victories over the struggles. They can come from behind. They can do something great even though they have faced hardship in some way. It reminds me that there is strength and growth in overcoming. I don't think I'm unusual in my loyalties. It is sweet to witness victory in what could have been defeat.

Pain can be a great teacher in that it brings out behaviors and thoughts we may have not even been aware of. It gives us something to work on—perhaps something to improve. After discovering infidelity, women have described themselves to me in these words:

"I didn't know I could get that angry! I never use words like that."

"I've never hit anyone in my life until now."

"My revenge is huge. I just want him to feel some of the anger and pain I have."

"Given what he did to me, I feel entitled to do whatever I want."

"I can't even believe I'm thinking the hateful thoughts I am."

"I am starting to hate myself."

If one is not going to block pain, the challenge is to face it, to learn from it. That is not an easy choice and is often the catalyst for reaching out to a therapist or pastor. People who cannot feel pain are in danger of self-harm. How will God use their pain to teach them something, to grow them up in some way? How will he use us as a helper in their life to overcome the trauma and grow through the pain?

A BRIEF HISTORY OF TREATING PAIN AND SUFFERING

Stephen Joseph (2011), a researcher and professor of psychology at the University of Nottingham, summarizes the development of modern psychology in his book, *What Doesn't Kill You*. He states that while the idea that positive change could occur from adversity and trauma, it lay dormant during most of the twentieth century while the more popular focus on psychology was to study the distress and dysfunction of clients. The goal was to relieve symptoms of suffering, not necessarily to move clients toward happiness and contentment. Joseph further states that Sigmund Freud brought the medical model of treating patients to his psychoanalysis, thus perpetuating the focus on disorders, symptoms of trauma, and treatments to relieve pain.

An exception to the early focus on relief of stressful symptoms was Viktor Frankl, a psychiatrist and psychotherapist who survived the Holocaust of World War II. His study of survivors eventually led him to write about the meaning in suffering in *Man's Search for Meaning* (Frankl 1959). Frankl's theories became known as Logotherapy, suggesting that the most powerful drive for all human beings is to find meaning in life. He notes that one can find meaning in three different ways: (1) by creating a work or doing something good for someone, (2) by experiencing something significant or interacting with someone who profoundly affects you, or (3) by the attitude you have when faced with suffering. Frankl believed that despair was experienced when suffering had no meaning. He saw that there were two sides to suffering, noting that there was nothing inherently good in adversity, but that perhaps there could be something good to extract out of adversity.

During the post-WWII era, the field of psychology was emerging, and other psychologists were beginning to study the factors that contributed to well-being and growth. Abraham Maslow was known for his work with self-actualization and saw the both/and of suffering. He proposed that the most important lessons for people came from traumas and tragedies because they forced them to look at new perspectives. The pain from traumas was painful *and* good (Joseph 2011).

A great advance in medicine occurred after the Vietnam War when post-traumatic stress disorder (PTSD) was named as a medical diagnosis. Veterans returning with painful physical symptoms were finally diagnosed with PTSD and treated to reduce symptoms of anxiety, sleeplessness, panic attacks, recurring thoughts, hypervigilance, dissociation, and more. Once again, well-being was synonymous with eliminating physical symptoms that caused suffering. There was a growing belief that triggering events would inevitably lead to PTSD, from which patients would never recover.

Although models of psychological growth and resilience were quietly emerging, the medical model dominated psychological treatment until the late twentieth century. Psychological health was simply defined as the absence of suffering, and few focused on the potential of growth from adversity. However, psychologists began separating themselves from the field of psychiatry (a component of the medical model), and in 1999 Positive Psychology was born. Martin Seligman, the newly elected president of the American Psychological Association, founded the movement with a desire to study the science of human strengths, virtues, happiness, and what makes life worth living. The movement did not advocate that only positive aspects of living were important to well-being. Psychologists were recognizing that it was naïve to seek a life in which there was no sadness or misfortune, but that the pursuit of happiness must include learning how to live with and learn from adversity (Joseph 2011).

TREATMENT MODELS FOR ADDICTION/COADDICTION

During the development of the medical model for treating physical symptoms and the emergence of the field of psychology that was attempting to separate itself from the field of psychiatry, a number of models were developed to treat addiction. Alcoholics Anonymous was created by William Gustavus Wilson (Bill W.) in the summer of 1935 (Kurtz 1979) when he accepted fellowship with another struggling alcoholic to manage his drinking problem. The model was birthed from alcoholics helping other alcoholics. They accepted their power-lessness over drinking. They believed there was a power greater than themselves that could help, and thus, they practiced surrendering their self-sufficiency.

They became brutally honest about their character defects and owned them with others. They took responsibility for the hurts they caused others on a regular basis. And then they committed to take all that was learned to help other people. This process for healing an alcohol addiction became known as the twelve steps or the addiction model.

Sexual addiction was originally identified in an extended paper written by Patrick Carnes in 1976 (Carnes 1983). He recognized that out-of-control sexual behaviors presented the same issues that alcohol had caused: unmanageability, tolerance, progression, and medicating of painful histories. And he created a program of tasks which offered a sexual addict a path out of addiction to well-being. There was also research developing regarding the system in which the sexual addict lived. It was noted that the spouse or friend of an addict became so involved in the life of the addict that he or she became as disconnected from reality as the addict. Carnes (1983) noted that a partner would participate in degrading, self-destructive, or even profound violations of their own values and thus become part of the problem too. Thus, in the early years of treatment for sexual addiction, there was a great emphasis on treating the disease of coaddiction.

In 1987, *Codependent No More* by Melody Beattie was published, further labeling the loved ones and partners of addicts as "significant others" and "codependents," suggesting they needed their own recovery process to get well. Research was also emerging noting that family of origin trauma (sexual, physical, and emotional) for both an addict and a spouse were similar, and therefore both partners had significant work to do to understand that pain and how it impacted life choices. The desire was for growth and healing for both an addict and spouse (Carnes 1983). Unfortunately, this assessment and labeling potentially left a betrayed spouse feeling unheard about his or her pain and loss, and it was common for a partner to feel blamed for the infidelity and addiction. Perhaps these labels and the proposition that partners needed help led many away from opportunities to grow.

My story of attending Family Week at Mark's treatment center in 1987 was filled with that reality. I had heard before arriving that the therapists were interested in seeing how codependent I was. At the time, I knew little about what that meant, but it seemed to indicate that something was wrong with me. While I didn't speak up about it, internally I was reeling from the pain of betrayal and loss and had no desire for anyone to look at my faults! It was enough that I showed up at all. My motivation was to support Mark. Period. I might have been inclined to run from it all, but because I was many miles from home, it did not seem like a viable option. Thankfully, I stayed and began to learn about addiction and that it wasn't my fault—I didn't cause it, I couldn't control it, and I couldn't cure it. That information helped me to be heard and to feel less threatened. When I returned home to my own counseling process, the gentleness of my therapist and therapy group helped me to be regularly heard and understood about my losses and pain. In addition, they encouraged me to join them on the journey of self-examination—a life-changing gift.

The trauma model was introduced to the sexual addiction community in 2009 by Steffens and Means to acknowledge the pain of a sexually betrayed spouse. Their belief was that the addiction model failed to properly acknowledge the trauma that relational betrayal causes to a spouse and, thus, was doing great harm to partners of sexual addicts. The pain, confusion, distress, reactions, and fear from sexual betrayal were categorized as natural responses to trauma. This model acknowledged the pain and loss of a partner caused by sexual addiction and validated the reality of betrayal without labeling the partner as a coaddict or codependent.

In the trauma model, infidelity was considered an attachment injury or psychological or relational trauma. Steffens and Means (2009) stated that it caused intense emotional and physical pain for a spouse, including many symptoms of posttraumatic stress that could lead to posttraumatic stress disorder (PTSD). They believed that "PTSD could last a lifetime with sufferers developing painful coping mechanisms that would burden their lifestyles and become ingrained in their personalities, or they may develop physical symptoms" (p. 8). Treatment from this perspective focused on eliminating symptoms of distress and creating safe boundaries. The trauma model did not necessarily encourage exploration of historical trauma, nor did it focus on the growth that could be available from crisis. Its focus was on describing the details of how trauma was experienced and justifying the physical and emotional responses that are natural when subjected to a relational trauma. Reestablishing safety and security were primary goals of healing.

Both models have their contributions and their shortcomings for helping a betrayed spouse heal. The twelve-step model, or addiction model, quickly encourages a betrayed partner to look at her own history, pathology, and areas for growth. However, it can miss the *suffering in the growth*. The trauma model can offer wonderful empathy for emotional and physical pain caused by addictive sexual behaviors. However, it can miss the *growth in the suffering*. A model that could synthesize the two would be best—a model acknowledging both pain and growth. This model has emerged: the Posttraumatic Growth Model (Tedeschi and Calhoun 1995).

We prominently display many ampersands (&) in our counseling office. We know that an ampersand represents the both/and rather than the either/or.

We also know that truth is complicated. Black-and-white thinking keeps us stuck in accepting one thing or the other. It is too simplistic. In the merging of two models, both of which were lacking a significant component, the posttraumatic growth model presents truth about the healing journey of a betrayed spouse: Trauma and transformation can coexist. Adversity is painful and it can provide growth. You do not need to negate one for the other to be true.

THE POSTTRAUMATIC GROWTH MODEL

Studies began in the 1980s to look at the meaning of suffering. While there had been significant evidence regarding the negative physical and psychological consequences of traumatic life events, research was validating that pain could have positive impact on a person's life. Tragedy could be a springboard to transformation. Pain could potentially bring growth and transformation. Many terms were used: *perceived benefits, stress-related growth, thriving,* and *flourishing* to name a few. But *posttraumatic growth* (PTG), used by Richard Tedeschi and Lawrence Calhoun in 1995, became most popular. Posttraumatic growth refers to positive psychological change experienced as a result of the struggle with highly challenging life circumstances. In 1996, Tedeschi and Calhoun created the Posttraumatic Growth Inventory (PTGI) to measure the positive changes occurring in people who had experienced traumatic events, allowing their assumptions regarding growth to be tested in many adverse life situations.

In their research on posttraumatic growth, Tedeschi and Calhoun gathered results of other researchers who were using the PTGI to study many crises, including the death of loved ones, cancer, heart attacks, war, natural disasters, incest, rape, and more. They saw that the results were consistent for all crises and that growth resulted in these five areas: (1) a stronger sense of self, (2) richer relationships, (3) spiritual growth, (4) changed priorities, and (5) new opportunities.

Tedeschi and Calhoun found that trauma can be transformational. But not all trauma led to growth. In other words, believing "time will heal" would not in and of itself create growth. Tedeschi and Calhoun identified these resources that supported posttraumatic growth: community/social support, disclosure of truth, cognitive restructuring, and spirituality and hope.

A major finding in research of posttraumatic growth was that the distress of a traumatic event was highly correlated to the shattering of one's assumptive world (Janoff-Bulman 1992). The beliefs about self, others, and the world were disrupted by the traumatic event and led to emotional pain and physical symptoms. Tedeschi and Calhoun found that when thoughts are shattered, there is turmoil in trying to figure out the truth, and thus, recurring thoughts disrupt one's sleeping and waking hours. The process of sorting out distorted beliefs caused by a trauma and the truth is miserable. It is painful. And it can also lead to new beliefs and truths, which we call growth. According to Tedeschi and Calhoun, "This process of assimilating the trauma into the life narrative and into the fundamental assumptions about life or changing the narrative and assumptions to accommodate what has happened involves great effort" (1995, 40).

There are two ways that newly shattered beliefs can be processed (Hollon and Garber 1988, as cited in Joseph and Linley 2005). Either the information must be *assimilated* within the existing schemas of the victim's model of the world, or the model of their world must *accommodate* a new schema. The following is an example of assimilating: A woman who discovers her husband's pornography use might believe she is not sexual enough and therefore caused him to pursue pornography. Her negative core belief that says, "I'm not enough" may have formed from many previous life experiences. *Assimilating* it into her recent traumatic experience with pornography would help her make sense of her current world.

In *accommodating* pornography use that is traumatic, a woman may accept that she is feeling violated and unchosen and deserves a faithful spouse. She may decide that despite culture's belief that "all men look at pornography," she believes that pornography is not healthy (a new worldview). Accommodation of trauma-related information can be processed either positively or negatively (Joseph and Linley 2005). For instance, increased pornography use (sexual sin) may be viewed in one of two ways: (1) Pornography is ruining the world—a negative accommodation that leads to a negative worldview of hopelessness and psychopathology, or (2) exposure to pornography is leading many people to get help and change their lives—a positive accommodation that leads to positive changes in worldview and growth. According to Joseph and Linley, "All trauma theorists are in agreement that recovery involves some form of cognitive restructuring" (2005, 276).

But why do people respond to trauma differently? Janoff-Bulman stated that "it is how an event is understood that ultimately determines whether it will be traumatic or not" (1992, 52). We once again are reminded that cognitive restructuring is essential to changing a posttraumatic stress response to posttraumatic growth.

Joseph & Linley (2005, 2008) are psychologists and researchers who have been interested in looking at both posttraumatic stress and posttraumatic growth, as both present legitimate concerns for well-being. In their distinction, psychological well-being (PWB) refers to a person's characterological strengths, meaning and purpose in life, and psychological maturity following adversity, whereas subjective well-being (SWB) refers to the positive and negative effect of adversity and overall life satisfaction or happiness. These differences are important in that theories of posttraumatic distress are theories of SWB and theories of posttraumatic growth are theories of PWB, according to Joseph & Linley. When a model of healing trauma is focused primarily on decreasing symptoms of PTSD (which does, in fact, lower distress and raise SWB), it does not necessarily lead to growth (PWB). In regard to trauma, however, when growth is experienced over time (PWB), eventually symptoms of PTSD decrease as well (which is experienced as an increase in SWB).

As the twenty-first century began, the birth of Positive Psychology and the research results of Tedeschi and Calhoun's PTGI, Joseph and Linley, Janoff-Bulman, and others were emerging to confirm that trauma and transformation could coexist. PWB, not just SWB, developed when support was present to complete emotional processing that was shattered from a traumatic event. It was an exciting new direction in psychology. Good could come out of painful life situations. Life was more than survival (establishing safety and security) and relieving symptoms of posttraumatic stress. Adversity could propel any of us to thrive, to be better, and to live with meaning.

RESEARCH FOR RELATIONALLY BETRAYED WOMEN

In 2017, Laaser, Putney, Bundick, Delmonico, and Griffin published the first research study using the Posttraumatic Growth Inventory (PTGI) for relationally betrayed women. As I mentioned earlier in this chapter, the PTGI had been used in other studies to study growth in crises and adversity, however, this was the first research study to look at posttraumatic growth for women who had been relationally betrayed. Relational betrayal was defined as "a violation of an expectation for emotional and/or physical (sexual) exclusivity in a committed relationship" (Whisman and Wagers 2005) and included these sexual behaviors: pornography, prostitution, physical affairs, emotional affairs, chat rooms, exhibitionism, voyeurism, sexting, one-night sexual connections, and more. Although relational betrayal can be experienced in all types of relationships, our study focused on women who were betrayed in a committed, heterosexual relationship. The study involved survey responses from 202 adult women who had experienced relational betrayal. The vast majority (96%) of women reported that their relational betrayal was at least a *very traumatic* experience; for 56.7%, it was "the most traumatic event in my life"; 31.8% described it as "extremely traumatic," and 7.45% "very traumatic."

Janoff-Bulman's (1992) research found that when people were victimized by a traumatic event, there was a significant relationship between levels of posttraumatic stress and a subject's cognitive beliefs about themselves and their world.

In other words, the more an individual developed negative core beliefs about a trauma, the more posttraumatic stress symptoms they would experience.

Participants in our research survey were asked what their perceptions or beliefs were when they discovered relational betrayal. There were eight items on a checklist, and these six were reported by at least 20% or more of the participants:

- "I can never trust my partner/husband again." (67.8%)
- "My marriage is ruined." (52.5%)
- "I will never recover emotionally from the pain and devastation of the betrayal." (49.0%)
- "I caused my husband's/partner's betrayal." (27.8%)
- "Nothing good can come out of this adversity." (25.3%)
- "My life is ruined." (23.8%)

The Core Beliefs Inventory (CBI) (Cann et al. 2010) was used to further measure the shattered beliefs of women who had been betrayed. The CBI was created to measure the level of disruption of a range of one's core beliefs following a traumatic life event, including beliefs about spirituality, human nature, relationships, meaning of life, and personal strengths and weaknesses. It consisted of nine questions such as, "Because of the event, I seriously examined my assumptions concerning why other people think and behave the way that they do," and "Because of the event, I seriously examined my beliefs about my own value or worth as a person." Responses were made on a six-point Likert scale ranging from "not at all" to "a very great degree." This assessment tool demonstrated adequate internal consistency and reliability when correlating disruption of one's core beliefs and the amount of anxiety, stress, and coping experienced following a traumatic life event. In our study, it was found that posttraumatic growth was significantly and positively correlated with the disruption in core beliefs.

To further examine the intensity and depth of physical and emotional symptoms of relational betrayal, we asked questions to determine whether criteria for PTSD were met. Symptoms of posttraumatic stress were assessed, such as intense fear and helplessness; recurrent images, thoughts, or perceptions of the betrayal; difficulty sleeping; irritability and outbursts of anger; difficulty concentrating; hypervigilance; panic attacks; avoidance of activities, places, or people associated with the betrayal; diminished interest in activities; and more. In 60.89% of the respondents, criteria for PTSD as indicated in the DSM-5 were reported. Our study also found that shattered core beliefs and posttraumatic stress symptoms were positively correlated. Our results indicated that the greater the shattering of one's assumptions about self, others, and the world, the greater the levels of distress (PTSD).

We asked women in the study to tell us what advice they received that was not helpful. The following are the top six selected out of nine choices on the survey:

- "You need to forgive him and forget the past." (34%)
- "Leave your partner." (31%)
- "He will never change." (30%)
- "Pornography is not considered betrayal." (24%)
- "You just need to get over this and everything will be fine." (22%)
- "If you had been more sexual/available, he would not have betrayed you." (17%)

When relationship betrayal was first discovered, 28.8% of our participants first approached therapists/counselors for help. Using our scale ranging from "hurtful" to "extremely helpful," 8.3% of their interactions were "hurtful" or "extremely unhelpful," while 52.7% were "very helpful" or "extremely helpful." Additionally, 15.1% of our survey participants first talked to clergy regarding their traumatic discovery. Responses in 26.2% of their experiences were either "extremely unhelpful" or "hurtful," with 13.7% being "very helpful" or "extremely helpful."

Resources that were helpful to betrayed women were also assessed. Participants chose four of the most helpful resources out of our list of twelve with the following results:

- Individual counseling (72%)
- Full disclosure (50%)
- Couple's therapy (49.5%)
- Educational materials (47%)
- Forgiveness (44%)
- Support groups led by peers (40.5%)
- Spiritual mentoring/support (38.5%)
- Intensive workshop/treatment (29%)
- Intentional separation (23.9%)
- Therapy group led by professionals (21.5%)
- Disclosure to children (12.2%)
- Disclosure to parents (10.7%)

Our participants' length of time in recovery postbetrayal ranged from less than two months (10.6%) to five-plus years (15.1%) with an average of 4.2 years. Despite the somewhat shortened amount of time to seek help and engage in available resources (52.9% were involved two years or less in their therapeutic journey), 80% or more of participants reported at least some degree of posttraumatic growth in each of the five subscales: Personal Strength (88.7%), Spiritual Change (87%), Relating to Others (86.2%), Appreciation of Life (85.3%), and New Possibilities (83.5%).

Of the twenty-one questions asked in the PTGI, the following are examples of growth to a "great degree" or "very great degree" for our research subjects:

- "I have more compassion for others." (62.4%)
- "I know better that I can handle difficulties." (61.9%)
- "I have a stronger religious faith." (60.9%)
- "I discovered that I'm stronger than I thought I was." (59.9%)
- "I am more likely to try to change things which need changing." (59.4%)
- "I have a better understanding of spiritual matters." (56.4%)
- "I am more willing to express my emotions." (53.0%)
- "I have a greater appreciation for the value of my own life." (52.0%)
- "I put more effort into my relationships." (52.0%)
- "I changed my priorities about what is important in life." (46.5%)
- "I am better able to accept the way things work out." (44.1%)
- "I established a new path for my life." (41.6%)
- "I have greater emotional intimacy with my spouse/partner." (40.8%)
- "I more clearly see that I can count on people in times of trouble." (40.6%)
- "I am able to do better things with my life." (37.7%)
- "I have a greater sense of closeness with others." (33.2%)

RESEARCH RESULTS

The results of this study indicated that with time, use of resources, and engagement in therapeutic activities, relationally betrayed women reported significant posttraumatic growth. An important finding was that posttraumatic growth was significantly and positively correlated with disruption in core beliefs. Advice to a newly traumatized woman can contribute to more negative core beliefs and despair when they may not be true. Thus, the first response to a traumatized person is critical; shifting the responsibility to them, intentionally or unintentionally, only exacerbates the shame they feel and deepens the trauma they carry. Moreover, it was found that Core Belief Inventory (CBI) scores were higher for those who met the PTSD criteria as compared to those who did not. Therefore, it can be concluded that when there is more pain, there is also more possibility for growth.

The results of the study confirmed that transformation and growth following relational betrayal is not only possible, but likely. These findings suggest that even in the most traumatic of betrayal situations, clinicians can provide hope that posttraumatic growth is possible. It is the ampersand, the both/and, that untangles the confusion: two things that appear to be in great opposition can be true at the same time. Distress and growth can coexist. We do not need to negate one to accept the other.

The timing of interventions is crucial, then, to address both realities of betrayal. It was shown that over 60% of the participants met the criteria for PTSD and, therefore, it is important for clinicians to offer guidance and therapeutic modalities to treat those symptoms immediately. Those treatments could include EMDR, cognitive behavioral therapies, medications, and empathy from safe community and/or a safe therapeutic relationship. The results indicated that for women who met diagnostic criteria for PTSD, the passage of time as well as therapeutic support to work through cognitive restructuring were significant factors in the development of posttraumatic growth following a relational betrayal.

These results remind us that women need ample time to process their emotions and experiences following betrayal. Yet it is a delicate balance for clinicians to neither rush a woman through her own experiences, nor to allow her to remain paralyzed by the relational betrayal and miss the opportunity of growth. Clinicians can promote posttraumatic growth by suggesting and offering resources to support the process of hearing and healing pain while holding the hope for growth.

RESILIENCY VERSUS RESOURCEFULNESS

It is often said that posttraumatic growth is equivalent to *resiliency*. A person who is labeled "strong" and "resilient" can manage crisis and trauma in life. It may be helpful to look at a definition of resilience to assess whether that is what we mean by posttraumatic growth. In the Merriam-Webster Dictionary, resilience is defined as: (1) the capability of a strained body to recover its size and shape after deformation caused especially by compressive stress; (2) an ability to recover from or adjust easily to misfortune or change. I think the word *recover* is significant here. They denote that there is a return to what was—not a movement toward something new.

I see resiliency as something like Kilz paint, which is used to block out stains before you add a coat of a beautiful paint color. It covers up the problem. To an outsider, it may never be known that there was anything else going on under that paint. It does the job! It also doesn't require you to seek help from another or admit there is a problem. It works quickly and allows you to get on to other things. It may be that resiliency grows independence and pride, not deeper self-awareness and changes in behaviors and beliefs. It may allow you to endure, to block out, to avoid seeing or feeling something, or to miss understanding the deeper cause. It may develop self-reliance, which can be interpreted as "I can handle anything!" There are times when being resilient can be helpful, but perhaps on its own, it is not the essence of posttraumatic growth.

Perhaps *resourcefulness* is a better word to describe the growth clients have available through adversity. I see resourcefulness as finding new ways to handle a problem. Recovery involves using new resources to grow, and as helpers we are responsible for providing at least a few of those resources. It may be resourceful for a betrayed partner to connect to others who have experienced a similar situation and who are further down the road of life—or what we call "safe community." It may be talking through those shattered beliefs that come from traumatic life events and reauthoring them for the future. It may be developing other choices about next steps and new possibilities for what to do or what has been learned. It may be asking for help from God and others, depending upon them in a way you have never experienced before. It may be learning to surrender what cannot be controlled to God, whose knowledge of what is needed and whose timing of things does not operate on human terms. It may be creating empathy and a new perspective for others who have faced the same experiences. It may be the unnatural process of forgiving someone who caused deep hurt. Resourcefulness leads to strength of a different kind. It leads to richer relationships. It leads to spiritual growth. And it is an essential focus of the help we offer to those whom we provide clinical or pastoral care.

Recovery for a betrayed spouse is a process of sorting out how they want to live through the troubles life brings; it is yet another both/and, ampersand truth. Resiliency improves in-the-moment pain management. Resiliency is the ability to bounce back, to return to prior conditions. In recovery, we help clients build resiliency when hard things come their way. *And* they may experience posttraumatic growth when they remember that resourcefulness will lead to new community, new skills, new beliefs, and especially, a new dependence on God.

BIBLICAL TRUTH

The Bible has offered wisdom about suffering all along. Perhaps psychology and our models for treating pain are finally catching up to God's truth. Maybe it is true that there can be joy in our suffering and that adversity can mature us in ways that a "happy" life cannot: "Consider it pure joy . . . whenever you face trials of many kinds, because you know that the testing of your faith produces perseverance. Let perseverance finish its work so that you may be mature and complete, not lacking anything" (James 1:2–4). If trials are to grow and mature us, then maybe even the trauma of relational betrayal can lead to something good. That is the hope: that one can be better, not bitter, from betrayal.

When an individual is in so much pain from trauma, they may think they are at the end of their rope. They can be in great despair. They might also experience the great hope of their faith: "Even though I walk through the darkest valley, I will fear no evil, for you are with me" (Ps. 23:4). It may be that they know this truth intellectually. They have read about God's presence in the Bible, and have sung about it in worship. But to watch God deliver a solution or fill a need or offer some solace when they are totally out of options—that may be the moment when they *really* experience God's presence with them. He desires to grow them in dependence on him and spiritual character if they will be patient with him. We can help clients learn to surrender to his plan and his timing, which is very different from adopting an identity as a victim of difficult circumstances.

Instead of "Why me?" in the face of their adverse experiences, we help them learn to ask the healthy parts of themselves, "What would you have me learn?" "How will I need your help?" "What do I need to surrender today?" and "What is my next right step?" We might help them ask God, "What in this world could you possibly resurrect out of these shambles? How will you mature me to be complete in you?"

BECOMING MORE CHRISTLIKE

The character growth we strive to facilitate in those we serve is "unnatural"— Christlike—not the usual human responses to pain and crisis. Human nature wants to control, to figure everything out, to hurry things along, to judge our worthiness by how others treat us, to hold grudges, to look to a spouse for all our needs, and to be pain-free. This is especially true in the context of betrayal trauma, and one's spiritual growth may include some very different aspects of living. Our personal spiritual growth and maturity as a helping professional is a critical antecedent in how we provide care for those who entrust themselves to us. Here are some of the many character changes we hope for a client to experience as they engage in a journey of healing:

- Accepting that unfairness is managed by God, not us.
- Learning not to personalize others' behaviors; they do what they do to manage personal pain.

- Slowing down our reactions and decisions.
- Becoming more intentional and proactive rather than reactive to life's circumstances.
- Caring less about what others think of us and more about God's opinion.
- Eliminating black-and-white thinking—allowing truth to be a both/and.
- Accepting God's timing of things, not controlling with our personal agenda.
- Forgiving those who hurt us.
- Allowing joy and pain to coexist.
- Surrendering to God those things we cannot control.
- Being still and listening for the Holy Spirit to lead instead of trying to figure it all out ourselves.
- Being vulnerable and authentic, not hiding the broken or embarrassing parts of our life.
- Living as a beloved child of God.

Ultimately, posttraumatic growth is a faith journey, coming to the end of what one thought made them strong and good and worthy. The superficial evidence of a successful life was not the healthy pursuit: being self-sufficient, living with monetary success, being liked by everyone, always looking good, working for worth, being a perfectionist, always being happy, or endlessly sacrificing oneself to be available to others. Maybe growth and well-being are not those things at all. Maybe turning deeper to supernatural living produces posttraumatic growth. If you remember, Tedeschi and Calhoun found these five areas of growth following adversity: individual strength, deeper relationships, new possibilities, changed priorities, and spiritual growth. Suffering can lead to maturing, not lacking anything in our spiritual character. In our work with those who suffer the pain of betrayal trauma, may we embody this same optimism as we strive to help them heal.

CONCLUSION

We all have things to change, ways to grow. As you walk the path of healing with those whose relationships have been impacted by sexual addiction, you will have an important question to keep at the center of the help you provide to them: "Are you, a betrayed spouse, willing to go there?" The helpful resources that are an inherent part of PTG will help you take clients there: cognitive reframing, safe community, disclosure of truth, and spiritual support. It is a privilege to co-participate in the process of healing with betrayed spouses, to help them discover the truth that they are not responsible for their husband's behavior, *and* there is opportunity for growth in the pain. In this process, we have an opportunity to help them become a better version of themselves, to be the woman God created them to be.

Adversity, trauma, and crisis can shake up our beliefs—about ourselves, others, and the world around us. They create doubts, fears, and needs that cause much emotional and physical pain. To find a sense of balance, we sometimes analyze the past, trying to make sense of it. Other times, we might catastrophize, imagining all the ways we must prepare for the bad things yet to come. The paradox of adversity is that it can initiate growth; it doesn't just destroy things. Out of loss there is gain. "In all things God works for the good of those who love him" (Rom. 8:28). This message of hope is one that must permeate the work we do with those in recovery, regardless of the outcome of their journey.

The healing journey involves helping betrayed spouses live in the present, one day at a time. It is equipping them to listen carefully for the Holy Spirit to inform them of the next right step. It is reminding them that God's grace is sufficient for today and identifying the ways he is showing up to take care of daily needs when their pain blinds them from this truth. It is a process of modifying the inaccurate beliefs they have come to hold about themselves and reminding them of these foundational truths: You are loved. God is always near. Pain will not be wasted. God will meet all your needs (Phil. 4:19). You can let go of worries (Matt. 6:34). You can find peace and joy now, knowing the truth of eternity. You don't have all the answers now, but one day you will be able to see the world with God's perspective (1 Cor. 13:11–12). You can use suffering to build character, to change your priorities, to become more dependent on Christ, to allow others to serve you (that's hard!), as well as to have a different filter in understanding others, to grow patience, to practice thankfulness in all situations, to live with the hope that God is in all your living. God will use everything in your life to work on maturing your character. Everything cries holy!

After thirty-plus years in my own healing journey and years of working as a clinician in the field, I can truly say that the path to healing and wholeness is so much more than focusing on sexual addiction—or on any specific traumatic life event. Each adversity is an invitation to work on becoming the best version of yourself, the man or woman God called you to be. Progress continues as traumatic life events are reframed as the problem for the pain and struggles of life.

As Virginia Satir, a renowned family systems therapist, once said, "Problems are not the problem; (unhealthy) coping is the problem" (Andreas 1991). Helping clients understand their thoughts, broaden their coping skills, identify their feelings, express their needs, share their deeper desires, and discern the truth about a problem will lead to greater self-examination, conversation, and growth.

Studying the fruit of the Spirit (Gal. 5:22–23) is a helpful spiritual self-assessment of how a client's growth is progressing. As a helper, your objective insights into these areas of growth for them are equally important. What is their current experience of love, joy, peace, patience, goodness, kindness, gentleness, self-control, and faithfulness? There is nothing like a traumatic life event to upset this basket of fruit. When we are not receiving love, it is hard to love. When life is hard, we can barely find anything to be joyful about. When our thinking is scrambled from adversity and we are trying to figure out what to do and what to think, we have little peace in our lives. When we desperately want life to get better and to get out of pain, our patience grows thin. When we're focused on our own survival from hardship, it is hard to take time to spread good things to others. Our own emotional roller coasters can lead to irritability and a loss of kindness for anyone. When we feel threatened by trials, it is extremely hard to have gentle responses. When we feel out of control with pain, it is hard to train ourselves to turn to God. Faithfulness takes practice. The fruit of the Spirit gives you a beautiful vision of where trials in this life might take you. As we walk with those who have been impacted by sexual addiction within their marriage, these principles become a helpful cluster of attributes to focus on throughout the healing journey.

Research on posttraumatic growth has confirmed the truths of our faith: we can live assuredly that trauma can be transformed. It is not a mistake that problems are part of our lives. In fact, it is through the difficult times of facing adversity that we are offered new pathways to becoming more Christlike and living for the eternity of being with him forever—with no pain. Adversity also gives us a new filter to look at others, knowing that they, too, are struggling to find healthy ways to express deep pain: "Be kinder than necessary because everyone you meet is fighting some kind of battle" (Barry n.d.).

As you journey toward beauty and wholeness, remember the words of Elizabeth Kubler-Ross from *Death: The Final Stage of Growth*: "The most beautiful people we have known are those who have known defeat, known suffering, known struggle, known loss, and have found their way out of the depths. These people have an appreciation, a sensitivity, and an understanding of life that fills them with compassion, gentleness, and a deep, loving concern. Beautiful people do not just happen" (1975, 96).

REFERENCES

Andreas, S. 1991. *Virginia Satir: The Patterns of Her Magic*. Palo Alto, CA: Science and Behavior Books.

Barry, J. M. n.d. "Be Kinder Than Necessary." Retrieved from www.goodreads.com/quotes /245536-be-kinder-than-necessary-because-everyone-you-meet-is-fighting.

Beattie, M. 1987. *Codependent No More: How to Stop Controlling Others and Start Caring for Yourself.* Center City, MN: Hazelden.

Cann, E., L. Calhoun, R. Tedeschi, R. Kilmer, V. Gil-Rivas, T. Vishnevsky, and S. Danhauer. 2010. "The Core Beliefs Inventory: A Brief Measure of Disruption in the Assumptive World." *Anxiety, Stress, & Coping* 23, no. 1: 19–34.

Carnes, P. 1983. *Out of the Shadows: Understanding Sexual Addiction.* Minneapolis: CompCare Publishers.

Janoff-Bulmann, R. 1992. *Shattered Assumptions: Towards a New Psychology of Trauma.* New York: Free Press.

Joseph, S. 2011. *What Doesn't Kill Us: The New Psychology of Posttraumatic Growth.* New York: Basic Books.

Joseph, S., and P. A. Linley. 2005. "Positive Adjustment to Threatening Events: An Organismic Valuing Theory of Growth through Adversity." *Review of General Psychology* 9, no. 3: 262–80.

Kubler-Ross, E. 1975. *Death: The Final Stage of Growth.* Hoboken, NJ: Prentice Hall.

Kurtz, E. 1979. *Not-God: A History of Alcoholics Anonymous.* Center City, MN: Hazelden.

Laaser, D., H. Putney, M. Bundick, D. Delmonico, and E. Griffin. 2017. "Posttraumatic Growth in Relationally Betrayed Women." *Journal of Marital and Family Therapy* 44, no. 3: 435–47.

Steffens, B., and M. Means. 2009. *Your Sexually Addicted Spouse: How Partners Can Cope and Heal.* Far Hills, NJ: New Horizon Press.

Story, L. 2012. *What If Your Blessings Come through Raindrops?* Brentwood, TN: Freeman-Smith.

Tedeschi, R. G., and L. G. Calhoun. 1995. *Trauma and Transformation: Growing in the Aftermath of Suffering.* Thousand Oaks, CA: Sage.

———. 1996. "The Posttraumatic Growth Inventory: Measuring the Positive Legacy of Trauma." *Journal of Traumatic Stress* 9, no. 3: 455–71.

———. 2004. "Posttraumatic Growth: Conceptual Foundations and Empirical Evidence." *Psychological Inquiry* 15, no. 1: 1–18.

Whisman, M., and T. Wagers. 2005. "Assessing Relationship Betrayals." *Journal of Clinical Psychology* 61, no. 11: 1383–91.

CHAPTER 12

TREATMENT STRATEGIES FOR COUPLES

Mark Laaser, PhD, and Debbie Laaser, M.A., LMFT

W e were young when we married: twenty-two and twenty-one. We were high school sweethearts who, despite our intense desire to be together, went to different colleges. Our primary focus was on graduating so we could get married and finally "live happily ever after"! In both of our families, parental financial support ended as soon as you married. So we both rushed through college in less than four years, sharing life through endless phone calls and frequent letters to one another, believing the life of marital bliss was just ahead of our daily grind.

Our life as newlyweds did bring much joy and adventure—and also much change. We were living halfway across the country from our families in the beautiful town of Princeton, New Jersey. Mark was in seminary, and Debbie was searching for teaching positions in an overly saturated professional environment. We had little money. We had little community. We were "leaving and cleaving," but neither of us knew how to do that well. Change abounded in our new life, some of which we orchestrated well and through some of which we reverted to our old and familiar ways of individually coping.

As we became educated about such things as coping, Mark brought his sexual addiction into the marriage to cope with difficult emotions and a history of being sexually abused. Debbie brought several significant coping strategies to manage her anxiety, loneliness, and frustration, including withdrawing and not talking about difficult issues and keeping busy with projects and work. We used our coping strategies silently, of course. Thus, the slow sliding away from each other began. The "knowing" of each other emotionally and spiritually—in other words, sharing all our feelings, perceptions, needs, and beliefs—was replaced with surviving, each in our own way. We both carried secrets about these internal places of our lives, and we missed opportunities to grow our love for fear that we would disappoint the other.

Our journey to God's greater design for our marriage began with a "crash and burn," as we've come to call it (described in chapter 11). This was the discovery of Mark's sexual acting out and his eventually being labeled a sexual addict. That was over thirty years ago. Thankfully, with the wise encouragement of a recovering alcoholic who witnessed Mark's intervention, treatment was found and initiated immediately for Mark's sexual addiction. We had no idea at the time that our spiritual journey as a couple had begun. We were both wracked with fear, shame, sadness, and uncertainty. But we stepped onto the ride, the wildest roller coaster imaginable, as Mark left for inpatient treatment for thirty days and Debbie joined him for Family Week midway through.

Slowly, slowly, James's vision in James 1:2–4 became possible: "Consider it pure joy . . . whenever you face trials of many kinds, because you know that the testing of your faith produces perseverance. Let perseverance finish its work so that you may be mature and complete, not lacking anything." While many professionals and support groups will primarily focus on changing sexual behaviors, we know that treatment—or well-being—is so much more. In this chapter, we will focus on the bigger picture of allowing something traumatic to become transformational for a couple.

For the purposes of this chapter, we will refer to the husband as the sexual addict and his wife as the betrayed spouse, since this represents the dynamic of most of the couples we work with. Given that our story involves Mark's recovery from sexual addiction and Debbie's recovery from betrayal, it is most natural to reflect that in our writing here. We certainly know that the principles here are applicable to other addiction/betrayal relationships. The strategies we discuss to help couples heal and grow have developed from years of our own professional help and years of counseling others as professionals ourselves in the field.

COUPLES' DEVELOPMENT

The idea that a thriving marriage is developed over time is foreign to most couples. Typically, there are many distorted beliefs operating in a couple that are not truths. These are beliefs that we bring into a relationship, ones that we may call the original status quo. The following are distorted beliefs we hear:

- Being together and unhappy is safer than being alone.
- Good couples don't argue.
- Being married should not have to be a lot of work.

- If my spouse really loved me, he or she should know what I need.
- Being sexual is equal to being intimate.
- Successful couples don't have problems.
- If we are a good couple, we will agree on everything.
- Couples that do well have the same interests.
- We have problems because he or she won't change.
- If I let my partner know who I really am, what I've done, or what I'm feeling, he or she will leave me.
- We are not good parents because our kids have struggles.

We believe that a husband and wife have many commonalities in the initial stage of relationship. Feelings that are often unspoken are much the same for both: loneliness, sadness, frustration, disappointment, fear, anger, shame, and more. Needs are difficult to articulate for both spouses. They expect the other to "just know": "If you really loved me you would know what I need!" Desires for the relationship are similar for both: to be heard, to be affirmed, to be loved unconditionally (blessed), to be safe, to be touched in healthy ways, to be chosen, and to be included (Laaser and Laaser 2008). Both members of the couple are choosing ways to cope as "desires of the heart" are unmet. Their choices are just different. Both live with secrets, hiding parts of who they are and lying about behaviors, feelings, needs, and desires. Neither partner is living in total honesty.

The truth for both is that a relationship is hard work. No one enters marriage and lives happily ever after. All couples need guidance, safe community, and encouragement. Life is difficult, and merging two separate lives with all the baggage that each will bring to the new relationship is complicated. If we do not explore the beliefs that comprise our being, we will reactively live them out in our relationships. Trying to build a healthy marriage from two unexamined lives is like walking through a field with land mines. Detonation will occur at the most unexpected times.

Finally, we believe that couples' development in recovery occurs in three distinct stages and that in each stage there are specific "tasks" of healing that can be helpful. Although we categorize these tasks, this process of healing from betrayal and growing together is not a linear process.

STAGE 1: CHAOS

With discovery of new information, all couples enter the chaos of the first year of recovery. Beliefs about oneself, each other, and the future are stirred up and need to be redefined. Often this stage is described as a roller coaster of emotions, information, and behaviors. It can feel out of control and unpredictable. Change and loss abound. One of the most hated words around our counseling center for husbands is the word *patient*. Addicts are not inherently patient—many have ADHD. They tend to want to manage this stage and hurry it along. In this phase, in addition to staying sexually sober, addicts are more profoundly working on their anxieties and, therefore, their need to please.

For the betrayed spouse, the ups and downs can be moments of knowing she loves her husband and moments in which she is angry and despairing beyond words. She is capable of outbursts and endless questions.

The truth, while incredibly painful, serves the purpose of shattering the old beliefs of "happily ever after" in the status quo phase of the marriage. Some couples find that talking about the truth is refreshing because at least it is honest. They may enter a brief period that we call the "honeymoon phase." They are now talking all the time and, for some, having a lot more sex than they ever had before. It can be a time of feeling connected to one another, despite the pain of betrayal. The following tasks are key to stage 1.

Take Responsibility for Yourself

Building any relationship or improving yourself will always start with you. It starts with accepting that you and only you are responsible for the person you are. Period. No one else makes you feel or act the way you do. You can be agitated or angry or sad by another person's choices. You can feel rejected by their behaviors. You can feel manipulated by another person's words or actions. You can be abused by what others are doing to you. *And* you still get to decide what you will believe and what you will do in any situation. You are the captain of that ship. The beginning of change starts with accepting responsibility for yourself.

Commit to Ongoing Sobriety

If we are to help couples heal from the pain of sexual addiction, the addict needs to find ongoing and permanent sobriety. This involves his program of recovery including counseling, counseling groups, support groups, and couple's counseling. Growing the marriage can't proceed if the addict is not sober. It is no different than trying to do couple's counseling when one of the partners is an active alcoholic. We don't require a specific length of sobriety before we initiate marital counseling (e.g., six months), but we do require that the addict is sober and continuing to work on it. When there is not sobriety, we find that marriage counseling reverts to those issues, and he remains the identified problem. Our expectation for all the men we counsel is that permanent, ongoing sobriety is possible. There is much talk in sex addiction support groups of how hard or even impossible that is. Many wives have been told that their husband will never be fully sober. That is so discouraging! We personally experience sobriety in our relationship and expect it of others. Expectations are important to state clearly. How else can hope be a reality and trust a possibility?

Commit to Three Equal Pieces of Recovery

We find that couples do better when there are three equal pieces to their recovery plan: his counseling and safe community of men, her counseling and safe community of women, and counseling for their relationship. Our symbol for this is a three-legged stool. It will topple if one leg is missing. Likewise, if a couple is not pursuing their individual recoveries and couple's recovery, the marriage won't stand either. A recovery program for the two spouses typically includes individual counseling, group counseling, and support groups (such as Sexaholics Anonymous, S-Anon, Celebrate Recovery, or other Christ-centered groups at churches). The couple's piece typically includes couple counseling and the possibility, though rare, of couples' support groups.

Full Disclosure

Couples can grow and thrive through adversity if they live in truth with one another. We create what we call a "new foundation" for the marriage by encouraging our couples to go through full disclosure (Laaser and Laaser 2017). We have a three-step process to guide couples through disclosure, which we believe is best done in the context of therapy. Since we work with couples as a couple, the addict/offender will work with Mark to establish a complete timeline of all sexual development, sexual behaviors, physical and emotional acting out, and sexual offending (if applicable) from birth to the present. This is an offering of information to the spouse which is often very different from the previous methods of her gathering information from questions and detective work. It can be hurtful, but it is far more harmful to let her live with a reality that is not true. We also believe that starting from birth is important to add context to the story of addiction—and hopefully empathy for the hurt that was done to the addict in his early life.

Briefly, our belief in full disclosure is based on fact that it is the only way to establish full intimacy. Relational intimacy depends on total honesty. The ability of the spouse to trust is only possible if there is ongoing total honesty. Shame is foundational to addiction, and one of the core beliefs of shame is "If you knew me you would hate me and leave me." In fact, there is a subprinciple based on that core belief: "The person I'm the most afraid of losing will be the person to whom I'm least likely to tell the truth." For shame reduction to occur and for the couple to be ready for greater intimacy, full disclosure must happen. We have found and research has confirmed that couples who go through this process are most likely to stay married (Schneider and Corley 2012). Couples living in truth will know that "she knows everything about what I've done, and she is still choosing to stay with me." That is a very different message for an addict who has believed that no one would love him as he was.

We are not regular proponents of lie detector tests. We mostly find that if the addict is willing to go through disclosure from birth to the present and if the addict is broken and humble, the spouse will sense that the whole truth is being told. There are times when this process is not adequate to build trust about truth-telling for a spouse, and a polygraph exam may help create a foundation of honesty. We do not feel that further polygraphs are helpful in most cases. We desire to help a couple build trust and safety through watching heart changes, behavioral changes, building trust in your own "spiritual knowing," and in trusting God.

Finally, we believe that disclosure to children is also important. Children, like adults, are very intuitive. As they watch and listen to the world around them, they absorb problems, tension, and unexpressed feelings. When they are not told the truth, they begin to create beliefs about themselves, you, and their world which, most often, are not correct. This can create a craziness for them that leads to confusion, anxiety, depression, and acting out behaviors of their own. You may remember stories from your own families in which you knew something was happening but no one was willing to talk to you about it. As parents, we can believe we are protecting our children, but we are actually hurting them by not allowing them to validate their reality. Of course, we must be wise about age-appropriate conversations. Too much detail is not necessary. Not enough information is confusing. Seek counsel to discern what is right for you. Modeling honesty will usually lead to greater respect and will also give a child greater resources to deal with any of their own problems, current or future.

Commit to the Relationship

The process of recovery in the first year is chaotic, as we have mentioned. There is tremendous fear that if there is enough anger or hopelessness, one of the spouses will leave the relationship. This fear can lead back to lying, hiding, and placating—the very issues that brought pain in the first place. If there is a desire to be brutally honest in the marriage, it will also be important to remove the threat of divorcing, at least for a time. We recognize that the decision to reconcile after betrayal is a complicated one. It will be made with time to allow for changes, with careful awareness of what is changing, with trust that God is directing the next steps. We generally ask our couples to consider a minimum period of one year to close the door on threats or decisions to divorce so the process of recovery has a chance to work. We know that truth-telling and building emotional and spiritual intimacy depends on the ability to feel safe that divorce is not imminent.

Learn to Be Safe People

If you want people to draw close to you, you need to be safe. It is that simple. Safety is experienced in many ways: emotionally, physically, sexually, spiritually, and financially. We have found that when there is significant lack of safety in a relationship, it is impossible for people to communicate well or even live together. The harm that is done to another is immeasurable. We cannot force growth or move forward in marriage when there is not safety. Therefore, we consider this a vital task of stage 1 of recovery.

Suffice it to say, no one is safe one hundred percent of the time. This is something everyone can continue to work on this side of heaven. We believe that safety involves being responsible for your own recovery, as we have said. It also involves a great deal of ownership. Safety is not present when we continue to blame our spouses for our problems. It is not trying to prove one's own point and to be right all the time. It is not controlling another person. When there is criticism, contempt, defensiveness, shutting down, or stonewalling of our spouses, there is not safety (Gottman 1999). Safety breeds vulnerability. Vulnerability breeds relationship.

Redemptive Separation

For some of our couples, there is so much toxicity in the relationship that it may be necessary for them to separate from each other for a time. It is not unlike sending your child to a "time out" when their behavior is unacceptable. Couples emotionally harm each other with yelling, blaming, using sarcasm, criticizing, using profanity, avoiding, shaming, using "always" and "never" statements, and stonewalling or refusing to talk for days. Physical harm is easily identified as hitting, slapping, or punching someone. But it also involves restraining someone or not allowing them to leave when they desire to do so. Sexual abuse occurs when someone is expected to give their body without their consent to provide sexual gratification to another. It is a taking from someone, not a sharing with someone. It is not just about sexual intercourse. And financial unsafety arises when money is withheld in the relationship or there is a refusal to share financial information with a partner.

Nothing good comes from ongoing abuse. We have created a process we call Redemptive Separation to help couples take a time out from the relationship to work on becoming safer with each other and to learn things about themselves (Laaser and Laaser 2017). We use the word *redemptive* because its purpose is to build something new: a thriving relationship. When two people take their focus off growing their marriage and instead put the focus on growing as individuals, we find they can come back to the relationship with healthier ways to contribute.

Address Underlying Disorders

As Daniel Amen, psychiatrist and pioneer in brain imaging, tells us, "If your brain is not working right, you are not working right" (Amen 1998). You will have difficulty making good decisions when your brain is not healthy. Fifty percent or more of the men coming to our counseling center for help with sexual addiction struggle with ADHD/ADD. We find that the second leading diagnosis among our male clients is anxiety, followed by depression and dysthymia, obsessive-compulsive disorder (OCD), and mood disorders such as cyclothymia and bipolar. Men who have experienced significant invasion trauma—sexually, emotionally, or physically—may also be diagnosed with posttraumatic stress disorder (PTSD).

For betrayed spouses, research indicates that the acts of betrayal also create PTSD symptoms (Laaser et al. 2017). These symptoms are important to acknowledge and to treat as quickly as possible. Any spouse who experienced significant invasion trauma while growing up may have previously developed PTSD. As for our male population, betrayed spouses have often struggled prior to marriage with mental health issues such as anxiety, depression, OCD, and mood instability.

Healing from addiction or betrayal requires attending to brain function. It is important to get accurate diagnoses for both. When a couple can afford to do so, we find great benefit when one or both spouses can get a brain scan (amenclinics.com). This is an expensive assessment; however, we believe that looking at the organ you are trying to treat is more effective than developing a treatment plan based on subjective symptomatology. Healing of these issues is not an automatic prescription for psychiatric medications. Doctors will focus on the benefits of exercise, nutrition, supplements, psychotherapy, meditation, and medication to support brain health. Regardless of the path to diagnosis, we know that attending to mental health struggles is essential to getting well personally and relationally.

STAGE 2: SEEING MORE CLEARLY

The presumption of this stage is that the addict has now been sober for at least one year. The roller-coaster ride of the first year has gone from a mega coaster to a gentler one, still with bumps but not with breathtaking ups and downs. We believe this stage takes place in the second and third years of recovery. It is a stage to work on your emotional, physical, and spiritual life together. It is a stage of repair to careers and finances. It is a time to practice talking about triggers and being safe with each other. It is also a stage in which the couples are not focused on the establishment of sobriety but on their personal growth and the growth of their relationship. We find the following tasks to be key to stage 2.

The Problem Is Not **the** Problem

One of our great teachers and a family systems therapist, Virginia Satir, was fond of saying, "The problem is never the problem, coping with the problem is the problem" (Satir and Baldwin 1984). A couple's conflict can develop over issues that are only symptoms or expressions of deeper issues. That can be true for sex addiction. Sexual acting out is devastating, but it is always a symptom of deeper pain. That is why the twelve-step literature will say to a spouse, "You did not cause his addiction, you cannot control it, nor can you cure it" (Al-anon, n.d.). The behaviors are about deeper pain. When a couple battles over sexual acting out issues or other problems, there is no resolution because the deeper thoughts, feelings, and needs are not being addressed. Counselors can help couples see that they are fighting over issues that are symptoms of the actual problem. When we are counseling a couple, we steer them away from superficial arguments. Instead, we help them walk through deeper levels of understanding by using Satir's Iceberg Model (Laaser and Laaser 2008).

When we help a couple look beyond the symptoms of a problem or trigger, we want each person to think about these deeper layers of feeling and thinking. We start by asking what he or she was triggered by—what was the situation that initiated his or her emotional response? Then we want to hear some of the words that would describe his or her *feelings*. "Were you sad, mad, afraid, disappointed, lonely, and/or ashamed?" There are many words that could be used.

Next, we want to know how he or she would have managed those feelings in the past. What *coping* (unhealthy) behaviors or substances would have been used? This is a statement of ownership: "When I feel this way, I tend to ask you a lot of questions," or "When I feel rejected, I withdraw and don't talk to you."

A next important layer of the iceberg is the *perceptions, meanings, and core beliefs* we have about the situation or problem. We often call this the "story in my head," as it is often not true, but if we don't stop and examine what we are thinking, we can act as if it is true. If someone has forgotten (again) to do something I asked him or her to do, I can perceive that he or she does not care about me. The story in my head could also develop, saying that you only do what you want to do and that you are selfish and will never change. The perceptions can be many, and often, they are not truths.

Continuing down Satir's Iceberg Model, we come to *expectations*, or needs we have. We react to situations because we need something—it is that simple. Figuring out what a need is and then asking for it can be difficult. Most people are not good at either one.

As we move someone down to yet lower levels of the Iceberg, we come to the deeper *desires of the heart*. We have identified seven of these desires, believing that all problems are really issues of unmet desires (Laaser and Laaser 2008). We believe that all men and women desire to be heard and understood, affirmed, blessed (unconditionally loved), safe, touched in nonsexual ways, chosen, and included. When we help someone identify a deeper unmet desire (or several) in any given problematic situation, he or she begins to understand why they were so reactive.

Finally, it is important to discuss the *truth* of each person involved (both husband and wife) and the truth of the situation. These are often very different than the "story in my head" that was originally believed.

When we teach clients how to use this model, we are also interested in encouraging them to know how they would serve each other when they have finished the vulnerable sharing of the iceberg layers. Since all sharing is done in "I" language and is solely about the feelings, thoughts, needs, and truth of the individual triggered by a situation, it can be received as a safe conversation. Learning to talk about problems and triggers in this way can transform relationships, especially a marriage.

Own Your Own Triggers

Triggers are emotional reactions to behaviors or stimuli in life. We know when we are triggered because we feel something: sad, mad, fearful, bored, or something else. For those in their addiction or their betrayal trauma, this awareness of triggers is typically quite diminished. Triggers are not just about sexual stimuli. All people experience these reactions as they live their lives, but often, they don't talk about them. You could be triggered when your son doesn't thank you for all the money you gave him (mad). You could be triggered because you were not invited to a neighborhood party (sad, rejected). You could be triggered because you thought your husband looked too long at a beautiful woman in church (anxious, angry). Because most people do not know how to talk about triggers in a healthy way, they usually blame others for the feelings they are having, they criticize, they try to control something or somebody, they ask a lot of questions, they shut down and don't say anything, or they distract themselves with work or something else. In other words, they find some way to cope.

Clients who do not have space to talk about their triggers often feel as if they are walking on eggshells. It is obvious they have some emotions flowing through them but keep their words and thoughts to themselves. In many Christian families and churches, the rule about emotions is quite simple: Don't talk about them. Under this rule, many people expect others to notice that something is wrong without having to express their experience or trigger, passively experiencing their suffering and hoping it is eventually seen. Recovery equips the individual to talk about what is triggering them and offers information to another person in a vulnerable and emotionally connecting way. It creates the ability to share what is being felt about the trigger, what the story being told in one's head is, and expresses a legitimate need. In this way, recovery work in individual or group therapy or pastoral counseling provides a way for a client to begin owning their triggers by initiating a conversation using the layers of the Iceberg Model.

In recovery, a person can learn to identify triggers and talk about them in a counseling group or with safe people. Eventually, it will be easier to practice with a spouse. Here is an example of a trigger we mentioned in the previous paragraph: "I am anxious and angry that you looked so long at that beautiful woman at church. The story in my head is that I'm not good enough for you. I also assume that you may not be sober and will eventually leave me. The truth is, I have a lot of old pain about not being chosen, and you've given me no reason to believe you will leave. I need to know whether you are working on this in your recovery program and would be willing to change your behaviors of looking too long." Getting clients to come to this place of self-awareness, emotional regulation, and attuned communication is the goal of recovery, and helpers play a significant role in fostering growth in these skills.

As we say, "Triggers are the gifts that keep on giving." Over time, triggers can be a gift to those in recovery to learn to examine what they are trying to reveal about one's emotions, thoughts, current and older pain, and what they need today. As a helper, these triggers are a goldmine of information about the client's interior world, emotional regulation skills, relational responses, and many more dimensions that are pertinent in the healing process. Although most clients, especially betrayed spouses, would like for it to be possible, eliminating all triggers in a client's life is not possible, and therefore not the goal of the therapeutic process. Anyone who is a living and breathing participant in life will get triggered in their recovery. As one gets healthier, they will be able to talk about triggers more quickly, understand from where in their personal narrative the triggers have originated, and manage them more successfully.

Heal Personal Trauma

Personal trauma refers to significant experiences in our earlier lives that affected our beliefs about ourselves, others, and the world. It is not possible to live life and not be impacted by those around you. Sometimes hurt happens from abusive situations. Sometimes it occurs from neglect. In either case, clients who have never had a chance to talk about them and reframe some of the thinking acquired from these situations carry their core beliefs and pain into their relationships. Marriage is no exception. Counseling is a place where trained professionals validate and draw out feelings that have been internalized and move forward with corrected beliefs. When we don't do this work, clients will carry the pain of the past with them into the future, blaming the current situation for all the pain. We call that projecting. No one likes to have someone's old pain projected upon them.

Debbie counseled a woman who had grown up in a family with four brothers. She came to our counseling center because her husband had been looking at pornography and was seeking other women from online dating profiles. He was committed to an extensive recovery program, had been sober for nearly two years, and had a heart change to be a new man. She found that she could not make progress in trusting him, despite the many changes he was making. One day as she got in touch with her earlier life story, she shared with Debbie that she had been sexually abused by all four of her brothers, and her dad had been unfaithful to her mom. She was weeping. She said, "I have been so hurt by the men in my life that I don't know if I can ever trust a man again." She was working through her core belief that had been birthed out of her past. Slowly, she began trusting her husband and his new choices.

Personal trauma is usually old, deep, and powerful. Dealing with it requires skilled intensive counseling programs and skilled trauma specialists. When individuals feel stuck in their recovery or their growth as a couple, we encourage more work on past trauma. There are a variety of methods of doing this kind of therapy, such as experiential therapy, cognitive behavioral therapy, and EMDR. For every professional, and especially pastors, knowing your training, skills, and, most importantly, boundaries, as you walk with clients in recovery is essential. The well-intended but otherwise incompetent attempts at helping that result in harm compound an individual or a couple's trauma and prolong their timetable for recovery.

Become Companions

When Eve was created in the garden of Eden, God promised Adam that she would be a companion fit or suitable for him. That is what we are supposed to be in God's design of one-flesh union. Companions are equals. Companions are patient with each other. We encourage both husband and wife to consider that they are on equal journeys. They need to do their own work, own their own problems, own their own triggers, and aggressively work on being safe. This means that even though the addict has betrayed the relationship in a destructive way, both husband and wife will come to accept that he is not the "identified problem" but that the responsibility for the growth of the relationship is a challenge for both. When a couple is experiencing companionship, they will intuitively know that their spouse wants what is best for them. They will know that each believes, "I am for you."

Find a Spiritual Journey Together

We work with couples from a wide background of Christian faith traditions and occasionally with couples from Jewish faith traditions. As Christian counselors, we believe it is our job to encourage our couples to practice spiritual disciplines such as praying, studying Scripture, reading devotionals, finding a place of worship together, or reading spiritually based books together. It has been our experience that most of our couples come in and typically have an individual spiritual journey, including individual spiritual disciplines. The challenge is finding a spiritual journey together. Since spiritual development focuses on our most important values and beliefs, working on this growth together is critical to creating companionship.

Serve, Not Submit to, One Another

In Ephesians 5, Paul teaches us that we are to become like little children and to lead a life of love just as Christ loved the church and gave up his life for the church. At the end of the chapter, he then quotes Genesis 2 and says that a husband and wife become a one-flesh union. This, Paul says, is a "great mystery" but is like the relationship of Christ to the church. This means, we believe, that couples are not to submit to each other from a place of fear or power with one being more dominant, but that they are called to serve each other sacrificially and submit to one another mutually in love. Again, we are to serve out of love rather than out of anxiety. We are not to serve based on fear of what will happen if we don't serve our spouses. We are to serve because we genuinely love each other. Serving is sacrificial.

Develop Healthy Sexuality

Both Hebrew and Christian tradition are rich in teaching about healthy sexuality, yet we rarely hear it taught today. Basically, we believe that sex is the expression of spiritual and emotional intimacy. One of the words used for sex in Hebrew Scriptures is *yada*, which means "to know" (Gen. 4:1). The word *sex* is never used in Hebrew or Christian Scripture, but the word "to know," *yada*, is. The verb *yada* is used by David in the Psalms to mean to truly know God (Ps. 44:21; 46:10; 69:19). If partners truly "know" each other, they will experience connection emotionally and spiritually. And if emotional and spiritual connection is established in the relationship, whatever physical or sexual connection occurs will be enough.

As we help couples develop healthy sexuality, we find that a period of sexual abstinence is often helpful in accomplishing two things: first, it helps the addict detox from the neurochemical tolerance addiction creates; second, it helps couples get the order of intimacy straight (Laaser and Laaser 2017). If emotional and spiritual intimacy come first, then sex will be an expression of it. The only way for sex to be satisfying is if it is an expression of intimacy. It is essential for both partners to have a mutual understanding of sexual abstinence.

Christian couples may be more vulnerable to some of the historic theological beliefs about sexuality concerning a spouse's "duty" to satisfy their partner sexually. We, sadly, have seen numerous situations in which the sexually betrayed spouse has been spiritually abused by church leaders into believing that sexual acting out is his or her fault. Additionally, submissive sex for a sexual addict can feed the addiction—we call it marital sexual addiction. Before sacred sex can be experienced, understanding how to heal sexual addiction and helping reframe these theological beliefs will be important.

Finally, we believe some couples will need to get professional sex therapy if the patterns of sexuality in the relationship have resulted in sexual dysfunctions. It is important to heal old wounds from sexual and physical abuse. Couples may simply need to learn new and more fulfilling ways to enjoy sexuality. Particularly after abstinence, they may need help in "getting back" to sexuality, something our colleagues Bill and Ginger Bercaw call Sexual Reintegration Therapy (Bercaw and Bercaw 2010).

Forgive One Another

In a relationship hurt by sexual addiction and infidelity, it is understandable that forgiveness of those acting out behaviors is a necessary step for healing the marriage. Forgiveness is a process, in our opinion, not an agenda item to hurriedly check off the list. It is a decision to live out forgiveness for the hurt someone else has caused you. It will include knowing how you have been hurt (the facts of the wrongdoing) and taking time to feel the emotions of the hurt with safe people who can hear you.

With forgiveness, there will be a decision to not keep a record of the wrongs of the past (1 Cor. 13:5), to not punish your husband for those hurts, and to not seek revenge. It does not mean you forget about the pain of those wrongs, as feelings will come up when memories of the past surface. Deciding not to act on them is a matter of discernment and knowing who and when to talk to about it. It may simply mean taking the pain of the hurt to God and allowing him to embrace you in that place.

Forgiveness is also a separate decision from reconciliation and trusting another person. When a wife is ready to relinquish bitterness, resentment, and pain from being hurt, forgiveness will allow her to move on to relational growth if she also desires reconciliation. When she sees her husband working on becoming trustworthy and living with a changed heart, she can begin to trust again.

Growth as a couple, however, involves greater forgiveness than just this step. It is not possible for two people to grow close together without hurting each other at times. That is the nature of intimacy. When we are hurt by someone as we get close, our natural tendency is to pull away and create distance, often without talking about what it is that hurt us. Or sometimes we get big and loud and scare away the person that hurt us so they will stop their behavior. Either way, hurt people continue to hurt people. In many marriages, those hurts eventually lead to divorce. If we choose to keep moving toward each other, it is important to engage in forgiving each other for the little and big ways we cause pain to the other. This requires ownership of what you do, which requires continual self-awareness and an offering of forgiveness. As the tenth step of the twelve steps encourages: we continue to take personal inventory, and when we are wrong, we promptly admit it.

While it can be easy to offer words of forgiveness to each other for the hurtful behaviors we bring to the relationship, we believe it is far more difficult to stop those behaviors for which we have been forgiven. Continuing to display the same damaging words or behavioral choices may lead to a spouse deciding not to reconcile after continual hurt. He or she may choose, instead, to create a healthy boundary from being hurt again. Forgiving one another must include changing how you live as well.

Have Fun Together

As Ecclesiastes says, there is "a time to weep and a time to laugh" (Eccl. 3:4). Having fun together is a vital part of growing together. For most couples, it is not difficult to have fun together in the first stages of the relationship: meeting, dating, and infatuation. As life grows in complexity, responsibility, and disappointment, it gets harder to take time to just play together. Some people learn that you do not play until all the work is done. And as an adult, the work is rarely done. Others find it hard to play when they are sad or mad because it might mean they cannot have those feelings anymore. For others, playing is simply not something they do very well. They know how to work hard; they just don't know how to laugh and play and not be productive.

Couples that heal together practice putting fun into their relationship. They learn to hold the complicated feelings of weeping and laughing. For many couples, the only way they have experienced playfulness with each other is through sexuality. We encourage them to learn how to laugh and enjoy each other in other ways. Our little selves often know how to do this best. So our suggestions might start with swinging together, jumping in piles of leaves, rolling down hills, sledding, and building sandcastles. You get the idea—these activities don't take a lot of money or time. As you experience the value of having fun, your ideas will expand, and relaxation and connection will become a regular part of your life together. Couples that do well will get good at playing.

STAGE 3: THRIVING

The third stage is one in which sobriety is now well cemented and many repairs have been made. Tools of communication have been practiced. Both husband and wife have solid recovery plans and are taking responsibility for the people they want to be. In this stage, couples experience greater serenity and peace, and the deeper spiritual path of recovery can be pursued. In general this begins by the end of the third year. The following tasks are key to stage 3.

Find Purpose in Your Pain

Thriving is a matter of flourishing and prospering. Some may think of it as a matter of acquiring wealth or possessions, but as Christians, we believe this is a matter of finding meaning in life—a purpose for being here. What is your story teaching you about life? Love? Glorifying God? Did you learn lessons primarily when life was comfortable and easy? Or are you finding that trials and adversity have taken you deeper in your character growth toward Christlikeness?

We believe that God doesn't waste our pain. In our trials, he is helping us to become more mature, not lacking anything (James 1:2–4). He is using difficult experiences to strengthen our character, to develop richer relationships through helping and empathizing with one another, to create new possibilities, to grow appreciation of our lives, and to deepen our spiritual walks (Tedeschi and Calhoun 1996). When we can accept the despair of trials and the potential growth they can bring, we can become companions in knowing our story has purpose. A wise person at one of our Couples' Workshops recently said, "Being broken and alone is hard. Being broken and together is hard and better."

Give Back

In the tradition of the twelve steps, the twelfth step is that "having had a spiritual awakening as the result of these steps, we try to carry this message to others." We believe that in this third stage, couples will be open to sharing their stories with others, thereby encouraging them and offering them the hope of what they have experienced. This could mean a variety of ways to carry the message. It might mean simply meeting two-on-two with another couple, sharing with a small group, and even telling your story in a Sunday morning testimony. This may sound intimidating, but we have seen it happen numerous times. The wider church has been silent about sexual problems historically. God has a call on many of you to use your story. He can redeem any painful story, and you have an opportunity to share that hope. Amazingly, when couples choose to give back to God's people, it creates passion and meaning for the marriage. It leads to thriving, not just surviving.

Create Vision

Vision is a matter of being intentional. We use that word often in our counseling. If we do not know where we want to go, we will submit ourselves to a life of reactivity. For many couples, the ideal of creating vision together was lost after the initial phase of infatuation when they dreamed of many things for their relationship. Others simply never thought about vision; they only lived for the moment.

As life builds in complexity—careers, children, responsibilities—it is easy to live day-by-day, one problem, one paycheck, or one event to the next. It is a life of reactivity, being pulled along by the current circumstances. Soon the spark of joy is gone. The passion of marriage is snuffed out by the difficulties of each day.

Vision, however, is being proactive. It is deciding what is important. It is giving time, attention, and money to those things that provide purpose and passion. The idea of creating vision is often difficult because it is perceived as something all-encompassing. So we have created a vision wheel with fourteen different slices of vision, breaking down the process into smaller segments. Couples spend time creating statements about each slice and then come together to create a vision statement together—something to work toward in their marriage. We include many different areas of life such as parenting, finances, careers, education, physical well-being, emotional well-being, spirituality, recreation, social life, and sexuality (Laaser and Laaser 2017).

The problem for some couples is that each partner may have an individual vision, but those visions do not complement each other. It is important to create vision as an individual. However, the couples that only have two separate visions experience *division*. Couples' work, therefore, must help a couple develop a vision that both partners can embrace and pursue. Once a vision statement has been created, taking action steps or setting goals begins. Working toward something meaningful infuses the marriage with joy and passion.

Surrender Living with a Perfect Spouse

When we stand at the altar to profess our love to one another in marriage, we most likely believe that we have found the person who will meet all our needs and heart's desires. *I will be complete. I will be cared for and protected. I will be chosen and treasured as the "one and only." It will be a perfect union.* Most of us expected that our spouses would be the answer to all our problems. Sex addicts genuinely hope that marital sexuality will be the answer to their sexual sins. Both spouses expect that the other will be the answer to all their desires for love, nurture, and attention. We soon find out that our spouse isn't meeting those expectations. This leads to resentments and, for the addict, the sense of entitlement to act out. For spouses, too, there are choices to manage the disappointment of marriage (which we call coping).

Since the fall of humanity in the garden of Eden, there has been no perfect human being other than Jesus. And thus, there is no possibility of a perfect spouse. No matter how hard we might try, we cannot give another person all they need and desire. In fact, we believe God would never want it that way even if he decided to create us with that capability. Why would we ever turn to him and learn to depend on him if there was another human being who could give us all we needed? No doubt, we would not.

Learning to love someone with imperfections and shortcomings is perhaps our greatest earthly challenge. (And please do not interpret that as tolerating the intolerable behaviors of others.) God can and will serve us with all the desires of our hearts when our earthly relationships fall short. We come to the realization that there is no such thing as a perfect spouse. We must depend on God and take our spouses off the pedestals. We practice loving another for their beautiful parts and their flaws. We stop searching for the next right person or relationship to satisfy deep desires that only God can satisfy. This is an act of deep spiritual surrender.

REFERENCES

Al-anon. (n.d.). "The Family Disease of Alcoholism." Al-Anon Family Groups of South Carolina. www.al-anon-sc.org/the-family-disease-of-alcoholism.html.

Amen, D. G. 1998. *Change Your Brain, Change Your Life*. New York: Three Rivers.

Bercaw, B., and G. Bercaw. 2010. *Couple's Guide to Intimacy: How Sexual Integration Therapy Can Help Your Relationship Heal*. Pasadena, CA: California Center for Healing.

Gottman, J. M. 1999. *The Seven Principles for Making Marriage Work*. New York: Harmony.

Laaser, D., H. Putney, M. Bundick, D. Delmonico, and E. Griffin. 2017. "Posttraumatic Growth in Relationally Betrayed Women." *Journal of Marital and Family Therapy* 43, no. 3: 435–47.

Laaser, M., and D. Laaser. 2008. *Seven Desires: Looking Past What Separates Us to Learn What Connects Us*. Grand Rapids: Zondervan.

———. 2017. *A Toolkit for Growth: Practical Recovery Tools for Individuals and Couples*. Minneapolis: Faithful & True.

Satir, V., and M. Baldwin. 1984. *Satir Step-By-Step: A Guide to Creating Change in Families*. Palo Alto, CA: Science and Behavioral Books.

Schneider, J. P., and M. D. Corley. 2012. *Surviving Disclosure: A Partner's Guide for Healing the Betrayal of Intimate Trust*. Charleston, SC: CreateSpace.

Tedeschi, R. G., and L. G. Calhoun. 1996. "The Posttraumatic Growth Inventory: Measuring the Positive Legacy of Trauma." *Journal of Traumatic Stress* 9, no. 3: 455–71.

CHAPTER 13

SEXUAL REINTEGRATION THERAPY

BILL BERCAW, PhD, CSAT, CST

Recently, a woman named Jessica gave us a call asking for help with her marriage. She told us that the main challenges she and her husband were facing related to sexual betrayal, specifically his compulsive use of online pornography and his occasional visits to massage parlors. Now, thirteen months postdiscovery, Jessica said she was hopeful because her husband had been going to individual treatment and to meetings. She had started down a similar path, but she was still in shock and couldn't imagine ever fully trusting him again. The specific thing motivating her to reach out to us was her and her husband's ongoing bedroom struggles. They had been working on things for over a year, but they just couldn't seem to get on the same page sexually. It scared both of them.

This is a familiar profile we first noticed many years ago: we would see both spouses working their individual and couple's recoveries well, but none of the work they were doing translated into meaningful improvement in the bedroom. These couples were not reporting that they felt free, relaxed, and present in sexual situations with each other. Prerecovery dysfunction or dissatisfaction was not melting away as couples moved further into their recoveries. Previously unbalanced patterns of initiation were not automatically balancing themselves, and previously dormant sex lives were not naturally resurging. This left many spouses with the same fear Jessica shared with us during her initial call.

Along with this scenario typically came other complications: some addicts swung in the opposite direction of their compulsivity by shutting down sexually to manage their fears of being compulsive, sometimes showing symptoms of sexual anorexia. Spouses tended to move in one of two directions: they would shut down sexually because sex had become too loaded and threatening, given the recent disclosure or discovery regarding their partner's acting out behavior, or they would become hypersexual as a way of managing their fear of losing their partner if their partner's sexual needs were not satisfied and as an attempt to control their spouse's acting out behavior.

Each partner seemed to be walking along opposite sides of a river, and even when they were doing great work in their recovery, they struggled to find a bridge to each other, to take that next step in their journeys where they could connect through the sensual/sexual realm of their relationship. These couples grappled with the same basic question: What do we do now? One of the greatest challenges facing recovering couples is learning how to be emotionally and sexually intimate after the fabric of the relationship had been severely damaged. And sexual intimacy is an undeniably crucial thread in that fabric. Unlike many other addictions, one can't simply cut sexual intimacy out of one's life and marriage and be better served by the removal.

The net effect of these complicated variables often leaves couples feeling as if they're on their own. Many times, they have been told or they assume that if they just work their programs, the sexual piece will work itself out. However, the only way their sexuality can be reclaimed in a healthy way is if they address it directly and intelligently. That fact is straightforward enough, but it leads to a difficult question: How?

SEXUAL REINTEGRATION THERAPY

When we began pondering this question in the early 2000s, we realized that when it came to working with couples recovering from sex addiction, there were no specific treatment protocols for addressing how spouses and partners can move toward a new sexual and emotional intimacy. We sometimes thought of the parallels between this lack of protocols for recovering couples and life before antibiotics. We knew about the unhealthy agents responsible for all the disease and suffering, and we knew of some ways to manage the symptoms, but we lacked an effective program with which couples could experience the deep healing they desired together. We recognized the need for a specific bridge to help recovering couples find connection in the bedroom while strengthening their intimate relating with each other. We needed to help couples fill the gap between *How do we understand what happened?* and *How does our relationship get to the other side?*

Given this need, we developed Sexual Reintegration Therapy (SRT), a structured way to help couples cross the bridge to the other side of the gulf that formed between them where they are truly creating a new relationship. There, they can experience their healthy, sexually integrated selves in the context of an emotionally and sexually healthy marriage. On the other side of the bridge is a capacity for connecting with each other and being able to trust and be more fully present, both inside and outside the bedroom. There, partners experience increasing feelings of hope, safety, and competence in rebuilding their sexual relationship. They know (for perhaps the first time) what it feels like to embrace a passionate and satisfying sex life while retaining their integrity and being more present with each other. Spouses begin to live abundantly and consistently choose to risk vulnerability with each other as part of that abundance. When couples are introduced to SRT, they begin to see a clear path toward approaching the final frontier of their healing journeys.

SRT is a step-by-step, structured, exercise-based program for couples who have done the hard work of early recovery and are ready to take the next step in their healing and address what may seem like the most daunting area of all: their sexuality. SRT is about more than just helping recovering couples claim and create a healthy and satisfying sex life. Many recovering couples need to recommit to their relationship, which means building their commitment from the ground up. That is usually much different from how they originally entered into relationship with each other, which was often for less conscious reasons and in a less deliberate way. This rebuilding project begins with the ground floor, the couple's emotional foundation. Another strength of the SRT program is that it addresses these two relationship cornerstones—emotional intimacy and sexual intimacy—simultaneously and thereby facilitates their integration with each other. This integration of intimacy with sexuality can be elusive for even the most resolutely committed recovering couples.

Furthermore, there is a strong spiritual component to SRT, characterized by the powerhouse team of reclamation and redemption. Reclamation comes in the form of a shared resolve to reclaim the bedroom, separate from and superior to previous sexual acting out experiences. And as each couple moves toward reclaiming what is rightfully theirs, they can seek and find redemption for the pain and sorrow they have encountered. "To all who mourn in Israel," reads Isaiah 61:3, "he will give a crown of beauty for ashes, a joyous blessing instead of mourning, festive praise instead of despair" (NLT). Very good things can grow out of very bad. We all have the potential to find purpose in our losses so they will not have happened in vain. And we've seen this powerful transformation happen countless times with the couples with whom we've been blessed to work.

In the pages that follow, we will discuss what an effective approach for sexual reintegration for recovering couples looks like, emphasizing the following:

- the parameters of healthy intimacy and sexuality upon which this approach rests,
- the goals and challenges associated with this work,
- the benchmarks we use to determine when couples are ready to begin SRT,
- and a sample of specific exercises that make up each phase of the applied program we've developed.

WHAT IS HEALTHY SEXUALITY?

We have always approached this question through the lens of what most of our clients are looking for and how our model fits within that framework. Our clients are typically looking for roughly the same thing: a mutually satisfying sex life in the context of a closely connected, exclusively committed relationship. They are looking for what we call "sexual abundance." This comes from the momentum of a thriving coupleship, gaining its energy through the connection between a consistently energized living room (emotional intimacy) connection and a consistently energized bedroom connection. As the positive energy circulates between those rooms, it creates its own flow and becomes self-reinforcing.

When a couple is enjoying sexual abundance, they take comfort in the security that their sex life is enough. For many recovering addicts and spouses, this is a major paradigm shift from the days of the recovering addict feeling like he or she can never get enough and the spouse or partner fearing they will never be enough. This shift represents the beginning of a whole new era for the couple. We tell our clients all the time that they are in a position to know the best sex they've ever had because it's the most connected, most intimate, and most spiritual sex they will have had.

However, if both partners keep nurturing the relationship—meaning they keep showing up and being real, vulnerable, responsible, and empathic—there will be some variability regarding their experience of sexual abundance. That is why we remind our recovering couples that variability is a good thing. It is the opposite of addictive/compulsive sexuality, where sex typically is rigid in terms of how it's approached and how the acting out actually happens, and where only one person's sexuality is considered (even when acting out with another person). But a healthy couple's sexuality necessarily varies because two partners are joining together as equals, sharing preferences, negotiating differences, and adjusting to changing conditions and experiences. As they do, they overcome autopilot sexuality and establish a conscious, deliberate, recovery-based approach to healthy sexuality.

COUPLEFLOW VERSUS COUPLEDRIFT

Another concept that relates to SRT is the idea that any couple at any given time is either in a state of flow or a state of drift. These are two contrasting types of relationship dynamics. Where CoupleFlow represents the positive stream of relational energy that enables sexual abundance, CoupleDrift describes the negative stream of relational energy that creates distance between partners.

CoupleDrift is characterized by reacting instinctively to situations with one's partner and being swept away from one negative interpretation and response to the next. It lacks self-awareness and drives a wedge between partners, creating a rising tide of negative assumptions, resentment, and sexual dissatisfaction that gains momentum as it continues. It is often quite subtle, with layers of distance slowly accumulating until it becomes more obvious that there is a problem. Sexual acting out is probably the quickest way to accelerate CoupleDrift.

The living room and the bedroom begin working against each other in CoupleDrift so that instead of sexual abundance, each partner finds an abundance of evidence to support negative beliefs about each other and their relationship (e.g., "He doesn't care about me," "She's always mad about something," "There's no way to keep him happy," and "I'll never be good enough for her"). Sharing a life together presents a steady stream of potential challenges that can accelerate the cycle of CoupleDrift, and couples recovering from sexual betrayal are presented with a heavy additional layer of challenge. Finally, it is important to note that all couples fall into some degree of CoupleDrift once in a while. But in its advanced stage, it becomes a way of life, reinforcing recurring arguments and leading partners to blame each other when things go wrong.

CoupleFlow is the opposite, with intentionally relational behaviors yielding consistent connection and partnership. As the transition takes place from prerecovery's CoupleDrift to secondary recovery's CoupleFlow, a powerful interactive process happens between the two spouses' brains. It's what Dan Siegel calls "interpersonal integration." Thankfully, neither spouse needs to be a neurobiology expert to have a direct impact on the other's brain. Sending affirming or flirtatious text messages, gazing deeply into each other's eyes, slowing down to savor a caress or to communicate more empathically, revealing some vulnerability—each of these actions can facilitate deep resonance between spouses' internal worlds (interpersonal integration) and promote a secure attachment bond. And thanks to recent brain research, we know these loving behaviors are not only good in the moment, but they also strengthen the neural connections in our brains so we are likely to repeat the behaviors.

During interpersonal integration, most of the action takes place in the right hemispheres of the brain. This is where nonverbal information, like an open posture or a compassionate facial expression, is perceived and given meaning (e.g., "My partner is here for me, and it is safe to share this with him/her"). It is also in the right hemisphere where emotion is accessed, allowing partners to connect in ever-deepening ways with each other. When our right hemispheres resonate with each other, we feel an energized bonding that keeps us coming back for more. We feel safe with each other. We can respect our differences and give each other the benefit of the doubt. When we argue, no one walks away feeling like a loser. We trust that our partner is with us—not necessarily perfectly tuned in to us, as that's not realistic for anyone, but consistently tuned in to us, mindful of and responsive to our preferences, struggles, and experience of things.

When this attunement works in both directions, it leads to mutual feelings of empathy and compassion and to shared positive experiences that strengthen the fabric of one's relationship. During such moments of attunement in the living room and bedroom, our brains are awash in bonding and pleasure neurochemicals like oxytocin, vasopressin, and dopamine. When our brains develop a taste for these powerful hormones, they want more. Who knew being hormonal could be such a good thing?

On the flip side, when we experience mis-attunement, which includes everything from name-calling to stonewalling to criticizing, our brains are affected in the opposite manner. They release the stress hormone, cortisol. The limbic regions of the brain (e.g., amygdala and hippocampus), where painful emotional memories are stored from our earliest days, is susceptible to being triggered. In a flash, it can feel like our partners are our enemies instead of our allies. In the absence of empathy and compassion, we look warily at each other. From this place, our brains are prone to slipping into an aggressive state (fight), an avoidant state (flight), or a dissociated, checked-out state (freeze). These primitive states severely limit our ability to relate in a respectful, adult manner with each other, creating a sense of drifting apart.

Clearly, there is a lot going on behind the scenes when partners are cultivating closeness or drifting apart. When working with couples recovering from sexual addiction, everything should be geared toward bringing their brains (especially the right hemispheres) closer together. This will bring them into the state of CoupleFlow they both want.

Ultimately, the goal of the SRT program is to guide partners toward experiencing the best versions of themselves with each other in their closely connected relationship—two people who are separate and responsible for themselves but also in a consistent and interactive state of flow as a couple. Through this state of flow they can experience the best versions of their sexual selves with each other and thereby add the final stone to the foundation of their new relationship.

So that's where we want to lead our couples. Yet before moving on, we should mention two items that will pave the road to successful treatment outcomes: a boundaries workshop and coherent narrative.

Boundaries Workshop

This is usually one of the first things we share with our new SRT couples. It blends concepts with practice and is based on the work of Pia Mellody (see *The Intimacy Factor*). Since intimacy is the process of sharing oneself respectfully and being available to nondefensively receive one's spouse's communications, we need a set of skills in place to facilitate a healthy experience of all this sharing. This workshop provides that skillset and addresses the reason relationships are not easy: they require a specific, critical proficiency in an area where few people have received any formal training.

Think about it. What other highly important project or job would we take on with so little training? In what other project or job would we depend on a partner with a similar lack of training? Would you ever even imagine getting on an airplane with a pilot who had no formal training? Absolutely not. What if he had seen a lot of movies or TV shows with cockpit scenes? No way!

That's exactly what happens in most relationships: we take off fast, go with what we know, and hope for the best. It's no wonder we have so many crash landings. However, if we receive the training needed and acquire that essential relationship skillset, then things become much more hopeful and safer between spouses.

Coherent Narrative

Another foundation of successful SRT treatment is helping our clients develop what Dan Siegel calls a "coherent narrative." This involves knowing the key events and influences in one's life as well as the affect surrounding them. Knowing the story of our lives reveals how we got to this point. Understanding the effects of all the things that have happened to us, our adaptations to what happened, and the influences of choices we have made empower us to be the active authors of the next chapters in our lives.

This process goes a long way toward undoing default ways of interpreting, feeling, and reacting. We strive to make the unconscious conscious by identifying messages we received about how we mattered, our family rules and roles, and what we learned about trust in close relationships. Sometimes spouses can see how the messages they each received intersect with each other, creating a setup for chronic fear-based and shame-based interpretations, mistrust, and distance-creating behaviors. Many times, it is shame- and resentment-reducing for a couple to see clearly how the deck was stacked against the likelihood of healthy intimacy and sexuality. It can make restacking the deck in their favor seem more like a joint project characterized by shared commitment and mutual investment.

GOALS OF SRT

The following four items are the main goals of the SRT program.

1. *To establish a new kind of coupleship characterized by consistently intimate relating.*

   Living in fear of one's spouse is a terrible way to go through a marriage. Nevertheless, this is the root of all intimacy disorders: a fundamental fear of relating with another human being in a deep and meaningful way. Typically, that default programming predisposes one or both partners to consistently and unintentionally create distance in response to the "threat" posed by the other. But if it's true that intimacy runs on the fuel of vulnerability, both spouses will need support throughout the SRT program to consistently take smart risks with each other and tolerate the vulnerability those risks generate. Thus, a significant paradigm shift in the SRT model involves learning to trust a new style of relating as vulnerable partners as not only safe but as the new normal.

2. *To develop a shared vision and plan for sexual reintegration and CoupleFlow.*

   We are learning through recent research about the brain's ability to grow new neural networks when it experiences certain processes of change. One of those is the process of visualization. Just as many world-class athletes have discovered and used the technique of visualizing success as a key component of their actual success, so too can recovering couples. SRT helps couples create a vision of a new life together, both inside and outside the bedroom.

3. *To provide planned opportunities to connect with each other in relaxed, enjoyable ways inside and outside the bedroom.*

   More than any other variable, spouses' abilities to schedule their time with each other and honor their commitments to those times are the variables most highly correlated with success in the SRT program. In order for any good to come from a program that involves two people working closely together, both people must first show up at the same place and the same time, prepared to work together. Because this is so fundamental, we do not leave it to chance. We strongly encourage couples to become good schedulers with each other, planning the dates and times for their exercises just as they would plan anything else that is a priority. And when they do, each partner sends a message to the other: "I value you and our relationship enough to prioritize this time in our busy lives."

4. *To embrace the tension that normally exists in romantic relationships as an opportunity.*

To be in relationship with another person means your needs often will be in competition, values will differ, and opinions will be at odds. This is normal and expected. What becomes problematic is when couples develop a pattern of avoidance strategies or unboundaried communication styles to cope with these situations. As spouses develop the skillset required to negotiate their differing needs, wants, and preferences successfully and respectfully, they gradually realize they do not need avoidance strategies to protect themselves from the inevitable disappointments they experience. In this way, spouses achieve another paradigm shift: "I can move toward my spouse with authenticity instead of hiding my authentic self behind my fears." This shift also becomes a powerful force in our recovering couples' efforts to engineer a shared sex life they both feel good about.

BARRIERS TO SRT

As we accumulated data from our clients' experiences with SRT through the years, themes began to emerge around challenges couples encounter. The following section details some of the commonly cited barriers that can arise during the SRT program.

Difficulty Communicating Directly about Specific Sexual Preferences, Insecurities, or Obstacles

Couples in recovery from sexual betrayal and addiction experience more frequent sexual dissatisfaction and dysfunction than the general population. One reason for this is understood through the lens of Patrick Carnes's fourth core belief: "Sex is my greatest need" (1983, 148). This changes everything as far as sexual satisfaction is concerned because sex works best when it is free of any demands, pressures, or performance expectations and is not one's primary source of validation or security. When sex is elevated to the top of one's needs hierarchy, it takes on more than it can be expected to handle, and we see more sexual dysfunction and complaints.

One of the goals of SRT is to put sex back in its place. Couples do this by deliberately deciding how to be in a healthy sexual relationship with one another. Doing so represents another paradigm shift: evolving from being sexually reactive to being sexually proactive. This evolution is characterized by each spouse being intentionally mindful about how to claim their healthy sexual selves and how those healthy sexual selves can enjoy each other. And that is best accomplished by directly and respectfully sharing one's sexual preferences as well as one's insecurities or obstacles.

Unresolved Trauma

Most people struggling with problematic sexual behaviors, as well as many of their spouses and partners, carry unresolved family-of-origin trauma into their relationships. This leads each spouse to be vulnerable to relating through child wounds, creating unhealthy communication patterns and CoupleDrift. This preexisting trauma is bound to be activated while the couple is attempting to heal, including during the SRT program, and is often expressed via overreactions or avoidance strategies. Thankfully, there are a number of highly effective trauma resolution techniques available, including EMDR, Somatic Experience, and Pia Mellody's Post-Induction Therapy (see www.healingtraumanetwork. net). Furthermore, it is widely accepted that spouses and partners carry betrayal trauma, an additional layer of trauma stemming from the betrayal itself (Skinner 2017). Again, there are established treatment protocols to support spouses and partners in healing from the trauma they experienced.

Comorbid Psychological Concerns

In most cases, we need to be as sure as we can that other clinically significant conditions (e.g., mood disorders, cross-addictions) are being managed directly and that each spouse is stable enough to tolerate the demands of a program like SRT (see chapter 12).

Preexisting Sexual Dysfunction or Sexual Dissatisfaction

Many (if not most) of our SRT couples report varying levels of prediscovery sexual dissatisfaction and/or dysfunction. We validate this as normal and emphasize that they are on the cusp of creating the mutually satisfying shared sex life that has felt elusive for so long.

Cybersex

When part or all of one's sexual acting out behavior involves online porn, we must confront the reality that many recovering addicts miss the sexual intensity that only cybersex can provide. As one recovering addict said, "When you've memorized every square inch of your favorite porn star's body but you don't know your wife's body half as well, that's a big problem." The tradeoff of intensity versus intimacy is one many couples will work through during their SRT process. Many spouses and partners worry they were not and will not be enough to meet their spouse's sexual expectations or preferences. That is why it is critically important to distinguish between addictive and healthy sexuality. When a recovering sex addict can consistently articulate the difference between the two, it reinforces that he or she truly wants to discover and build a new sexuality grounded in honesty, vulnerability, and presence. And there is plenty of room for sexual playfulness, novelty, seduction, and yes, intensity between spouses in their new sexual relationship.

Heightened Emotions

As people recovering from problematic sexual behaviors and betrayal trauma move into their respective healing, they are bound to become more connected to their emotional worlds. This is a necessary development, yet it can lead to the experience of some big feelings. Commitment to boundary practice allows each spouse to own and respectfully share their emotions and empathically receive their spouse's emotions.

Negative Reactions to Structure

Some people have an initial or ongoing resistance to the level of structure involved in SRT. Some people struggle with it feeling artificial or mechanical. We try to validate that many people feel some discomfort in response to a clearly defined and structured format, and we try to understand where their discomfort is coming from. For example, in relationships where sex has served as a primary source of validation, people tend to have anxiety around giving up unimpeded access to their sexual security blanket, and it often manifests as resistance to the structure.

WHAT SRT IS NOT

Here are a few things we designed SRT to specifically avoid. SRT is not . . .

Cookie-Cutter

This is a highly structured and defined treatment approach, but it is not one size fits all. Therapists need to know where, when, and how to make adjustments from one couple to the next. For example, for the couple where the recovering spouse struggles with negative self-comparisons to the prostitutes her husband has been with or the porn-star bodies he's been masturbating to, the therapist would be wise to let her set the pace on any exercise involving caressing each other's bodies (or any state of undress). If it's too much anxiety and pain for her to tolerate, we don't want to rigidly adhere to assigning it just because it's the next exercise in the program. In that scenario, perhaps we come back around to it in another month. Or perhaps we look for opportunities for her to gradually regain confidence in her attractiveness by setting up situations that would help that along. The therapist would strive to balance her entirely understandable insecurities with the need to lean into them and would need to tailor the progression through the SRT program accordingly.

Two-Become-One

The goal is not to achieve perfect harmony by molding two separate people into one seamless being. Sexual codependence should never be the goal of a therapeutic intervention, and this is true of SRT as well. Instead, SRT strives to increase the sense of connection and attunement within the coupleship while maintaining a healthy degree of *differentiation*. Differentiation, or the ability to hold appropriate boundaries in a healthy relationship, is a constant growth edge in couples' sexual recovery, both inside and outside the bedroom. The goal is to nurture a consistent connection marked by empathy and compassion, while leaving plenty of room for differences.

Perfection-Seeking

The instructions for the exercises are direct and clear. However, this does not mean it is possible to complete the exercises perfectly. We know there will be huge variances regarding experiences between couples and from exercise to exercise. Some couples will become too attached to doing things by the book. One example is the man who said his biggest problem with one of the caressing exercises was that he kept dropping the book! So, we tell our clients to read the instructions together, put the book down, and relax. Move into the experience together and know that something entirely organic is about to happen despite the structured setup.

READY, SET . . . NOT SO FAST

Despite SRT's proven track record and the many couples who have benefitted from it, we don't just start couples in SRT whenever they ask for it. From many couples' perspectives, it's as if they've been rushing to get to the airport, an urgent desperation driving them to make their flight. It's understandable that as soon as they arrive at the gate, they want to get up in the air together. This couple is often clear when expressing their treatment needs—for example, "We need help with our sex life more than anything else. That's our main need right now."

Sometimes, we might assess the couple and agree with them: "Yes, based on where you are in your recoveries, this looks like a great time to squarely address rebuilding your coupleship, including your sexual intimacy. Let's begin SRT."

But other times, we might need to paint a picture of recovery over time and convey that now is the time to position themselves for SRT by focusing on the things they each need to work on before starting. Most often, one or both spouses would benefit from individual work. The betrayer often needs support in setting up his program and in understanding how to compassionately embrace his spouse's betrayal trauma responses while she typically needs support in dealing with her betrayal trauma (or vice versa depending on the gender of the betrayer and betrayed spouse). Whenever we get a new couple, we have a checklist of couple's tasks that help us determine their readiness for SRT:

1. *Safety/Boundary List*

    This is the betrayed spouse's list of boundaries detailing the actions that would either help her or him feel safer in the relationship or would trigger a consequential response. An example of the former would be, "Continue with weekly individual and group therapy." An example of the latter would be, "Any acts of dishonesty or deception would indicate a need for you to participate in an individual intensive." This list requires therapeutic support in both its preparation and delivery. The betrayer also needs therapeutic support to prepare to hear the list nondefensively and to respond compassionately. Sometimes specific items need to be negotiated (e.g., internet usage, business travel).

2. *Boundaries Workshop* (See the section with the same title above in the CoupleFlow vs CoupleDrift section of the chapter.)

3. *Formal Disclosure*

    This is the betrayer's opportunity to give a full accounting of his or her acting out behavior. Therapeutic support is necessary to provide guidance regarding how to structure the document and regarding appropriate levels of detail. Coordination between each spouse's therapist is essential so that the betrayed spouse's specific questions are addressed. The disclosure statement is meant to be read aloud by the betrayer to his or her spouse in a therapist's office, typically with both spouses' therapists present. Dan Drake and Janice Caudill's (2019; 2021) workbooks *Full Disclosure: How to Share the Truth After Sexual Betrayal*, volumes 1 and 2, are an excellent resource to assist clients through this crucial process of healing for their coupleship.

4. *Impact Letter*

Occurring following disclosure, this is the betrayed spouse's written account of the specific areas of traumatic impact that the betrayer's acting out behavior has caused. It is not designed to shame the betrayer but instead to honor the betrayed spouse's pain. Again, therapeutic support is required for each spouse and for the couple.

5. *Emotional Restitution*

This is the betrayer's response to the impact letter. In it, he or she addresses each specific aspect of the impact letter, striving to own responsibility for their hurtful behavior and to validate their spouse's feelings each step of the way.

6. *Coherent Narrative*

The level of self-awareness and understanding typically gained through trauma work allows people to develop a coherent narrative. (See above.) It can be a significant and powerful trust-building exercise for the betrayers to read their narrative to their spouses because there is a big difference between, "Trust me, I'll never do that again," and "Now that I understand the connection between my early trauma and why I turned to acting out compulsively, why I was able to compartmentalize as I did, and how I was able to rationalize going so far outside my values and my commitment to you, I am actively pursuing healing the wounds that made me vulnerable to all that dysfunction. I know what to look out for in my mind that could represent the leading edge of a relapse."

As helpful as this can be for the betrayer, completing the same exercise holds great promise for empowering the betrayed spouse as well. When both spouses are willing, the SRT exercise that guides them in creating their couple's narrative affords them the opportunity to integrate their life stories and to see how they fit together—usually in some ways that are healthy and some that are not. This is not an absolute prerequisite for beginning SRT, though it is highly desirable for couples to complete this exercise at some point in the process.

While some couples may be frustrated by not being able to start SRT on day one, there is a simple reason for the checklist of couple's tasks that we communicate to our clients: we are not going to let you get started until you are set up for the kind of success that you can trust and maintain as long as you are together. But once a couple has reached the specific benchmarks, by all means, it's time to get started!

THE FIVE PHASES OF SRT

Once a couple has completed the couple's tasks, they are well positioned at the SRT starting line. We then ask them to read the *SRT Playbook*, which introduces the structure of the program. It describes the categories of exercises, called Planned Intimate Experiences (PIEs), as being either communication, caressing, educational, or some combination of those three. It also details the roles they will alternate between during the caressing PIEs (caresser/receiver) and the spirit and philosophy surrounding each role. Finally, it prepares the couple for the typical arc of a PIE, including scheduling, preparation/initiation, and discussion.

The following is a synopsis of each of the five phases of SRT and a sampling of the over forty PIEs:

Phase 1: Shared Commitment

The main goal of the Shared Commitment phase is establishing a solid base of mutual investment in the healing process and a shared experience of pulling in the same direction toward the same goal: a new relationship both spouses are grateful for and proud to be part of. In this phase, there is no prescribed touching (that comes in the next phase). Instead, the emphasis is on Communication PIEs to . . .

- Create an atmosphere of trust and mutuality (SRT Couple's Contract, Recovery Check-Ins)
- Reinforce CoupleFlow momentum via affirmation (Attraction in Action)
- Establish consistent, intimate connection (Daily Shares)
- Expand hope through vision work (Past, Present, Future)

Recovery Check-Ins (RCI)
- Type: Communication
- Purpose: Facilitate a consistent, structured sharing of basic recovery information between partners via a mutually crafted outline of check-in topics.
- Benefit to the betrayer is he or she can (1) feel empowered to share about one's recovery on one's own terms, on a predictable schedule and (2) seize an opportunity to be vulnerable and demonstrate follow-through with commitments.

- For the betrayed spouse, the healing process is often an exercise in tolerating anxiety. Knowing that an RCI is on the calendar often helps to bind one's anxiety between check-ins. It not only gives betrayed spouses a chance to experience their spouse being vulnerable, it also gives them a chance to hear from their spouse on high-value topics and action steps regarding their recovery. The betrayed spouse also benefits from the scheduled opportunity to ask questions.
- Testimonials: "They help her feel a lot better and less stressed, which helps me feel a lot better!" "I like not having to ask him how he's doing or to look for signs of what he's doing. I know every Wednesday night at 8:00 he's bringing it to me."

Daily Shares

- Type: Communication
- Purpose: Jumpstart intimate connecting (as little as five minutes) via a powerfully efficient four-step check-in process.
- Because of its efficiency and consistent results in enhancing connection, it helps couples stay in the habit of connecting. If couple's recovery is a chance to reorder how we relate, the Daily Shares PIE is an intentional step in that direction.

Past, Present, and Future

- Type: Communication
- Purpose: This PIE helps couples look across seven elements of their relationship from three dimensions of time, helping to create a vision of a new life together, both inside and outside the bedroom.
- We are learning through recent research about the brain's ability to grow new neural networks when it experiences certain processes of change. One of those is the process of visualization (see above). This PIE takes advantage of that process in the context of a couple's relationship.

Phase 2: Courageous Discovery

- Focus begins to include the physical and sensual aspects of intimacy.
- The first of the caressing PIEs are introduced with each one emphasizing presence (Hands and Feet Caress; Face Caress; Back Caress; Sensual Bathing; Quiet Cuddle; Body Caressing 1).
- Slowing down enough to notice each other and to notice what's happening for each person can be challenging for some, but that is where great potential lies for vulnerability and connecting (Mutual Gaze; The Other Side of the Door; Mirror, Mirror).

- Couples also engage in self-assessment and sharing about long-standing sexual attitudes, beliefs, and body image (Sexual Image Assessment).
- The physical PIEs purposefully heighten sensual experience and bonding through shared pleasure by a more intentional approach, expanding beyond genital/intercourse/orgasm focus (which typifies compulsive sexuality) to a more holistic experience.
- The cornerstone for many of these physical PIEs is a technique called *sensate focus*, originally developed by William Masters and Virginia Johnson, then furthered by Helen Singer Kaplan. Sensate focus involves a sloweddown, pressure-free approach to physical pleasuring so partners can enjoy a higher quality connection to their senses during their time together. Sensate focus is also a great way to promote one of the basics for sexual arousal: relaxation.
- When partners are not adequately relaxed and instead are experiencing anxiety, the sympathetic nervous system is triggered, and the body directs blood away from the genitals and erogenous zones and toward the body's core. There is then a tendency to rush through the act and/or to struggle with sexual responsiveness. But a relaxed body and mind are primed and ready to experience pleasure in an uninhibited way. The parasympathetic nervous system is engaged and blood flows freely to the genitals and erogenous zones. There is a strong, present connection to bodily sensations and a tendency to give in to the moment.
- Many people are pleasantly surprised by how much they enjoy the slower approach of these sensate focus PIEs and by how happy they are to have a more varied menu for pleasure.
- Testimonial: One recovering sex addict, a seventy-year-old man, reported, "I told myself, 'This seems kind of silly, but I guess I have to go with the program.' A few minutes later, I was shocked at the tears flowing down my cheeks while my wife caressed my hands while looking into my eyes. It was so simple and not at all sexual, but the connection was pretty powerful."

Hands and Feet Pleasuring

- Type: Sensual Caressing
- Purpose: Introduce couples to a new type of sensual touch and to the roles of "caresser" and "receiver."
- Many people are pleasantly surprised at how pleasurable and connecting the experience of caressing each other's hands and feet can be.
- The challenge (and the opportunity) is to slow down in order to increase one's capacity for a wider range of sensual pleasure.

- The environment is intended to be free of demand or pressure of any kind with an emphasis on experimenting with pleasurable touch.

Front Door, Side Door

- Type: Communication
- Purpose: Assist couples in exploring how they typically get their needs, wants, and preferences met in relationship with each other and in identifying potential adjustments to maladaptive styles.
- The front door represents a direct and honest communication style, whereas the side door represents indirect or even non-existent communication. Most people who struggle with sex addiction also struggle with direct communication of their needs, wants, and preferences.
- The goal is to support them (and their spouses) to find the courage to consistently use the front door despite what may be a well-worn path to the side door.
- **Example 1.** Here is one man's side-door (default mode) experience of an ordinary interaction with his wife: "In the past, I would let my wife's appetite dictate whether I ate or not. I would ask her, 'Are you hungry? Do you want to eat soon?' If she said yes, we would eat. If she said no, we wouldn't. When she said no and I was hungry, my resentment would build as the time went by, but all the while I would not say anything." This PIE guided him in envisioning how this same situation might be different if he were to use a front door approach: "I am getting hungry, and I would like to eat soon. What time were you thinking of having dinner? If you're not hungry that's okay; I'll have a quick snack to tide me over." In this way, he found a way to be true to himself while communicating clearly and respectfully, steering clear of resentment.
- **Example 2.** A couple needed curtains for their living room windows. For the last three years, they had the curtain rod and valence installed, but no curtains. The whole time, the husband was thinking, *I would really like to have some curtains on the windows.* But his side-door default mode led him to the safety of silence, so he never said anything to his wife about this. Every time he was in the living room, he resented his wife because they still had no curtains. Here's what his front door transformation looked like: "I would like to have the curtains installed on the windows. I would like for us to look at some options and make a decision on ones we both like." His wife was shocked to hear this because they had gone years without curtains, and she had no idea it made a difference to him whether they had curtains.

Phase 3: Revelation

- This phase focuses on a spirit of curiosity and learning about one's own and one's partner's sexuality. This includes not just sexual anatomy but each person's unique sexual response cycle as well (Sexual Experience Graph).
- It pulls for vulnerability in the context of a safe, structured environment as spouses are guided in sharing and teaching each other their sensual and sexual preferences (Adult Show and Tell, Hands-on Lesson).
- Couples typically experience deeper levels of trust, intimacy, and self-acceptance via the process of revealing themselves to each other. This often stands in sharp contrast to the previous years' enduring less pleasurable touch, either due to the embarrassment or fear of direct communication or because they simply did not know their bodies well enough to share their preferences.
- Couples are guided in consolidating their SRT experiences to this point and in sharing them with each other (What I Know Now). This process reinforces the significant progress that the couple has made at about the halfway mark of the SRT program.

Sexual Experience Graph

- Type: Communication/Education
- Purpose: Provides information regarding sexual response and guides couples in creating a graph that captures their typical sexual responsiveness through the four phases (excitement, plateau, orgasm, and resolution). It allows couples to develop a better sense of their sexual selves and to share what they are identifying with each other by walking each other through their sexual response graphs.
- Also helps each spouse to identify and share the erotic moments and obstacles that occur during a typical sexual experience.

Here are the responses from one couple's Sexual Experience Graph:

JULIE

1. **Excitement phase.** My first erotic moment is a faint sense of sexual desire followed by a spontaneous thought about being sexually intimate. My first obstacle occurs immediately after my erotic moment when I think, *I am not sexy/pretty/adventurous enough for Jeff,* and I then feel shame. I know where this obstacle comes from: *It was your years of sexual avoidance and*

lack of initiation and then discovering that you were getting your sexual needs met elsewhere. I run into my next obstacle when the fight within myself begins: *Do I ask for what I want, or do I play it safe and say nothing? I want to move toward him, perhaps with a suggestive touch, but how will he respond? Will he want to go further or give me one of his "good friend" hugs before pulling away?*

2. **Plateau phase.** I encounter several obstacles in this phase: first is removing my clothes and being naked. I'm so sure you do not like what you see, and I wish I was twenty pounds lighter like I was before three kids. Another obstacle is when things start progressing sexually, and something is happening that I don't like or is not pleasurable. I am afraid to say anything for fear of how you might react. But if part of our foreplay involves oral stimulation, it is definitely an erotic moment. When you do that for me, it's a slam dunk, always an amazing experience. When I can see and feel signs of your arousal, it's another erotic moment for me, as it usually gets me even more sexually aroused because I know you're turned on by me.

3. **Orgasm phase.** If you can't delay your orgasm until I've had mine, I say it's okay, but I don't feel okay, so I guess that's a bit of an obstacle. Just some minor frustration. After your orgasm, you manually and orally stimulate me to orgasm, which is great and definitely an erotic moment. I just have to be careful to ignore negative thoughts and feelings about not having simultaneous orgasms during intercourse because they become obstacles.

4. **Resolution phase.** I'm not sure this is erotic, but I guess it kind of is: I love the sense of closeness after we've had sex and we are holding each other. It's nice when you are not in a rush to get out of bed, because then I feel like you want to enjoy that quiet, vulnerable time with me.

JEFF

1. **Excitement phase.** My first erotic moment is kissing you, holding you, and feeling your body lean into mine. It tells me you really want to be with me. I also like it when you are the one who makes the first move.

2. **Plateau phase.** Undressing you or watching you undress and then seeing you naked is a huge erotic moment. So is touching you sexually and having you touch me. Sometimes though, if I notice that you aren't lubricating, I think, *I need to make it more pleasurable for her.* So this obstacle is about me feeling inadequate and responsible for your sexual

responsiveness. I don't say anything because I'm afraid I would need to say it perfectly (and even if I do say it perfectly, you still might have a negative reaction).

3. **Orgasm phase.** My next obstacle occurs as soon as we begin intercourse. I am afraid of reaching orgasm too fast and not being able to slow down. And when I can't, I feel like a failure. This fear has even led me to avoid sexual intimacy with you through the years, even when I really want to be with you. But you are always very nice about it when it happens. I enjoy helping you have your orgasm after I've had mine—definitely an erotic moment. But in the back of my mind, I fear you're unhappy with my inability to control my orgasm so we can both have one during sex.

4. **Resolution.** Holding you after we're done is really nice. Sometimes I wish we had more time to just lie there together, but usually one or both of us has to get to our next thing. I usually feel very relaxed physically and emotionally, but I wonder if me getting there too soon is something you silently resent.

It's helpful for the therapist to help each couple process what surfaces during the sharing of their graphs. Julie and Jeff are a great example of a couple who needed to talk more about their sexual realities, and doing this PIE opened up some new dialogue for them. For example . . .

- It was meaningful for Julie to hear directly that Jeff actually enjoys some of the things she assumed he did not. It was important for her to know that she is enough for him, and he does desire her. A critical clarification was to understand that it is his fear of inadequacy and fear of reaching orgasm too quickly that has been responsible for his sexual avoidance. Talking about his long-standing source of shame therapeutically led Jeff to seek treatment with a sex therapist for premature ejaculation.

- It was important for Jeff to learn from their discussion that her lubrication is not an indication of her enjoyment. Also, as a function of talking directly, Julie was able to give Jeff the green light to reach for the lubricant whenever he wanted. She also clarified that, while he is involved in her sexual responsiveness, she absolutely does not think of him as being responsible for it.

- This PIE motivated Julie to ask her women's group about sexual expectations and responsiveness. One surprising bit of feedback was that the women told her they all need clitoral stimulation to reach orgasm, that it does not just happen through intercourse. Julie was surprised to hear that and resolved to begin experimenting with more direct clitoral stimulation during intercourse.

- They both realized they needed more experiences to know their preferences better. This is significant because this is a couple who has been married thirty years and realize they need to have more time together to figure out what they each like and to continue communicating directly with each other.

Phase 4: Enhancement

- This is where things really start to gel. Couples are able to clearly identify tangible gains in both emotional intimacy and in their progress toward sexual abundance. These noticeable gains are fueled by vulnerability, with each spouse taking smart risks with each other, allowing themselves to be known and feeling much closer as a result.
- The goal of this phase is to enhance each spouse's ability to share their sexual realities with each other. Toward that goal, there is an emphasis on experimenting with each other to see what feels pleasurable as well as on teaching each other about what one is learning about their touch preferences (Total Body Caress II).
- Having fun and keeping things light in the bedroom is a strong theme in this phase. (Surprise Me, Bedroom Soccer).
- Momentum should be building throughout this phase. That is not to say there won't be any obstacles, but overall we expect to see couples feeling more confident and hopeful that they are moving on to the vision they have for their reinvigorated relationship.

Just a Kiss

- Type: Sensual
- Purpose: Utilize an everyday form of affection to rekindle passion and intimacy.
- Time and time again, we hear from the women we work with that "we just don't kiss anymore." Indeed, one of the first types of affection that typically declines during the course of a marriage is passionate kissing. One reason some women avoid initiating kissing is that they don't want to "mis-signal" their husbands that they are interested in having sex when all they are interested in is kissing and cuddling. In this scenario, she wants to avoid the dynamic where she feels like she is turning him down, and then he feels rejected. Along the same lines, one reason some men stop initiating kissing is that they only do so when they hope it will be merely

a stepping-stone on the way to sex. Kissing is like a sculpture in the attic that has been discovered while packing for a move. You have it appraised only to find it's worth more than you ever dreamed. It was there all along, for years—perhaps even decades—losing its luster and fading from your conscious awareness. But when you dust it off and properly display it, you once again appreciate its value.

- One couple, Jon and Mary, had been married for fifteen years. After kids and after discovery of Jon's acting out behavior, kissing was all but nonexistent. For a while, Mary had no desire to kiss Jon, but over time as they were both on track with their recoveries, Mary expressed an interest but also a concern about how to approach it.

- The structure of this PIE helped both of them manage their expectations and allowed them to enjoy being in the moment and having fun with kissing again rather than thinking of where it would or wouldn't lead.

- They both reported a freedom in the moment and heightened feelings of emotional intimacy as they realized they were sharing something special and intimate with each other. At this time, Mary told Jon about her previous concerns about mis-signaling him in the past and her desire to kiss for the sake of kissing. Jon agreed that he would like to experience that as well and also expressed some sadness in realizing Mary had chosen not to kiss in the past based on his reaction or pressure he might have put on her.

Phase 5: Integration

- Entering this fifth and final phase of SRT, couples have likely made significant changes to how they think about sexuality both as individuals and as a couple.

- Couples are typically acutely aware of the contrast between former, dysfunctional ways of interacting and the new, intimacy-centered way of interacting (What I Know Now II).

- Couples are beginning to trust that these changes are real, and they are becoming more adept at dealing with roadblocks, channeling a spirit of partnership, and drawing on enhanced resilience. PIEs pull for recognition of progress made in these areas and the shared appreciation that usually accompanies it (Gratitude Letter).

- By this point in the SRT program, the sensual and communication exercises have positioned couples to begin adding intercourse to their menu of shared pleasure (Putting It All Together).

- Couples are guided in identifying and appreciating their shared spirituality (My Spiritual Moment).

- This last phase is about recognizing and claiming victories as well as planning for the ongoing work to be done (Lifetime Blueprint).

Gratitude Letter

- Type: Communication
- Purpose: To harness the power of gratitude to enhance mutual positive regard and thereby strengthen the felt connection between spouses.
- Nothing reinforces and enhances abundance like gratitude. At this point in the SRT program, couples have plenty of tangible accomplishments and victories they can point to and celebrate.
- This PIE asks spouses to capture their feelings of gratitude—for each other and for how far they have come together—via letter they are guided in writing to each other. Sample questions include the following:
  - Think of a direct request that you have made of your partner during this process. What has your partner done that has been helpful to you?
  - Were there times you saw your partner stretching him/herself to be relational in a way that may not come naturally?
  - Were there times when your partner was there for you during a difficult part of the program?
  - Were you aware that your partner kept showing up and being present throughout the process?
  - Note: These are suggestions, and the couple is not limited to these ideas.

Lifetime Blueprint for Emotional Intimacy and Sexual Abundance

- Type: Communication
- Purpose: To consolidate all of the practices and experiences each spouse has come to value into an inventory (e.g., protecting time together, practicing functional boundaries in order to share more deeply, kissing for the sake of kissing, doing RCI's and Daily Shares, and more) and then convert that inventory into a series of action steps, which constitutes the couple's Lifetime Blueprint.
- The SRT program has been building toward helping each spouse create a new way of being in relationship with the other: an emotionally intimate and sexually abundant relationship. By now, this relationship is more energized, present, respectful, resilient, and hopeful than ever before. Because there is a new system in place, these highly valued characteristics are renewable and sustainable as long as the system continues to be engaged.

- The couple uses this blueprint to guide their check-ins with each other as well as their periodic check-ins with their couple's therapist. The blueprint can be modified and adjusted to encompass each couple's growth and advancement through the years.
- We encourage couples to review their blueprint together on a monthly basis to see how it's working and how closely they're following it and to see if any modifications are needed.
- We also encourage couples to review this plan with their couple's therapist on at least a quarterly basis.

Here is a sample Lifetime Blueprint:

1. We will schedule our upcoming PIE times for the week every Sunday at 8:00 p.m.
2. We will meet for RCIs on the first and third Sundays of the month at 8:15 p.m. (following PIE scheduling; Jack initiates).
3. We will meet for Daily Shares every night at 8:30 (except Wednesday, which will be at 9:00 p.m. to accommodate Jack's meeting; alternate responsibility for initiating on weekly basis).
4. We will reserve two PIEs per week for pleasuring that leads to intercourse and one PIE that does not.
5. We will define successful experiences by how present and connected we feel, not by how intense the experience is.
6. We will kiss passionately on a regular basis, just to enjoy kissing, not only during our sexual times.
7. We will use the Boundaries Communication Guidelines when we feel uncomfortable or anxious or want or need something. This works for us!
8. We are each responsible for our own pleasure. We will redirect and welcome redirection in keeping with this principle.
9. We will take one weekend per quarter for our marriage (go to a bed and breakfast, camping trip, hotel on the beach). We will both participate in the selection and planning of each destination.
10. We will each continue to work our recovery programs.
11. We will review this Lifetime Blueprint at our first Daily Share of the month and ask, "How are we doing?" (then use our Boundaries Communication Guidelines).
12. We will meet with our therapist every three months to review our Lifetime Blueprint.

A FINAL WORD: HOPE

Some of our clients, in moments of despair, have asked, "Do you think there's hope for us?" Despite all the pain they have experienced, we believe the answer largely depends on what they are willing to do. If they each are willing to follow a program designed specifically to address their unique challenges, even and especially when confronted with imposing obstacles, then yes, absolutely there is hope. And that hope is a flame that must be kept alive and fueled in order to reclaim what is rightfully theirs and to find redemption for the pain they have experienced in the form of a new relationship for which they are both grateful.

REFERENCES

Carnes, P. J. 1983. *Out of the Shadows: Understanding Sexual Addiction.* Minneapolis, MN: CompCare Publications.

Caudill, J., and D. Drake. 2021. *Full Disclosure: How to Share the Truth After Sexual Betrayal-Volume 2 for Partners: Preparing for Disclosure on Your Terms.* Independently published.

Drake, D., and J. Caudill. 2019. *Full Disclosure: How to Share the Truth After Sexual Betrayal.* Independently published.

Mellody, P. 2004. *The Intimacy Factor: The Ground Rules for Overcoming the Obstacles to Truth, Respect, and Lasting Love.* New York: HarperCollins.

Skinner, K. 2017. *Treating Trauma from Sexual Betrayal: The Essential Tools for Healing.* Orem, UT: GrowthClimate Incorporated.

PART 3

TREATMENT STRATEGIES AMONG SPECIAL POPULATIONS

CHAPTER 14

MAKING ADVANCES:

Reclaiming Sexual Wholeness for Female Sex and Love Addicts

Marnie C. Ferree, MA, CSAT

O nly a few years ago it would have been unheard of to include a chapter about women who struggle with sexual addiction in a Christian-based treatment guide. As the issue was explored and the treatment field evolved in the 1980s and '90s, the focus was solidly on men. Males were the ones identified as sexually addicted, and male pronouns dominated the early self-help books and clinical articles. Like many health disorders, whether physical or mental, early research also focused on men, as they presented most frequently for treatment and were generally believed to far outnumber the few females who might grapple with this disorder.

When the faith-based community began to address sexual addiction, largely prompted by the pioneering work of Mark Laaser, who published *The Secret Sin: Healing the Wounds of Sexual Addiction* (1992), women again were left out of the discussion. Indeed, Christians seemed even less likely to consider that females could be among the sexually addicted. When I challenged one popular Christian writer and speaker who was addressing men's battle with pornography in the mid-1990s about including women in his illustrations, the scoffing answer was that women didn't deal with this problem. I received the same response from multiple Christian publishers when I was finishing the original version of *No Stones*, my book about women's experiences as sex and love addicts. Finally, one honest editor admitted he believed that women struggled, but the topic was "too hot" for his publishing house to tackle. I self-published the book, originally titled *No Stones: Women Redeemed from Sexual Shame* (Ferree 2002) rather than "women

287

redeemed from sexual addiction" based on strong feedback that women would never buy a book that called them sexually addicted. Eventually, after significant grassroots success, the book was picked up by InterVarsity Press, and a second edition was published in 2010 properly subtitled *Women Redeemed from Sexual Addiction* (Ferree 2010). I am grateful we have made advances in recognizing women's experience as sex and love addicts and including them in treatment resources, including Christian ones.

What has not changed enough is the lopsided balance of information, and especially resources, available for female sex and love addicts (FSLAs). A group of female colleagues collaborated to meet this need with the publication of *Making Advances: A Comprehensive Guide for Treating Female Sex and Love Addicts* (Ferree 2012), which I was privileged to edit and cowrite. Although today book chapters, and certainly clinical articles, consistently address sex and love addiction in women, this population is still widely underserved. As the authors of *Making Advances* explore, women are different from men (of course!), and treating women is very different from treating men. This distinction is especially true when it comes to the uniquely intimate issue of sexuality, including its addictive presentation.

Early clinical thought was based solely on women's experience as sex and love addicts, later expanding to include the experience of those who treated them. These treating individuals were also largely sex addicts themselves, as the field followed the path of alcoholism, where those who were personally afflicted by the disorder were motivated to receive psychotherapy training in order to help other sufferers. The writers of *Making Advances* recognized the gender gap in research and developed a Women's Sexuality Survey to compare the women who self-identified as sex and love addicts with those who described themselves as nonaddicts (Corley and Hook 2012).

As expected, the impact of FSLA (the initials will also identify female sex and love addiction as well as female sex and love addicts) was clearly demonstrated (Ferree 2012, 21). In a cohort of almost 500 women, 261 identified as either sex and love addicts or sex addicts, compared with 230 women who did not. Among the sex or love addict group,

- 67% reported feeling bad about their sexual behavior.
- 70% felt degraded by their behavior.
- 49% reported they could not control their sexual desire, compared to 10% of the nonaddict group.
- 71% reported withdrawal symptoms such as irritability, anxiety, and depression when not able to act out.

- 45% reported their sexual behavior had interfered with family life and personal responsibilities.
- 62% made failed efforts to stop the behavior.

Clearly, women who struggle with sex and love addiction are hurting and need compassionate, trained therapists and clergy who can assist them.

SHAME AND CULTURAL MESSAGES

Although there is a clear neurobiological component to sexual addiction, which Bill Struthers explains in chapter 2 of this text, at its core, sex and love addiction is a shame-based disorder. In the insightful book *The Soul of Shame*, psychiatrist Curt Thompson (2015) explores this debilitating emotion and belief that "I am a horrible, terrible person who is deeply flawed and thoroughly unlovable." Shame creates a perpetual loop of reinforcing experiences. Shame causes us to hide from others out of fear of being known—of being revealed as the despicable humans we are. However, this deep isolation feeds the very shame we seek to avoid.

For the woman struggling with sex and love addiction, shame is her relentless stalker. After nearly twenty-five years of treating FSLAs, the comment I still hear from them more than any other is, "I thought I was the only one!" A fear of being all alone in battling this issue keeps many women silent about their problem. With only a handful of notable recent exceptions, specifically the graphic memoir *Getting Off* by Erica Garza (2018) and the movie *Unlovable* by Charlene deGuzman (Roskind and Yoonessi 2018), the decidedly male face of sexual addiction fuels FSLA's belief that they are somehow uniquely flawed.

Compounding the shame is a persistent cultural double standard about men's and women's sexual behavior. Although the #MeToo movement is holding men more accountable, males have long received a cultural pass for sexual impropriety. Their sexual proclivities were excused as "just a guy thing" that women had to tolerate or overlook. Even at the highest level of political office or media fame, men might have been criticized, but they were rarely held responsible.

For the Christian woman, the shame around sexual problems is intensified. Within religious circles, the judgment for female "sinners" is usually harsher. In fact, when a husband fails to control his sexual impulses, a finger is often pointed at his wife, who is encouraged to be more sexual with him to keep him at home. It is unheard of for a man to be implicated in his wife's acting out.

Culturally, a woman is in a sexual double bind. Kelly McDaniel (2012) outlines four damaging feminine messages in Western culture:

- "I must be good to be worthy of love."
- "If I am sexual, I am bad."
- "I am not really a woman unless someone desires me sexually or romantically."
- "I must be sexual to be loveable."

These conflicting messages are a setup for problematic sexual behavior. Being sexual proves a woman is desirable and loveable, yet being sexual also proves she is bad. Add the Christian emphasis on sexual celibacy until marriage, without much accompanying exploration of healthy sexuality and relationships, and a woman is adrift in a toxic sexual sea she is not equipped to navigate. Yet she is punished when she fails to live up to sexual expectations of purity.

The pervasive messages of pornified culture add to the shame as women are bombarded daily with eroticized images of females. Women internalize these images as normal—desirable—and they come up short in comparison, which in turn shapes their sense of self, namely, their self-concept (how they think about themselves) and self-esteem (how they feel about themselves), as well as what expectations they perceive others hold for them. Any sense of unworthiness these airbrushed expressions of femininity awaken in her add to the sense of shame she carries and the lies she believes about herself, namely, "I am not pretty enough. I am not sexual enough. I will never be enough."

Again, the church unintentionally adds to the shame of FSLAs by largely ignoring them in Christian literature and public conversation and even excluding them from support groups for those struggling with sexual addiction. While initially gender-specific groups are helpful, ones for women are rarely available within faith-based environments. Women are also prohibited from taking part in a Christian sex addiction recovery group with men, so where can an FSLA turn for help? She is often abandoned by the faith community that shames her.

IDENTIFYING SEXUAL ADDICTION IN WOMEN

The presentation of female sex and love addicts has changed since I entered personal recovery in 1991. In those days, women largely fit my experience, which was the more relational form of primarily "love" addiction with occasionally some "sex" addiction thrown in. Even with the introduction of the internet and its sexual opportunities, most women engaged in romantic or sexual chat rooms—activities that provided a pseudo-relationship. In my early days working in the field, it was relatively rare for women to act out in more stereotypically male ways such as compulsive masturbation or anonymous sex. The pornography women viewed was more erotic than explicit.

These "softer" presentations have definitely changed. Today, in fact, women's sexual acting out almost completely parallels men's, especially among the technology natives—those young women who have grown up in the digital age. For over a decade, statistics have held steady: one in three visitors to a pornographic website is female. What is changing is the kind of pornography these women are viewing and the age they began viewing it. Gail Dines, a leading antipornography feminist and author of the disturbing book *Pornland: How Porn Has Hijacked Our Sexuality* (Dines 2010) describes how the cybersex landscape has become decidedly violent. Christian organization Covenant Eyes similarly reports that 88% of online porn contains violent sex (Covenant Eyes 2018). According to a Barna Research study commissioned by Josh McDowell Ministry (Barna 2016), teens and young adults are the largest consumers of internet pornography— almost all of it free. Therefore, from an early age, entire generations are being conditioned to think that misogyny, demeaning acts, and sexual violence toward women are acceptable and even normal. Young females believe they must endure discomfort and even pain in order to be sexually pleasing to a male partner.

It is most helpful to consider sexual addiction (overall, not just in women) as an umbrella term that covers a variety of presentations. Some women relate to the relationship, love, or fantasy addict description and report serial or simultaneous relationships, if only in their minds. Other women recognize themselves as pornography or cybersex addicts, including sexting and sending or receiving sexual videos. Women also masturbate compulsively, exhibit themselves (including in socially acceptable ways), trade sex for money or drugs, and partner with another sex addict in an addictive relationship.

Identifying sexual addiction in women is often more difficult than it is in men. As previously mentioned, shame prevents women from volunteering their acting out history. It is crucial that every intake session (with men, as well) ask specifically about pornography use and problematic sexual behavior. Use a screening instrument like the Sexual Addiction Screening Test Revised (SAST-R, available online without charge at www.sexhelp.com) or the identification questions from the twelve-step sex addiction fellowships. Most women will answer no if asked whether they have anonymous sex, but if the question is reframed to "Are you ever sexual with someone you just met in a bar or elsewhere?" a woman is apt to say yes if that description fits. Some FSLAs are fueled by the power they feel around successful seduction or sexual activity.

It is always appropriate to examine a woman's problematic sexual behavior through the standard addiction grid of obsession, compulsion, continuation despite negative consequences, and tolerance. These characteristics determine if a woman is truly addicted and not simply feeling shame for acting outside her value system. Women face the same consequences as men when it comes to out-of-control sexual behavior. These include health compromises from sexually transmitted infections, depression, anxiety, economic or job loss, relational disturbance, and spiritual distress or disconnection. An obvious difference between the genders is women's ability to become pregnant, which is an especially complicated situation if it results from her addictive sexual behavior.

THE PROBLEM BENEATH THE PROBLEM

The presentations of sexual addiction are only the tip of the iceberg. Christian helpers must go beyond beaming the light of truth on a woman's addictive behavior and flood the light of God's compassion on the problem beneath the problem, which is unrelenting pain. Sexual addiction is not about sex at all; it is about a desperate search for "love," connection, attention, affirmation, and approval.

For most women, the roots of sexual addiction can be traced to experiences from childhood. There has long been an understanding that childhood sexual abuse is correlated with later addictive behavior, and untreated sexual trauma is a significant risk factor in multiple treatment failures and relapses for substance abusers. Carnes's (1991) early research showed that 81% of sex addicts reported childhood sexual abuse, and that statistic has been reflected in the population of sex addicts attending Bethesda Workshop retreats. Most sexual abuse is committed by someone the child or adolescent knows and trusts, like a family member, friend, teacher, coach, minister, or someone in a similar position of authority. Like little else, childhood sexual abuse creates great confusion between sex and love, autonomy and consent, and sometimes gender or orientation. The overt sexual activity escalates early sexual awakening, which has often been kindled by exposure to pornography. Connecting the dots between sexual abuse and sexual addiction, then, is not rocket science.

Other less obvious family dysfunction can influence a woman's development and provide a setup for unhealthy relationships and expressions of sexuality. Boundary issues are of particular note, where families can be either enmeshed or disengaged. Enmeshed families struggle with differentiation among members, where children are not allowed to separate in developmentally appropriate ways. Often there is a parentified child who plays the role of surrogate parent in the absence of a healthy marital relationship. In this form of emotional incest, the child meets the parent's needs instead of the other way around. Because the child is put in a partner role, a sexual undercurrent taints the relationship even without any overt sexual contact. Being melded to another person feels like love, which is a characteristic of the relationship addict.

Carnes's research indicates the majority of sex addicts come from what the Circumplex Model (Olson, Sprenkle, and Russell 1979) describes as "rigidly disengaged families." This atmosphere provides rigid rules, expectations, and structure, but lacks emotional connection. Clinical observation suggests that most unhealthy Christian families, especially those who describe themselves as evangelical or fundamentalist, fall into the rigidly disengaged quadrant of the Circumplex Model. The environment is performance based rather than relationship based. Love feels conditional. Sex or an intense relationship becomes an attempt to generate connection.

Current clinical focus considers disrupted or impaired attachment as a key etiological factor for sexual addiction, and this construct is described in chapter 4 of this book. Affective neuroscience shows that early caregiver attunement shapes the infant's attachment system and that, without secure attachment, a child lacks the capacity for effective self-regulation (Katehakis 2012, 2016). Like drugs or alcohol, sex and love offer a compelling way (albeit a destructive one) to manage her dysregulated nervous system.

Based on the form of insecure attachment, an avoidant/dismissing woman may seek anonymous, emotionless sex for the rush of dopamine that masks her internal numbness. A woman with a preoccupied attachment style never learned to manage her impulses, and thus tends to behave in uncensored ways, including sexually. The avoidant/fearful attachment style (also associated with disorganized attachment in some models) ricochets between fear of engulfment and fear of abandonment. Her inconsistent history contains people who were both a source of protection and threat, and her sexual and relational behavior reflects that duality.

A contrasting viewpoint to this "classic" form of sexual addiction, which is influenced by abuse and attachment injuries, is a "contemporary" form of rapid-onset sex addiction that has emerged with the proliferation of internet technology (Riemersma and Sytsma 2013). The contemporary model is characterized by the Three Cs of chronicity, content, and culture. Chronicity refers to a rapid onset of sexual addiction that largely affects the "Gen-Sext," who are raised with unparalleled access to graphic sexual material. The resulting overproduction of dopamine alters the sexual arousal setpoint, which disrupts normal neurochemical, sexual, and social development. The second C is highly arousing content that is easily accessed and infinitely novel. As described earlier, this content is also increasingly violent and nonnormative. The content itself activates powerful neurofeedback loops of anticipation and arousal. The third C is culture, which has also been previously explored as saturated with sex and conflicting messages about sexuality. Those who experience the "contemporary" form of sexual addiction often lack the overt sexual trauma that is characteristic of the better-known classic "trauma model." However, both models support the neuroaffective underpinnings of sex addiction when culture is (accurately) identified as the trauma.

A key task for Christian helpers is to understand the underlying issues that drive an FSLA's behavior. These wounds comprise the desperate pain that demands relief and the repeated attempts to get it through sex and relationships. Recognizing and honoring this pain is an enormous gift for the FSLA and often provides the window into her shame.

RECOVERY FOR THE FEMALE SEX AND LOVE ADDICT

The roots of sexually addictive behavior just described are equally applicable to both genders. As detailed earlier in this chapter, although fewer women reportedly struggle with sexual addiction, few differences exist today between men's and women's forms of acting out. Why include a separate chapter devoted to female sex and love addicts? The answer lies in the differences in treatment for women. Unique therapeutic considerations factor into working with FSLAs, and the best practices that are standard for treating men are harder to implement with women.

Like their male counterparts, female sex addicts need multidimensional help. Recovery from sexual addiction can be illustrated by the dual rails of a train track: one rail represents recovery from cultural, trauma, and attachment wounds, and the second rail signifies arresting acting out and healing the collateral damage in the addict's life and relationships. The typical protocol in treating addiction is to stop the problematic behavior or substance use first and then to focus on the underlying issues. The intimacy disorder of sexual addiction, however, often requires a simultaneous emphasis on trauma and acting out or even attention to the trauma alone at first.

Sometimes, especially for attachment-injured and emotionally dysregulated FSLAs, a modified harm reduction model is required. In this case, initial treatment encourages lower-risk behaviors, such as no sexual encounters with strangers, while the client heals from trauma and works on affect regulation. Building a support system is usually required before women achieve sobriety, which is a catch-22, since being known by other women is one of FSLAs' primary fears. The Christian helper may find this treatment approach uncomfortable, since the sexually addictive behaviors are antithetical to Christian values. As someone who is personally in recovery from sex and love addiction fueled by years of sexual abuse and deeper attachment trauma, I attest that this seemingly unconventional approach saved my life. The best practice for long-term healing is often the treat-trauma-first tactic.

Helpful modalities for addressing trauma include EMDR, somatic experiencing, experiential work, psychodynamic therapy, and Internal Family Systems. Activities like constructing a genogram, Trauma Egg, or telling her story (repeatedly) serve to reduce shame and foster understanding. The trauma work central to recovery is fairly consistent for both genders, so this section focuses primarily on behavioral and relational recovery for FSLAs.

Therapeutic Considerations for Women

First, however, the Christian helper must be aware of foundational therapeutic considerations that are specific to treating women, especially female sex addicts and their debilitating shame. If sexual addiction is correctly viewed as an attachment-based intimacy disorder, the importance of the therapeutic relationship, which has long been considered the key factor in a successful clinical outcome, becomes more critical. When you understand the way women are wired to prioritize relationships and how growth for women develops through relationships, the bond between an FSLA and her helper escalates in importance.

Women especially need to attach to their therapists in order to risk the unique pain of exploring the possibility of sex and love addiction and their inner world. A clinician or spiritual supporter must be attuned to the client's nonverbal expressions, aware of any attachment breaches in the relationship, and willing and able to repair them.

Those familiar with sexual addiction treatment will recognize the work of Patrick Carnes and his Thirty Task Model (Carnes 2009) as the standard of care. These tasks generally focus on the first period of recovery and are important for achieving sobriety and calming supercharged neurochemistry. The Task Model, though, is best suited to a male brain. The cognitive-behavioral approach of the early tasks jives well with a male orientation to get things done and make progress. Females need a slower, more relational approach. When timed correctly, the tasks can be equally helpful for women, but that timing is crucial. Initially, certain tasks like making a secrets list or a romantic timeline are best done jointly during a session rather than as homework. They can provide concrete ways to bond and connect, but they are best used sparingly in the beginning of treatment.

Creating a safe therapeutic setting is the clinician's most important responsibility. An FSLA's first experience with complete safety may be with you, her helper. Gender is a complicating factor with many nuances. Some heterosexual FSLAs seek a female therapist to avoid the possibility of sexual or romantic intrigue. Others distrust women and may seek a male therapist, while some may intentionally look for a male clinician because they are used to manipulating men and unconsciously may see seduction as a healing path. Regardless, the therapist must maintain scrupulous boundaries. She or he must also be aware of personal vulnerabilities and maintain honest, supportive personal relationships, including peer consultation and supervision if counter transference issues arise.

Exploring the Addiction Cycle

The classic cycle of addiction is a helpful construct for all addicts. The specific cycle Carnes details (2001, 2005) is particularly useful in deconstructing the unconscious patterns that comprise the intimacy disorder of sexual addiction, especially when adapted for women.

Without help, most FSLAs (and addicts in general) have no idea what leads to their acting out. The love/relationship addict reports that she "woke up" (metaphorically, but sometimes actually) and found herself in another affair or simultaneous relationship. The cybersex addict says she only intended to hear a podcast or check an app, and suddenly (it seemed) she was immersed in pornography or an online sexual encounter. In a combination of denial and naivete, the FSLA is often unaware of how she wound up acting out again in a way that brings her little pleasure beyond a momentary jolt and lots of lingering pain.

Understanding the predictable cycle of addiction is a behavioral key to achieving and maintaining sexual and relational sobriety. The cycle starts with the wounds and resulting core beliefs (including cultural ones) that lead to an addict's debilitating shame messages, as described earlier. Next comes a trigger, which can be either an internal state or an intrusion from the environment. Some triggers are specific to an individual such as a particular date, song, or scent. Others, like loneliness or stress, generalize to everyone. Becoming aware of frequent triggers allows an FSLA to be alert to her vulnerability.

When a trigger intrudes, a woman begins to preoccupy or obsess about obtaining relief from the distressing state or indulging in the euphoric recall of some prior acting out. She fantasizes about feeling better or reenacting some remembered pleasure. Remember, acting out is mood altering, and even at this beginning of the addictive cycle, neurochemistry begins to ramp up in anticipation and arousal.

Most addicts believe they can stop their behavior if they "really want to" or "try harder." Intervening at the acting out stage almost always fails, which leads to more desperation and shame. For most addicts, especially FSLAs, the missing puzzle piece is a recognition of their rituals. These decipherable behaviors are the bridge between being triggered and acting out. Most women are not conscious about the seemingly unimportant or everyday decisions they make that are part of their addictive cycles. Many of these choices are ingrained and culturally supported, especially those involving appearance. Clothing, makeup, hair style, and accessories, which are heavily promoted as characteristic of being feminine or attractive, are often part of a woman's ritual. The way she moves, makes eye contact, touches, texts, and flirts can be part of her addictive dance. Being independent and powerful, or conversely, dependent or helpless, creates a certain sexual aura.

The woman who acts out in more overtly sexual ways like viewing pornography or engaging in cybersex usually has shorter, simpler rituals. Online acting out requires only an internet connection and sufficient privacy. Alcohol or drugs may be a factor for the woman who meets anonymous partners. Help an FSLA identify her rituals by backing up her actions from the point of acting out. Ask her, "What happened before that? And before that?" Examine every minute detail. Encourage her to take responsibility for these seemingly preprogrammed choices.

Explore the emotions and cognitive distortions that are also part of the progression. Challenge her denial that "all women act like this" or the belief "I'm nobody unless I'm sexually desirable." Support her through the pain of loneliness or self-debasement ("I'm a horrible person") that energizes her addiction. Teasing out the FSLA's rituals is an ongoing process, and usually a lengthy one. However, once she is clear about her rituals, denial is much harder to maintain. She recognizes that "just calling" a former acting out partner is a ritual of reconnection or that keeping her phone in her bedroom overnight is a setup for acting out online.

The recognition of triggers and rituals allows an FSLA to use the tools of recovery when they are most likely to be effective. Establishing multifaceted boundaries are critical—and never easy for the recovering woman. They need to be put in place at the preoccupation and fantasy stage, before the woman slides into her ritual. The "bottom line" boundaries of sobriety are usually easy to identify, like "I won't look at pornography," or "I won't have sex with _____," or "I won't send or receive sexts." The *how* of keeping those boundaries is the challenging part, and determining the intermittent specific boundaries that support sobriety is another crucial task of recovery.

Boundaries are what make these theoretical goals into practical achievements. Like rituals, break down big-picture boundaries into behavioral steps that are concrete and measurable. Boundaries need to be identified for every form of acting out. Instead of "I won't have contact with so-and-so," detail how that distance will be maintained. Examples include "I'll block that phone number and email address," and "I'll change my own contact info if necessary." Another boundary might be "I'll find a different gym or grocery store from those he frequents."

The ubiquitous nature of technology makes recovery harder for the FSLA who acts out online. When the drug is always available at your fingertips (or even in your own mind), sobriety is challenging. Today, it is very difficult to navigate life without a smart phone and home wireless internet service. Limiting physical access to devices overnight or during unstructured or alone times can help. Blocking and monitoring programs can offer a stopgap between preoccupation and acting out. Tools like the Three Circles of Sex Addicts Anonymous are helpful in codifying behaviors that are off limits (inner circle), those that are ritualistic or questionable (middle circle), and those that support recovery and healthy living (outer circle) for all individuals in recovery, women and men alike.

Boundaries need to be multifaceted and comprehensive. Instead of punitive forces, which is how addicts usually view them, boundaries are benevolent guardians of safety. They should cover physical practicalities like the steps described, and they also should include the mental and emotional measures needed to safeguard sobriety. Examples here include being careful of triggering music and media, as well as refusing to entertain fantasies about acting out in any form. Harder still, boundaries will likely be costly for the FSLA, at least emotionally and practically, if not financially. It is her responsibility to enforce her own boundaries (a novel concept for most women), and she may have to take inconvenient steps to do so. Recovery is hard work!

Resisting the Pull of Egypt

At this stage, the issue of willingness usually appears or reappears. The FSLA who is in the throes of addiction or negative consequences is usually motivated toward change. (Pain does that, which is a grace.) The woman who has experienced the relief of telling her story without judgment or the deeper healing from some of her trauma can get complacent about recovery practices. When she realizes transformation is a lifelong process of living life differently—and especially when it sinks in that "different" means avoiding things and people that have felt like life for her—the idealism of recovery often fades. Replacing any early enthusiasm is a depressing landscape of loss. She may not have enough tools on board to mitigate the withdrawal symptoms and grief she is feeling. She is caught in the in-between space of "not yet." She has opened her hands to let go of addiction, but she has not yet had them filled with the benefits and gratitude of recovery.

This FSLA is in a dangerous place, and the Christian helper must be attuned to her vulnerability. She is at risk for a slip or relapse, which are a part of recovery for almost all sex addicts. She may return to people, places, and things that were part of her rituals and test the waters to see if she can get by without acting out.

The love or relationship addict may ache for a former affair partner and search for him online or in his favorite hangouts.

This period is a good time to remind the FSLA of the story of the children of Israel. After years of captivity and misery (the definitions of addiction), they were delivered from bondage and made their way to the promised land. It was not an easy journey, but eventually they found themselves at a defining moment: on the banks of the Jordan River with the choice to risk fighting the giants in the promised land or to give in to fear. The Israelites chose poorly; they rallied to forgo the promises ahead of them and *return to Egypt*.

It is an apt metaphor for the journey of recovery. Addicts know how to survive the slavery of Egypt. It may not be a pleasant survival, but it is familiar. When the pain of addictive behavior is eased a bit but the full benefits of a life of integrity are not yet realized, the cost-benefit balance of recovery can feel like it has shifted. At this stage, it helps the FSLA to review the cost of her acting out and revisit the pain of bondage. Perspective and perseverance are key here.

Using the Tools of Recovery

If sexual addiction is best described as an intimacy disorder, then the obvious solution is to find healthy connection. Community is a core tenet of addiction recovery, but it is difficult to establish for the recovering FSLA. The thing she needs the most is something she most fears. Perhaps surprisingly, many female sex and love addicts are uncomfortable around other women, especially hetero-sexual FSLAs. Women are the competition for men, and many FSLAs compare themselves to other women and objectify both self and other. Regardless of the discomfort, intentionally connecting with women through regular calls and texts is important. Face-to-face connections are better.

Recovery rooms are the best place for a woman to find recovering sisters. A twelve-step sex addiction fellowship is ideal, because those females understand the unique pain of a woman addicted to sex and relationships. Indeed, being part of a twelve-step group is a core component of recovery. Meetings offer a safe place to know others and be known—to risk vulnerability. When an FSLA tells her shameful secrets and receives acceptance, she has a corrective antidote to the core belief, "If you really knew me, you would leave me." When she receives grace from human hands, a shame-based woman begins to open to the possibility that she might truly receive grace from God.

Beyond simply attending meetings, working the twelve steps is another valuable tool. The steps provide a structure for admitting powerlessness, embrac-ing surrender, practicing honesty and accountability, accepting responsibility, and walking in a new way of life. Completing the written inventories is a good prompt toward the practice of journaling, which is helpful for releasing pent-up emotions. Recovery is a new way of life, and using the tools of recovery make it possible to achieve and maintain sobriety.

RECOVERY IN THE SPIRITUAL REALM

Recovering spiritually may not be as obviously needed as achieving sobriety and healing from trauma, but it is just as important and often more difficult. Many FSLAs are spiritually wounded. For some, the wounds began in childhood with an environment of rules-based religion instead of relationship-based spirituality. Perhaps parents attended religious services (or sent their children), but positive values were not practiced in everyday life. The disconnect or even hypocrisy influenced the FSLA's thinking and eventually behavior. It might have contributed to her justification of her sex or love addiction.

Some Christian homes use Scripture as a spiritual bypass around painful feelings or situations. They misinterpret Bible passages to dismiss or prohibit normal, God-given emotions. They do not allow developing adolescents to wrestle with faith or the existential questions of life. Children must blindly accept their parents' viewpoint, maybe even down to the specific denominational form of Christianity that is acceptable. A woman from this kind of rigid, shaming faith environment is apt to rebel, and acting out sexually is a powerful way to assert herself.

Perhaps an even more painful situation is when a woman is abused or exploited by someone who is a spiritual authority figure. The priest who makes sexual advances, the youth minister who flirts and touches inappropriately, the deacon who is fired for his use of pornography, or the pastor who commits clergy sexual abuse by being sexual with members of his congregation—all deeply taint her view of God. How can she believe that God, who is the ultimate spiritual authority and healer, is willing to be anything but unconcerned (at best) or exploitive (at worst) of her challenges around sexuality? If spiritual leaders can sexually abuse with impunity, including from other spiritual authorities, then why can't the FSLA escape consequences? On the other hand, as stories continue to unfold about horrific sexual abuse of children by priests within the Catholic Church while leaders reportedly knew and did nothing of substance to protect children, why would an FSLA turn to God for rescue? Certainly, other Christian churches have experienced this leadership failure, but the extremely public nature of the vast scandal in the Catholic Church is painfully triggering for those others, even if they are not Catholic themselves.

We human beings tend to base our perceptions of God on our experiences with fellow humans. If our earthly father is kind, available, affirming, and full of grace, we more easily trust that God is similar. If parents and spiritual authorities are shaming, judgmental, and unforgiving, we lack a positive model we can extrapolate onto God. Why expect that God will treat us any differently?

The strong patriarchal culture further complicates a woman's healing. When men, including public figures, demean and openly brag about objectifying women, it is easy to internalize the misogyny. Women learn young that sex can be the equalizing factor that provides them more power in a masculine-tilted world. Yet when faith communities demonize women's sexuality as a near-irresistible temptation and then put women in charge of managing men's lust, which is an unfortunate stance of many evangelical churches, the double bind is inescapable.

The persistent patriarchy flourishes especially within religious communities. Many religious men and institutions believe the Bible endows them with inherent, God-given authority, rather than understanding that the Bible was written in a time when women had little to no status, and it simply reflects that culture. Jesus was astonishing in his encounters with and acceptance of women. He chose a woman (and a sexual sinner) as the first recorded missionary to proclaim his arrival as the Messiah. The average stage on Sunday morning, however, is notably absent of female pastors, and far fewer women are in bona fide organizational leadership.

The spiritual implications of patriarchy are enormous. If the church does little more than provide lip service to the value of women, why should an FSLA believe the church cares about her sexual struggles, especially when they are clearly viewed as sin? An FSLA is especially challenged when twelve-step recovery encourages her to connect with a power greater than herself and turn her will and her life over to the care of God. She is likely to hold (perhaps unconscious) spiritual beliefs like the following (taken from *No Stones: Women Redeemed from Sexual Addiction* [Ferree 2010]):

- "God couldn't possibly love me after what I've done."
- "God has abandoned me just like all the other men in my life."
- "God says it's not OK to be a feminine woman or one who enjoys sex."
- "God says I must be in second place—I must be the caretaker for everyone else or the one who submits my desires to others'."
- "God won't give me second chances. If I blow it, He'll condemn me."
- "It's up to the female to keep men at bay. I am 100% responsible for the sexual purity of my relationships, and if there's a problem, it must be my fault."
- "I can't begin again. I can never be pure."

The strong portrayal of God as father and references to God with only masculine pronouns is another spiritual wound for countless women. On the one hand, if a biological father has not been safe or available and men in general have not either, it is difficult to look to a male higher power. On the other hand, heterosexual women view males as potential sources of affection and sex, which triggers a complicating "Ekk!" reaction for a woman hoping to connect with God. Once again, she is in a double bind.

Christian helpers could be instrumental in expanding a woman's view of God—provided they are so enlightened themselves, of course. The Bible is full of feminine metaphors for God, and the theology of the Trinity supports God-as-being as much as God-as-father. Many FSLAs also suffer from what Kelly McDaniel (2012) terms "mother hunger," which means a longing produced by the absence of an available, nurturing mother. Seeing God as a nurturing mother is enormously healing for the woman who did not experience a good enough mom. Christian feminist writers can be helpful in showing an FSLA a different view of God that is still rooted in sound theology. This paradigm shift helps practically, as well, as the recovering FSLA is more inclined to connect with other women as supportive sisters in her healing.

RECOVERY FOR MALE PARTNERS OF FSLAS

In the same way that women get strong cultural messages about being female, men receive potent messages about what it means to be male. Being the husband of an unfaithful wife is completely counter to the strong, virile image of masculinity. What is the matter with a guy who can't keep his wife at home? Men of FSLA wives endure more embarrassment and shame than wives of male sex and love addicts. Husbands are subjected to isolation and derisive speculation by this reverse situation, and there is no ready place for them to turn.

Male partners are generally unrecognized and underserved. The literature about partners of sex addicts is filled with feminine pronouns, and almost no research has been done about men married to FSLAs. Male faces are rare in support groups for partners (other than the occasional gay man) and few men are open about their experiences. Husbands face the same betrayal trauma that crushes wives of male sex addicts, but they must navigate it with limited resources.

A difference is that a husband is often immediately encouraged to divorce his straying wife, whereas betrayed wives are frequently pressured to forgive and stay with their unfaithful husbands. He rarely is encouraged to get individual help for himself, and Christians naively assume that if the wife becomes sober, their relationship challenges will be over. Husbands, though, are not immune from the personal issues associated with an addictive family system.

Our experience at Bethesda Workshops is that husbands of FSLAs share some common denominators of unhealthiness. Early limited research showed that 71% of male partners of FSLAs were also sexually addicted (Schneider 2001). The husbands who attend Bethesda's Healing for Partners Workshop almost always report a personal struggle with pornography even if they have not crossed the flesh line to act out with another person. Other male partners report a long-standing history of compulsive masturbation. Some of these husbands are more understanding of their wives' addiction and are better able to support her recovery. Others, though, seem so undone by the betrayal that they lack any empathy for their wives, despite the husbands' personal problems around sex.

My clinical experience is that husbands who are not themselves addicts generally fall into one of two categories. The first group is extremely angry, often even dangerously full of rage. Female partners are also angry, of course, and both genders have every reason to be. Male partners, though, are apt to cross the line into physical and sexual abuse on top of verbal abuse, which is more typical of female partners. Husbands may berate and demean their wives, then wake them in the middle of the night to demand rough sex. They become oppressively controlling and authoritative and misuse Scripture to demand that their FSLA wives "submit." This group of angry male partners is extremely hard to engage in their own therapy and recovery process.

Conducting a formal, full disclosure is an important part of any sex addict's recovery, but this process requires special consideration if the male partner is extremely angry. An FSLA may be putting herself at risk for domestic violence if she discloses her unfaithfulness. It is vital that the Christian helper thoroughly assess the situation and provide informed guidance and structure to the disclosure process. Specific training in this area is crucial.

The second group of male partners is avoidant. These passive men are likely to deny, minimize, or excuse their wives' behavior. They are often shut down emotionally and are relationally disengaged. Some husbands overfunction in the relationship and tolerate unacceptable behavior without enforcing any boundaries or consequences. The clinical work with these male partners is to get them in touch with their anger, which may be deeply buried. They need to find their voices and to develop the ego strength to establish boundaries, which is a gift both to themselves and to their sexually addicted wives.

Like disclosure, a sexual abstinence period is also a clinical challenge with male partners. Many husbands are extremely resistant to a mutually agreed on time of marital sexual abstinence, which is a normal protocol for recovery.

Sex provides a one-up position in the relationship, a way to control the FSLA and to reinforce the husband's position as the one with the power. Men, especially, tend to feel punished or deprived when a wife insists she needs a total timeout from sexual activity as part of her recovery. A marital sexual abstinence period is just as important for the relationship as it is for the recovering woman. The relationship needs a reset, too, as the FSLA rebuilds trust and the couple learns deeper skills for emotional intimacy. A well-trained couple's counselor is crucial in this area too.

SPECIAL CHALLENGES FOR FSLAS

Recovery from sexual addiction is never easy. Female sex and love addicts, though, face unique challenges as they journey to live in integrity and authenticity and to repair their relationships. The hardest challenge is the fewer number of women in recovery from sex and love addiction. A woman is often either the only female or one of only a handful of women in support or twelve-step groups. Her innate pull toward relationships makes it difficult for her to focus in a male-dominated environment. It is hard for an FSLA to stay emotionally present and out of her preoccupation and intrigue. The meeting and the men attending it may be safe (and usually are), but the FSLA herself is not safe, especially in the beginning of her recovery when she is trying to establish and maintain sobriety. Phone meetings are a good work-around for this challenge. Most of the major sex addiction fellowships offer women-only phone meetings. Even if the meeting is mixed gender, it is easier to stay present in an audio-only format.

The smaller pool of potential female candidates makes it hard for women to find a female sponsor. Online recovery meetings usually have more women participating, but there remains a chronic shortage of women with sufficient sobriety to sponsor other women, especially in a face-to-face setting. Many FSLAs must settle for an online or phone relationship with a sponsor. Women's challenges with other women further complicate the situation. Gender-specific group therapy is a wonderful avenue for women to learn to engage with and trust other women. In a safe therapeutic environment, females can practice the vulnerability and direct communication that normally eludes them in other settings.

HOPE FOR WOMEN

Despite the shame, influence of a sexually saturated culture, and the dearth of resources and openly recovering women, it is possible for the female sex and love addict to walk in newness of life. She can use the tools of recovery to achieve sobriety, and she can rebuild trust. With the help of the loving God and Great Physician, she can heal from trauma. Redemptively, she can even come to find meaning in her struggle as she reaches out to help other women seeking recovery from sexual addiction. Slowly, the church and Christian helpers are making advances in being avenues of grace for a female sex and love addict.

REFERENCES

Barna Research. 2016, April 6. "Porn in the Digital Age: New Research Reveals 10 Trends." www.barna.com/research/porn-in-the-digital-age-new-research-reveals-10-trends/#.

Carnes, P. J. 1991. *Don't Call It Love: Recovery from Sexual Addiction*. New York: Bantam Books.

———. 2005. *Facing the Shadow: Starting Sexual and Relationship Recovery*. 2nd ed. Carefree, AZ: Gentle Path.

———. 2009. *Recovery Zone, Vol. 1. Making Changes That Last: The Internal Tasks*. Carefree, AZ: Gentle Path.

Corley, M. D., and J. Hook. 2012. "Women, Female Sex and Love Addicts, and Use of the Internet." *Sexual Addiction and Compulsivity* 9, no. 1–2: 53–76.

Covenant Eyes. 2018. *Pornography Statistics*. www.covenanteyes.com/pornstats/.

Dines, G. 2010. *Pornland: How Porn Has Hijacked Our Sexuality*. Boston: Beacon.

Ferree, M. C. 2002. *No Stones: Women Redeemed from Sexual Shame*. Fairfax, VA: Xulon.

———. 2010. *No Stones: Women Redeemed from Sexual Addiction*. 2nd ed. Downers Grove, IL: InterVarsity.

———, ed. 2012. *Making Advances: A Comprehensive Guide for Treating Female Sex and Love Addicts*. Royston, GA: Society for the Advancement of Sexual Health.

Garza, E. 2018. *Getting Off: One Woman's Journey through Sex and Porn Addiction*. New York: Simon & Schuster.

Katehakis, A. 2012. "Best Practices for Addressing Attachment Injuries." In *Making Advances: A Comprehensive Guide for Treating Female Sex and Love Addicts*. Edited by M. C. Ferree, 188–214. Royston, GA: Society for the Advancement of Sexual Health.

Katehakis, A. 2016. *Sex Addiction as Affect Dysregulation: A Neurobiologically Informed Holistic Treatment*. New York: W. W. Norton & Company.

Laaser, M. R. 1992. *The Secret Sin: Healing the Wounds of Sexual Addiction*. Grand Rapids: Zondervan.

McDaniel, K. 2012. *Ready to Heal: Breaking Free of Addictive Relationships*. 3rd ed. Carefree, AZ: Gentle Path.

Olson, D., D. Sprenkle, and C. Russell. 1979. "Circumplex Model of Marital and Family Systems: Cohesion and Adaptability Dimensions, Family Types, and Clinical Applications." *Family Process* 18, no. 1: 3–28.

Riemersma, J., and M. Sytsma. 2013. "A New Generation of Sexual Addiction." *Sexual Addiction and Compulsivity* 20, no. 4: 306–22.

Roskind, J., producer, and S. Yoonessi, director. 2018. *Unlovable*. Motion picture. United States: Orion Classics.

Schneider, J. 2001. *Back from Betrayal*. 1st ed. Tucson, AZ: Recovery Resources.

Thompson, C. 2015. *The Soul of Shame: Retelling the Stories We Believe about Ourselves*. Downers Grove, IL: InterVarsity.

CHAPTER 15

CONSIDERATIONS WHEN WORKING WITH CATHOLIC CLIENTS

Fr. Sean Kilcawley, SLT, PSAP

began talking about pornography in 2014. I had recently returned to the Diocese of Lincoln, Nebraska, from studies in Rome, where I earned a graduate theology degree in marriage and family. My first task as director of the office for religious education was to write a new chastity curriculum for use in our Catholic schools. After writing those lessons, I was convinced the new curriculum would be a game changer! Then I sat in the confessional for a couple of months and had a new realization: my chastity program was not going to work.

In the years I had spent in Rome (2009–2013), the whole world had shifted. Students who once were distracted by sending text messages on their push-button flip phones now were using smart phones with access to everything the internet had to offer. So I had to ask myself the question, "How do I teach the truth, beauty, and goodness of God's plan for marriage and human sexuality to a generation that is consuming the anti-message?" How does one sow the seed of the word of God in the rocky soil that results from early exposure to pornography? This reality led me to shift my focus to educating parents on the dangers of pornography and how to protect their children online. As I gave talks to parents, many of the adults in attendance were moved to seek help for their own problems. In turn I sought out further education in the assessment and treatment of sexual addiction. Currently, I spend much of my time traveling and speaking to other priests about how to help their people who find themselves enslaved to sexual sin.

In this chapter, I hope to pass on what I have learned through this experience so it may benefit other priests, pastors, and Christian therapists when working with Catholic clients. Although I will be speaking from my experience within a Catholic culture, I believe the principles will be transferable to anyone who wishes to accompany others in a journey of Christian recovery. By Christian recovery, we are speaking about a facilitated conversion that happens in a discipleship relationship. Our challenge is that we often work with clients who have professed faith in Jesus Christ and are living according to the faith to the best of their abilities. All the externals of faith practice are present, but another part of them is still enslaved to sin. So we are attempting to facilitate conversion in a person who may believe they are already converted.

In Catholic culture, we use the term *new evangelization* to describe this dynamic. In *Redemptoris Missio*, Pope John Paul II provides a deep reflection on the distinctions and relationship between evangelization *ad gentes* (the evangelization of peoples who have not heard the gospel preached), pastoral care of the faithful who have received the gospel, and new evangelization of those who have already heard Christ proclaimed. In Catholic culture, these might be people who were baptized and raised as Catholic but have fallen away. They may be people who have never subjectively appropriated the objective truths of the faith that they learned in religious education classes. When considering the Christian porn or sex addict, we are often working with someone who professes belief in Christ but struggles to live a life that is congruent with their belief system. We can also consider this to be a person who has not subjectively appropriated what they objectively believe.

So this work is the reevangelization of members of our churches who have not yet turned away from sin to embrace the gospel in its fullness—or more fundamentally, those who have not yet embraced the person of Jesus in his fullness. For the Christian addict, recovery and conversion are convertible terms, and the therapist, priest, or pastor are evangelizers of their clients as we attempt to prepare their hearts to receive the gospel in its fullness, in a way that will move them to live in congruence with their belief system. I will begin with a brief summary of what the Catholic Church teaches about the virtue of chastity and how it is violated, propose a vision for recovery as a work of evangelization, and then address some specific pitfalls for Catholic clients as they integrate their spirituality with their recovery.

HEALTHY SEXUALITY IN A CATHOLIC CONTEXT

According to the Catechism of the Catholic Church (CCC),

> Chastity means the successful integration of sexuality within the person and thus the inner unity of man in his bodily and spiritual being. Sexuality, in which

man's belonging to the bodily and biological world is expressed, becomes personal and truly human when it is integrated into the relationship of one person to another, in the complete and lifelong mutual gift of a man and a woman. The virtue of chastity therefore involves the integrity of the person and the integrality of the gift (CCC 2337).

People who possess this virtue have no division in them. They are free of compulsive behaviors. They are free to say no and free to say yes at the appropriate times. According to Catholic teaching, chastity means there is no genital sexual expression outside of marriage. Given this standard for chastity, Catholics are most at home within the twelve-step fellowship Sexaholics Anonymous, where the sobriety definition is "no sex with anyone except for my spouse, including myself."

According to Catholic teaching, sexual expression is sacred. It is a moment in which a husband and wife become cocreators with God. There are two ends to the marital act. The unitive end binds the couple together, and the procreative end allows their love to multiply. Both the unitive and procreative ends of the marital act bring an incarnate experience to the Scripture: "That is why a man leaves his father and mother and is united to his wife, and they become one flesh" (Gen. 2:24). Here it must be emphasized that both ends of the marital act are to be present. The moral principle is found in the document *Humanae Vitae*: "This particular doctrine, often expounded by the magisterium of the Church, is based on the inseparable connection, established by God, which man on his own initiative may not break, between the unitive significance and the procreative significance which are both inherent to the marriage act" (Paul VI 1968, 12). So every instance of conjugal intimacy must be open to both the unitive and procreative ends of the act. The couple must be open to bonding and the possibility of life in that particular moment. For this reason, faithful Catholics do not practice artificial contraception. The only morally licit means of spacing childbirth is by monitoring the fertility cycle of the woman and abstaining during the fertile periods, also known as natural family planning. Several fertility awareness methods are currently available to assist couples who discern to avoid pregnancy, and many Catholic dioceses have a full-time employee to coordinate fertility awareness education.

For faithful Catholics, the practice of natural family planning is both a blessing and a challenge. Couples who follow this teaching are already practicing abstinence to some degree. The challenge comes for many couples when working on sexual reintegration after betrayal. Practicing natural family planning involves charting the woman's cycle to discern which days of the month the couple might be intimate without risking pregnancy. Those days, often referred to as "green days," can turn into expectations for recovering addicts who are still seeking sex as a reward for sobriety, which in turn can be a trigger for betrayed spouses who are still early in their own recovery work. This is an additional dynamic that must be addressed with couples as they navigate their recovery work.

In addition to contraception, chastity is violated by lust, fornication, prostitution, rape, pornography, and masturbation. Definitions for all of these can be found in the CCC, but two are worth including here for reference. First, the CCC contains a robust definition of pornography:

> *Pornography* consists in removing real or simulated sexual acts from the intimacy of the partners, in order to display them deliberately to third parties. It offends against chastity because it perverts the conjugal act, the intimate giving of spouses to each other. It does grave injury to the dignity of its participants (actors, vendors, the public), since each one becomes an object of base pleasure and illicit profit for others. It immerses all who are involved in the illusion of a fantasy world. It is a grave offense. Civil authorities should prevent the production and distribution of pornographic materials. (CCC 2354)

It is also worthwhile to include the Catechism's treatment of masturbation in its entirety.

> By *masturbation* is to be understood the deliberate stimulation of the genital organs in order to derive sexual pleasure. "Both the Magisterium of the Church, in the course of a constant tradition, and the moral sense of the faithful have been in no doubt and have firmly maintained that masturbation is an intrinsically and gravely disordered action." "The deliberate use of the sexual faculty, for whatever reason, outside of marriage is essentially contrary to its purpose." For here sexual pleasure is sought outside of "the sexual relationship which is demanded by the moral order and in which the total meaning of mutual self-giving and human procreation in the context of true love is achieved."
>
> To form an equitable judgment about the subjects' moral responsibility and to guide pastoral action, one must take into account the affective immaturity, force of acquired habit, conditions of anxiety or other psychological or social factors that lessen, if not even reduce to a minimum, moral culpability. (CCC 2352)

The strength of these teachings is that they provide clear boundaries for chaste living. For the addict, these boundaries can seem overwhelming. While these teachings are clearly laid out in the CCC, they are not commonly taught to the faithful in a religious education classroom setting. If someone attends a Catholic school, the teaching regarding pornography and masturbation is not typically given to young people until their junior year. With the average age of first exposure being between eight and eleven years of age, many young people have already developed the habit of pornography and masturbation before being instructed about the morality of these actions. This has been a grave negligence on the part of church leaders and educators that is slowly being corrected in various parts of the country. For example, in the Diocese of Lincoln, Nebraska, the topic of pornography is introduced in the fourth-grade curriculum, and masturbation is addressed beginning in the fifth-grade curriculum.

The principal reason these teachings are not given in a formal way in religious education is that "the Church has always affirmed that parents have the duty and the right to be the first and the principal educators of their children" (The Pontifical Council for the Family 1995, 5). More recently, Pope Francis expanded on this idea while specifically addressing the need to educate young people about the dangers of pornography:

> Sex education should provide information while keeping in mind that children and young people have not yet attained full maturity. The information has to come at a proper time and in a way suited to their age. It is not helpful to overwhelm them with data without also helping them to develop a critical sense in dealing with the onslaught of new ideas and suggestions, the flood of pornography and the overload of stimuli that can deform sexuality. Young people need to realize that they are bombarded by messages that are not beneficial for their growth toward maturity. They should be helped to recognize and to seek out positive influences, while shunning the things that cripple their capacity for love." (Francis 2016, 281)

While the teachings of the church are clear, their implementation has often been weak. I have already mentioned that it is common for a young person to have little to no education for love (a common term for sex education in Catholic culture used to distinguish it from that provided in secular environments which is often incongruent with Catholic and Christian values; some other education programs call it Education for Affective Maturity) at home or in school and at the same time to be exposed to pornography between eight to eleven years of age. When they finally learn that pornography and masturbation are sins against chastity, this can be the cause of great shame and may be received as a small-T trauma within the person's psychosexual history and religious narrative. Here there is an important moral principle to follow: we are not culpable for things we do not know. For instance, I cannot be found guilty of breaking a rule I am ignorant of.

In sum, there is a rigorous standard set by the Catholic Church coupled with silence regarding how to live it practically. This cannot help but to elevate the level of shame experienced by Catholic addicts. It is also common to find members of the parish who are very faithful to their devotional life, yet continue to fall into pornography and masturbation regularly. I have already stated that recovery and evangelization are convertible terms. So, to facilitate recovery, a new evangelization is required. In fact, all recovery tools and programs should be considered "preevangelization programs" that are a necessary part of our evangelizing mission.

RECOVERY AS EVANGELIZATION

Pope Francis, in an early interview, stated that the church was a field hospital.

> The thing the church needs most today is the ability to heal wounds and to warm the hearts of the faithful; it needs nearness, proximity. I see the church as a field hospital after battle. It is useless to ask a seriously injured person if he has high cholesterol and about the level of his blood sugars! You have to heal his wounds. Then we can talk about everything else. Heal the wounds, heal the wounds. . . . And you have to start from the ground up. (Francis, "A Big Heart Open to God," 2013)

It seems like hyperbole when he says, "It is useless to ask a seriously injured person if he has high cholesterol and about the level of his blood sugars!" However, when we consider what the church has actively done to address the hypersexualized culture since the time of the sexual revolution, the analogy is fitting. I have heard many people say, "We just need to teach young people about the virtues, and they won't want to look at pornography," or "We need a really good theology of the body program, but we don't talk about pornography or masturbation." Essentially, we are just talking about the superficial without addressing the wound.

For example, as a priest, I might address a group of young people regarding the great love that our Lord Jesus Christ has for each of them: "Jesus loves you!" Unfortunately, the interior response of many of those young people may be, *Father, if you knew what I was doing in my room between 11pm and 1am, you would not be telling me Jesus loves me right now.* Until we say something like, "Jesus loves you even though . . ." or "Jesus loves you even when . . . ," we are not speaking into the wound. When working with addicts, we must remember the basic core beliefs they carry:

I am basically a bad, unworthy person.
No one would love me as I am.
My needs are never going to be met if I have to depend on others.
Sex is my most important need. (Carnes 2015, 46)

In a religious context, we can rewrite these beliefs in the following way:

I am unlovable.
If people knew me, they would reject me.
No one, not even God, can meet my needs.
I have to meet my own needs.
Pornography, masturbation, sex, alcohol, work, even religious rigidity is the
best way to meet my needs.

In addition to these lists, I would add another common core belief: "Love is a reward for good behavior and withheld for bad behavior." When I was young, I remember my stepmother telling me that my sister was upstairs cleaning up my room. When asked why, my sister said, "Maybe if I clean up after him, then he will love me." As a child, this did not register as a problem, but reflecting back, I can see how this belief that love is a reward for when we behave but is withheld when we misbehave crept into our mindset. We were told, "Thanks for behaving while we had company; I love you," "Thanks for cleaning up the kitchen; I love you." But when we misbehaved, we heard only, "Go to your room." Then the next time we emptied the dishwasher: "I love you."

It can also be common for this distorted belief to enter the spiritual life. When it does, it takes the form of, "Jesus loves me when I am in the state of grace but withdraws when I sin." This belief, however, is in contradiction with the words of Jesus in the Sermon on the Mount when he says, "he [the Father] causes his sun to rise on the evil and the good, and sends rain on the righteous and the unrighteous" (Matt. 5:45). Love is not a zero-sum game. It always multiplies. The love of God is infinite and is never withdrawn or withheld. When we speak of sin, it is our own turning away from his love, and he is always waiting for us to turn back to him.

Discerning the Heart of the Person

The core beliefs of the addict are an indicator that they need evangelization. In the treatment of addictions, we also know that breaking denial is necessary in the early stages of recovery. For the religious person, they often refuse to see that they are not as advanced in the spiritual life as they claim to be. When this denial persists, they are often not disposed to the conversion that they are seeking. Some insights from Pope Francis and Pope John Paul II help us to understand this dynamic more clearly.

The field hospital image of Pope Francis is fitting for where we find ourselves in the world of Catholic recovery work. Carrying the analogy forward implies that we need to do triage assessment when we see a new client. In military field hospitals, people are put into three categories: expectant (those who will die), immediate and delayed (those in need of surgery), and minimal (those without serious injury). A similar process might happen in our work of evangelization, as in a certain respect we can use three categories for our Christian clients. Pope John Paul II does just that in the opening paragraph of his document on the family, "The Role of the Christian Family in the Modern World."

He speaks of the first group as families that "are living this situation in fidelity to those values that constitute the foundation of the institution of the family" (John Paul II 1981, 1). These are people who attend mass every Sunday, they believe everything the Church teaches, they are evangelizing others, and the fruits of the Holy Spirit are apparent in their lives. In other words, they have appropriated what they believe and are living in a way that is congruent with the teachings of the Catholic Church. They are converted.

The second category consists of doubters. "Others have become uncertain and bewildered over their role or even doubtful and almost unaware of the ultimate meaning and truth of conjugal and family life" (John Paul II 1981, 1). These people may attend mass but do not necessarily believe everything the Church teaches. They are often involved in their parish, but they might not agree with the Church's teachings with regard to marriage and sexuality. Perhaps they are part of their parish community but do not value the practice of going to confession regularly.

The third category is those who have suffered some form of injustice. "Finally, there are others who are hindered by various situations of injustice in the realization of their fundamental rights" (John Paul II 1981, 1). Here, John Paul II was probably speaking about various social injustices that make it difficult to live marriage and family life well in certain parts of the world. We might also apply it to the many familial and relational injustices that exist in our culture today. The wife who has been abandoned by her husband or has discovered her husband's pornography addiction, the adult survivor of childhood sexual abuse, the child of divorced parents, or the ten-year-old who is accidentally exposed to pornography on the iPhone his mother gave him for his birthday are all people who have suffered an injustice. These situations all constitute wounds, or traumas, which can impede one's capacity to love.

Leading with Love

Corresponding to these three groups of people, there are three methods for transmitting and passing on the faith. These are different ways of talking about the faith. Pope Francis refers to them in this passage about preaching, "A beautiful homily, a genuine sermon must begin with the first proclamation, with the proclamation of salvation. There is nothing more solid, deep and sure than this proclamation. Then you have to do catechesis. Then you can draw even a moral consequence. But the proclamation of the saving love of God comes before moral and religious imperatives. Today sometimes it seems that the opposite order is prevailing" (Francis, "A Big Heart Open to God," 2013).

The first method is the *kerygma*, or first proclamation of Christ's saving love. "Jesus Christ loves you; he gave his life to save you; and now he is living at your side every day to enlighten, strengthen and free you" (Francis, *Evangelii Gaudium* 2013, 164). The kerygma is the starting point for all of our evangelizing work. The second method is catechesis. In catechesis we explain what we believe and why we believe it. Catechesis presupposes that someone has already received the gospel and now is ready to grow in their intellectual knowledge of the faith. Finally, drawing a moral consequence is when we propose various situations and discuss their moral gravity or weight. In moral theology, casuistry was a practice in which theologians would debate difficult moral questions in order to assist confessors to discern the gravity of various sins and the culpability of the person who commits them.

These three methods of transmitting the faith correspond to the three types of people in our triage. The person who is already converted is ready to read deep theological treatises, evaluate moral consequences, and more. The doubter is in need of catechesis and needs to understand better what we believe and why. The one who has suffered an injustice needs the kerygma preached over and over again. Even the most devoted person who prays vigorously every day and then discovers their spouse's pornography use needs to be reminded that they are loved by our Lord, who will never betray them.

While this principle may seem obvious to some, it is definitely not followed by all. When Pope Francis says, "Today it seems the opposite order is prevailing," it is often prevailing in the way we talk about pornography. It is common in our churches to have education about pornography that focuses on the moral consequences rather than on the kerygma. Any time we do a presentation on the harms of pornography, the negative consequences—pornography leads to human trafficking and prostitution, pornography leads to domestic violence, and so on—we are talking about the moral consequences. In the initial stages of recovery, addicts who focus on the harm their behavior is doing run the risk of elevating their shame. While these arguments are helpful for social justice work and influencing law in the public sphere, they are not particularly helpful for an addict. (An exception to this principle is people who are in denial that their behaviors are doing any harm to themselves or to others.) The faithful male Catholic addicts I have worked with do not watch pornography because they hate women; they do so because they are afraid of women. They do so because they do not know how to be loved. When that is the case, they need the first proclamation of Christ's saving love again and again.

Mercy and Conversion

The first proclamation is one of mercy. Pope John Paul II writes on the relationship of mercy and conversion in the document *Dives in Misericordia*:

> The Church professes and proclaims conversion. Conversion to God always consists in discovering His mercy, that is, in discovering that love which is patient and kind as only the Creator and Father can be; the love to which the "God and Father of our Lord Jesus Christ" is faithful to the uttermost consequences in the history of His covenant with man; even to the cross and to the death and resurrection of the Son. Conversion to God is always the fruit of the "rediscovery of this Father, who is rich in mercy." (John Paul II 1980, 13)

Mercy leads to conversion. Mercy is an experience in which someone is surprised by love. We know mercy when we experience the love of the Lord at a moment in which we feel we do not deserve it—perhaps at a moment we feel particularly unlovable. We see a clear example of this in the eighth chapter of John's Gospel.

As we examine the story of the woman caught in adultery, we may begin by asking the question of how she got there. What is her story? I imagine she became a prostitute for the same reasons many women today become prostitutes. Perhaps her family was ruined in some way. Did her parents die? Was she abandoned? Was she abused or raped as a young child? It would be logical to imagine that whatever happened, she came to believe that she had no value in herself and that her only value was her bodily value. She may have believed she was unworthy of true love or a real marriage. Perhaps the best she believed she could do was to go from man to man and make some money along the way to take care of her basic needs. I imagine she hated that life and maybe even wished she would die before waking the next morning.

Then, according to the biblical narrative, she is caught in the act of committing adultery. She is brought before Jesus in the street, and a large crowd gathers. "Teacher, this woman was caught in the act of adultery. In the Law Moses commanded us to stone such women. Now what do you say?" (John 8:4–5). What was this moment like for the woman? She is completely exposed. Perhaps she believes that now she will finally get what she deserves. Everyone in that crowd sees her exactly the way she sees herself. It is a moment of vulnerability and shame.

How does Jesus respond? He bends down and begins to write in the sand. There are many commentaries on what exactly he wrote. For our purposes, it is important that he bent down to write in the sand because he was placing himself within the woman's gaze. In moments of shame, we all tend to look at the ground. In this case, Jesus places his finger where the woman is looking, as if to say, "Look at me; I see you; I know who you are—who you *really are*." Perhaps the woman notices Jesus looking at her and looks away.

Then Jesus stands up and says, "Let any one of you who is without sin be the first to throw a stone at her" (8:7). Immediately he returns to write again on the ground. This time he catches her eye. I imagine the woman now allows herself to look at this person who is looking back at her with love. In that moment, the woman starts to notice that he looks at her differently than anybody in the crowd. While the crowd looks in a way that confirms what she previously believed about herself, Jesus looks in a way that tells her something different. He looks into her, and he looks at her with love.

Perhaps at this point the crowd notices how Jesus looks at her: "How does Jesus just look at her eyes? I cannot stop looking at her body and thinking about what she has been doing. I want to kill her because she is an occasion of sin for me. I remember Jesus also teaching that 'anyone who looks at a woman lustfully has already committed adultery with her in his heart.'" They start dropping their stones. Finally, all that remain are Jesus and the woman.

Jesus says to her, "Woman, where are they? Has no one condemned you?" (8:10).

She answers, "No one, sir" (8:11). This is the most crucial moment. This is the moment that reveals that mercy in fact leads to conversion, because the "No one, sir" includes herself. Somewhere in the look of love that entered into her gaze of shame, she started to see herself the way Jesus sees her rather than the way the crowd sees her. Only then does Jesus say, "Go now and leave your life of sin" (8:11). Where does she go? She follows after Jesus. She shows up in the Pharisee's house and washes his feet with her tears. She is there at the crucifixion. She is the first to discover the empty tomb. She is transformed by love.

This is the encounter of mercy that leads to conversion. Every addict conversion happens when we allow Jesus to love us as we are. It is what twelve steppers call surrender. It is the moment when all of the other work done in therapy, accountability groups, recovery groups, and more comes to fruition. When working with Catholic clients, this is the experience we are trying to facilitate.

CATHOLIC PRACTICES AND RECOVERY

Confession

Of course, for the Catholic Christian, this is the experience we are meant to have each time we confess our sins in the sacrament of reconciliation. However, most Catholic clients have been going to confession regularly for the same sexual sins for an exceptionally long time with limited results. Looking at this practice in the context of the addiction cycle can be helpful for understanding why it has not been efficacious. A few adjustments may be necessary to help a client to benefit more from this important practice.

Confession is a ritual in the Catholic Church with a specific format to be followed. The penitent begins by asking for the priest's blessing and stating the length of time since their last confession. They then name the sins they have committed by number and kind. This means they should name the number of times they have committed masturbation, sent or received nude pictures, or had sexual intercourse outside marriage since their last confession. They should also confess the amount of time they spent watching pornography. Looking back at the woman caught in adultery, she receives a great mercy in a moment when she is completely open and vulnerable. Naming the things we are most ashamed of puts us in that place. Sometimes people are tempted to minimize when confessing, or they go to different priests each week to hide the frequency of their acting out. Having a regular confessor who knows them can be an important step in growing in vulnerability and openness to the grace the sacrament offers.

Another reason confession is not efficacious for some is that it has become part of the ritualization process of their addiction. Kevin Skinner (2005) suggests that a typical ritualization process always begins with a vulnerable time as well as a stimulus that awakens movement toward acting out. Vulnerable times include when we are hungry, angry, lonely, tired, agitated, bored, or stressed. They might be times of the year, like the anniversaries of deaths, traumatic experiences, or discovery days. Stimuli, or triggers, can be sexual or nonsexual. Sometimes they are places, as when a college student or seminarian returns home and stays in the room they used to act out in when they were in high school. The power of the trigger is dependent on the vulnerable time. When a person is in a vulnerable time, triggers have a greater impact and a stronger pull. If there are vulnerable times, the person in recovery needs to be more vigilant in avoiding triggers. A typical ritual for a Catholic man might look like this:

- Bored and alone at home (vulnerable time).
- Unfiltered internet available (trigger).
- Checks social media and notices that friends are together and feels left out.
- More loneliness (emotion).
- Rechecks social media.
- Looks at picture of girls.
- Looks at pictures of girls he does not know (chemical release starts).
- He wants more but does not want to look at porn (thought).
- Goes to YouTube and watches a video of the fifteen most inappropriate commercials of 2019.
- Tells himself, *I'm not looking at porn.*
- Breaks a sweat, feels excited, and more.
- Eventually he thinks, *I'm already lusting, so I might as well be looking at porn.*
- **Asks himself,** *Can I get to confession before Sunday?*
- After making a plan to go to confession, acts out.
- Feels shame.
- Acts out again.
- **Goes to sacramental reconciliation.**
- Resolves to never act out again.
- Feels vulnerable, alone, bored.

As is illustrated above, going to confession becomes part of the ritualization process. In this way, it is no longer an experience of Jesus's look of love entering into the gaze of shame. It has simply become a way of closing the ritual. In order to reclaim the power of the sacramental experience, we have to get the small-R ritual out of the big-R Ritual. Some simple ways of doing that are to begin to go to confession every week at the same time, preferably with the same priest. This will help the client experience the sacrament of reconciliation without having to confess a sexual sin. For many Catholic addicts, they have never had that experience. They only go to confession for sexual sins, which impedes them from making further progress in the spiritual life.

The Eucharist and the Look of Love

For Catholics, the Eucharist is the source and summit of the spiritual life. Everything flows from the Eucharist, and everything is ordered to the Eucharist. Catholics believe that the mass is a re-presentation of the sacrifice Christ made on Mount Calvary. So, we properly say that we are at the foot of the cross at each mass, which means we are entering into the moment of mercy at each mass. It is the moment when Jesus cried, "Father, forgive them, for they do not know what they are doing" (Luke 23:34). It is the moment in which he gave his life so we could live. We also believe the Eucharist is the body, blood, soul, and divinity of Jesus Christ. Therefore, in a mysterious way, the same Jesus who bent down to write in the sand so the adulterous woman would not miss his look of love continues to make himself present to us today.

Eucharistic adoration is a devotional practice in which the consecrated host is placed in a monstrance so the faithful can simply look at Jesus in adoration. One priest who was known for spending hours in adoration was asked what he does during his time. He replied, "I look at Him, and He looks at me" (CCC 2715). Eucharistic adoration is an important devotion for Catholics in recovery to engage in because it provides an opportunity to reflect on how Jesus sees us and loves us as we are.

Mary, Our Model and Mother

In Catholic tradition, devotion to the Blessed Virgin Mary has always been recommended for preserving chastity. There are two key ways this devotion can assist in the recovery process. She is a model, and she is our mother.

Mary is a model of surrender. In Luke's Gospel, we find the story of the annunciation, when the angel Gabriel tells Mary she will conceive a son. After Mary questions how this is possible, the angel explains that it will happen by the power of the Holy Spirit and that nothing will be impossible for God. Then Mary prays the words of surrender: "'I am the Lord's servant,' Mary answered. 'May your word to me be fulfilled'" (Luke 1:38). In the translation prayed in the Catholic devotion known as the Angelus, Mary says, "Behold, I am the handmaid of the Lord. Let it be done to me according to your word." Mary lives a life that is completely surrendered to the Holy Spirit. That is the goal of Christian recovery. Following this event, she goes to visit Elizabeth, who has also conceived—John the Baptist. In this encounter Elizabeth says, "Blessed is she who has believed that the Lord would fulfill his promises to her!" (1:45).

These words are particularly interesting coming from Elizabeth because her own husband, Zechariah, did not believe the words that Gabriel spoke (Cf. Luke 1:18). Mary's response gives us insight into how she was able to trust and entrust herself to the Lord:

> My soul glorifies the Lord
> and my spirit rejoices in God my Savior,
> for he has been mindful

of the humble state of his servant.
From now on all generations will call me blessed,
    for the Mighty One has done great things for me—
    holy is his name.
His mercy extends to those who fear him,
    from generation to generation.
He has performed mighty deeds with his arm;
    he has scattered those who are proud in their inmost thoughts.
He has brought down rulers from their thrones
    but has lifted up the humble.
He has filled the hungry with good things
    but has sent the rich away empty.
He has helped his servant Israel,
    remembering to be merciful
to Abraham and his descendants forever,
    just as he promised our ancestors. (Luke 1:46–55)

This song of Mary is known in Catholic culture as the Magnificat. When praised for her faith by Elizabeth, she immediately gives praise to the Lord, who has "done great things for" her. She then names several of these things: scattered the proud, brought down rulers from their thrones, lifted up the humble, filled the hungry with good things, and more. These can all be understood as events from salvation history. God scattered the proud as the Red Sea crashed down on the Egyptians, he brought down rulers and raised up the lowly as David became king, and he filled the hungry as he fed the people of Israel in the desert. In other words, Mary recognized that everything the Lord had done for the people of Israel, he did for her. Therefore, he is trustworthy.

When any Christian is struggling to surrender his or her life to the Lord, it is usually because they don't trust him. We forget everything he has done in the history of salvation, not to mention everything he has done in our own lives. Mary gives us a model of remembering who we are so we can entrust our own hearts to the Lord.

Mary is also our mother. Jesus said to the beloved disciple, "Here is your mother." He said to Mary, "Here is your son" (John 19:26–27). Each of them was suffering a loss. Mary's vocation was to be the mother of Jesus—to love Jesus and to ponder his life in her heart. At the moment of the crucifixion, she watched her son die and must have wondered, "Whom will I love when he is gone?" At the same time John, the beloved disciple, was the one Jesus loved. He had leaned against Jesus's chest at the last supper, listening to his heartbeat. He was the only one of the twelve who did not scatter as Jesus was crucified, because he never missed the look of love. He must have wondered, "Who will love me when he is gone?"

Jesus looked at them and responded by saying, "Here is your son"—love him. And "here is your mother"—she will love you. In this moment, Jesus gives his own mother to each of us who have lost a mother or had imperfect mothers. Catholics believe Mary intercedes for us with her Son. She is also available to comfort us in our sorrow and grief as she did for the beloved disciple. Cultivating a relationship with her in the spiritual life can open the door to restoring a proper appreciation of femininity, beauty, and care. So many addicts go to pornography looking for affirmation from a woman. True maternal affirmation is accessible through the intercession of Mary.

Devotion to the rosary is recommended as a way of connecting with her as we meditate on the life of Jesus. The rosary consists of five decades of prayers. Each decade consists of the Lord's Prayer, ten Hail Marys, and the Glory be to the Father, Son, and Holy Spirit. As one prays the rosary, there is a meditation on one event from the life of Jesus and Mary. There are four sets of mysteries that guide meditation on different days of the week. They are as follows:

- The joyful mysteries: the annunciation, the visitation of Mary to Elizabeth, the birth of Jesus, the presentation of Jesus in the temple, and the finding of Jesus in the temple.
- The luminous mysteries: the baptism of Jesus, the wedding feast of Cana, the proclamation of the kingdom, the transfiguration, the institution of the Eucharist at the Last Supper.
- The sorrowful mysteries: the agony in the garden, the scourging at the pillar, the crowning with thorns, the carrying of the cross, the crucifixion.
- The glorious mysteries: the resurrection, the ascension into heaven, the descent of the holy spirit at Pentecost, the assumption of Mary into heaven, the crowning of Mary as queen of heaven and earth.

Community Recovery

While Catholic culture has a rich devotional life and tradition, there has been a weakness in establishing recovery communities within the structure of the Church. Groups like Pure Desire and Celebrate Recovery have not taken root within many Catholic parish communities. Many Catholics, and I suspect other Christians, have a hard time with general twelve-step communities because of the more generalized usage of "higher power" rather than speaking directly about

God or Jesus. Sometimes there can be a resistance to seeking help outside of the faith community because of a distorted belief that if someone needs a program other than the spiritual program of their particular denomination, that implies there is something wrong with their religious denomination.

If this reluctance is present in a client, one way of addressing it is to point to the beatitudes and how they correspond to the twelve steps. As Jesus began his public ministry, he preached the Sermon on the Mount. The first thing he preached was the Beatitudes, which revealed their importance. Just as one must work the twelve steps of recovery in order, the beatitudes provide an order for walking through the conversion process.

"Blessed are the poor in spirit" (Matt. 5:3) implies that we must acknowledge our own spiritual poverty. We cannot save ourselves. We cannot run our own lives. We need a savior. This corresponds to the first step: "We admitted we were powerless over lust and our lives have become unmanageable."

"Blessed are those who mourn" (Matt. 5:4). When we truly come to believe we are powerless and cannot recover on our own, we have to grieve. We mourn the fact that we could not stop our sexual behaviors by the power of our will; we mourn the fact that we have to go to therapy, group, and get a spiritual advisor. We have to grieve the loss of our addiction, which has been our best friend for years.

"Blessed are the meek" (Matt. 5:5). To be meek means that we have to humble ourselves and follow someone. We have to take direction. Here we have a convergence with steps two and three: "We came to believe that a power greater than ourselves could restore us to sanity. We made a decision to turn our lives and our wills over to the care of God as we understood him."

"Blessed are those who hunger and thirst for righteousness" (Matt. 5:6). Now it is time to desire righteousness in all areas of our lives so we "make a fearless and searching moral inventory" in step four.

"Blessed are the merciful, for they will be shown mercy" (Matt. 5:7). In steps five, six, and seven, we "admit to God, ourselves, and another person the exact nature of our wrongs. We are prepared to have God remove all our defects of character, and we humbly ask him to do so." In that process, we receive mercy.

Then comes "blessed are the pure in heart" (Matt. 5:8). When a Christian struggles with purity of heart, it may be the case that he has not yet been poor in spirit. This is the sixth Beatitude, and the order matters.

"Blessed are the peacemakers" (Matt. 5:9). In steps eight and nine, we make a list of those we have harmed and make amends wherever possible.

Steps ten, eleven, and twelve are simply living in Christian discipleship. We continue to take inventory, and when wrong, promptly admit it; we maintain conscious contact with God through prayer and meditation; and we seek to carry the message to others. We become evangelizers. This approach reveals that the twelve steps are nothing other than pre-evangelization. They are an intentional way of walking someone through the beatitudes and should be seen as a complement, not a competitor, to the faith. The Catholic in Recovery program is in its early years at the time of this writing. It is a twelve-step fellowship that attempts to integrate elements of the Catholic faith more directly into a twelve-step format and can be found at www.catholicinrecovery.com.

CONCLUSION

"Whoever is not against us is for us" (Mark 9:40). Jesus speaks these words when his disciples show concern that outsiders are using his name to drive out demons. Jesus reminds them that no one who drives out demons in his name can say anything against him. As we translate this into recovery language, that means being willing to do whatever it takes in order to be free and to do whatever works to facilitate true conversion and surrender to our Lord Jesus Christ. All of the tools we use—various therapeutic approaches, prayer ministry, twelve-step groups, and internet filters—are ordered toward conversion.

Catholic moral teaching is clear and admittedly difficult to live into. But this is balanced when we place recovery in the context of new evangelization. When clients are given permission to begin again from the perspective of mercy, there is room for incredible growth, and they come to experience traditional Catholic devotions like confession, eucharistic adoration, and the rosary in a new and more connected way. As a priest, I am especially grateful for the opportunity to share in this work with so many committed therapists and other religious leaders as we seek together to help our people to encounter Jesus's look of love.

CLERGY, CELIBACY, AND SEXUAL ACTING OUT:

A Developmental Perspective

Kenneth M. Adams, PhD, CSAT

A monolithic perspective is often used to understand and rehabilitate Catholic clergy, who take vows of celibacy but find themselves acting out sexually with others or using pornography compulsively. This perspective often includes a primary assessment of moral failing and subsequent recommendations of a return to a stronger faith commitment as the solution to the sexual acting out. Many clergy entering clinical settings find themselves continuing in sexually acting out patterns in spite of increased spiritual and prayerful efforts.

However, pastors who commit to celibacy are not monolithic in their etiology and in the dynamics that have led to their acting out and crossing of implicit and explicit sexual boundaries. While some may find relief and resolve with a stronger faith journey, others will find themselves failing in their renewed prayerful commitments. Increased shame and a spiral of denial and secrecy often follow those who do not find renewal in their faith. A double life may emerge, displaying a public face of faith on one hand but privately losing control over sexual impulses and behavior on the other. This is fertile ground for despair, shame, and addictive patterns. The subsequent increasing collapse of sexual boundaries too often leads to dire consequences for the wellbeing of the pastor and others in his care.

While not monolithic in etiology, celibate clergy who act out sexually share common threads anecdotally observed in clinical settings that warrant discussion and consideration. One of those is the role of loss and grief that may be associated with sexual celibacy. Too often clinicians avoid exploring the role of vows of celibacy as a loss issue for fear that it could propel the clergy to leave his ministry and enter lay life. Unfortunately, this reluctance prevents the celibate clergy from properly grieving the loss of his sexual life. A mature and comprehensive reconciliation of the celibate life is not achieved. In its place, sublimation of desire is encouraged, and the grief is denied its needed expression, often leading to a secret double life of sexual acting out.

This section looks at sexuality as a biologically driven attachment and developmental experience in which celibacy has the potential to disrupt and lead to the grievance and entitlement we often see in this clinical group that emerges when grieving is not expressed. The exception, for the purposes of this section, is professed celibate clergy whose primary arousal is to children. The severe thinking errors, grossly distorted beliefs, denial, and negative personality traits (e.g., inability to experience empathy) of those attracted to children do not readily fall into this discussion.

SEXUALITY AND ITS DEVELOPMENTAL UNFOLDING

Sexuality is inherently linked to attachment and caretaking. An individual's sexual development unfolds within the developmental and attachment history with primary caregivers. Disruptions in healthy development may manifest in later sexual problems.

Since the development of sexuality is integral to early attachment and bonding experiences, it is part of the overall developmental process. Sexuality is a biological and experiential internal drive that is linked to individuals' relationships to their caretakers. Its expression is negatively influenced whenever there is significant disruption or trauma. The more disruption there is in the developmental years of childhood through adolescence, the more potential exists for later sexual difficulties to occur. Experiences that prevent sexuality from unfolding naturally can disrupt development and split, or disconnect, lust from love (Money 1986).

Research studies support the idea that various disruptions in attachment affect sexuality (Jore et al. 2016; Money 1986). Del Giudice (2009) notes that early stress leads to disrupted attachment and an increase in the number of sexual partners. Miller and Fishkin (1997), in a study that followed men over a thirty-year period, found that men with anxious and avoidant attachment styles desire more sexual partners compared to those with secure styles. Allen and Baucom (2004) have noted that (1) males with dismissive attachment styles have the highest number of sexual partners, (2) females with preoccupied attachment styles have the second highest number, and (3) both groups have significantly more sexual partners than securely attached counterparts.

The neurobiological component of attachment theory suggests sexuality is a neurobiological affective attachment mechanism (Creeden 2004; Katehakis 2009) that remains integral to the ongoing development of the individual. Developmental insults may leave an individual able to be sexual but not able to bond or align values and morality with sexual expression. Parts of the self become split off, and sexuality no longer serves to connect or to align with professed values and morality. Rather than sexuality becoming integrated with the development of all psychological parts of the individual, a dissociative or compartmentalized sexuality develops. Further weakened is the brain's ability to exert executive control over sexual impulses to align with stated values. Sexuality is now used to discharge the grievances associated with feelings of loss from a sexuality that has failed to integrate with their chronological age, indicating a type of immaturity in their psychosexual development.

Erotic feelings now more easily merge with other feelings, such as anxiety, anger, pain, and shame (Carnes 1991). When this happens, sex may become disconnected, dissociated from the individual's moral compass and executive control of the brain, functioning on its own. Sex is then used as a drug to medicate feelings. Developing sexually compulsive or addictive behavior can be compensatory for a developmental, emotional, and sexual landscape that contains loss and grief that has not been reconciled. The person turns to addiction as a soothing agent. Now, a part of the self is sexually addicted. Sexual focus has become truncated and dissociated and, therefore, separate from the moral values and vows to which a priest commits.

Schwartz and Southern (1999) have explained sexually compulsive behavior as the end point in a series of developmental events: early attachment difficulties cause subsequent overwhelming experiences and feelings that the child is unable to assimilate. As a result, he has affect dysregulation issues: poor social skills, a lack of perceived efficacy in negotiating relationships, limited empathy and compassion, and difficulty with accurate attunement to cues from others. His self-development is impaired; he has split himself into parts. He may have difficulty with gender-related behavior; for example, he may not feel confident in his masculinity. Developing sexually compulsive or addictive behavior becomes compensatory for an attachment disorder.

THE ROLE OF GRIEVANCE WHEN SEXUAL BOUNDARIES ARE CROSSED

Given the evidence that sexuality is a normal ongoing biological state that is directly impacted by developmental events, loss associated with a vow of celibacy must be considered as a factor in those clergy who act out sexually, addictively, or otherwise. This is especially relevant when the individual has entered religious life to escape unresolved identity and sexual issues. Focusing on the failure of maintaining a moral commitment as the central cause of the collapse of sexual boundaries may overlook the grief that the sexually acting out is masking. Consider the story of Father Mark.

Fr. Mark entered therapy because of complaints of alleged flirtatious behavior with a number of women in his parish. The complaints came to the attention of the bishop, who insisted that Fr. Mark get help. While he had wanted to date in his teen years, the calling to the priesthood kept him from pursuing his desire. At the age of twenty-one, Fr. Mark had entered the priesthood after an early adolescent conversion experience. Now thirty-one, he was steadfast in his faith and knowledge that the priesthood was his calling. In fact, he seemed to radiate a natural faith and a deep authenticity to his calling.

While expressing some confusion and shame regarding the allegations, Fr. Mark willingly opened up during the therapy sessions. He readily acknowledged that he enjoyed the attention of the young women at the parish but was clear that he had no intention of breaking any boundaries of sexual contact with them. He was genuinely uncertain why he was perceived as too flirtatious.

Over time, Fr. Mark revealed that he had a compulsive habit of viewing pornography and masturbating. In the therapy sessions, he readily expressed shame and regret and a desire to stop. He sought confession and spiritual direction on many occasions in his effort not to use pornography. He prayed often and sought help from the Lord. In spite of all his sincere prayerful and spiritual efforts, he was unable to change. At times, he would binge on porn and masturbation multiple times a day. Fr. Mark readily expressed a loneliness that he tried to cover up with the porn but could not find a way to stop doing what was bringing him increasing shame.

Fr. Mark had been using porn since his early teen years as a result of his difficulty with his alcoholic father and the struggles he witnessed between his parents. He would often intermediate during his parents' fights, trying to comfort them both and bring order to his family. Fr. Mark's porn use seemed an obvious attempt to comfort and soothe the distress and loneliness that began in his early childhood.

Understanding that his childhood loneliness was a driving factor, Fr. Mark began to make progress in using porn and masturbation less often. However, he was unable to stop completely, and when pressed about it, he began to admit that he didn't want to stop. Over time, he increasingly talked about feeling cheated out of love and intimacy during his childhood. Now a priest, he was uncertain how he would reconcile his unmet longings for love and companionship with his vow of celibacy.

Further sessions with Fr. Mark helped him begin to see that he carried grievances about feeling cheated out of the opportunity to find love and companionship. He was certain that his calling to be a priest was solid, but he was unclear how he would find peace with his desire for love. He also began to see that he wanted too much from his interactions with the women at the parish. He realized he was trying to make up for the lost opportunity for love and romance by pushing the boundaries with the women. Fr. Mark began to understand that his unmet needs for companionship were spilling over in his interactions with women. He also saw how his compulsive porn use fed his sexualizing of women. He now accepted the fact that it all had to stop.

In the end, Fr. Mark needed to come to terms with the missed opportunities for romantic love. Sublimating his desires to other platonic relationships as well as other spiritual passions was not enough. He had to grieve. While continuing to honor and reinforce his calling and all the joy it brought him, he began to openly grieve in sessions. He also surfaced and confronted his anger about his upbringing. By doing so, his grievances began to diminish. With the support of his sexual addiction recovery group, he set clear boundaries in his interactions with women and pornography use.

In his workbook *The Recovery Zone*, Pat Carnes (2009) details the breakdown of anger and loss as part of the addict's "grievance story" in a series of task assignments. In the detailing and writing of his grievance story, Fr. Mark saw more clearly how his history of unexpressed loss and grief led to his sexual acting out. In allowing active grieving, Fr. Mark remained mindful and vigilant of his vulnerability to relapse into addictive behavior, which can occur when a grievance story is activated and indulged.

In time, Fr. Mark became more reconciled to the vow of celibacy as he separated out past injustices and permitted his grief and anger to surface. More at peace and reconciled, he could more easily avoid the seduction of his "injustice list" of grievances and self-pity and more readily embrace the joy of his priesthood. The template Fr. Mark worked so hard to create of noticing and sharing loss and allowing grief when it arose (as opposed to sublimation) gave him the capacity to renew his vow on the daily basis that it sometimes required.

GRIEF, ACCEPTANCE, AND RECONCILIATION: THE PATH FORWARD

When those clergy who struggle to live within the vows of celibacy are not helped by a return to a stronger faith, expressing the grief and loss of not having romantic companionship is necessary for a more mature integration of celibacy. Critical awareness and tasks that allow the celibate clergy's path forward include:

- Accepting sexual desire as part of the longing for love and companionship that is an inherent part of one's lifelong identity development.
- Grieving and accepting the loss of sexual expression (as opposed to sublimating) adds to the resiliency needed to live a celibate life.
- Recognizing that the grief and loss surrounding sexuality is not static and will reemerge at different points in the lifespan.
- Resolving early developmental loss issues related to family-of-origin dysfunction.
- Naming, delineating, and monitoring the grievance story.
- Participating in treatment for porn or sexual addiction when needed.
- Recognizing the need for ongoing reconciliation with and recommitment to the celibate life as a fluid process requiring acceptance as a key aspect of the complexities that may present in living the vow of celibacy.

The renowned developmental psychologist Erik Erikson (1963, 1986) revealed in his research that identity development is not reconciled only at one stage but is a dynamic interaction between the individual's attachment needs and environmental experiences as he ages. The erotic desire inherent in the longing for attachment, love, and companionship is not static and reveals itself constantly across the life span. Celibate clergy must periodically return to grieving and reconciliation in order to avoid transgressing their vows of celibacy.

REFERENCES

Allen, E. S., and D. H. Baucom. 2004. "Adult Attachment and Patterns of Extra Dyadic Involvement." *Family Process* 43, no. 4: 467–88.

Carnes, P. J. 1991. *Don't Call It Love: Recovery from Sexual Addiction*. New York: Bantam Books.

———. 2009. *The Recovery Zone, Vol. 1; Making Changes That Last: The Internal Tasks*. Carefree, AZ: Gentle Path.

Creeden, K. 2004. "The Neurodevelopmental Impact of Early Trauma and Insecure Attachment: Re-Thinking Our Understanding and Treatment of Sexual Behavior Problems." *Sexual Addiction and Compulsivity* 11, no. 4: 223–47.

Del Giudice, M. 2009. "Sex, Attachment, and the Development of Reproductive Strategies." *Behavioral and Brain Sciences* 32, no. 1: 1–21.

Erikson, E. H. 1963. *Childhood and Society*. New York: W. W. Norton & Company.

———. 1986. *Identity Youth and Crisis*. New York: W. W. Norton & Company.

Jore, J., B. Green, K. Adams, and P. Carnes. 2016. "Attachment Dysfunction and Relationship Preoccupation." *Sexual Addiction and Compulsivity* 23, no. 1: 56–90.

Katehakis, A. 2009. "Affective Neuroscience and the Treatment of Sexual Addiction." *Sexual Addiction and Compulsivity* 16, no. 1: 1–31.

Miller, L. C., and S. A. Fishkin. 1997. "On the Dynamics of Human Bonding and Reproductive Success: Seeking Windows on the Adapted-for Human-Environmental Interface." In *Evolutionary Social Psychology*. Edited by J. Simpson and D. Kenrick, 197–235. Mahwah, NJ: Erlbaum.

Money, J. 1986. *Lovemaps: Clinical Concepts of Sexual/erotic Health and Pathology, Paraphilia, and Gender Transposition of Childhood, Adolescence, and Maturity.* New York: Irvington.

Schwartz, M. F., and S. Southern. 1999. "Manifestations of Damaged Development of the Human Affectional Systems and Developmentally Based Psychotherapies." *Sexual Addiction and Compulsivity* 6, no. 3: 163–75.

Skinner, K. 2005. *Treating Pornography Addiction: The Essential Tools for Recovery.* Provo, UT: GrowthClimate.

CHAPTER 16

EFFECTIVE INTERVENTION FOR SEXUALLY COMPULSIVE ADOLESCENTS

Floyd Godfrey, PhD, CSAT

M any adolescents who are sexually compulsive will progress toward complete sexual addiction. The psycho-emotional dynamics that foster sexual compulsivity in adolescents are often the same dynamics found with adult addicts. Repeated compulsive behaviors over time become deeply ingrained as neuropathway development occurs. Once these pathways are firmly established and the adolescent reports a coping "need" for the sexual behavior, we can say it has moved into the category of addiction, just like an alcoholic who reports the "need" for alcohol to cope with stressors.

Although compulsivity can be difficult to mitigate, addictive behaviors have generated neuropathway connections that make it even more difficult to manage. The patterns become memorized in the brain, and the limbic system defaults to these behaviors instinctively as a mechanism for coping. It's helpful for adolescents to know that their compulsive patterns can be changed before they become completely addictive, but it's difficult to determine whether they are engaging compulsively or addictively. Fortunately, the strategies and interventions for these two situations are often similar.

INGREDIENTS FOR SUCCESS

There are three critical aspects to be considered for successful programs to be successful: developmental needs, systemic intervention, and collaboration. Each of these areas require specific planning and organization. Therapists must understand the developmental stage of the adolescent they are working with. The intervention must be systemic and have measurable progress points for the adolescent, their parents, the therapist, and others involved in treatment. And the intervention must involve collaboration with therapists, family, and supportive mentors.

Developmental Needs

Understanding developmental needs of adolescents is paramount to successful programming. Without a keen understanding of the adolescents in your care, any approach will be ineffective. You cannot approach an adolescent in the same manner you approach adults. There are so many changes happening in their lives that they are often confused. Yet this is also when they begin behaving as if they are full-fledged adults. This can be puzzling for adults trying to interact with them, so let's talk about the major changes occurring during adolescence.

The most obvious changes during this period are physical changes to the body, such as primary and secondary sexual characteristics (Greenberg, Bruess, and Oswalt 2017). Adolescents' bodies are growing into something more mature. Primary characteristics include such things as increased growth, body hair development, changes in the voice, and genitalia development. Testosterone increases for boys, causing sperm development. Estrogen increases for girls, causing menarche. And for both sexes, these and other hormones cause secondary sexual characteristics (Greenberg, Bruess, and Oswalt 2017). Romantic feelings and fantasies emerge, as do curiosity about others' bodies and a desire for experimentation. All these changes can be exciting and repulsive at the same time to an adolescent. Some feel perplexed, some engage the rush of new emotion, and others experience an awkward repulsion to the changes. All these changes bring a flurry of confusion that adolescents must manage without years of adult experience. The physical and emotional changes are novel.

As mentioned earlier, there is an increased curiosity about romance and sex at this stage. Hormone changes bring them to a place of inquisitiveness about things that are different. Some Christian adolescents feel ambiguous about this curiosity, as they may have been taught to "flee from sexual immorality" (1 Cor. 6:18). Although this is sound biblical advice, it runs contrary to the impulses and curiosity now filling their minds and bodies. Similarly, some adolescents are curious about the same sex, and it is important to acknowledge that this is increasingly reported by adolescents in Western cultures. Therapists must use caution labeling these curiosities and hold space for exploring the story underneath the disclosure. The realization that something they perceive as wrong is also something they can't stop thinking about can create internal shame. This will be important to address during intervention.

The capacity for increased compassion and emotional intelligence is another change that occurs during adolescence. Although sometimes adolescents appear snarky and self-centered to their parents or adults, their ability to feel for others has expanded. Usually this shows itself first within social circles. However, their general ability for empathy has increased. Additionally, they begin to experience self-awareness of their emotional experiences. Though they can't always put labels on them, they start to identify various feelings and emotions that motivate them.

The brain of an adolescent has an increased capacity for abstract concepts. They can start to think hypothetically and formulate theories. They have an increased ability for moral insights and existential thinking. This often causes them to have a heightened awareness of right and wrong. Sometimes it feels like they've become moral police officers, observing injustices in society, at school, at home, or at work. They consider religious teachings and embark on their own journey for spirituality, often involving perceptions of God and morality.

Adolescents also experience an increased motivation for social bonding experiences. They are concerned for the welfare of their friends. Sometimes they may feel as though friends are more important than family. This is a normal stage of bonding and attachment for every adolescent, sometimes at the expense of family relationships.

A strong desire for independence is another marker of adolescence. They learn to think on their own, develop their own opinions, and generally seek to function without adults. Typically, they aren't capable of the independence they want and still rely upon parents, family, or adults to support them. However, the desire for independence often causes them to pull away without asking for help and to seek their own solutions without support.

One final developmental aspect to consider is the development of their sense of confidence and self-esteem. Most youth search to identify things they like about themselves and things they feel confident about to develop a sense of identity from perceived strengths and weaknesses. This stage of self-esteem formation sets the stage for adult life. They need mentors and healthy adults who can help them manage weaknesses and insecurities, while focusing on strengths and positive qualities.

In summary, when a therapist understands these various developmental changes, it's easier to identify adolescents' "needs." Consider the following when developing your approach:

- They need safe adults other than parents with whom to talk and share.
- They need safe adults to teach them about puberty and sexuality.
- They need to be affirmed by safe adults about their budding sexuality.

- They need help identifying emotions and feelings when confused.
- They need space to formulate their own opinions without criticism.
- They need opportunities to develop strong social bonds.
- They need space for independence, while living within healthy boundaries.
- They need encouragement as they identify strengths and form their identities.

Establish a Systemic Approach

Because there are so many changes during adolescence, the most effective interventions for sexual compulsivity are systemic. In other words, the therapist should have the overall picture and develop a system for implementation. A systemic approach involves an organized treatment plan that typically is held together by eight different pillars.

Pillar 1: Support Network Development. Ideally, this network at a minimum should include parents, an adult mentor of the same gender, and therapists. Sometimes the network can be expanded to include additional family members, religious leaders, and possibly some mature peer friendships. It is important to have various people within the network supporting them in their goals for treatment because it's extremely difficult to overcome compulsive sexual behaviors in an atmosphere of isolation. The adolescent should be taught that recovery happens within community; it's a team sport.

Pillar 2: Shame Reduction. Sometimes adolescents carry toxic shame instead of healthy guilt. They might believe they're flawed and defective, that something is innately wrong with them. They may be confused about sexuality and believe they are bad because they are tempted in this way. In whatever way the toxic shame speaks, it must be reduced and eliminated as much as possible. Toxic shame fosters addictive patterns. Some have said that shame is the lifeblood of addiction. You must effectively deal with shame to heal the emotional undercurrent that drives the compulsive behaviors.

Pillar 3: Recovery Education. The adolescent must acknowledge the struggle and give the therapist the opportunity to teach them about recovery. They must acquire a basic knowledge of how their current struggle came into existence and understand the basic concepts of addiction and recovery work. When they learn recovery basics, the sobriety tools they learn will be much more effective. Otherwise, they won't understand why they're doing what they're doing in recovery. They will make limited progress.

Pillar 4: Social Skill Development. Many youths struggle to fit in and connect socially. Sometimes youth have experienced wounding around social activity, further increasing a sense of shame and insecurity. Because they have a strong need for bonding and social engagement, a deficit will increase compulsivity. They may need social coaching or help in developing meaningful friendships.

Pillar 5: Sobriety Skill Development. Adolescents need to learn some basic skills to keep away from the compulsive behavior. It's often hard to address deeper emotional undercurrents when they act out in ways to mask the discomfort. Getting sober from the acting out is important.

Pillar 6: Self-esteem Development. Therapists must help the adolescent focus their mind and energy on personal strengths. You may need to help the teenager identify their strengths and find ways to engage them. This is especially true if they come into your program without strong familial support or adult mentorship. They must learn to love themselves as unique individuals, to develop a sense of identity based on confidence and security.

Pillar 7: The Family System. The home and family environment must be evaluated to identify changes that need to be made toward a healthy structure. Adolescents can make wonderful progress in counseling, but if the home environment is toxic, they will often default to old patterns of coping. Family therapy is often required for this aspect of treatment. Similarly, parenting classes can be useful, or a monthly parent group to discuss helpful changes in the home. In some cases, you might need to help parents and family understand that changes in the system doesn't mean they've done something wrong but rather that the teenager needs something a little different.

Pillar 8: Emotional Awareness Development. Therapists must help adolescents identify emotions and healthy forms of expression. Sometimes this includes ways of coping with difficult or stressful emotional experiences. Bottling up the emotion can increase compulsivity. The bottled-up emotions fuel the fire.

When considering these eight pillars of treatment, you can combine interventions to accomplish several at the same time. For example, if the adolescent is involved in group therapy alongside individual therapy, you can accomplish shame reduction as well as social skill development. Therapists must learn to identify various aspects of treatment to make the biggest impact on their young clients.

Develop a Collaborative Approach

Collaborating with other therapists, parents, and mentors will provide the best outcome for intervention. Each has their own unique role influencing the teen's life. When the program collaborates with different aspects of the teenager's life, the most success will be achieved.

Good Therapists

Finding the right therapist to work with adolescents is important when developing a collaborative approach. Most therapists do not have the natural finesse teen programming requires. Consider the following when choosing a therapist:

1. Therapists who are good with teens know how to lightly banter. They're mature enough to hold good boundaries and be directive, but they can also be light and playful.
2. A good therapist for teens understands they're stepping in and out of transference with their client. Sometimes the teenager needs a counselor and sometimes they're hungry for a mentor. A good therapist for teens can observe the need and step into each as appropriate.
3. A good therapist is comfortable and confident when speaking with parents. They must be capable of teaching recovery concepts and challenging parents when appropriate. Some parents need boundaries, as their interaction with their child has been unhealthy. A therapist must be able to confront those issues honestly while holding a boundary with parents.
4. A good therapist can hold the privacy of the teen they're working with. It's not uncommon for parents, family members, or clergy to become overly inquisitive. For example, they might seek extra information that was given to the therapist in confidence. If the therapist loses the teen's trust, treatment impact will be immediately reduced. Within the realm of sexuality, not every graphic fantasy needs to be disclosed to parents. A good therapist knows how to keep the teen's privacy without jeopardizing safety.
5. A good therapist receives feedback for growth and improvement. They actively seek advice and ideas for working with adolescents.
6. A good therapist understands recovery concepts and can adequately teach them off-the-cuff lessons. Sometimes the best therapists have a personal

experience with these issues, making it easier for them to relate to the teenagers. However, when this is the case, it's important the therapists have a stable and enduring recovery pattern in their own lives.

Parents and Mentors

One of the most important things for parents and mentors to learn is basic communication. Many parents become highly defensive and frustrated trying to talk to their teens. When youth are snarky and pressing for independence, they tend to push buttons. It can be frustrating for parents and mentors to interact with them. However, getting defensive only makes matters worse. Parents and mentors need to learn patience in responding. Here are a few basic communication skills they can learn to better understand and connect with adolescents.

1. Learn their language. Teens often have their own jargon for describing life and difficulties, so parents must get on their channel to understand the dialect. Try to communicate in their language when appropriate. Best attempts that result in humorous failure can be a bonding experience with teenagers.

2. Remember their friends. Because teens seek social bonds, attention to their friends sends a caring message. Adults should memorize friends' names and interests. This way adults can restate the information at appropriate times. If you care about their friends, adolescents will notice.

3. Be able to discuss teens' music and media interests. Find out what they enjoy and familiarize yourself with it. Listen to it occasionally to get an idea of what they like. Be prepared at the right opportunity to discuss it with them and aspects you enjoy. Even the fact that you tried will send the message you care.

4. Be willing to try their hobbies. Find out what special interests the teen has and engage them. Whether it's sports, crafts, or some hobby you are unfamiliar with, look for opportunities to enjoy it together.

5. Ask the teenager to teach you something. Perhaps it's the hobby you've investigated, the music they're listening to, or something from school. Let them be the professional at something and teach you. Let them recognize their strength in that area.

6. Ask the adolescent their opinion about something. The topic doesn't matter, but be prepared to hold your opinions to yourself and just listen. Show a curiosity in what they think, but don't debate. Watch your body language to avoid sarcastic eye-rolls. Actively listen to see what they think about different topics.

7. Take time to play with the teen. Find things to do together that bring laughter and a relaxed atmosphere. It doesn't matter the activity; just make time together without distractions. This might require putting away electronics.

8. Ask questions about their reality like the following: "What's it like these days going to high school?" "What is the peer pressure like at your school?" "What do kids think nowadays about religion?" "Do you think teenagers care about politics?" Whatever questions parents and mentors ask, just remember it's about your curiosity, *not* an opportunity to lecture or teach.

Morals are a limited motivational tool. Teaching kids right and wrong might be essential for healthy development, but shaming them for doing something wrong will have the reverse effect. Adults often make things worse by doing this. Bible-thumping and acting as a morality police aggravates the situation. Parents must learn to listen and teach on deeper levels about *why* they believe something is wrong. Teens want to understand the deeper why rather than an abstract concept without rationale.

Parents should ask themselves, *Why am I concerned about my teen?* Limiting their own motivations to moral judgments is emotionally hazardous. Adults must be capable of teaching healthy aspects about what's going on—the deeper why.

Creating Safety with Adults

Youth often describe the need for "safe" adults who can listen without passing judgment. They avoid inducing further shame by simply avoiding adults who make them feel that way. Therapists need to teach parents and mentors on these points. Additionally, therapists should teach teenagers how to discuss these points with adults in their support network. Consider the following list of common statements from youth looking for safe adults:

- "I need someone to listen to me without lecturing or criticizing."
- "I need someone who can hear my embarrassing things without flipping out."
- "I want safe adults to know that sometimes it freaks me out to tell anyone; I'm used to keeping things a secret. It's a big deal that I am sharing."
- "I want safe adults to promise they won't tell my personal stuff to other people—no gossip between adults or other youth."
- "I want to know that an adult isn't disappointed in me and that they'll support me."

- "I want to know that an adult cares about me, will check up on me, and will take an interest in me."
- "I want an adult to promise they won't give up on me, even if I keep messing up or give up on myself."
- "I need an adult to be encouraging and compassionate, because sometimes I get discouraged."
- "I need an adult to be patient with me."
- "I need an adult to understand that sometimes I just want to make my own decisions and have my own opinions."
- "I need an adult to ask me specific questions without avoiding the embarrassing ones."
- "I want an adult to learn about my problems so they know how to talk about it with me and help me along."

Teaching Parents and Mentors Attunement

Teaching parents and mentors how to listen and communicate with teenagers is essential. Some will struggle with it more than others. However, a beginning step toward a good relationship is the adult's ability to stay tuned-in to the teenager. We call this *attunement*, literally "the feeling of being met and understood" that emerges from secure attachment. (van der Kolk 2014, p. 113). This concept is different than empathy but requires connection and attention. It's about the adult's ability to engage another person and stay present for them. There are four basic communication tools that help create attunement:

1. **Listen without responding.** You don't necessarily need to talk. Teens get talked at most of the day between school and extracurricular activities. What they don't get is someone listening to their thoughts, ideas, and feelings. In other words, adults must learn to truly listen. Listening does not mean mentally preparing a rebuttal while the teen is talking or feigning interest while working on other tasks. It means providing undivided attention while listening without interruption to what they have to say.
2. **Use "I" statements.** Don't be afraid to talk about your experiences. In other words, share about how things have impacted you, while being sure to not project onto them. Avoid "you" statements, as these are often filled with blame or shame. Simply share your perspective as the adult—no judgments. For instance, "I am noticing a few changes since your parents got divorced and I am wondering how you are feeling about that" is better than "You keep acting up at school and your grades are falling; what's the problem?"

3. **Reflect back before responding.** In other words, repeat back to the teenager what you think they've said. This a helping skill that every parent needs in their toolbelt as it can help prime empathy. Make sure you have it right in your mind before you formulate any response. Take your time; don't be reactive or impulsive.

4. **Ask permission before responding.** Adults can say something like, "Would you like my input on this?" or "Could I share something that worked for me?" When a teenager simply wants to be heard, any response from an adult could be misperceived as controlling or shaming. Asking permission before responding helps them feel respected.

Some final thoughts for parents and adults:

1. **Be cautious with your tone.** Teenagers can quickly detect sarcasm. If you roll your eyes or talk down to them, you reinforce any walls the teen builds. Keep your tone patient and curious. Avoid condescending gestures and facial expressions.

2. **Keep your emotions in check.** Teenagers tend to push adults' buttons. But anger and frustration will not help the communication. Likewise, your own anxiety can get in the way of the relationship. Get support for yourself when needed so you can keep your emotions in check.

Helping Parents and Mentors Avoid the Fear Cycle

Many parents and mentors fall into anxiety and fear about their child's sexual behavior. These things make it extremely difficult to think clearly and rationally. In some cases, adults have their own wounds around sexuality: abuse, molestation, or marital infidelity. As such, understanding and resolving one's own sexual story is an important part of parenting well (Bowman, 2013). In other cases, parents are simply scared about the long-term ramifications of compulsive sexual behavior. There could be countless reasons that any adult would fall into a fear cycle, so it is important to teach them how to recognize and stay out of this cycle. Again, examining one's own sexual story is imperative when working with anyone, especially teens, who struggles with problematic sexual behavior. This applies to parents as well.

One indicator that adults may be falling into a fear cycle is general anxiety or panic. Typical anxiety symptoms include a pounding heart, racing thoughts, and difficulty breathing, just to name a few. In this situation, parents must be taught to acknowledge the symptoms and to relax. Deep breathing, meditation, or mindfulness techniques can help ground them so they can think rationally. Most parents do not want to make decisions from a place of fear.

An important tool to escape this cycle is to reach out for support from trusted friends or family. This should include the spouse when possible. Soliciting encouragement and support from other adults can help ground the parents. It also provides a sounding board for decision-making.

Once parents are more grounded, it's helpful to analyze where the fear might be originating. For example, is it possible the parent's wound around their own molestation is coming to the surface? In that case, is the fear directly related to unhealed trauma or to a message of impending danger about the child? Another example might be related to the parent's moral standards as a Christian. In other words, do fears of hell or condemnation rise to the surface? Wherever the fear originates, the parent should find support to resolve it.

As these issues are processed with a therapist, parents will need to consider their options in helping their teen. Do new rules or boundaries need to be established in the home? Is there an appropriate way of interacting with their teen that will reduce emotional drama? What options do parents have to support their teen? It is important for parents to consider options without the fear cycle influencing ultimate decisions.

Once all options have been considered, parents can clearly communicate to their teenager without emotion and drama clouding the process. It may take practice. Many parents will need to rehearse in session with a therapist.

CONSIDER THE TEEN'S INTERNAL RESPONSE

Most teens have confused feelings about compulsive sexual behavior. On one hand, friends at school may be telling them it's fine, no worries. On the other hand, parents and pastors might be communicating concern with sexual behavior outside a marriage relationship. The mixed messages can generate confusion.

The most common experience for teens in this situation is guilt. They believe the behavior is wrong and deep down are conflicted about it. This is especially true if they've been unfaithful in some committed dating relationship. On some level, the behavior seems wrong, but the physical sensations are exciting. Teens feel torn inside about physical pleasure for something they believe they're not supposed to enjoy. This can escalate into spiritual confusion, causing them to wonder why God would give them such strong feelings for something that is wrong or sinful.

Youth in Christian contexts tend to magnify feelings of guilt and morph them into a sense of toxic shame. Rather than sensing that the behavior is wrong or unhealthy, they begin to feel as though something is wrong with *them*. Instead of seeing sinful behavior as a mistake, they believe they must be a mistake. Or instead of categorizing the behavior as bad, they interpret themselves as inherently bad or unworthy. This sense of shame must be separated from guilt and acknowledged as unhealthy. Often, the intense feelings of toxic shame generate compulsive energy and maintain the cycle.

When shame is deeply embedded, the struggling teenager moves into patterns of hiding and secrecy. These become the hallmark of potentially addictive behavior. Their ability to keep others from knowing what's really going on and from knowing who they really are is deeply unsettling. Thoughts of disclosure and transparency—that someone may know their deepest, darkest secrets—can bring panic. This anxiety process tends to repeat itself, and shame thrives.

Ultimately, the hiding and secrecy generates patterns of isolation. A teenager increasingly becomes lonely. This isolation can be literal or emotional. They might be popular and have many friends, but the secrecy about their inner struggle keeps them from connecting on deeper levels. The hiding and secrecy become forms of isolation. In other cases, youth feel segregated from others and don't feel like they have any friends.

Therapists must remember that toxic shame destroys self-esteem. It is emotionally painful and drives people toward isolation. The messages that happen inside the teen's mind erode their confidence. It confuses their ability to set healthy boundaries as guilt would require. Instead, they perpetuate messages like, "I'm bad," "I'm a mistake," or "Something is wrong with me."

THERAPEUTIC PROGRAM SUCCESS

If you're creating a program within a clinical context, it will be important to consider factors that increase programming success. You'll need to do considerable planning ahead to address each of these issues. Successful programming requires time, planning, and collaboration with others working with teens.

One of the first important considerations is whether you would accept juvenile sex offenders into your program. It's not uncommon for adolescents who are experimenting with pornography or other compulsive sexual behaviors to be referred to you for treatment. In some instances, these teens have moved beyond pornography and simplistic acting out into illegal behavior. For example, a young man with compulsive pornography problems might someday start asking a younger sibling to do sexual things with him. This isn't typical, but it's not uncommon. Our experience has been that most sex offender teens need a different type of treatment and are often disruptive to successful programming.

They need intervention that addresses their specific needs. Although there might be some overlap in the course of treatment for compulsive sexual behaviors, it's unwise to mix the two groups. Teens who cross this line of sexual interaction with younger children need a different treatment.

A successful program will also incorporate regular engagement with parents, mentors, and any religious leaders who are directly involved with the teen's support network. A monthly parent group is a good option that allows for support, education, and updates about their teen's progress. After obtaining consent from the parents and the youth, both mentors and religious leaders can also be included. This helps to generate a dynamic team working to help the adolescent.

A successful program for teenagers will also resonate with them. In other words, you must ensure that the program speaks to adolescent culture. You'll want to incorporate logos, posters, music, and other items that reflect pop culture. Obviously, you'll need to make sure these items are appropriate but also effective to create an atmosphere that's engaging. A word of caution here: teens can detect even the slightest hint of inauthenticity. In your attempts to be culturally relevant with them, be authentic.

Also, be sure to plan ahead to prepare the system. Such details might include making sure the therapist facilitating the program has read the material and understands what is taught. Confirm that you have a room reserved so the group can use a consistent space. Acquire all the parental consent forms before the first day. Have program handouts, workbooks, forms, and other paperwork prepared ahead of time. Take the time to consider all the possible details. You'll be in trouble if you simply pull a group of youth together on a day without adequate planning and consideration of details.

As you prepare the system for your program, make sure you're collaborating with other therapists. It's easy to know what's happening for each individual teen when all the individuals in your group are your clients. But if you have teens in your program working with other therapists, you'll need to collaborate with those therapists. The program will have much more success if you go into group with some ideas about what the participants need to do individually. In some cases, you may need to have the parents sign a release of information so you can openly discuss with the other therapist any current needs or status of treatment. You also want to know what this other therapist is teaching. If the concepts and tools you're teaching within the program are inconsistent with another therapist's teachings or philosophies, the teenagers and their families may become confused or derailed in their progress.

The most successful programs have written materials, handouts, or workbooks for participants to complete. Sometimes these can be completed within group, and other times the teen should work with their therapist to complete them. My experience has been that a combination of both will have the most impact. A framework for learning content—a workbook, journal, or something else—will help them stay on track and will help the parents know what their children are learning so they can reinforce the concepts outside the office. If you can't locate some type of workbook material, a blank notebook and handouts can work too.

I have found it to be helpful to create a rank system so teens can track their progress. Similar to Boy Scout programming that includes earning merit badges and progressing through ranks, when participants in your program have smaller tasks to mark off their lists toward higher ranks, they report feeling encouraged by the visual indicator. It gives them a sense of traction and momentum in their progress. This also gives parents some gauge as to how their teens are doing when they can see the chart.

Your program will maximize success when participants engage both individual and family therapy outside of group. Youth will get stuck on different concepts you teach in the program, so it's important to have individual time to help them understand and integrate the concepts. They should make recovery concepts part of their new lives, which usually requires individual attention. Also, their family systems often need adjusting. Parents may need to learn additional parenting skills. Siblings may need to learn new communication skills. Family members need to learn how to interact with one another in ways that are more supportive.

One final piece of advice for successful programming: use external motivators. Youth don't have the same intrinsic motivation as adults. Many adults are extremely concerned about the escalation of their behavior, as it could involve divorce, loss of employment, financial distress, religious consequence, or other measures deeply impacting their lives. Lacking these heavy consequences, some teens appreciate external motivators that encourage them to complete their goals. For example, you might have a competition on a specific week to see how many tools each participant can use on a given day. You might have a group competition and plan a pizza party if everyone stays sober throughout the week. If you've established rank advancements, you might consider gift cards or special prizes to celebrate the success. These external motivators are especially useful when they incorporate working together. The positive peer pressure keeps their momentum going.

GROUP FORMAT SUCCESS

Most successful programs include a group therapy format, so here are a few items that create success within the group context. Establishing parameters for general group format provides structure and direction.

Make sure that you always create safety whenever you bring new members into the group. Create an atmosphere that makes the group feel like a team. There are many ways of doing this, so decide on a procedure and keep it consistent. For example, you might go around the group and ask everyone to share their stories, then let new members share how they can relate to each story. For another example, you might ask veteran group members to share what they need to feel safe in the group, and then ask the new member what they need to feel safe. Open this up for further discussion and you'll create a safe container.

Safety should also include verbalizing the need for confidentiality and respect. With prolific social media, this aspect of group safety must be reinforced regularly. Similarly, teasing or joking will destroy the sense of respect group safety requires.

Remember that facilitating group therapy for teenagers is more different than with adults. It's best to keep things moving every fifteen to twenty minutes. If you expect teens to sit and talk for ninety minutes, you'll encounter resistance and little interaction. Try to shake up the format.

Before group begins each week, provide gathering activities. For example, you might set up board games, a dartboard, a ping-pong table, or other activities that allow for youth to move around and relax. These activities get them into motion interacting with one another. It sets up an atmosphere of engagement. This makes it easier to move into group discussion about personal issues because you already have engagement momentum. I also suggest that you play music that teens enjoy during gathering time. Set the tone and make things fun and upbeat right when they walk in the door.

If your group meets right after school in the afternoon, consider having snacks available. Youth are often starved after a school day. It's difficult to do any kind of emotional work or instruction on an empty stomach.

As a rule, keep check-in brief. When group begins, each person should check in about their week with whatever criteria you've established. It shouldn't be a long, drawn-out story. Sixty seconds per person is all you need. Save long stories for personal processing time.

To keep engagement momentum with your group, consider doing a warm-up immediately after your lesson or check-in. This is some kind of icebreaker that continues the interaction between group members and gets them out of their chairs, moving, talking, and interacting with one another. Sometimes warm-ups can go deeper and start bringing up personal issues. If you move in that direction, give it ample time.

Successful groups always include a lesson or teaching piece. The youth need mentors who can instruct them on lasting recovery concepts. It is the facilitator's job to dynamically teach in a way that the youth can hear what's taught. As a group, you can work on a workbook assignment or watch a recovery video and discuss how it applies to each of them. But always make a lesson and teaching part of the group format.

Any good group will allow for time to do personal processing. This could address questions the youth have about life or unique challenges. If they don't verbalize a need to address any problems, the facilitator can bring up issues from individual counseling that need to be addressed as a group. But always be sure to give each person ample attention as needed. When your group grows larger, be especially mindful of quiet or withdrawn teens who stop talking. Make sure everyone has a chance for attention. Remember that you will also be tapping into their developmental need for attention and guidance. If anyone is regularly overlooked, they may slowly lose traction in their recovery.

A successful facilitator ensures that every group member is engaged in the process. If youth are falling asleep, check to see if the group is moving to something new every fifteen to twenty minutes. Ask yourself if the content and the format is sufficiently engaging to keep them involved. You may need to make changes to what you're doing. In other instances, you'll need to challenge the youth to stay present and participate in all the group discussions. You may decide to require that they leave their phones off when they come to group. Or they can all leave their phones on a table at the door.

A progress chart will help teens visualize their progress as they come each week and check off tasks. As discussed previously, make sure your programming includes tasks they can work on between sessions. The chart becomes a visual reminder and keeps the pressure going to accomplish their goals. It also provides validation about their work and progress. This chart can be a way for them to show their parents they're making progress.

As the group becomes cohesive, encourage them all to connect outside of group time. Successful recovery throughout their lives will involve learning how to connect in various ways for support. For some, this will include learning how to socialize and connect generally. Group texts are helpful, as well as phone calls to discuss accomplishments or challenges during the week. Also encourage participants to hang out so they have a time to talk about stuff unrelated to their group work. Parents might choose to sponsor a hangout night offering pizza and games. Encourage outside group interaction to maximize the group success.

As mentioned earlier, make sure that the group is fun. The facilitator's interaction should be playful, warm, and engaging. If group members are arriving early each week and you have a difficult time getting them to leave at the end, then you've created a successful group format.

An increasingly sexualized culture requires more effective intervention and treatment for youth falling prey to compulsive sexual impulses. We can help teens avoid serious sexual addiction by developing successful programs. Such programs will adapt to the developmental needs of the adolescent, develop a systemic approach, and engage collaboration with parents, mentors, religious leaders, and other professional therapists.

CONCLUSION

An increasingly sexualized culture requires more effective intervention and treatment for youth falling prey to compulsive sexual impulses. We can help teens avoid serious sexual addiction by developing successful programs. Such programs will adapt to the developmental needs of the adolescent, develop a systemic approach, and engage collaboration with parents, mentors, religious leaders, and other professional therapists. However, this process of helping must begin with the willingness to examine our own sexual development and experiences, then doing the work in our own lives necessary to repair any unresolved wounds from the past.

REFERENCES

Bowman, T. 2013. *Angry Birds and Killer Bees: Talking to Your Kids about Sex*. Kansas City: Beacon Hill.

Greenberg, J., C. Bruess, and S. Oswalt. 2017. *Exploring the Dimensions of Human Sexuality*. *6th ed*. Burlington, MA: Jones & Bartlett Learning.

van der Kolk, B. A. 2014. *The Body Keeps the Score: Brain, Mind, and Body in the Healing of Trauma*. New York: Penguin Group.

SUBJECT INDEX